Personal Identity, the Self, and Ethics

Personal Identity, the Self, and Ethics

Ferdinand Santos
and
Santiago Sia

with best wishes,
Santiago

palgrave
macmillan

First published 2007 by
PALGRAVE MACMILLAN
Houndmills, Basingstoke, Hampshire RG21 6XS and
175 Fifth Avenue, New York, N.Y. 10010
Companies and representatives throughout the world

PALGRAVE MACMILLAN is the global academic imprint of the Palgrave
Macmillan division of St. Martin's Press, LLC and of Palgrave Macmillan Ltd.
Macmillan® is a registered trademark in the United States, United Kingdom and
other countries. Palgrave is a registered trademark in the European Union and
other countries.

ISBN-13: 978–0–230–52203–9   hardback
ISBN-10: 0–230–52203–3   hardback

This book is printed on paper suitable for recycling and made from fully
managed and sustained forest sources. Logging, pulping and manufacturing
processes are expected to conform to the environmental regulations of the
country of origin.

A catalogue record for this book is available from the British Library.

Library of Congress Cataloging-in-Publication Data

Santos, Ferdinand.
  Personal identity, the self, and ethics / by Ferdinand Santos and
  Santiago Sia.
      p. cm.
  Includes bibliographical references and index.
  ISBN 0–230–52203–3 (alk. paper)
  1. Self (Philosophy) 2. Identity (Philosophical concept) 3. Ethics.
  I. Sia, Santiago. II. Title.

  BD450.S277 2007
  126—dc22   2007023318

10   9   8   7   6   5   4   3   2   1
16   15   14   13   12   11   10   09   08   07

Printed and bound in Great Britain by
Antony Rowe Ltd, Chippenham and Eastbourne

Contents

List of Abbreviations

1. Charles Hartshorne's works

BH	*Beyond Humanism: Essays in the Philosophy of Nature*
CAP	*Creativity in American Philosophy*
CSPM	*Creative Synthesis and Philosophic Method*
DR	*The Divine Relativity: A Social Conception of God*
IO	*Insights and Oversights of Great Thinkers*
LP	*The Logic of Perfection*
MVG	*Man's Vision of God and the Logic of Theism*
NT	*A Natural Theology for Our Time*
OO	*Omnipotence and Other Theological Mistakes*
PPS	*The Philosophy and Psychology of Sensation*
PSG	*Philosophers Speak of God*
RSP	*Reality as Social Process: Studies in Metaphysics and Religion*
WM	*Wisdom as Moderation: A Philosophy of the Middle Way*
WMW	*Whitehead and the Modern World*
ZF	*The Zero Fallacy and Other Essays in Neoclassical Philosophy*

2. Alfred North Whitehead's works

AI	*Adventures of Ideas*
MT	*Modes of Thought*
PR	*Process and Reality: An Essay in Cosmology*
SMW	*Science and the Modern World*
PNK	*An Enquiry Concerning the Principles of Natural Knowledge*

Prologue

Much of present-day literature upon this subject is based upon notions which, within the last hundred years, have been completely discarded. The notion of the fixity of species and genera, and the notion of the unqualified definiteness of their distinction from each other, dominate the literary traditions of Philosophy, Religion, and Science. Today, these presuppositions of fixity and distinction have explicitly vanished: but in fact they dominate learned literature. Learning preserves the errors of the past, as well as its wisdom.

Each single example of personal identity is a special mode of coordination of the ideal world into a limited role of effectiveness. This maintenance of character is the way in which the finitude of the actual world embraces the infinitude of possibility. In each personality, the large infinitude of possibility is recessive and ineffective; but a perspective of ideal existence enters into the finite actuality. Also this entrance is more or less; there are grades of dominance and grades of recessiveness. The pattern of such grades and the ideal entities which they involve, constitute the character of that persistent fact of personal existence in the World of Activity. The essential coordination of values dominates the essential differentiation of facts.

> Alfred North Whitehead on Personal Identity;
> "Immortality," in *The Philosophy of Alfred North Whitehead*

I have sometimes sat looking at a comrade, speculating on this mysterious isolation of self from self. Why are we so made that I gaze and see of thee only thy Wall, and never Thee? ... How would it seem if my mind could but once be within thine; and we could meet and without barrier be with each other? And then it has fallen upon me like a shock – as when one thinking himself alone has felt a presence – But I am in thy soul. These things around me are in thy experience. They are thy own; when I touch them and move them I change thee. When I look on them I see what thou seest; when I listen, I hear what

vii

thou hearest. I am in the great Room of thy soul; and I experience thy very experience. For where art thou? Not there, behind those eyes, within that head, in darkness, fraternizing with chemical processes. Of these, in my own case, I know nothing, and will know nothing; but my existence is spent not behind my Wall, but in front of it. I am there, where I have treasures. And there art thou, also ... I can imagine no contact more real and thrilling than this; that we should meet and share identity, not through ineffable inner depths (alone), but here through the foregrounds of common experience.

William Ernest Hocking on the Self and the Other
in *The Meaning of God in Human Experience*

Introduction

The questions and the context

What does it mean to be "oneself" or to be "the same" person? What does being a "person" or a "self" mean? What is "personal identity"? How do these notions relate to ethics? Many, influenced by the postmodernist talk of "the fall of the self," have sought to show that these questions are unanswerable and even irrelevant. There is a trend to convince us that since there is no self in reality, despite the claims in much of traditional philosophy, we should disregard all talk connected with this illusion and devote our attention elsewhere.

This work takes a different stand. It seeks to address these questions in order to maintain their continued importance in philosophy and in other disciplines. In fact, in the recent issue of *The Economist,* the question "Who do you think you are?" is given extensive coverage, and the articles dealing with the question attest to the increasing and widening need to examine it closely.[1] Identifying some of the problems which have been brought about by the traditional answers, this book provides another conception of person, personal identity, and the self. More specifically, it is an investigation into the approach that process philosophy brings into the discussion. Our goal, therefore, is to develop a philosophical anthropology based on process philosophy, in particular as set out by Charles Hartshorne.[2] Since process philosophy at its core is a metaphysical system, this work is also a metaphysical inquiry. Again, it should be noted that metaphysical thinking as developed here is not to be aligned with traditional metaphysics, which has been subjected to much justified criticism. Metaphysics as pursued in process philosophy is quite distinctive.

Process metaphysics purports to be existential, i.e., it holds that its theoretical constructions are grounded in human experience, which it takes as the starting point as well as the yardstick of its general view of reality. As human experience is the point of departure for Hartshorne's metaphysical speculation, it is in human experience that our discussion must find its first foothold. This is why we have chosen to concentrate on a particular experience common to all human beings, namely one's experience of one's own identity. The question that lies at the heart of this experience is in fact the central issue as well as the starting point of any metaphysics of the human person. It is the most common question concerning personal identity. *What am I?*, i.e., What kind of being, what kind of entity am I? What is the referent of the term "I"? What constitutes my "person"?

Ipse-identity and *idem*-identity

There are two related issues connected with the topic of this work. One is understanding identity in terms of personhood or selfhood and comprehending it in terms of that specific character which defines any entity, specifically a human being. The second is the issue of personal identity as sameness. Contemporary expositors of this more specific field of discussion understand it as the problem of specifying conditions for identifying a person at a particular point in time as the same person at another point. Paul Ricoeur uses two related Latin words to distinguish these two ways of considering personal identity. The first kind he calls *ipse*-identity (*ipse* meaning "himself" or "itself"; hence the emphasis on "selfhood" or "nature"), while the second he terms *idem*-identity (*idem* meaning "the same"; hence the emphasis on transtemporal sameness).

The kind of entity a person is cannot be separated from the issue of sameness. That one will even be interested in asking the question *What am I?* presupposes that one has an awareness of being the same *I*. Likewise, praise, blame, reward, punishment, conversion, and other similar human experiences are all anchored onto the same issue of *idem*-identity. At the same time, the issues involved in the question about the nature of person encompass a larger domain than the mere issue of transtemporal sameness. And while the stability that underpins transtemporal identity is a key element to an adequate description of personhood, it remains but an initial step. The answer to the question *What am I?* must be sought within a larger domain of discourse which involves the concept of person itself.

The relationship between these two issues notwithstanding, there is a distinction between them. This distinction is particularly evident in present discussions which separately treat the problems involved in each issue. A vast literature exists on the question of *idem*-identity. It has become a clearly distinct and separate area of inquiry from that of personhood, with some authors relegating the latter to a domain belonging properly to psychological inquiry, which has little or nothing to do with the former. Nonetheless, we believe that, although useful, such a way of proceeding proves to be ultimately detrimental to both areas of inquiry.

Concerning *idem*-identity, for instance, the primary difficulty with the contemporary debate is that most, if not all, of the contending theories are attached to the idea of an unchanging substrate. The two major perspectives, namely, the *strict* view and the *nonstrict* view of transtemporal identity are both grounded on this notion. The strict view, which holds personal identity to be ultimately nonproblematic because of its unanalyzable character, ends up positing the existence of an entity akin to a Cartesian *ego*, which is not only distinguishable but also stands apart from the bodily and mental states which it has. While personal identity is ultimately irreducible to its physical and psychological states, and a person is finally much more than his bodily and mental components, the clear-cut distinction which leads to the positing of a "third" term is, as we shall try to show, untenable and unnecessary.

Also questionable is the fundamental presupposition of theories which fall under the nonstrict view: a substantialism which does not involve the entire person itself but its constituent parts. Avoiding the necessity of positing a third term, but working with the psychological and physical "components" of person, the nonstrict view treats these in quite the same way that the strict view treats personal identity in its totality, namely, as substrata of change. In this way, one makes sense of the multiform transformations that an entity undergoes in the course of its lifetime in terms of either bodily or mental criteria which are rooted in an unchanging conceptualization of body, on the one hand, or mind, on the other.

Thus, if the strict view of personal identity is based on the idea of an unchanging spiritual substrate distinct from and irreducible to body or mind, the nonstrict view of personal identity hinges on the notion of an unchanging material substrate. The nonstrict view is analyzable in terms of either its physical (as it is expounded for instance in bodily theories of identity) or psychological (as it finds expression in theories which use memory as a key concept) manifestations. The strict view relegates the person, not to its "components," but to a third term, while the nonstrict view reduces it to either one of its components: body or mind. Moreover, some contemporary theories that equate personal identity with mind are actually anchored onto a physicalist view, which locates the mind's reality within the material locus of the brain. Both views reduce the reality they intend to describe to a term founded on the idea of an unchanging entity—the strict view, to that of a spiritual substance, and the nonstrict view, to that of a material substance.

Despite the difficulties involved in dealing specifically with *idem*-identity, the idea of transtemporal identity remains an important component of the global picture of personal identity, as it allows for the possibility of asking the question of personhood. However, if the criteria presently given to describe what constitutes transtemporal identity are in fact substantialist, then the notion of person that would result from using the *idem*-identity question as the starting point would be substantialist as well.

Is it possible then to ground criteria of *idem*-identity on a concept other than substance? This investigation into the notion of personal identity intends to add a clarifying and perhaps unifying note to the dissonant and competing voices, as the search for such a criterion can find a better grounding that is more attuned to the actual experiences of persons themselves and more cognizant of better conceptualizations of reality than the notion of substance. Both the strict and nonstrict perspectives on *idem*-identity will therefore be rejected.

But why does an investigation into personal identity matter? There are three reasons. The first is the concern for one's future. However one may deny it, and whatever elements one wishes to include, e.g., loved ones, family, etc., concern for one's own future appears to be qualitatively different from one's concern for others'. Death, for instance, can never be vicariously experienced. Nor can its full impact be grasped by observing—however attentively—the deaths of other persons. This concern for a personal future is tied up with a second concern: survival. Shall we continue to be the persons that we are 5, 10, or 15 years hence? Survival is a notion that seems to be founded on that gut instinct that we are the same individual we were years ago and will remain such many years from today. The concern to survive, intuitive and unarticulated as it often is, nevertheless finds expression in that universal desire for immortality. Religion has always been the prime expositor of a theoretical account of the desire to survive, not only within a specific period, but forever. Finally, there is the idea of ethical responsibility, and with it, the requisites of praise and blame, reward and punishment. This third reason, tied especially to the fact that survival, as an ultimate concern for the greater part of humanity, has very intimate links with the ultimacy of responsibility—among the great monotheistic religions at least—becomes especially important in this regard.

These three common experiences are the reasons why the issue of personal identity matters. Moreover, they do not only collectively bridge the strict and nonstrict perspectives on identity, but they also allow for the connection between *idem*-identity and *ipse*-identity. These experiences also serve as the background for Hartshorne's reflection on personal identity and his rejection of an ontology of substance as the foundation for it. To the question, therefore, as to why personal identity matters, our answer is that only a notion of personal identity that unifies in a coherent theory transtemporal sameness and personhood can account for these features of experience which go beyond the simply intuitive.

Hartshorne's method and theory

What would pass as a coherent notion of personal identity though? It is first and foremost one that escapes the charge of substantialism. Hartshorne's critique of theories of identity as mere sameness is based on his view that the identity of not just persons but of any entity cannot be fully described by an ontology of substance. The positing of an aspect of an entity that remains the same throughout the manifold changes in its history may be useful and indispensable, but the full reality of an entity, human or not, defies the simplicity and reductionism of substance. That "something remains the same" may be an important presupposition in describing identity, but it cannot be the only or even the most important one.

About concern for one's future, a substantialistic basis for a theory of personal identity would certainly appear, initially at least, to be a better explanation of why one cares more for one's own future than for another's. What it fails to recognize, however, is the fact that one's very finite nature precludes an infinite designation to this "future." Biologically, the most one can hope for is a limited slice of time extending from the present moment one considers one's own future, to the moment of one's death. The fact is, outside the realm of religion, no infinite future is vouchsafed to us. Why care for the future then? According to Hartshorne—contrary to the notion implicit in most theories of personal identity—concern for the future is not founded on the sameness of substance. Concern for one's own future is founded not on the fact that it is one's self that makes the future a matter of concern, but on the fact that it is the future itself that matters, be this one's own or not. The future that matters is not one's own, but any future one can influence, have sympathy for, and, to some extent, regard as good or bad *for someone*. Ultimately of course, Hartshorne identifies this all-embracing future, with God, as the all-inclusive reality into whose storehouse of memories all lives and all experiences are taken.

There is a breadth and generality to Hartshorne's view that stands in stark contrast to the myopic vision of a concern for the future founded primarily and often, solely, on the fact that it is one's own. This is why the experience of being concerned for one's survival cannot be built on a substantialistic foundation. To connect such concern with the continued existence of a self-same substance is to be doomed to the rather bleak and depressing prospect that eventually every "I" becomes nothing at all, or what is for all purposes the same in value terms: a heap of dust. One obviously does not survive one's death. Shall we limit the domain of personal identity then from the moment of birth to the end of one's biological existence? Or shall we extend it to cover one's legacy and the judgment that history shall pass on us? We need to look further than these alternatives.

If what changes are mere external accessories, attached to an unchanging core, then the raising of the issue of *idem*-identity becomes less than interesting. This is why Hartshorne's metaphysics, which explains the relation between stability and change, provides a clarifying note to the discussion. As subsequent chapters will show, his metaphysics is based on a consideration of contrasting concepts that relates them to one another in a manner that first considers each one's relative importance to the other. As mutually dependent pairs, these concepts stand or fall together. Neither one by itself is capable of describing reality. This symmetrical relation, however, is inserted into a broader relation of asymmetry which Hartshorne takes to be the fundamental relational category of reality.

The experiences of stability and change need to be reconciled in order to give a better metaphysical foundation to a theory of transtemporal identity. Otherwise, we find ourselves either having to posit a third term, as in cases of strict-identity theories, or attributing identity to an unchanging and ultimately material substrate, as in cases of physical and psychological theories. Both ways merely postpone having to answer the inevitable question, *what then does change?* According to Hartshorne, this is exactly what substance metaphysics does. It moves the question of whether or not an entity, in its very nature, can be said to change, farther and farther into the margins of our theories. It locates change as far away as possible from the very character defining an entity. For him, unless the core, i.e., the very nature of an entity, can be said to change, change cannot be regarded as real. It cannot be said to have the same ontological status as stability. This for him immediately violates the canon of symmetry and mutual dependence governing the relation between contrasting concepts.

Furthermore, Hartshorne reverses the very relation by which stability and change are usually conceived. Although they are symmetrically related and mutually dependent, he holds that one term expresses the global reality of the relation. And the other in fact acquires its content by being inserted into the descriptive domain of the more concrete concept. Change, he says, is the more original and concrete experience out of which we abstract the derivative notion of stability. An ontology of substance cannot articulate this fact.

Does this, however, agree with our everyday experience of things and persons? Is not our immediate and initial experience of things and persons that of stability? This is an observation which will later be addressed more fully. Still, it must be acknowledged that comparing the identities of persons and things is not unproblematic. A person loses a limb but remains the same person that he was prior to the loss; a table gets one of its legs replaced and remains the same table. The difficulties arise, however, when we begin asking the question as to how much an individual must retain to be regarded the same, and how much of the original table can be replaced for it to be considered the same. Moreover, comparisons between persons and nonhuman entities start to break down when the issue of mind comes up. Things do not have "selves" the way persons do. But persons have brains. Is it not possible then to ascribe the manifestation of a "self" in a human being to the fact that it has a brain—a material entity? Certain physicalist accounts of mind do reduce the psychological aspect of selfhood to the fact that humans have brains. Not only are the two hemispheres of the brain, for instance, capable of functioning independently of each other, but individuals who have had one hemisphere damaged by a stroke can survive, since the other hemisphere manages to combine the functions of both. Is there still identity if only part of the brain is functioning? Perhaps as long as enough of the individual's past experiences and memories are retained and remain operable?

The storage capacity of computer hard drives has increased tremendously since the first one rolled out in 1953, when they had no more than a 5-megabyte capacity (the same size as two MP3s), weighed a ton, and were the size of two big refrigerators. Today we speak of gigabytes and terabytes. What if a storage device eventually becomes available that can store not just a fraction but all of an individual's memory and experiences after the body dies? Would it be possible to speak of a device that can store every single bit of information in a human brain as somehow "identical" with the departed person? However, even in this case the question arises, is the memory of an individual captured in a supercapacity storage device an individual at all? Would it not be a mere elaborate, perhaps interactive, video of that individual's history? How much of *himself* must a person retain to remain himself? Here again, the question of the constitution of the "self" arises. Is it body? How much of it? Is it mind? How much?

Even with regard to things, a similar question can be asked. The story of the *Ship of Theseus* is a clear illustration. Theseus has a ship that requires a major overhaul. He has it dry-docked while he rebuilds it piece by piece. After a year of working on it, every plank, bolt, and beam has been replaced. Now suppose one of his old rivals decides to steal and hide all the parts that Theseus had disassembled from the old vessel and puts these together piece by piece and in the same order so as to make a second ship. When both are finished, which ship is the original one?

The commonsense view of identity, whether of persons or things, is not as unproblematic as it initially seems. This is why Hartshorne, while regarding the commonsense view as the starting point of a reflection on identity, holds it to be just that—a starting point. For he holds that the mind, in its initial approach to whatever it is that immediately confronts it, abstracts from the complexity of the real in order to give it a firmer grasp of its object. Its initial foothold therefore involves a drawing back from the overpowering richness of reality in order to render the real more manageable and manipulable. However, as William Wordsworth says in *The Tables Turned*, "we murder to dissect." The abstracted reality, the "unchanged," is no more than a pale reflection, a mere shadow of the concrete and more complete reality which is the "changing." The commonsense experience of identity is not the primary experience. It is already the result of a second-order reflection on reality, albeit still a vague and yet-to-be-fully-articulated one.

Theories which deal with both *idem*-identity and *ipse*-identity would benefit from being loosened from their bonds with a substantialistic metaphysics. Of course, it must be admitted at the outset that *ipse*-identity theories will benefit more from this endeavor. The issue of *idem*-identity, at least initially, requires the application of the notion of substance in its methodology, although even this eventually gets bogged down in a lot of difficulties that are traceable to the notion of an unchanging substrate. One such difficulty for instance is the proliferation of incredible, puzzling cases whose counterintuitive and contrary-to-commonsense nature makes them rather amusing, given the fact that they are all supposedly founded on a commonsense view of identity.

The major difficulty with present theories of personal identity, especially those that concern *idem*-identity, is a failure to generalize beyond the narrowness of the starting point, i.e., the useful idea of an unchanging substrate. It is analogous to the inability, for instance, to generalize beyond what seems to be one's most immediate experience or encounter with reality: stability. However, as Hartshorne would argue, it is only by going beyond what appears to be the initial approach to the real, i.e., by seeing that there is in fact much more to the so-called commonsense view, that the genuinely original and initial approach can be discovered. This, according to him, is an experience of change. Therefore, in place of a metaphysics of substance, he puts forward a metaphysics of event which articulates the primacy of change and reconciles it with the experience of stability. One makes sense of the fact that stability is a factor in our experiences, often as if it were the primary or initial one, because it is a genuine factor of experience, not because it is *the* primary experience.

Hartshorne's theory of personal identity is based on the notion that the alleged locus of stability—the unchanging substrate—is an abstraction from concrete realities. A selfsame ego is the abstract correlate of the concrete reality, which is the self that is different at every moment. This is not a denial of enduring individuality or of a specific subject possessing definite experiences. It is rather an assertion that each new experience undergone by a subject means a new actuality for that subject. The persistent identity itself is an abstraction, while the subject of these experiences is concrete. Consequently, he says that a new subject is present at every moment, and this subject—this "I"—is not just "I as subject here," but also "I as subject here and now." Spatial and temporal considerations are intrinsic to one's concrete reality. However, the concreteness of this "I" depends upon the sequence of experiences which make up this "I." He calls such a sequence a "society" of experiences, and these experiences he calls "events." The stable "I" which is the referent of common sense is a mere limited slice of the entire society of experiences. This is why he holds it erroneous to argue that each individual is always simply the same subject or the same entity even if it must likewise be admitted that each individual is the same. Persons are identical and selfsame throughout their lives as individuals, but not so in their concreteness. Concretely, there is a new person at each moment, and to recognize the sameness of a person, we must disregard that which is new at every moment. Personal identity then is the persistence, not of an unchanging substrate, but of certain "defining characteristics" in a very complex reality which is in the process of constant change.

The ontology of event is the foundation of Hartshorne's conception of identity in general and personal identity in particular. He would agree with the notion that personal identity is different from the identity of nonhuman entities. The similarities between a theory of personal identity and a theory of the identity of things go only so far; at a certain point the differences become clearly manifest. The question that Hartshorne would ask, however, is, what kind of differences are being referred to here? It is obvious that the experiences of persons—that things, as well as themselves, remain the same—constitute the starting point of an inquiry into the general structure of identity. And it is from within this general structure that the more specific structures emerge, namely, those that properly govern identity of the human type. Hartshorne's concern, however, lies with the general structure. He seeks to find out its underlying presuppositions, since he argues that these presuppositions require reconsideration and critique, based as they are on an ontology of substance.

An event for Hartshorne is a spatiotemporal slice of any experience that constitutes the ultimate building block of reality. Substances too, have been regarded as such. The difference between the two, however, lies in the structure that governs the coming-to-be of each. A substance, while it is susceptible to being modified, is stable and fixed. Moreover, its modifications are external accretions, induced from the outside, while its very nature remains intact. Nothing in an event, as a basic *descriptum* of reality, remains fixed and stable except for a vague outline of its coming-to-be, a blueprint that does not determine its future reality, but creates and guides its future possibility. It is therefore teleologically ordered, but only to the extent that the creation of future possibility belongs to its very nature. It is self-ordered in its creativity. It creates itself. This self-creativity, however, is not an absolutely undetermined kind. For the coming-to-be of an event is itself governed by a structure. This, in Hartshorne's philosophy, is the structure of creativity, which is best described in terms of an asymmetrical or unidirectional causality.

Memory

Hartshorne turns to memory and its role. He does not take issue with the Humean dictum that sense perception alone is incapable of disclosing any causal connectedness. In the natural world all that is ever really perceived is the continual, and at times repetitive, succession of events. Causal relations are not directly observable. However, Hartshorne rejects Hume's skeptical conclusion that what are commonly called causal relations are no more than constant conjunctions. He thus appeals to our experience of memory, which, he says, lends support to a theory of real causal connectedness. Memory, more than being the presentation of the past in the present, is more properly the modification of the present by the past. Memory is influence. Past experiences that are remembered impose restrictions upon the present subject. Memory preserves something of the ideas, emotional qualities, and valuations in prior experience. These in turn achieve integration in the present subject doing the remembering.

Hartshorne's purpose, however, is not the elucidation of a theory of memory, nor a theory of personal identity based on the evidence afforded by memory—as in the case of Locke's account for example. Memory is a means, a tool which he intends to utilize as an explanation of causal connectedness. But in order to do this he has to expand its meaning, i.e., generalize beyond its commonsense understanding and use in order to make it applicable to all types of experience, human and otherwise.

This expansion is done via his generalized comparative psychology, in which various psychological concepts are made cosmic variables—i.e., notions possessing an infinite range of value—and are thus applicable to all entities regardless of their simplicity or complexity. This method, first and foremost, strips the concept of memory of its denotation of consciousness and awareness—aspects which belong properly to its human manifestation. "Memory" is a technical term for Hartshorne, which first means a past actuality's being taken into account by a present one, before it becomes the conscious remembering of a past experience by an entity whose temporal locus is the present. It is for him a metaphysical concept first and only secondarily an idea that belongs to the domain of the specifically anthropological.

Now this "being taken into account" has itself a structure—an asymmetrical one. The causal relationship, according to Hartshorne, displays an asymmetrical character. To experience something is an essential relation. This means that a subject is internally related to its object and is therefore constituted by it. At the same time, however, the object is externally related to the subject. In the relation $X R Y$, for instance, X is externally related to Y when X would have had the same nature apart from this relation. The absolute term in this relation is the externally related and, hence, independent cause. On the other hand, the relative term is the internally related and hence dependent effect. That one remembers one's grandparents puts one in a relation of causal dependency on them, but does not in any way put them in any relation of causal dependency on one. However, although there are such real necessary, albeit unidirectional, relations, these are not such as to make any presently existing entity necessary. That one had one's particular set of grandparents is an absolute fact; that one was to turn out to be their grandson is not. What a real necessary relation commits us to is simply to hold that a certain set of existing entities (relatively, but not absolutely particularized) shall not remain a null class.

Moreover, since the causal relation goes one way and not two, it is the past that is objectively immortal in the present. But it is so not on account of its having absolutely determined this present, but because present reality takes "into account" past actuality as data upon which it feeds in its ongoing process of coming-to-be. The present is inherently "parasitic" on the past, since in the order of becoming, the present relative to the past is the latter term. And it is the latter term that includes the former, not the other way around. The subject includes the object as the effect includes the cause. According to Hartshorne, the generic nature of the temporal-causal process is cumulative; i.e., it enriches the sum of the determinateness of reality.

A present experience which "feeds" upon past data is itself eventually taken into yet another experience, a later one, thereby becoming past. The coming-to-be of a present experience which is parasitic upon the past escapes the charge of determinism because inherent in its very nature, i.e., embedded at the heart of its process of "consuming" its past, is an element that escapes the causal relation. "The many become one and are increased by one"[3] is a dictum of the process philosopher Alfred North Whitehead, used by Hartshorne to explain the theory that present actuality includes in it an inescapable element of creativity summed up in his notion of synthesis. The creativity of present becoming actuality is constituted by the unification of past data into a novel whole that in its totality escapes the very influence of such data. Creativity is synthetic, and synthesis is creative. The newly emergent whole is ultimately irreducible to the innumerable factors that have been gathered together in order to give it birth. It is simply a new actuality. What this demonstrates is that what is "taken into account" by present reality is already in the past. This is why Hartshorne says that the structure of memory is the paradigm of experiencing. What we experience is always and already in the past. Following Whitehead, he calls the present a "specious present"—the term denoting the evanescent and slippery character of the present moment. On the one hand, this shows the fleeting character of the present, while, on the other hand, it points to what he calls the "objective immortality" of the past. Past experience, as an objective datum consumed by present actuality, is immortal in that it will forever be part of whatever it is that results from the entire sequence of experiences. This sequence, in both Hartshorne and Whitehead, finds its consummation in the memory of God.

This interpretation of memory is the key to understanding the structure of Hartshorne's event ontology. An event—being a minimal unit of some actual process—is, for Hartshorne, the ultimate unit of reality. It is what he calls the "basic descriptum" of the real, i.e., that which all true characterizations correctly, and at least indirectly, describe. A particular human experience is one such kind of unit. Any particular moment abstracted from an entire sequence of events can be characterized by one or more predicates. However, Hartshorne insists that this does not mean that the idea of an identical subject possessing *changing* qualities is equally applicable to the event-concept. Rather, an event is characterized by so thoroughgoing a mutability that subjectively, it is gone as soon as it becomes what it is. In a paradoxical way, it could be said that it *is* only when it is no longer.

Objectively immortal in the present drops of experiences that feed on them, events nonetheless "perpetually perish subjectively." This often-misunderstood Whiteheadian concept is key to a more adequate understanding and systematic exposition of the structure of a Hartshornean event. An event for Hartshorne is an actual entity, i.e., it possesses all the requisites of something that fully exists. Like anything that exists, however, it is always in the process of striving toward novel forms of becoming, new ways of actualizing itself. When an entity concludes this striving, this process toward becoming itself, its character as subject perishes and it becomes an objectively immortal datum—"fodder" for later experience. In this guise, it becomes, in Whiteheadian terms, the objectively immortal "superject." "Subject" and "superject" are two analytical phases of an event's process of coming-to-be. And thus they also correspond to the two phases of each event. An event is first of all a subject arising from the fundamental process of becoming, which aims at arriving at what Whitehead calls "satisfaction," the achievement of unity or the synthesizing of all previous data of experience. The subject therefore is not already given and presupposed by these previous experiences, but rather is the process itself of these experiences. It is not in itself given as a datum to which experiences are superadded, but is the very striving toward achievement of a "subjective aim" or individual purpose. When this has been achieved, the subjective phase is transcended and the entity enters into a new phase. Its subjective guise is shed and it discloses itself as the superject, which is the arrival of an entity-in-the-process-of-becoming at that stage in which it has acquired objectivity, i.e., where it is a permanently completed "being." The superject represents that stage which embodies the now-fulfilled aim, the reaching of what Whitehead calls an event's own "absolute self-attainment."

An event is first the actual entity in the process of achieving its aim—a teleological perspective. When this aim is reached, the event then becomes the very transition between this earlier phase and the next phase. The subjective phase has the nature of a process which only comes to an end when it is transformed into the superject, which is both objectively immortal as well as unchanging. An entity then becomes a permanently completed "being." But the story does not quite end here. For the event that has reached this stage finds itself again hurled into a further and newer event, by being taken into another subject in the process of becoming. The two phases overlap; there is a mutual immanence between them. It belongs to the nature of the superject that its objective immortality is characterized by being taken in as a datum, which, together with a host of other data, is synthesized by yet another event in the endless advance of the creative process. The two phases belong to the nature of an event. They are the two poles which stand or fall together in an event's description. Neither one can be left out. However, it is obvious that the domain occupied by each is not the same, for the processive phase encompasses both itself (the changing) and the unchanging. And the latter in fact is only truly itself when it finds itself once again hurled into yet another trajectory of becoming in the creative unification of itself, together with all other objectively immortal data of experience, by a still later subject.

Applied to the concept of a person, this doctrine entails that an individual's nature or character is never fully determinate in content until his death. And the self-identity of a person cannot be dependent upon the existence of some unchanging substrate that possesses an unchanging content. Instead it is founded first of all upon the permanence of the defining characteristic, and second, upon the mutual overlapping of the phases in its process of coming-to-be. But there are no defining characteristics, fixed and determined beforehand as to their minutest details. There is only a relatively defined outline because of the element of novelty and creativity that characterizes the synthesizing activity of later events, and yet defined nevertheless because of the objectively immortal data which these later events *must* feed upon and synthesize.

To be "remembered" in Hartshorne's scheme therefore means two things. First, it is to be taken account of, to be "consumed," "synthesized," and made part of any later event. Every event in this regard is a "remembered event." The structure of the concept of personal identity in Hartshorne follows that of an event. Personal identity is not constituted by an underlying substantial self that remains the same throughout an individual's lifetime. Identity in the concrete connotes change. It is an affair of difference along a continuous historic route of events, made self-identical by its defining characteristics which embody their own subjective form. Concretely, the general notion of identity as well as the more specific concept of personal identity, for Hartshorne, can be rightly called "mnemonic identity." We prefer to use the word "mnemonic" to the term "remembered" as this latter term is loaded with connotations of conscious awareness. The term "mnemonic" is derived from the Greek word $\mu\nu\eta\mu\alpha$ (*mnema*), $\mu\nu\epsilon\mu\epsilon\iota o\nu$ (*mnemeoin*) which is a memorial or record of a person or thing, especially one that is already dead (a tombstone for example). It is from this that our English words "memory" and "remember" are derived. The identity of an individual is akin to a memorial, a tombstone, the trace of a past whose reality can never be undone, because it will forever be "remembered" by a present actuality.

As a mnemonic type of identity, personal identity is structured in the manner of an event in the process of coming-to-be. It is dipolar, i.e., it has both a stable as well as a changing aspect. The stable pole is embodied and expressed in the events that are objectively immortalized (the superjects) in the unifying activity of later events belonging to a particular event-sequence. The changing pole is the process of continuous transformation from subject to superject, back, and so on, which a person undergoes throughout the course of a lifetime. It is easy to see that the processive dimension is the more comprehensive one, embracing in itself both stability and change. It is also the more concrete pole, for it includes, in its comprehension, each individual event in the series. It is only abstractly thus that personal identity can refer to a continuity of character that an enduring object exemplifies in the course of its life history. This character is a mere pattern of unity, a defining characteristic guided by an entity's subjective aim expressed in its manner of behaving or in its way of responding to what it encounters.

Relatedness

It is within the orbit of these metaphysical notions that not only a theory of personal identity but also a theory of person is found within process thought. This account, however, will remain incomplete if it does not include the other part of the twofold description that Hartshorne gives to reality. To be remembered according to Hartshorne means to be related. The real is not only processive; it is also, at its core, a community of sorts. The very process of transformation and mutual overlapping of subject and superject is made possible by the fact that every event is related and is set on its path of becoming *itself* by first being related to what is an other to it. All of reality is characterized by a dynamic responsiveness to what is other. A society of events, i.e., a set of events that are united by a specific defining character and subjective aim, is also a society of interrelated events whose relationality is constituted not only by later events in the sequence synthesizing earlier ones, but also by events in that particular sequence relating themselves to a sequence different from their own.

This notion echoes the existentialist thesis that there is no existence without coexistence. But it is also a deepening of this notion. For it situates the relational element in the very nature of every individual and is able to do this by *stating* the fact of an individual's relational nature, or explaining coexistence by means of external coordinates such as socialization, the learning of language, the witness of social artifacts, the development of culturally and environmentally influenced thought patterns, etc. More importantly, it offers an account of *why* and *how* an individual is social or relational. The key once again is found in the structure of the coming-to-be of an event. A person, according to process philosophy, is genuinely relational because it is part of a world made up of an indefinitely extended plenum of interconnected events that cannot be isolated from one another.

An event is both processive and relational. A person, being a society of such events, cannot be otherwise. Its individuality consists in the mnemonic structure of the events that make it up, and this mnemonic structure is shot through and through with sociality. However, if events supremely exemplify the processive nature of the real, it is on the level of event-societies, i.e., persons, that the relational character of the real truly comes to the fore. And it is also here that the mnemonic structure of events transcends the level of the purely conceptual. The mnemonic structure of reality becomes imbued with consciousness in persons and thus becomes a coordinate of a philosophical account of the human being, an anthropology. Moreover, it is also on this level that the relationality and sociality which are internal structures of person-events begin to involve other event-societies in much more complex ways and are thus transformed into external structures of community. Hence, personal identity is not merely a "remembered" identity; it is also, and more importantly, a relational or "communal" one. It is not something a person has by or in oneself alone. One has one's identity only within the larger context of one's manifold relations. This communal dimension adds an even greater complexity to the process by which a person's concrete identity is ascertained as well as established.

Toward a process anthropology

A process philosophical anthropology involves these two elements, namely, the mnemonic and relational character of personal identity. And one who sets out to discover the relational dimension of personhood by means of considering the mnemonic element at the root of personal identity finds out eventually that this is finally grounded in relationality itself. The chapters that follow represent an attempt to clarify this insight and develop the claims made.

Chapter 1 contextualizes this work by looking at the first and most systematized account of personal identity, namely, that of John Locke. Contrary to a number of Lockean critics, one can make adequate sense of Locke's notion of personal identity only when it is evaluated vis-à-vis his ontological and ethical concerns. Such concerns are also to be found in Hartshorne's account. Chapter 2 moves from an evaluation of Locke's notion of personal identity to the manner by which his critics have appropriated his theory, specifically in dealing with the question of transtemporal numerical identity. Locke himself sought to avoid reducing the "person" to a "substance." Those who followed him sought either to push his theory to its logical conclusion, thereby loosening the bonds of identity with the unity and integrity of the self, or to return to a substantialistic view if only to safeguard this integrity. This chapter will highlight the substantialism that serves as the foundation for such subsequent theories.

Chapter 3 discusses Hartshorne's critique of the ontology of substance vis-à-vis his rejection of P.F. Strawson's substantialistic concept of person and Strawson's notion of personal identity in terms of a body that can be situated within a clearly defined spatiotemporal locus. Chapter 4 traces the roots of the popularity of substance ontology as well as the subsequent reaction of ontologies of event to the notion of nature, as constituted by particles that are simply located within a definite spatiotemporal locus and isolated from every other particle or component of nature.

The next chapters attempt to develop an alternative to the substance ontology that informs and underpins the previous discussion. Chapter 5 discusses the structure of Hartshorne's philosophical method and the two pillars of his metaphysical doctrine, namely, the principles of asymmetrical relationality and the universality of experience, both of which arise from a thoroughgoing rejection of any ultimate metaphysical dichotomies. Chapter 6 is an analysis of the ultimate constituent units or *descripta* of reality, which Hartshorne holds are not independent and isolated substances but event-actualities. The coming-to-be of such events is characterized as being atomic or "epochal" on the one hand and relatively dependent on the data of past events on the other. It is in memory that we have an exemplification of the asymmetrical structure of the causality which underlies the becoming of events and the pastness of the data which present acts of creativity synthesize.

Chapter 7 develops the process view further by discussing this conception of person in the context of the process category of "memory." It explains how "memory" is a conceptual apparatus that discloses to us, by means of its causal structure, the interrelatedness of reality. It unpacks the implications of this conception for ethics. Chapter 8 extends the discussion of this conception of person further by focusing on its transcendent and social dimensions and shows its importance in enabling a better understanding of the place of persons in society.

1
The Lockean Account of Person and Personal Identity

Personal identity as an issue

John Locke (1632–1704), whose writings initiated the modern quest for an account of "personal identity," once noted that to find out what personal identity is, one must consider what "person" stands for. Accordingly, this chapter will discuss personal identity within the more complex and inclusive notion of person. It will discuss the issue of personal identity not only from the perspective of Locke's account, but also with a reference to some of the problems that have arisen in present discussions.

There are a number of rival theories of personal identity, some of which bear a close resemblance to one another. A very rough dividing line can be drawn between theories supporting a physical determinant of identity and those that espouse some sort of psychological factor. Within the first group is the general theory—although with some modifications—which holds that entity 2 at time 2 is the same as entity 1 at time 1 if and only if entity 2 has the same body which entity 1 had. For the second group, i.e., the psychological side of this division, memory and other elements of consciousness are taken to be paradigmatic criteria of personal identity over time. Especially since Locke—whose writings have influenced most contemporary psychological theories of identity—the continuity of an entity existing at present with an earlier or later stage of itself has been viewed in terms of the link that memory affords. Briefly, the memory criterion holds that entity 2 at time 2 is the same entity as the entity 1 at time 1 if entity 2 at time 2 is linked by a continuity of memory to entity 1 at time 1. Like the bodily criterion, the memory criterion is also a more general theory which admits a number of modifications.

At the root of this division is the concern to specify the criteria by which an entity can be said to be *the same* at distinct points in time. This concern becomes even more important if we consider that physical and psychological theories of identity are themselves part of the larger theory of "nonstrict" identity. This conglomeration of theories is founded on the idea that the identity of persons is a concept that is further analyzable by means of the constituent parts of an individual—this roughly translates into the body, on the one hand, and the mind, on the other. They are to be distinguished from "strict"-identity theories, which do not allow such reduction and insist instead that personal identity is a "further fact." That is to say, personal identity is a concept that stands over and above any attempt to explain it in terms of an appeal to criteria of either bodily continuity or memory.

Our discussion here on strict and nonstrict theories[1] as well as the physical and psychological criteria is intended to show that there are basically two ways by which personal identity questions can be described. We shall call the first the "question of transtemporal identity," or simply, the "question of sameness", and the resulting theory, that of *idem*-identity. The second description has to do with identity as "individuality," "distinguishing character," "defining characteristic," or "selfhood." It is analogous to what Paul Ricoeur calls *ipse*-identity.[2] Its primary query, as distinguished from that of the first description, is: *What am I?* This we shall label the "question of defining character," referring to the concepts of nature, individuality, or selfhood. In contrast to the first description, which concerns itself with how to describe what remains the same in the midst of change, the second description asks what makes it possible to even conceive that there is something that remains the same. Hence, while the problem of identity in general is usually regarded as a problem for logic, the question of the "identity of persons" represents a much wider concern.[3]

This shows a disagreement we have with some philosophers discussing personal identity who also make the distinction between these two kinds of sameness. Such philosophers, however, not only attempt to isolate one area of discussion from the other, but also argue that the only kind of identity that is the proper subject of philosophical discussion is sameness, relegating the discussion of selfhood to psychology, which is typically concerned with the kind of person someone is or wants to be.[4] This sharp distinction between the two ways of understanding identity is due to the ambiguity inherent in the concept of personal identity itself.[5] The ambivalence in the use of the phrase "same person" means that it can be used to refer either to the identity of a person as an entity that persists or to the personality of a particular individual. The first reference alludes to the retention of identity throughout the course of change; the second, to the personality or selfhood that is made to appear as the locus of stability.[6] In view of this, we hold that such perspectives misrepresent the issue of personal identity. The question of sameness and the question of selfhood are intertwined. To separate them is to preclude the mutual illumination by each distinct but related discussion.[7]

Transtemporal identity refers to that which is stable, that which remains the same. Can the body be regarded as the locus of this stability?[8] If the body of an individual undergoes numerous transformations, can that individual still be regarded as the same individual? What remains the same?

If not the body, could it be the mind, or as Anthony Quinton calls it, "a particular bit of psychological apparatus"?[9] But if an individual's stock of experiences keeps expanding—thereby adding to the store of memories—does that individual remain the same individual? What remains the same? If neither the body nor the mind taken on its own is the locus of such stability, could it be something else? Is there a substrate, a "third term," that underlies all these changes, albeit one that implicitly reintroduces either of the two categories? To this question, a number of theories of personal identity give an affirmative answer.[10] In fact, this conception of an unchanging substrate is implicit within the bodily and memory criteria themselves.

It is this notion of an unchanging substrate that we hold to be detrimental to any attempt to enunciate an adequate view of the person and which precludes a resolution of the problem of personal identity. When the metaphysical foundation of a theory of person is primarily substantialistic, the ensuing theory of personal identity, whether this be understood in terms of selfhood or sameness, will also be substantialistic, thereby failing to do justice to the complexity and richness of the reality it describes.

Theories of personal identity

Proponents of strict-identity theories hold that there is nothing else about personal identity that can be discussed. In their view, it is "an utterly unproblematic notion"[11] and "an ultimate unanalyzable fact, distinct from everything observable or experienceable that might be evidence for it."[12] As far as they are concerned, the only identity relation that obtains is one that consists in the strict Leibnizian sense, whereby identity is a relation that an object can have *only* with itself. David Lewis describes this perspective in this way: "Everything is identical to itself. Nothing is identical to anything else. There is never any problem about what makes something identical to itself; nothing can fail to be. And there is never any problem about what makes two things identical: two things never can be identical."[13]

It is certainly the case that what is at stake is not simply the *similarity* that a particular stage in the life of an entity has with an earlier or later one, but also the *identity* of these. Still, the relations that hold between these distinct stages cannot be one of complete identity, for obviously no two points in an individual's life are identical. Applied primarily to the question of the identity of persons, this last observation entails that personal identity is different from the identity of things.[14] But it also implies that persons must be regarded as subjects which, while possessing bodily as well as mental states, must nevertheless be regarded as distinct from and irreducible to these persons.[15] And third, it claims that personal identity is a "further fact," ultimately irreducible to the other facts which are a person's bodily and mental states.[16] It is, moreover, different from everything that can be observed or experienced, which might be regarded as evidence for it, e.g., bodily or mental states. Geoffrey Madell argues that the fundamental error of many theories of personal identity, such as those of strict identity, is precisely to treat persons as simply another kind of object constituted by parts—a mistake, he says, that is bound up with the failure to give due attention to the first-person perspective.[17]

Nonstrict identity theorists, for their part, hold that transtemporal identity is constituted by the holding of *other facts* to which personal identity is then reduced. Hence, some authors use the term "reductionist" to describe this viewpoint.[18] These "facts" concern physical and/or psychological continuity. The existence of a brain and a body, as well as the occurrence of a causally interrelated chain of mental and physical states, constitutes a person's existence. Persons cannot be regarded as separately existing entities over and above the existence of an entity constituted by mental and physical states. This is in spite of the fact that a person can be regarded as existing and having experiences. To attribute these facts to persons is not required in describing the facts in which personal identity consists, since an "impersonal" description of personal identity is possible. Although numerical identity is an all-or-nothing affair that does not admit of degrees, indeterminate or gray areas are not altogether ruled out: i.e., so long as it is understood that such indeterminacy is merely semantic rather than metaphysical. This means that in the question regarding whether or not a person at time 1 is the same person at time 2, there is no indeterminacy in reality itself.[19] Instead, the indeterminacy lies with the application of the descriptive term that covers both situations.[20] The concept of person is a vague one which is not covered by any specifying conditions clearly stating what counts as a person, or as the same person over time. However, if and when all the facts concerning the matter do become known, then any remaining identity question will already be an empty one. This means, it is no longer a genuine question about different possibilities but a case where seemingly conflicting answers are merely different descriptions of the same facts.

To these assertions of the nonstrict theories we will have to add Derek Parfit's unique contribution to the discussion. In 1971, he published an article entitled "Personal Identity," in which he claimed that most people hold a set of intuitive beliefs about transtemporal identity, which require correction.[21] This work has had a major impact on much of the contemporary debate on the problem of personal identity. Parfit's later works have, to a considerable extent, been a further elaboration and defense of the theses he put forward in this article. He says that these intuitive beliefs center around three major themes: (i) the notion that personal identity is a "further fact" (the key idea behind strict identity theories), (ii) the idea that it is always possible to decide whether or not personal identity has been maintained, and, the most important factor in evaluating the possible outcome of a situation, (iii) the question with regard to whether the same person continues to exist. The correction of such beliefs, Parfit holds, will lead to concrete changes in our judgments about what can be done with reason. He makes a distinction between numerical and qualitative identity, the first being concerned with an entity being one and the same as it was at an earlier point in time, and the second, with the characteristics of two entities which have the very same features.[22] Our common intuitive beliefs have to do with the presumption that, in spite of the obvious lack of *qualitative* identity over time, a person continues to be *numerically* identical throughout his life. Such belief, he says, comes to the fore in one's concern for one's own future. Parfit argues that there is no basis for belief in such a continuing numerical identity or in being concerned about it. It is only a person's characteristics and circumstances that really matter, and even with these, what counts are merely relations of degree.[23] These are, according to him, "the facts in which personal identity consists."[24] When these change, an individual's identity changes with them, and there is nothing further than these simple facts.

The Parfitian thesis that personal identity is not what matters in survival is significant for our purposes. Like Hartshorne's own account it seems counterintuitive. Indeed, there seems to be important lines of intersection in both their theses, concerning the identity of persons. What is perhaps the most striking of these is Hartshorne's idea that one's *own* future is not all-important but only that one is able to influence *a future*, be this one's own or not and Parfit's notion that what is important is that there will be someone in the future, who will be psychologically continuous with me, as I am now.[25] What in Parfit is a particular person, is for Hartshorne God as that entity whose future—because I can influence it—is somewhat continuous with mine. There are significant differences, of course, the most striking one being that, for Hartshorne, a statement such as "my identity does not matter" does not mean the same as it would in Parfit. For Hartshorne, *identity does matter*, but the question is, *what kind of identity?*

John Locke also had a theory of personal identity. For him identity *does matter*; his only qualification to this being that the identity of persons is a unique kind, different from the identity of other entities, but not totally different from these either. Hence he allowed for analogies between human and nonhuman identity, all the while emphasizing the difference between persons, whose identities possessed an ethico-religious implication, and nonpersons (organisms and nonliving entities), for whom identity did not bear such an implication. Thomas Reid and Joseph Butler shared Locke's view concerning the importance of personal identity but regarded it as an ultimately, unanalyzable fact, different from and not susceptible to analogies with the identity of nonhuman entities. Hence, they criticized Locke for the manner by which he applied the concept of identity to persons and things.

Hume, who also delved into the problematic of identity, represents a more radical rejection of the importance of personal identity. For him, no real bond exists among the distinct perceptions that make up our mental life. And the identity we ordinarily take as unproblematic is shown to be a mere quality which we attribute to them. This leads Hume to reject in a similar fashion the notion of an abiding, substantial self, since he believed that no single impression is available to us from which the idea of a self could be derived. What for Locke was merely problematic, Hume deemed nonsensical.[26] Hume's rejection of the substantial self is close to Hartshorne's rejection of it inasmuch as Hartshorne's idea of the relative unimportance (or importance) of identity is close to Parfit's view. And yet, Hartshorne does not subscribe to Hume's skeptical conclusion. There is, for him, a connection that is no mere illusion, but is actually implied by the very manner by which events flow into and succeed one another.[27]

This flow or connectedness which makes the issue of personal identity important is made explicit in Paul Ricoeur's notion of the relationship between "the identity of the self" and "the identity of the same." Ricoeur offers an alternative to the Parfitian way of looking at the issue of personal identity, by analyzing Parfit's account and laying bare the complex structure of the issue.[28] Like Hartshorne, Ricoeur seems to hold the relative importance of identity, reflected in the distinction he makes between *idem*-identity (a notion similar to, if not the same as, the idea of numerical identity of Parfit, Locke, Butler, and Reid) and *ipse*-identity (a concept treated, albeit tangentially by Parfit, Butler, and Reid, but an all-important notion for Hartshorne). Locke actually offers a rather comprehensive analysis of the notion of person; unfortunately, this has been largely eclipsed by the criticisms which have tended to obscure this larger Lockean framework with the more specific concern of identifying the flaws of his idea of numerical identity. The treatment given to the importance or unimportance of identity will be the most important thread that shall run through this chapter's discussions, the aim of which will ultimately be to answer the question: *What kind of identity matters to entities that are called persons?* This question will then lead to a consideration of the kind of entity that would give importance to its identity. Hence, the fundamental question is: *What is a person?*

Persons and things

There has not seemed—in either ordinary talk or philosophical discourse—a univocal notion of person. Instead, the word and its almost exact cognates in modern Western languages appear to have had numerous uses, which at times overlap with one another. Much contemporary use of the term applies it in a general way—as the word "thing" is used to refer generally to any object. In fact, when it is not used to call attention to the fact that its referent is a human being which should be treated as such, e.g., with respect, "person" is used in quite the same way as "thing" to refer or point to a particular entity. However, two important features of the concept "person" are, in fact, (i) its distinction from a thing and (ii) the different and special treatment accorded to its referents, i.e., persons, based on the very fact that they are not the same as things. Thus we have the Kantian stipulation, for instance, that persons—as contrasted with things—must be regarded as having an unconditional worth and that respect is an attitude which has application to persons only, never to things. A corollary to this view, of course, is that things are regarded or valued based upon the degree or kind of service they render vis-à-vis persons' goals and ends. Persons on the other hand, are never to be regarded *merely* in the same way, but in fact are "ends in themselves" and are valuable in and of themselves.

The proposal of the strict view of personal identity arises from the observation that persons are in fact not the same as things. Unfortunately, discussion of the issue has evolved in a way that focuses more on questions of individuation and identification. In addition, the idea that has provided its thrust, viz., an inherent difference between persons and things, which carries with it abundant implications, remains at the core of the discussion and manages to reassert itself in the works of many contemporary authors.

Consider the issue of sameness and identification. While it is relatively unproblematic to identify material objects like tables and chairs as the same at two different points in time, identifying persons is far more complex. The most common and simplest theory of identity hinges on the identifiability of a particular object as numerically the same at time 1 and time 2. Persistence may not necessarily consist in retaining the same matter—as ships and tables can be repaired, and even persons' bodily cells are renewed—but so long as an entity retains the same form, it is still numerically the same. With regard to the more specific question of the identity of persons, however, it is a different matter. The bodily criterion describing the identity of persons reduces this identity to the essentially same structures that characterize things such as tables and ships, an idea that has long been criticized as untenable and has in fact never been popular among philosophers.

Joseph Butler (1692–1752) referred to it as the "loose and popular" sense of identity and distinguished it from what he called the "strict and philosophical sense."[29] Thomas Reid (1710–96), likewise, distinguished between this popular sense and what he called the "fixed and precise" sense of identity. The identity commonly ascribed to things, Reid argued, is something which is called identity, merely "for conveniency of speech."[30] Both he and Butler argued that personal identity is different from that of objects, in that it does not admit of degree or change. Bodies, as distinguished from persons, allow for a great deal of change of the subject. When applied to things, however, identity has no fixed nature, and thus questions that arise with regard to their identities are usually questions about words. Nonpersons, Reid says, admit of a change to their very natures as well as to their parts.[31] This cannot be the case with persons as "it is impossible that a person should be in part the same, and in part different; because a person is a *monad* and is not divisible into parts."[32] Being indivisible, a person is truly irreducible to its constituent parts. One is always more than one's body, mind, and experiences put together.

The point of Reid's argument is the fact that persons are to be regarded as unified totalities, Leibnizian monads. From this vantage point, personal identity simply cannot subsist with the diversity of substance. Unlike non-human entities, a person cannot be regarded as having parts, or being identical or reducible to them. Now, while it is beyond question that one cannot be identified with any of one's bodily parts, the issue becomes complicated when "parts" do not simply refer to "body parts," but constituent experiences, for instance, that which characterize an individual's life history. An individual says, for instance, "I am not thought, I am not action, I am not feeling; I am something that thinks, and acts, and suffers. My thoughts, and actions, and feelings, change every moment; they have no continued, but a successive existence; but that self, or I, to which they belong, is permanent, and has the same relation to all the succeeding thoughts, actions, and feelings which I call mine."[33] These entities too cannot, in Reid's thought, be regarded as identical to the person himself, nor can two of them be identical with one another. Identity is primarily a relation an object can bear *only* to itself.[34]

Personal identity therefore is not something that can be divided or which consists of parts. Reid argues that this implies the continued existence of that indivisible thing which he calls the "self" which thinks, deliberates, resolves, acts, and suffers. Everything else that can be called a component part changes every moment. Instead of a continued or permanent existence that characterizes the self, these latter constituents have a "successive existence." The sheer idea of a "part" of a person, Reid argues, is absurd. A man may lose a limb, his health, his strength, and yet remain the same person that he was. He loses nothing of his personality.[35] This is true. However, the reason he gives for saying that the person remains the same after an amputation is rather dubious. He says: "The amputated member is no part of his person, otherwise it would have a right to a part of his estate, and be liable to a part of his engagements. It would be entitled to a share of his merit and demerit, which is manifestly absurd."[36] He regards this fact of nonentitlement as a reason for saying it is not part of a person. Now if none of those things which are in fact parts of persons are to be called "parts of persons," then nothing else can in fact be called parts of persons. As Noonan rightly observes, Reid's reason for denying that such body parts are parts of person is no reason at all. Whether something is a part of a person is a physical question, not a moral one. This renders Reid's considerations irrelevant. "All he establishes," Noonan argues, "is simply that for *moral* purposes a person (as opposed to families, organizations, etc.) is the smallest unit."[37] But it is exactly this point, i.e., the description of person as the smallest unit—"that indivisible thing" not further analyzable into constituent parts—that brings Reid to posit the existence of a third term, a "self" or an "I," to which these parts, be they physical or mental states, belong.[38]

Reid's (as well as Butler's) views are reactions to the theory of personal identity espoused by John Locke, who drew an analogy between what he called the "sameness of life" that constituted the identity of plants and animals and the "sameness of consciousness" that marked the identity of persons. Butler, who is traditionally regarded as the originator of the so-called "circularity objection," also argued—in line with Reid's criticism—for the untenability of the Lockean analogy, on the grounds that the word "same" is used in different senses when applied to plants and animals, on the one hand, and to human beings, on the other.[39] When applied to persons, the term "same," says Butler, can only be used in the strict and philosophical sense, which of course means that there can be no change in the parts of the entity to which the phrase is applied. And as applied to persons, he agrees with Reid that these are akin to Leibnizian *monads*.

John Locke's theory of personal identity

We now turn to the Lockean account itself, before going into a discussion of the criticisms of Butler and Reid, criticisms which in spite of being problematic are still defended today by strict-personal-identity theorists. With a view to discover the anthropology implicit in Locke's theory, we will discuss his account of personal identity in terms of consciousness and draw a possible defense against the Butler-Reid objection as well as a point of departure for a discussion of person.

Locke was responsible for clearing the ground as well as setting the stage and the terms of the modern debate on personal identity. His views remain highly influential and downright controversial.[40] Much of present-day philosophizing about personal identity is a reaction either for or against the theory he proposed in his work *Essays Concerning Human Understanding*, published in 1690.[41] The historical significance of this work is brought to the fore if we consider that less than 50 years after its publication, David Hume remarked that the problem of personal identity that the work raised had evolved into "so great a question in philosophy."[42] Locke's specific treatment of the problem is found in the chapter entitled "Of Identity and Diversity," which appeared in the second edition of his work in 1694.[43] Locke wanted to give an account of personal identity, which would represent his fundamental opposition to Cartesian philosophy dominant at that time, which held the indivisibility of the self or thinking substance as a self-evident truth. Locke also wanted a theory that was consistent with our knowledge of our identity over a specific temporal period and which was not susceptible to skeptical objection. Moreover, he wanted to explain why personal identity is something that cannot be a matter of indifference to us. The experiences we have had or will have, both good and bad, matter to us in a way that is different from the experiences of others. Finally, and perhaps most importantly, Locke intended to point out a vital fact which many who have considered the problem before him had neglected; namely, that the concept of identity has to be joined to some substantive notion, e.g., a plant or a person, in order to have any import at all. What enables us to say that a particular thing is the same depends on the kind of entity we are talking about.

However, there was also an undeniable religious motive behind Locke's project. According to Noonan, Locke wanted "to provide an account of personal identity which would make sense of the Christian doctrines of human immortality, the resurrection of the dead and the Last Judgment."[44] Unlike many present-day theories of personal identity, which would probably take some religious ideas he considered as "puzzle cases," e.g., immortality or the resurrection, Locke saw them as facts requiring a rational explanation. However, unlike theories current in his day, which attempted to explain these issues using either a dualist or a materialist theory, Locke attempted to find a middle ground that would accommodate the elements from both the metaphysical systems. The religious motive is significant as it is intimately bound up, in Locke's view, with questions of morality and law, the subject of which are, of course, persons. In rejecting materialist and dualist solutions to religious problems therefore, he was also rejecting views concerning persons, which followed either of these two lines of thinking. He rejected both, the idea that persons were mere bits of thinking matter,[45] as well as the Cartesian solution current in his time, which posited the existence of an immaterial soul, whose identity over time was secured apart from the fortunes of the body.[46] Thus, on the one hand, he stated that "matter cannot think ergo the soul is immaterial, nothing can naturally destroy an immaterial thing ergo the soul is naturally immortal,"[47] while on the other hand, he also declared that "all the great ends of morality and religion are well enough secured, without philosophical proofs of the Soul's Immateriality; since it is evident, that he who made us first begin to subsist here, sensible intelligent Beings [...] can and will restore us to the like state of Sensibility in another world and make us capable there to receive the retribution he has designed to men, according to their doings in this life."[48] Locke also saw the need to make sense of the fact that we have knowledge concerning our own identities. Wherever one finds oneself, he argues, "there another may say, is the same person."[49] But he rejects the idea that bodily continuity alone makes personal identity. This rejection is what lies behind his distinction between "man" and "person." He also repudiates accounts which ground personal identity in the identity of substance, whether material or immaterial. And he was especially keen to point out that to be the same person is not the same as having one persisting, immaterial, spiritual soul-substance.[50] Locke regarded both the living body as well as the supposed soul-substance as irrelevant to finding an answer to the question of personal identity because they are ultimately incapable of explaining the certainty one has that he is in fact the same person as the one whose actions he knows he has done and whose experiences he is conscious of having had.

Despite his repudiation of the Cartesian viewpoint, however, there remains implicit in Locke's thesis, an emphasis on the first-person perspective, which is supposed to afford a privileged standpoint from which proposals concerning the nature of personhood can be judged.[51] Indeed, concern for self-knowledge coupled with his refusal to accept Cartesian dualism and his rejection of the grounding of personal identity in the identity of substance are foundation to his enterprise. Self-knowledge is an important as well as an all-pervasive theme in his writings. In fact, the definitions he gives to the term "person" emphasize the point even more. Thus, he defines person as "a thinking intelligent being, that has reason and reflection, and can consider itself as itself, the same thinking thing, in different times and places; which it does only by that consciousness which is inseparable from thinking, and ... essential to it: it being impossible for any one to perceive without perceiving that he does perceive."[52] This is also evident in his definition of the "self" as "that conscious thinking thing ... which is sensible or conscious of pleasure or pain, capable of happiness or misery, and so is concerned for itself as far as that consciousness extends."[53]

This shows that somehow Locke did adopt a Cartesian conception of consciousness as necessarily entailing self-consciousness. For him, as it was for Descartes, it is not possible to experience anything without knowing that we are in fact experiencing it. Still several things need to be noted here. Locke is ultimately led to hold this perspective because of his ontological presupposition that makes a clear-cut distinction between the notions of substance, men, and persons. However, in spite of certain similarities, Locke's view is not so readily identifiable with the Platonic or Cartesian view.[54] He did feel some sympathy for this view,[55] but he emphatically did not accept it.[56] The perspective that Locke takes concerning the relation of "person" and "consciousness," more than showing his specific view on the "constitutive criteria" of identity, discloses the real motive behind his controversial and even problematic account of identity. This is the elucidation of a view of person in terms of both "individuality" and "forensic" personality.[57]

The Lockean tripartite ontology

Locke makes a distinction between "substances" (both material and immaterial), "men," and "persons." Persons, according to him, are not thinking substances, even though when a person thinks, it is a thinking substance that does the thinking for it. Further, men are not persons, for when a man is no longer conscious of a past action, he is not the same person as the one who committed the action despite remaining the same man. These distinctions in Locke's ontology constitute a central component of his treatment of identity. But it is also the source of a great deal of perplexity in the study of his ideas. According to Locke, by means of sensation and reflection, we obtain the simple ideas which we later unite to form the complex idea of a particular substance. The idea of a "thinking substance" is obtained by the combination of simple ideas of thinking, doubting, etc., which we obtain through reflection, with the vague notion of a substrate in which these physical operations inhere. However, we are not able to prove by reason the existence of an immaterial substance since it is "impossible for us, by the contemplation of our own *Ideas*, without revelation, to discover, whether Omnipotence has not given some Systems of Matter fitly disposed, a power to perceive and think, or else joined and fixed to Matter so disposed, a thinking, immaterial substance."[58] Locke's suggested option therefore was that God could add to matter either a power to perceive and think or that God could create a thinking, immaterial substance. This operation of "superadding" would not alter the nature of the matter to which thought or a thinking substance was added. In making this point, Locke went against the most commonly held conception at that time, which utilized an ontology of two substances, the essential properties of which do not cross over to one another.

This issue was brought up, for instance, by Edward Stillingfleet, who found Locke's notion objectionable and threatening as it not only seemed to confuse the ideas of matter and spirit, but also veered perilously close to materialism. Locke's reply was that no more does he confuse the idea of matter with spirit than he does the idea of matter with the idea of a horse, explaining that "matter in general is a solid extended substance; and that a horse is a material animal, or an extended solid substance with sense and spontaneous motion."[59] An animal or a plant, for Locke, is a combination of matter and biological processes. With animals, the matter of the body has other properties "added" to it, e.g., sense perception and mobility. Propagation in plants is another such "added" quality, as is gravity, which is the result of forces added to the material universe. This idea is used analogously to explain how thought or thinking substance can be "superadded" by "the good pleasure and Bounty of the Creator."[60] Finally, Locke insists that were sense and spontaneous motion not added by God to animals, they would in fact be no more than animal machines as Descartes had argued.[61]

Corollary to the distinction between thinking substances and material substances are the two senses in which Locke understands the term "substance" itself. First, he believes that there are clusters of qualities or "simple ideas," of which we cannot imagine how they subsist by themselves. This inability leads us to posit a substratum "wherein they do subsist and from which they do result."[62] For Locke, it was this notion of substance as a substratum necessary for the existence of qualities, which is the important sense of the word.[63] It represents the idea of substance in general which, in his own words, is merely a "supposition of he knows not what support of such qualities, which are capable of producing simple ideas in us; which qualities are commonly called accidents."[64] The idea of substance in general, therefore, is "nothing but the supposed but unknown support of those qualities we find existing, which we imagine cannot exist *sine re substante*, without something to support them, (and) we call that support *substantia*, which, according to the true import of the words, in plain English, 'standing under' or 'upholding.'"[65]

Here we must carefully note a few things. The notion of substance is an inference for Locke. From our encounter with qualities and accidents, we infer the existence of that "something" that supports them. What he is therefore talking about when he discusses substance is, first and foremost, the *origin* of our idea of substance and, only secondarily, the actual existence of such substances themselves. Still, it would be a misinterpretation of Locke to say that substance, for him, is nothing but a figment of our imagination.[66] For him, the supposition is warranted and the inference from qualities to substance is justified. But it remains an inference nonetheless.[67] We do not perceive substances; instead, they are inferred as the support of accidents or qualities, of which we are not capable of conceiving as subsisting independently.[68]

This general idea of substance must not be confused with the distinct ideas of particular substances. This is the second sense by which Locke understands the word. In this secondary sense, the idea of substance is nothing but several combinations of simple ideas, by which we represent particular sorts of substances to ourselves.[69] And he gives the example of our idea of the sun, saying, "what is it but an aggregate of those several combinations of simple ideas, bright, hot, roundish, having a constant regular motion, at a certain distance from us, and perhaps some other?"[70] The important point to note concerning the distinction between the idea of substance in general and the notion of particular sorts of substances is that like the former, ideas concerning the latter are formed by the supposition that in each case those sensible qualities involved in the idea of particular substances flow from what he calls "a particular internal Constitution, or unknown Essence of that Substance."[71] Thus when we see different things, Locke says that what we notice is that we postulate a different unknown essence for each distinct entity. We nonetheless remain incapable of specifying what exactly is peculiar to each of these entities except in an indirect way, i.e., in terms of the peculiar set of qualities that we perceive and which enter into our definition of the kind of entity we are looking at.[72]

Now concerning particular substances themselves, he says that there are only three kinds of which we have ideas: (i) God, (ii) finite intelligences, and (iii) bodies. God is a substance since any account of what exists requires mentioning him. The same goes for finite intelligences inasmuch as they cannot be conceived as made up of more fundamental entities. Finally, the same is true for bodies. Locke holds that identity is applicable to our ideas of substances and the modes and relations of these substances as well. Now concerning their identities, God, who is without beginning, is eternal, unalterable, and everywhere, has an identity which is beyond any doubt. Finite spirits and bodies, on the other hand, have a determinate time and place of origin, whose relationship to each of them determines its identity as long as it exists.[73] Concerning the idea of body, a distinction must be made between inanimate and animate ones. Inanimate bodies, Locke says, do not possess an organization toward a particular end. Hence, in our ideas of such entities, our only concern is the cohesion of particles of matter, however they are united.[74] The same goes for every bit of matter.[75]

The organizational structure of inanimate bodies is not important to their identity over time. Their identity remains the same, determined by their point of origin.[76] Locke holds that such entities will remain the same over time for as long as no addition or subtraction of matter takes hold of them.[77] The identity of inanimate bodies throughout a specific period of time depends upon the organization of their parts. Animate bodies, on the other hand, like plants and animals, are the same because of the organization of their parts and the directedness of this organization toward a particular end. The particles that constitute an organism—unlike in inanimate entities—are arranged in such a way that they contribute to the organism's overall purpose, which is none other than the continuation of the entity's life. What makes an organism identical to itself, therefore, is not so much the determination afforded by having the same time and place of origin—as in the case of substances, but in the participation by constantly fleeing particles of matter in one common life, by which it continues to be the same animal or plant.[78]

Now the identity of man, as a natural entity, i.e., an organism, is constituted in the same way.[79] Locke's account of how a human being, just like a plant or an animal, partakes in this common life is intended to show primarily how an organism may consist, at different times, of a variety of basic substances, which are united together into one single organization by an identity of life.[80] Man, therefore, is a certain kind of living organism whose identity depends upon its biological organization directed toward the continuation of the organism's life.[81] We should note here, however, that when Locke speaks of participation in a common life or continuity of life, he does not simply mean the spatiotemporal succession of particles united by a common thread. For even between a living man and one now dead, there is spatiotemporal succession of particles. And yet the dead man is no longer the same man but a corpse. Physical integrity is a requirement for man as an organism to remain the same. He must be possessed of a vital body, the parts of which have an organization directed toward a certain end. For as long as long as there is continuity of life, man will remain the same over time.[82] This explains why Locke makes use of the body, with its particular shape, as the most obvious and commonly used feature of what is called a "man."[83] However, men also possess minds. We observe our bodies; but we also observe our thoughts, beliefs, ideas, intuitions, and so on. Locke makes sense of this duality via his distinction between "man" as a biological term, and "person" as a forensic term.

The distinction between "man" and "person"

In his work *Reference and Generality*, P.T. Geach, makes a distinction between general terms which are either "adjectival" or "substantival."[84] He held that among terms which may be univocally applied to a great number of entities, we may distinguish those that characterize entities in a way that adjectives describe, e.g., brown, long, etc., as well as those terms that do not so much characterize or describe things, but tell us what kind or sort of thing an entity is, e.g., anthill, book, man, etc. This second type of terms are called "sortals."[85] This first distinction is followed by a second one, namely, between adjectivals, which possess a criterion of application, and sortals, possessing a criterion of identity. [86] To say that adjectival terms have a criterion of application means that whatever term one picks out, e.g., black, the question will be about which individuals would such terms be applicable to. On the other hand, the criterion of identity which covers sortals determines the conditions under which a particular individual to which the term "black," for instance, is applicable is *this particular individual*—the same or different from another.

Let us apply these distinctions to the terms "brown" and "book," each being applicable to a particular group of entities and not to others. The cover of a book may be brown; but so can be the bark of a tree, or dried leaves, as we see them in late autumn, or the flowerpot sitting on the windowsill. While they may all be brown, the fact remains that nothing in the meaning of "brown" can enable us to distinguish between a book, the bark of a tree, dried leaves, or a flowerpot. On the other hand, with the term "book" we have a criterion of application enabling us to distinguish a book from other entities. We can point to it, and say what sort of entity it is. One important thing to note here is that different sortals often, but not always, have different criteria of identity.[87] Thus the criterion of identity for books, for instance, would differ from the criterion of identity for leaves or for human beings. Locke was probably the first philosopher who, in considering the question of identity, had anticipated this point.[88]

It is obvious from the foregoing discussion that "criterion of identity"—at least the one we are interested in here—does not involve the question as to what could count as *evidence* for identity. Rather, we are describing the criterion which specifies the conditions which apply. It possesses not merely an *epistemic* status, as in the case of a retinal scan, for instance, which, although possessing an almost incontrovertible way of determining the identity of an individual, is not a criterion in the sense by which we understand it. It is, rather, a *metaphysical-cum-semantic* principle of identity, in that not only is it an important element in the meaning of any particular sortal, but it also enables us to have an idea concerning the fundamental nature of those entities to which the sortal applies.[89]

The distinction that Locke makes between man and person is founded on this notion concerning sortals and the fact that the two different sortal terms have different criteria of identity associated with each of them.[90] Locke, as James Baillie noted, was the first to realize that there was a philosophical problem with the notion bequeathed by Platonic and Cartesian philosophy.[91] In doing so, he recognized the conflicts inherent in the dualistic conception of human beings. Of course the question that arises is whether it becomes possible for two sortal terms to be applied to but one entity. Obviously not; as "book" and "flower pot," for instance, cannot be applied to but one thing. But what about man and person—the two sortals which Locke clearly distinguishes and regards as having different criteria of identity? An initial answer could be that though certain sortals are inapplicable to one and the same thing, some—like man and person perhaps?—are not as easily placed under this category. Is this in fact what Locke had in mind?

There are two interlocking threads that dominate Locke's treatment of identity as this notion is articulated in the *Essay*.[92] The first is his fundamental opposition to the Cartesianism that held sway during his time. And the second is his recognition of the ethico-religious import of the question of personal identity, and his intention to make sense of what he refers to as "the great ends of morality and religion."[93] The distinction he makes between man and person is consistent with this motive, for what he ultimately wanted to articulate was not so much the problem of finding a relation, e.g., memory, which would unite diverse ideas into one spiritual bundle (the question of personal identity), as much as how an individual could morally own, and thus be accountable for, *his own* thoughts, experiences, and deeds. The former is a third-person problem; the latter, the first-person problem of how a moral agent is rendered a *self* to *himself* over a specific period of time.

Nowhere perhaps does Locke's conceptual pragmatism come out more strongly than here. The distinction is put in a clearer light if we consider that he uses the idea of person to bring to the fore notions regarding reward and merit, accountability and recompense, which are not as readily accessible to the strictly biological perspective from which he regarded the sortal term "man." Alston and Bennett point out that Locke regarded it as a fact that concepts that best fit our interests are those which we ordinarily choose and utilize.[94] Now Locke believed that while it is possible for an individual to be indifferent and have little or no concern for the fate of others, he cannot be unconcerned about his own fate. In the same way that he cannot be unconcerned about the rewards or penalties he is to receive for deeds which he recognizes as his own.[95] Locke obviously wanted to highlight this fact. He distinguishes the two sortals and restricts the notion of person so that a statement about someone as the same person who had committed a crime or has done a good deed would imply accountability or merit without much room for dispute. He did see after all that what makes individuals accountable for their actions is their ability to recognize these as their own. And while the witness of others is recognized as vital, first-person recognition remains the most important element. This perspective, according to Locke, belongs properly to the sphere of the term "person."

The first-person viewpoint is therefore of great significance for Locke, neither in itself nor even because it enables us to get a glimpse into his understanding of personal identity. It is important for Locke because it allows him—in his moral theory and religious concerns—to emphasize that accountability is only possible with its just rewards and punishments if there is a *person*—a self-conscious individuality which is able to "own" thoughts, deeds, or experiences, which are worth rewarding or deserving of punishment. Every other so-called concern alleged of Locke's philosophy is secondary to this practical aim.

Scientific and moral concerns

For most practical purposes the identity of man, according to Locke, is on the same basis as that of plants and animals. The term "man" stands for a biological concept which includes in its comprehension: (i) its constitution, which is akin to that of both animate and inanimate entities,[96] (ii) its difference from inanimate entities, in that its constituent particles share in a common life directed toward economy and its continued existence (This is also his similarity with plants and animals.), and (iii) its difference from plants and animals, in that to its spatiotemporal continuity, which makes up its identity, may be added an element that is not found in plants, animals, and inanimate objects; namely, consciousness.[97] It must be remarked that this delineation of the concept man from both inanimate and animate entities is consistent with the analytical and pragmatic thrust of Locke's philosophy and his desire to be clear with regard to the identity of sortals. In this regard, we may make a distinction between a "scientific" (or "physical") as well as a "moral" interest that lies beneath the often unconventional distinctions he makes.[98]

Take the case of the sortal "man" and regard it vis-à-vis the distinctions and similarities it has with other entities. From a scientific point of view, man is first a body possessing a particular shape—just like an inanimate object. However, man is also a living body. Hence he is unlike a mere thing but like "an animal of such a certain Form"[99] and is composed of particles united in such a way as to share in a common life. Tie these analytical distinctions with Locke's view that identity is sortal relative, and we get to the bottom of his reason for insisting that we should not confuse the identity of man over time with the nonidentity of his body over time. For strictly speaking, a man's body—regarded as a mass of matter—is not the same over time; its constituent particles undergo quantitative change.[100] However, our common everyday form of discourse tends to fuse these two claims, viz., that man's body over time is the *same* body, and that over time, that body is *his*.

Against this too close an association, Locke insisted on the distinction in philosophic discourse between the ideas of identity and ownership. Why? For according to him, there is no such thing as identity over time of a human body as a mere mass of matter. The sortal term "body" may have such an identity (founded, like other bodies, on its origin); but not when it is also qualified as "human"; hence, his insistence that the identity of man not be equated with bodily identity.[101] For, in a strictly philosophical sense, and in a very scientific sense as well (cells are really replaced and renewed over time), a man's body in the course of a certain period of time is no longer the *same*, albeit remaining that man's *own*. While the distinction may in fact be somewhat artificial, it nevertheless draws attention to Locke's intention of being clear about the difference between the body understood as a collection of particles, and the body understood as unqualifiedly "human." The earlier term is different from the latter in that there is an element in the latter which for Locke is significant, namely, the element of possession or ownership.

What constitutes "ownership"? With this question, one leaves the realm of the specifically scientific and physical and enters the domain of morality and law. In this domain, Locke denies any ultimate relevance to shape, figure, and even organization toward an end, in a way that made these so vital to questions regarding biological constitution. Moral man is not only a body; he is also a rational creature. And it is in this way that he becomes subject to law.[102] The idea of moral man cannot therefore be regarded as merely coextensive with the scientific or physical idea of man. They are two different ways of speaking about the same individual.[103]

From this vantage point, emphasis is given not to corporeality or its purposive structure but to rationality. To the question then regarding the criterion of ownership, an initial key to finding an answer would be reason. Locke's concern to speak of man from the perspective of morals is clearly a legal one.[104] For him, a moral man is a corporeal, rational being who stands in relation to the law, and it is possible both that a human being might not be a moral man and that a moral agent might not be a human being.[105] What is important then in this regard is that an agent be a corporeal and rational entity standing in relation to the law. It is secondary, even inconsequential, whether this entity is a man or monkey,[106] as a monkey's constitution would likewise not matter at all should it be found to possess rationality.

The reflexivity and "concernedness" of consciousness

The idea of moral man, however, requires further qualification. Locke wanted to move his analysis to an even deeper level by asking how a rational and corporeal agent, i.e., a moral man, can attribute to itself deeds which will merit either reward or punishment. How does one become accountable? The key to Locke's answer is his notion of consciousness, which has two interlocking dimensions: reflexivity and, what he calls, "concernment". In his book *Studies in Words*, C.S. Lewis pointed out that in the English language of Locke's time, "consciousness" had two basic connotations, a weak and a strong one.[107] The weak sense puts the emphasis on the root—the second half—of the word's Latin origin; the first half, the prefix, is inactive. ("Consciousness" is derived from *cum*, meaning "with," and *scire*, meaning "to know.") In the weak sense, the prefix *cum* contributes nothing to the overall meaning of the word. The strong sense, on the other hand, stresses both prefix and root and is closer to what Locke means when he uses the phrase "conscious to himself." Lewis termed this the "consciring" sense, which emphasizes the element of being "conscious to oneself." To be conscious to oneself is to have knowledge of something that one shares with oneself alone, i.e., in the sense of being a witness to one's own deeds. It is therefore no less than knowledge of oneself, of one's thoughts, and one's actions.[108]

Locke's notion of consciousness lays heavy emphasis on this element of being a witness to one's own thoughts, acts, and experiences, being self-conscious—a Cartesian influence no doubt.[109] "Everyone," he says, "is to himself that which he calls *self*."[110] Consciousness is reflexive perception of thinking, "a second-order act; the perception of what passes in a man's mind."[111] This is a concept he stresses throughout his extended discussion of thinking in the second book of the *Essays*.[112] For one to be conscious in the strong sense of the word means that one is aware of oneself as the agent of a particular act that has been committed. Reflexive consciousness then is shared knowledge; it is none other than a shared awareness that a present state of oneself has with a past state of that self.

However, more important than this description of consciousness as reflexive is its implication for Locke's rational and corporeal agent. For that consciousness is reflexive means that it encompasses in it an element of what Locke calls "concernment."[113] By using this term, Locke is attempting to bring home the point that the domain of morality encompasses not only a reflexive awareness of one's thoughts and deeds, but more significantly, a concern for one's fortunes as this may be affected at the moment or at some future time. One is being responsible for the thoughts and actions he appropriates as *his*.[114] Hence, the questions "What constitutes ownership?" and "How does one become accountable?" are intertwined. For one becomes accountable and is the subject of either reward or punishment by owning the myriad thoughts, actions, and experiences he has had or will have. This is something one does through concernment whereby one "sympathizes and is concerned"[115] for one's thoughts, actions, and experiences. It is this that constitutes moral ownership as well as an individual's relation to the laws and the society or community to which one belongs.[116] But it is also this—*concernment*, being oneself a witness to one's own acts leading to one's owning up to them—that for many of Locke's critics, is constitutive of, and is for all intents and purposes indistinguishable from memory.

The role of memory

The distinction between consciousness regarded simply as reflexive awareness and consciousness as concern enables us to clarify Locke's notion of consciousness as memory and the usual interpretation of his theory of personal identity in terms of this category. We must note at the outset, however, that in spite of Locke being presented as the originator of the thesis of personal identity based on the criteria of memory, he himself never uses the word in any of the main expositions of his theory of the identity of persons. It is "consciousness" that he uses, not memory *per se*. And even if consciousness did have this connotation of memory, this does not in fact play quite the role in his theory as it is widely assumed.[117] One of the primary reasons why Locke has often been interpreted as saying that personal identity is constituted by memory is his notion of *concerned* consciousness. This type of consciousness, i.e., knowledge one shares with oneself alone, appears, in our ordinary way of understanding at least, to be exactly what memory is. Hence, Thomas Reid correctly observed that Locke "attributes to consciousness the conviction we have of our own past actions, as if a man may now be conscious of what he did twenty years ago."[118] Because of this, he says, it is impossible to understand the meaning of Locke's notion, unless "consciousness" is taken to mean memory.[119] Indeed, the only knowledge of the past that appears to be truly relevant for Locke's thesis is consciousness as memory knowledge.[120] However, that there are considerable difficulties with this theory—if in fact it were Locke's theory—was already clear to Joseph Butler and Thomas Reid.[121] Butler argues as well that to hold that remembrance of past thoughts, acts, and experiences are necessary to being the same person is to say that one "has not existed a single moment, nor done one action, but what he can remember: indeed none but what he reflects upon."[122] The crux of the argument of course is that personal identity cannot be made dependent upon memory because memory is unreliable. There are countless thoughts, acts, and experiences I can no longer remember. Surely, if my identity depended on my remembering these, then either I have lost my identity or it has been interrupted. Am I therefore to limit my identity only to those experiences I can remember?

Butler moreover brings in the objection which has now become a standard criticism found in literature dealing with Locke's theory. This is the so-called "circularity objection," which states that memory presupposes, and therefore cannot constitute, personal identity.[123] As knowledge in general presupposes truth, memory—since it presupposes personal identity—simply cannot occur as an ingredient in its definition. Indeed, not only do we normally take for granted that there is a distinction between a genuine and an apparent memory, we also have no difficulty in accepting the fact that people are capable of remembering having done things which they did not do and forgetting things which they in fact did. This point was driven home by Antony Flew.[124] Flew argues that Locke wanted to say that *P* is the same person who did or witnessed *X* if and only if *P* remembers doing or witnessing *X*. This, however, is not clear. The verb "remember" and its cognates, according to Flew, have a strong and a weak sense. In the strong sense, to remember something implies the correctness of the recollection, i.e., in everything except the minor details. In the weak sense, on the other hand, remembering simply implies an assertion of sincerity in making a memory claim. It is in this weak sense that we allow for the mistakes of memory. In fact, although we pay attention to what people claim to remember when deciding upon identity questions, the fact that one claims to have done or seen something does not show that he in fact did or saw it. Take the case of someone suffering from paramnesia; although sincere in his "recollection," he may in fact be mistaken. The classic example made popular by Flew is that of George IV, who in his declining years, "remembered" his gallant leadership at the battle of Waterloo, though he was never present on that field.[125] Given this fact, it would seem that if we are to say that *P* is the same person if he has the memory of *X*, we would have to mean that *P* has to remember *X* in the strong sense of the word.

However, difficulties immediately arise. How do we decide between veridical and apparent memory in a particular case? If a person's inner conviction is in fact unreliable, it appears that we shall have to take recourse in something other than simply a claim of memory. In ordinary circumstances we would have to appeal to the person's physical presence at the scene or scenes which he describes. This suggests not only that the memory criterion cannot stand on its own, but that it is in fact parasitic upon bodily continuity. This is a view held by some Lockean critics who see the need to augment memory with the bodily criterion.[126] However, Locke too emphasized the fragility of memory.[127] He was very much aware of the fact that there seemed to be a constant decline in our memories, even of the deepest and the most retentive minds. Memory can indeed be so weak at times that its contents might as well never have been there.[128]

If actual memory were taken as logically necessary and sufficient for personal identity—as many of Locke's critics present him as doing—then his views concerning its fragile and fleeting character could very well be taken as evidence for something like a person's "decay."[129] As memory fades, so does one's identity as a person whose decay, if there were in fact such a phenomenon, could be hastened by illness (as in the case of individuals suffering from Alzheimer's disease). Or this decay could be accelerated through a deterioration of the senses. As Paul Helm observes, "it is surely an extremely odd justification for looking at old diaries and photographs at regular intervals that one is striving to continue to be the person one once was. It is surely more reasonable, and more consistent with *Locke's overall view*, to describe the situation as trying to remember what one once did and was like."[130] That phrase—

"Locke's overall view"—is significant. For it must really be within its compass that the particular notions, e.g., "substance," "man," "person," "memory," "consciousness," etc., that we encounter in Locke must be understood and explained. Obviously, memory—because of its weakness—cannot be relied upon to provide a watertight account of personal identity, nor its constitution. However, that memory is constitutive of personal identity is precisely *not* what Locke's view amounts to. For him, the sole and sufficient condition of full identity is *consciousness*. Memory, because it is a dimension or aspect of consciousness, can provide evidence for identity, but not constitute it. The claims of memory have authority, provided they follow on observation; that is to say, observations cause memory claims to be authoritative (not too far from accurate).[131]

Memory and causal connectedness

For Locke, memory provides evidence of a causal connection, not necessarily a logical one.[132] Since personal identity is constituted by the spatiotemporal continuity of consciousness (in the same way that the identity of a plant is constituted by the spatiotemporal continuity), memory provides good evidence for such continuity, in much the same way that a student who sees a particular tree everyday on his/her way to the university is good evidence for the continued identity of that tree. In the case of persons, there can be no question with regard to the necessity of memory for personal identity. Memory is necessary because, as Paul Helm interprets Locke to say, a person must be able to "consider itself as itself, the same thinking thing in different times and places." However, "it is not logically necessary for being the same individual as someone in the past that one remembers things in the past."[133] This shows that there is an inherent ambiguity in the idea that memory is logically necessary for personal identity. If it were understood in the sense of memory being logically necessary for an entity to be a person at a particular time,[134] then Locke's notion of consciousness commits him to this view; but if it were taken to mean that the recollection of doing a particular act is logically necessary for being that person who in fact *did* the act, then there is no evidence that Locke held this view.[135] The first instance merely provides evidence, the second constitutes personal identity. The first is the Lockean view; the second, a misinterpretation of it.[136]

Moreover, what is required by memory as an evidence for identity is that a person is able to recall some action in the past, not that he *does* recall it. Locke was not, strictly speaking, a memory theorist. That alone suffices to show how his theory was misunderstood by both Berkeley and Reid. Their objection, first of all, neglects the transitive character of identity.[137] Stressing and adopting such transitivity is in fact one of the ways that neo-Lockeans have tried to defend his theory against Reid's misinterpretation.[138] This allows for Locke's account to be understood no longer in terms of "psychological connectedness" simply, but in terms of "psychological continuity", in which case a person at a later time can be regarded as the same person at an earlier time, just in case the person at a later time is linked by a continuous experience-memory to the person at an earlier time.

The transitivity of memory aside, however, the interpretation of "can remember" as "can in fact remember" opens the possibility for many other contrived absurdities not too different from Reid's. For instance, one can say that one's identity varies from hour to hour. If one were alert or in a reminiscing or nostalgic mood, for instance, one can say that one's identity can extend farther back in time than it would be an hour later when one can recall very little because of being drowsy or simply being tired. Having said these, however, we must insist that in order to be faithful to Locke's notion of consciousness as concern, the response that must finally be given to Reid's objection is that (i) consciousness should not be regarded as equivalent to memory and (ii) the question of personal identity in Locke must not be separated from the distinction he made between the sortal terms "man" and "person," nor should these two be regarded as identical or interchangeable. A murderous youth who undergoes conversion and in later life becomes a saintly old man remains (from the scientific/physical point of view) the same "man." From the perspective of Locke's idea of *concerned* consciousness, however, he would no longer be exactly the same "person." In this regard, moreover, consciousness as concern does not readily establish a transitive relationship. As Behan puts it, "In order to be the same person with the person who performed an earlier action, a moral man must remember the action as his *and* re-appropriate the action as *his* through concerned consciousness."[139] He does not have to remember everything that he has done, thought, or experienced, but only some portion of it. As an evidential criterion, perfection is not required of memory. Although not perfectly reliable—something Locke himself recognized[140]—human memory, under normal circumstances, has the power to remember some, if not a great deal, of the thoughts, acts, and experiences an individual has had. If persons could in fact recall very little, this would really be a serious difficulty. However, for the most part, and in most cases, persons are quite successful in recalling their pasts. Antony Flew points out that a distinction must be made between "genuine remembering which necessarily involves the truth of the proposition said to be remembered, and honest memory claims which do not."[141] And he brings in the possibility of paramnesia to stress his point concerning the possible changes on alternative interpretations of "can" and "remember."[142] In doing so Flew intended to lay greater stress on the inherent weakness of memory and thus put the spotlight on the inadequacy of the Lockean account. His main question is: How are we to decide between a genuine and an apparent recollection in a particular case?

On the errors of memory

Since it is constricting to limit personal identity to actions and experiences that an individual can actually remember, we should perhaps qualify what was asserted earlier by explaining that *X* is the same person who committed an act if, and only if, he can remember it. This would allow for a greater flexibility in the requirement of memory. In a strong practical sense, "can" would imply that if X in fact committed the act, there is something we can do—a set of procedures such as hypnosis perhaps—which might induce an individual to recall whatever it is that he saw or experienced. However, even with such procedure or other, there is no way to be sure that the individual's memories would in fact be true. Even false memories can be insinuated into the minds of persons undergoing hypnosis. If "can" were not understood in this way, we have to ask what its use here contributes. What difference is there between "actually remember" and "can remember"? It is, of course, possible that the latter phrasing were simply another way of saying that X is the one who committed the act if, and only if, he were the person to whom the application of hypnosis or psychotherapy is appropriate. However, this is also problematic. It could be false since even before discovering who committed the act in question, our "procedure" would have been applicable to any likely candidate anyway, and not to X alone. Or it could be merely a surreptitious way of saying that X is actually the person who committed the act so that nobody else "can remember" it. This brings us all the way back to Butler's circularity objection. For, in this argument at least, it does seem that the concept of memory presupposes personal identity, and not the other way around.

In this instance, it must be admitted that the vagaries of memory would indeed pose serious problems for an account such as Locke's. However, it would only be truly problematic if Locke's theory in fact made memory a constitutive criterion of identity. While the criticisms are valid, they cannot be directed against Locke for his theory of personal identity does not involve this manner of understanding memory. It is a fundamental flaw of many criticisms against him that they assume his account to do so.[143]

What about lying (conscious disavowal) or a claim not to remember at all? And what of paramnesia which, according to Flew, is not just a logical possibility but a real phenomenon?[144] Memory is not only weak and often unreliable, but it can also be manipulated. Locke was not unaware of the problem paramnesia posed. Thus, he discusses the question why "one intellectual substance may not have represented to it, as done by itself, what it never did, and was perhaps done by some other agent."[145] As a scientist and physician, Locke was very well aware of such a situation, pointing out that its impossibility "will be difficult to conclude from the nature of things."[146] And from the scientific viewpoint, he in fact considered this phenomenon significant.[147]

Concerning the problem of paramnesia and lying or conscious disavowal, let us consider them as two sides of the same coin: the falsehood of a particular memory claim, paramnesia being the "innocent" mistake; and conscious disavowal, the "sinister" one. While significant from the scientific/physical point of view, paramnesia was considered significant by

Locke from the perspective of morality only with a certain qualification. Moreover, if there is in fact significance to false memory claims such as callous disavowals, and even paramnesia itself, this must be approached and considered from within the entire orbit of Locke's ethico-religious concerns. The madness such as that which afflicted George IV, was not *in itself* morally significant for Locke, as an individual cannot, from the vantage point of *concerned* consciousness, be held to be morally accountable. If there is any significance to this phenomenon in the realm of morals, it would be, according to Locke, thanks to the goodness of God who "as far as the happiness or misery of any of his sensible creatures is concerned, will not, by a fatal error of theirs, transfer from one to another that consciousness which draws reward or punishment with it."[148] Were an individual to be afflicted with this particular type of madness, God's goodness[149] will safeguard him from being held accountable. Memory is first, and at best, a *ground* for the experience of the continued identity of a person; it is not what personal identity consists in. In addition, for Locke, present ascriptions of personal responsibility based on the likelihood that a memory claim may actually be reliable are *provisional*. This makes it possible for honest but false memory claims as well as ascriptions of responsibility. This also explains, in Locke's mind, why a court of law can punish a drunkard for committing a crime of which he may not have been aware at the time, in which case the deed was not, strictly speaking, his *own*. A human court justly punishes the drunkard "because the fact is proved against him, but want of consciousness cannot be proved for him."[150] Human ignorance brings about this situation, for a human court cannot give the drunkard, accused of a crime of which he was not aware, the benefit of the doubt. Locke invokes the Christian notion of the Last Judgment and says that on that "Great Day, wherein the secrets of all hearts shall be laid open, it may be reasonable to think that no one shall be made to answer for what he knows nothing of, but shall receive his doom, his conscience accusing or excusing him."[151] On that day, Locke imagines a situation in which the weaknesses and vagaries of memory will be set right; where one cannot deny having done something which he had in fact committed but may have forgotten; and where one who remembers having done an act which he in fact did not commit will realize his error. In this ideal future domain, Locke believes that there is nothing that an individual *can* remember of which he will not be made to recall should this be needed for the forensic purposes of that day.[152]

This shows why Locke's theory does not explicitly allow for a hardhearted refusal to admit a past wrong committed. If a man, here and now, were in fact able to remember a past act and yet also be unwilling to own it as *his*, it may be that the act may have already been pardoned and his guilt may have already been absolved. In this case he has good grounds for refusing to appropriate the past deed. Thus Paul the apostle, speaking of his "new life in Christ," was able to say: "It is *no longer I* who live."[153] On the other hand, he may simply be stubborn and is merely refusing to accept responsibility by *owning* the deed. Against the callousness of a hardened heart, Locke's theory has no secure check. Ultimately, however, even the result of such stubbornness is temporary. In the end, one can only avoid accountability for so long. The coming of "the Great Day" will see to it that a rectification of the situation does take place.

A great deal of the objections leveled against Locke's theory, most especially those criticisms that hinge on the fact that memory has gaps, is based on an inaccurate reading or interpretation of his account. The objections such as those of Butler, Reid, Flew, Mackie, and Bernard Williams are valid. However, they are also inaccurate inasmuch as they argue that Locke maintains either that memory is *constitutive of* personal identity or that it is a *criterion* of personal identity in the strong sense of the term. As we have tried to show, Locke did offer a theory of personal identity; but memory does not play quite the role in it that is commonly assumed. It is consciousness that was of paramount importance to Locke's theory. And the role of consciousness in this theory is logical and metaphysical. Personal identity at any particular time, i.e., at that moment where a "punctual self"—to use the phrase Charles Taylor employs to describe the idea of "person" in Locke[154]—exists, is constituted by consciousness at that time while personal identity over time consists in the spatiotemporal continuity of an individual consciousness. It is consciousness that guarantees that there is in fact one person (or more) who exists where there is a man at a series of times and places t_1P_1 ... t_nP_n. On the other hand, the role of memory is epistemic; it affords one sort of evidence for personal identity, its vagaries notwithstanding. It enables us to know whether or not there is in fact a person that exists in that series of times and places t_1P_1 ... t_nP_n, where there is a "man". Insofar as it is reliable, memory affords evidence of the spatiotemporal continuity of consciousness which constitutes personal identity. It is the imperfect and incomplete recaller of this continuity of individual consciousness. Hence, when Locke describes memory by using the phrase "as far as this consciousness can be extended backwards to any past action or thought, so far reaches the identity of that *person*," he is using memory to retrace the previous spatiotemporal history of that individual consciousness. What becomes obvious is that the distinction between consciousness and memory is tied up with the distinction between man and person, and that all these are in turn bound up with the moral as well as legal thrust of Locke's notion of the identity of a person as an accountable self.

Person as individuality and property

Just as participation in a unified life directed and organized toward preservation and economy is the hallmark of the identity of plants and animals, so participation in a unified consciousness directed and organized toward the appropriation of its thoughts, actions, and experiences, is the hallmark of the identity of persons.[155] This analogy between life and consciousness furnishes the matrix of the Lockean thesis that a moral agent's identity has nothing to do—conceptually at least on any particular notion at the substantial level—with the nature, number, and continuity of whatever it is that underlies that phenomenal identity.[156] Just as life is an organizing principle unifying a host of fleeting or constantly changing parts into one continuous entity such as an animal, so consciousness is that principle which brings into one coherent identity what could very well be an entire gamut of thoughts, actions, and experiences which a particular individual had.

Consciousness is able to unite into a coherent pattern the identity of person in the same way that life unifies the identity of man, animal, and plant. Consciousness not only possesses a reflexive character, but it also has an appropriative role. "Concerned consciousness"—the term we shall give to Locke's notion of "concernment"—enables a moral agent to *own* as genuinely *his*, thoughts, actions, and experiences, thereby recognizing these as his moral property. This moral property then is what a person speaks of as himself, or *his* self. Thus Locke says: "Self is that conscious thinking thing ... which is sensible, or conscious of Pleasure and Pain, capable of Happiness or Misery, and so is concern'd for it self, as far as that consciousness extends."[157] I, as a moral agent, speak of those which I have appropriated as my very own, as my *self*. This is obviously a first-person point of view, which Locke contrasts to the third-person perspective, which sees this *self* which I have appropriated and labels it "person." Thus, Locke states that person "is the name for this self. Wherever a Man finds what he calls himself, there I think another may say is the same Person."[158]

We must be clear as to the nature of the Lockean strategy. Instead of one concept—an individual for instance—which includes in its comprehension two criteria: one dealing with "man," the other with person, what we have are two distinct sortal terms, two distinct concepts, each possessing its own criterion. This apparent tidiness, while representing a radical departure from common everyday usage and understanding of these terms, simply confirms what has already been intimated on several occasions earlier in this discussion; namely, that Locke's real concern is to articulate a theory of moral agency and a description of what it means to be a moral agent. Ultimately for him, persons are the only real moral agents. This is disclosed by his calling "person" a "forensic term,"[159] which of course is meant to lay stress on the fact that "the interests which best explain our employment of this particular method of classification" (i.e., the Lockean strategy) are those of morality and law.[160]

The second point that needs to be noted concerning Locke's strategy is the fact that, owing perhaps to his desire for greater and greater clarity, his method is characterized by a progressive delimitation of concepts. This was already made evident by the copious distinctions we have so far encountered. What we see now is that the notion of person itself contains within its comprehension the further distinction between its substantive use and its use as a forensic term describing the nature or character of a moral agent. This divergence is not without its historical moorings. C.C.J. Webb in his book *God and Personality* has pointed out that the seeming ambiguity with regard to the notion of person—which stems from the divergence between substantive individuality and forensic personality—has its roots in the Greek and Latin mindset, which expressed the rational nature by the term *persona* and the individual subsistence by the term *hypostasis.*[161] Webb goes on to say that the history of the notion of person which has involved a constant oscillation between these two ideas,[162] was first crystallized in the thought of Boethius, who defined person as "the individual substance of a rational nature": *Persona est naturae rationalis individua substantia.*[163]

The substantive use of "person" then refers to the moral agent as an "independent and fundamentally unchanging individuality"; *this* moral agent, and not *that* one. The forensic use, on the other hand, refers to the same moral agent, but primarily as one whose *ownership*[164] of the elements that constitute his *self*, establishes his personality through social relationship and voluntary activity. Here again, yet another distinction is possible, viz., that of forensic personality as owner of its thoughts, acts, and experiences, and that of forensic personality who, as the owner of these constituents of self, stands as an agent who plays a role[165] within a community of other agents and whose membership in this community puts him in a relation to its norms and laws.

These two qualifications of a forensic personality, "owner" and "role-player," are encompassed by Locke's notion of person. A citizen is one who plays a role or shares in the life of that aggregate of persons to which she belongs. Now while a citizen's private life is his/her own, i.e., ideally at least his/her citizenship is the only face she presents to the public. However, not everyone who is a member of the community is recognized as fit to play a role in its public life. There are criteria by which one is admitted to the rights and privileges of citizenship. Satisfaction of these criteria is what establishes one as a citizen or a person in the legal sense. Indeed in legal terms, "persons" are regarded as subjects of legal rights and duties.[166] What counts for the legal concept of person is in fact the relation an individual has with the law, such that whatever characteristics that particular individual may have apart from such relation is deemed inconsequential.[167] Commonly, a necessary condition for having the rights and privileges of citizenship is responsibility and accountability for one's actions. Rights are ascribable only to persons, and thus, persons alone are responsible and accountable. (It is in this sense that children and the mentally handicapped for instance are covered by a different set of norms and regulations governing accountability and responsibility for acts committed.)

From the foregoing discussion, it becomes obvious why the forensic nature of person is the key to understanding Locke's thesis that consciousness, *concerned* for its *self*, constitutes personal identity. The problem of personal identity, from the vantage point of *concernedness*, is not a third-person problem concerning either unity or substance. Rather, it is a first-person problem that concerns the manner by which I, as a moral agent, become accountable to myself for my thoughts, actions, and experiences. Charles Taylor describes this type of situation as a kind of weaving of who or what one is (identity), and one's moral orientation.[168] But the problem of personal identity is also the problem of how these constituents of a moral agent's *self*—what is *his*—become, and over a definite period of time continue to be, *his own*. It is within the framework of Locke's moral philosophy that his theory of personal identity must be comprehended. And it is his notion of *concerned* consciousness that must be regarded as a solution to both problems, as it is this that provides the basis for moral ownership, which, for Locke, is a necessary and sufficient condition for accountability.[169] Hence, it is within such ambit of moral concern that our discussion of the issue of the identity of persons must find its locus. We shall bear this in mind as we now turn to issues that have arisen from more contemporary discussions of the problem.

2
Personal Identity and the Unity and Uniqueness of the Self

David Hume's "fictitious identity"

A thoroughly "fictitious" notion is how David Hume would characterize personal identity. And to search for it would only lead to despair due to the utter impossibility of precisely and introspectively locating it. Although beginning with a limited view of both experience and reflection, Hume nevertheless attempted to discover the self by attending to his own experiences and tried to catch himself having them. He of course ended up concluding that there was no such thing apart from the stream of experiences that the self was supposed to own.[1] The "I," he realized, refers not to an ego that owns thoughts, actions, and experiences, but simply to the causally connected series of thoughts, actions, and experiences, whose connections are at best problematic.[2]

By focusing on consciousness from the perspective of experience as a succession of atomistic and discrete states that are mediated through the senses,[3] Hume was able to expose the difficulty inherent in the notion of a substantial self. Indeed, if this substantial self were no more than the element that remained unchanged throughout a series of changes, then the series taken by itself would disclose nothing more than a succession of members that need not be connected with each other.[4] With the possibility of a unifying center being rejected, the varied perceptions that Hume speaks of are ultimately left without anything to pull them together into a coherent whole. Still, this does not faze him. The idea of a substantial self, he insisted, is no more than a philosopher's invention.[5] It was, he thought, both unintelligible and unnecessary, even if we have in fact become so accustomed to using it for purposes of facility whenever we find ourselves reflecting on our ideas of particular things.[6] But there simply is no unchanging and stable underlying entity, for the self is no more than a bundle of varied perceptions in rapid and perpetual flux.[7]

In this regard Hume's thesis represents a more radical reaction to Descartes's thought,[8] although it could also be said that his was a more radical playing-out of the consequences of the Cartesian *cogito*.[9] Whereas Locke, for instance, merely intended to overcome the excesses wrought by the theory of the Cartesian *cogito* and in fact draws from it elements that he regarded as acceptable,[10] Hume believed that because there is no single impression from which our notion of self could be derived, there can be no such idea. Thus, he is explicit in his denial of the existence of such an entity.[11] Furthermore, whereas Locke makes a close connection between personal identity and the continuity of consciousness (memory), Hume regarded memory as the source of our fictitious belief in an abiding self.[12] He explains the idea of an abiding self as he would explain all natural beliefs; namely, as a product of the habitual workings of the imagination. He held that the operation of the imagination is consistent with the principles of the association of ideas. Hume clarifies this point: "Our ideas of bodies are nothing but collections form'd by the mind of the ideas of the several distinct sensible qualities, of which objects are compos'd, and which we find to have a constant union with each other."[13] However, as there is no real connectedness among the distinct perceptions which make up our mental life, whatever connections there may be are mere qualities which we *attribute* to these atomistic perceptions on account of the union of their ideas in the imagination, when we reflect upon them.[14] This thesis concerning all natural beliefs is then applied to the idea of personal identity.[15]

Hume held that the principles underlying the alleged union of varied perceptions are the relations of *resemblance* and *causality*. These are the ones that give rise to our belief in the substantial self. Resemblance is produced by memory, the faculty which creates images of our past perceptions. The existence of many resemblances among many of the past perceptions that make up a person is explained in terms of the many past experiences that a person has had. Because an image resembles its object, the production of memory images coupled with their being frequently placed in our chain of thought, will inevitably lead to the rise of what to the imagination would seem like the continuance of one object.[16] In the case of personal identity therefore, what arises is something that seems like a continuous identical self. Hence, memory does not merely provide access to one's past, but it also gives one a sense of one's endurance through time. Memory in Hume's account of personal identity not only discovers the identity but also contributes to its production by producing the relation of resemblance among the perceptions.[17] Memory does not so much produce as discover personal identity by disclosing the relation of cause and effect among diverse perceptions.[18]

Hume is in basic agreement with the Lockean thesis that memory affords us with some awareness of that causal chain which constitutes a person.[19] However, he considers this Lockean account inadequate and even misleading. He holds that once one becomes aware of that causal chain, one can extend the same chain of causes and extend one's identity as a person beyond the limits of one's memory. Thus he argues: "'Twill be incumbent on those, who affirm that memory produces entirely our personal identity, to give reason why we can thus extend our identity beyond our memory."[20]

There is no denying the weakness of memory. It has gaps. We do not even remember most of our experiences. And yet we do not think ourselves as not existing during those intervals we cannot recall. For instance, although we have no recollection of ourselves right after birth, we do not consider ourselves as not having existed at that point. This is why we hold that there is something else which makes it possible for us to think of the perceptions we cannot remember as also belonging to our abiding self.

This "something else," for Hume, is none other than causality.[21] Resemblance is therefore supplemented by our notion of cause and effect, and it is this that affords us with the idea of an abiding selfhood. The closeness of the members of any series of perceptions causes us to believe that there is a connection between them. This is how we come to think of ourselves as continuing to exist as identical persons throughout a certain period of time.

Yet even this account is problematic. For the manner by which resemblance and causation create a fictitious image does not provide a real explanation. Indeed, Hume says they enable the mind to "glide smoothly" from one perception to the next, but the way he explains it makes it appear as though one must envision oneself being confronted with an aggregate of perceptions and then being required to decide whether, collectively, they make up a single bundle. Some critics inquire how we come to know which perceptions belong to a particular bundle and which do not.[22] They add moreover that the mere fact that a number of items resemble each other will not in itself persuade us that they belong together in the same group or category, let alone that they constitute a single entity. This particular critique becomes even more pointed if we consider the fact that the possible way out—that is, because all such perceptions resemble each other they are said to belong to a particular self—is precluded by Hume's repudiation of a unified self.[23]

Hume, of course, eventually rejected his own explanation of how resemblance and causation lead to our idea of a continuing self. He came to believe that what they provided was no more than an explanation of the fact that *we do overlook* the numerical distinctness of perceptions, but they do not do away with this distinctness.[24] Of course, he could have exploited the fact that memory is a real factor in our having a notion of ourselves as existing through time. This was seen by Locke, for instance, and used by him in varying degrees. But Hume chose not to do so. Thus in the Appendix of the *Treatise*, Hume admits to being dissatisfied with his explanation of the principles that unite our successive perceptions in thought or consciousness and makes us attribute to them a real simplicity and identity.[25] And he makes the notable admission that he could only conceive of the alleged unity of the self if our perceptions either inhere in something simple and individual or if the mind perceives some real connection among them.[26]

This for all intents and purposes leaves him with a theory not far from that proposed by Butler and Reid that the only solution to the problem lies in a pre-Lockean, substantial conception of the self, a notion which he, however, had patently repudiated.[27]

Derek Parfit and the unimportance of personal identity

Unlike Hume, Derek Parfit regards personal identity, not as a fictitious notion but as a useful, although mistaken and ultimately unimportant, belief. If for John Locke the first-person point of view constitutes an important aspect of an account of personal identity, the same cannot be said for the theory espoused by Parfit who dismisses the normal recourse to an "I" in our notion of personal identity as a throwback to the theory of a Cartesian *ego*.[28] On the other hand, like Locke, Parfit's interest in the issue personal identity is grounded in ethical concerns. He calls into question an ethics based on the idea of a self that is interested only in its survival and well-being. And to the extent that personal identity is presupposed by this kind of concern, he holds the concept questionable. In this regard, his approach to ethics, which appears more in line with a "no-self" conception of a moral agent, is more conducive to a Humean or a Buddhist approach.[29] He claims, however, that he is not arguing for a Buddhist no-self view in which there would be no persons. He is simply trying to "free us from certain kinds of mistake" which tend to result when "we have only one scheme (*viz., the belief that we are entities separate from our mental and physical states*)" and thus are led to "take too seriously some elements" in it.[30] Nevertheless, he finds a compatibility between his reductionist view and the eclipsed view of self in Buddhism.[31]

According to Parfit, that we do take recourse to the first-person viewpoint is a *choice* we make on account of either convention or belief. It is not *per se* required by the experience we are trying to describe.[32] A person is no more than the occurrence of many other physical and mental events—a series of characteristics and circumstances which are normally described as a person and yet need not in fact be described as such. There is here an implicit rejection of the substantialistic thesis, and an obvious disavowal of the belief that persons are separately existing entities with a determinate identity over time. There is nothing more in which personal identity consists than the existence of a person's brain and his body, "the thinking of his thoughts, and the doing of his deeds, and the occurrence of many other physical and mental events."[33]

Is it possible to describe in impersonal terms a reality which for most of us and under the most ordinary circumstances is regarded as personal? To suggest that it is sounds counter-intuitive and even more contrary to commonsense than the suggestion that it is possible to describe the world without one's own perspective being already implicit in the description.[34]

Against this view, Parfit holds that it is possible to describe not only the world but even human life in terms that are completely impersonal. One of the central elements of his theory is the notion of quasi-memory, coupled with the related concepts of quasi-intention, quasi-responsibility, and other quasi-characteristics.

Quasi-Memory

Memories are the most direct source of knowledge we have of the past—*our* past. Parfit claims that "quasi-memory" is simpler as it is the more fundamental concept which underlies our notion of ordinary memory. The notion was first introduced by Sydney Shoemaker in an attempt to give an account of personal identity in terms of psychological continuity which is not vulnerable to the circularity objection.[35] While ordinary memory involves remembering only one's *own* experiences, quasi-memory is constituted by a person's remembrance of experiences without that person necessarily being oneself.[36] In this regard, ordinary memory can be regarded as a sub-class of quasi-memory, except with an additional condition; namely, that the experience an individual remembers is *his* experience.[37] That we do not experience quasi-memories is something Parfit acknowledges; all our memories are ordinary memories. At the same time, however, he points out that our ordinary memories come with a "separable belief" which is not constitutive of memory as such. This is the belief that "unless they are delusions, they are about *our own* experiences."[38]

Parfit clarifies his point by means of a thought experiment. Suppose memories were susceptible of being copied from one brain to another. If this were in fact possible—he does not think that this is a logically impossible technological development—our view regarding ordinary memory would change as we would no longer be able to hold the belief about the alleged personal character of our memory. Instead of presuming right away that a particular memory was of our own experience, we would eventually get used to asking whose experience it was. This imaginary situation he is proposing points to the belief that a memory of one's own experience does not necessarily belong to the nature of memory as such. Rather, it is something additional to it. As such, the essential features of memory can be described in an impersonal way, i.e., as the mere recollection of a past experience. No reference to oneself as the one remembering is necessary.[39]

Parfit believes that his impersonal scheme is both coherent and adequate, and he regards it as an alternative to the ordinary mistaken way by which we understand personal identity. The mistake is not the belief that there are persons, but that a person is a separately existing entity possessing a determinate identity over time. The impersonal scheme should not be understood to mean that Parfit rejects the idea that thought requires a thinker. He actually has no difficulty in admitting this.[40] But he denies that such requirement entails that a person should be more than the existence of his brain and his body as well as the events associated with these.[41] There is simply no need to speak of a "person" as a third term, i.e., as a separately existing entity over and above his body and mind. We may do so, but this adds nothing further to the description of the facts that are already made available to us by considering the person's physical and mental states. This constitutes the so-called Parfitian "no further fact" view of persons.

Identity as "no further fact"

Parfit supports the plausibility of his no-further-fact view by considering the possibility of "divided minds,"[42] which in turn he justifies by pointing to an actual datum of science.[43] The human brain is made up of two very similar hemispheres—a right and a left one, each playing a distinct role and exercising control over different parts of the human body. The right side of the brain controls movement of the limbs on the left side of the body and is in charge of processing information from the left side of the body and the eyes. It also plays a major role in such abilities as pattern recognition and artistic creativity. The left side of the brain, on the other hand, controls the limbs on the right side of the body, processes information from the right side of the eyes, and is the seat of linguistic and mathematical abilities. The two hemispheres are attached to each other by a band of commissural fibers called the *corpus callosum*.

The Nobel Prize–winning neurosurgeon, R.W. Sperry, in his September 1967 address to the American Psychological Association in Washington, D.C. detailed how in a study he conducted with a number of medical colleagues on advanced epileptic patients, whose *corpus callosum* had been severed in its entirety (a process called commissurotonomy), the patients displayed "an apparent doubling" of consciousness which he further elaborated as such:

> Instead of the normally unified single stream of consciousnes, these patients behave in many ways as if they have two independent streams of conscious awareness, one in each hemisphere, each of which is cut off from and out of contact with the mental experiences of the other. In other words, each hemisphere seems to have its own separate and private sensations; its own perceptions; its own concepts; and its own impulses to act, with related volitional, cognitive, and learning experiences. Following surgery each hemisphere also has thereafter its own separate chain of memories that are rendered inaccessible to the recall processes of the other.[44]

Extrapolating from this, Parfit asks that we imagine a situation in which we could be fitted with a device that would allow us to voluntarily divide and reunite our minds.[45] This of course raises the question, which part of one's divided mind would one really be? Or does one cease to exist as one self while divided, and instead be split up into two subpersons? Parfit argues that unless we give up the belief that personal identity requires the notion of a separately existing entity, these and other such questions will remain unanswered.[46] However, were we in fact to give up this belief, and acquiesce to his suggestion that our descriptions should be impersonal, the problem will cease as descriptions based solely on two series of thoughts in a divided mind exhaust everything that can be said or needs to be said.

A difficulty with Parfit's suggestion of an impersonal scheme is that it does not seem to do justice to the unity of self that we experience. Moreover, his attempt to explain human reality without this unifying element could reduce human life to a fragmented succession of self-contained events. The unity and continuity of self is a real experience for us. For one, with regard to brain bisection, even Sperry cautions that we should not think that one who has had his brain split in two is thereby anatomically divided in half. It is the functional qualities that are divided.[47] Our experience of the unity of consciousness is something that does not lend itself to easy problematization by means of the application of imaginary cases—even if these cases are anchored onto some actual scientific findings. This point is made by Roland Puccetti in his treatment of A.L. Wigan's long-neglected classic, *The Duality of Mind* published in 1844, and republished in 1985. Puccetti notes that it does not follow *necessarily* that if we have two brains we have two minds, anymore than it follows necessarily from having two nostrils that we have two senses of smell.[48] "One mind," he insists, "does not become two upon hemispheric disconnection."[49] And even authors like Thomas Nagel who seem sympathetic to the idea that recent discoveries among neuroscientists could eventually make us rethink whether or not our concept of a unified selfhood is an absolute datum or "merely another case of integration, more or less effective, in the control system of a complex organism," appear cautious when it comes to any suggestion that we should abandon the idea of our own unity.[50]

Psychological connectedness and continuity

As a matter of fact, Parfit himself acknowledges that an atomistic and fragmented succession of self-contained events would fail to make sense of the undeniable continuity that we experience in our lives. However, he also believes that his argument does not commit him to such fragmentary thesis, as his aim is simply to limit us to a description of the *degree* of that continuity, without having recourse to descriptions in terms of a continuing personal identity. This accounts for his introduction of the notions of psychological connectedness and psychological continuity, which are based upon a development and an enlargement of the Lockean thesis that personal identity extends just as far as consciousness does. Parfit defines psychological connectedness as "the holding of particular direct psychological connections," e.g., being able to remember at present experiences of the past.[51] However, the degree of such connectedness is highly variable, and because of this, we can think of situations in which there is a strong connectedness, e.g., an individual in his forties may have numerous connections with himself when he was in his early thirties, but we also have situations in which this is markedly reduced, e.g., the same forty-year old having a weaker connectedness with himself when he was eleven years old. Parfit posits an arithmetic formula which he uses to define this strong connectedness: "There is enough connectedness if the number of connections, over any day, is *at least half* the number of direct connections that hold, over every day, in the lives of nearly every actual person. When there are enough direct connections, there is what I call *strong* connectedness."[52]

The variable character of psychological connectedness indicates that there can be no transitivity among the *relata*. Even if most people are strongly connected from one day to the next, this is not an indication of their connectedness with themselves over a longer period of time. And he demonstrates what he means by this:

> I am now strongly connected to myself yesterday, when I was strongly connected to myself two days ago, and so on. It does not follow that I am now strongly connected to myself twenty years ago. And this is not true. Between me now and myself twenty years ago there are many fewer than the number of direct psychological connections that hold over any day in the lives of nearly all adults. For example, while these adults have many memories of experiences that they had in the previous day, I have fewer memories of experiences that I had twenty years ago.[53]

How then does he account for the series of *relata* in which each one is strongly connected with its predecessor but does not necessarily pass on that connection to its successor? Parfit uses the transitive notion of psychological continuity, which he characterizes as not requiring direct connections over the entire series, but requiring only that there be enough direct connections between each successive link in the chain of consciousness leading back to the past. This constitutes psychological continuity then, namely, the holding of overlapping chains of memory experiences, strong intentional acts and results, and mental contents such as beliefs or desires that are not merely momentary.[54] Hence, although one may be psychologically continuous with a past self at age four, one may not necessarily be psychologically connected with it.

Psychological connectedness, according to Parfit, is the more important concept both in theory and in practice. Our normal belief of course would regard psychological connectedness as a consequence of personal identity over time. Parfit points to two reasons which show why this belief is mistaken. First, while all types of identity by definition are transitive, psychological connectedness is intransitive. Second, while identity is an-all-or-nothing affair, psychological connectedness is a matter of degree. However, he does propose a way by which we can talk about our lives in terms of the psychological connectedness between a succession of selves. He says:

> On my proposed way of talking, we use "I," and the other pronouns, to refer only to the parts of our lives to which, when speaking, we have the strongest psychological connections. When the connections have been markedly reduced—when there has been a significant change of character, or style of life, or of beliefs and ideals—we might say, "It was not *I* who did that, but an earlier self." We could then describe in what ways, and to what degree, we are related to this past self.[55]

All other moments in a life would then be referred to as a past self or future self. This way of talking, Parfit, says, is often useful and natural in our own lives. Consider the example of a childhood friend whom John has left when his family decided to move to another city. Robert was six when John last saw him. All the memories he has of Robert are that of a six-year-old child that he used to play games with after class. Not having seen him for twenty-something years, John is fully aware that if they were to meet at some point, he would no longer be the six-year-old boy, but someone quite his own age. And yet when they did meet again a few years ago, this question spontaneously entered John's mind: "Whatever happened to that six-year old?" He could not avoid this thought from causing him certain degree of disorientation and perplexity: "This is not the Robert I know."[56]

On the one hand, Parfit recognizes the fact that every so often there would be a significant break or reduction of connectedness. On the other hand, in most circumstances, this reduction would only come gradually— the connectedness would become weak slowly without such dramatic breaks. Given this situation, he suggests that it would be better if instead of talking about successive selves, we were to "talk directly about the *degree* of connectedness."[57]

Parfit moves on to what he calls "Relation R," defined as "psychological connectedness and/or continuity with the right kind of cause," adding that "the right kind of cause could be any cause"[58]—hence, a much more "loose" type of connectedness. Relation R, Parfit suggests, is what truly matters.[59] He disagrees that personal identity is what unites the different experiences that together constitute a life.[60] And if we must use the term "personal identity," he argues, we should take it to mean no more than a particular condition placed on Relation R. This means that it not only holds between a present person and a future one, but that there is none of the sort of branching which would happen in cases such as that of divided minds—e.g., in the cases of brain bisection.[61] In short, Relation R is psychological continuity/connectedness in the widest sense. Noonan explains it further: "Whether the cause is the normal one, or even a reliable one, is completely irrelevant, for any cause is as good as any other, since it is solely the *effect* that matters. Thus I have a survivor, in the non-literal, Parfitian sense, at some future time *t* just in case (a) there is a person at *t* who is psychologically continuous and/or connected with me, and (b) this person's psychological states at *t* are *in some way or other* causally derivative from my present psychological states."[62]

It is Relation R, not personal identity that matters. Relation R is a functional term; it does not primarily say anything about the nature of identity as such. If anything, it drives home the point concerning what Parfit believes is the unimportance of identity. Relation R is a way of describing what the notion of personal identity attempts to answer, viz., the question about what unifies the different experiences of a lifetime. But it does so without taking recourse in the conception embedded deep in our normal belief about personal identity, namely, the idea of a fixed and static entity separate from and standing over and against its mental and physical states. This constitutes what Parfit calls the "reductionist" thesis, of which he distinguishes three types: "Constitutive Reductionism," "Identifying Reductionism" and "Eliminative Reductionism."[63]

The self as states

What these reductionist views have in common is that they all reduce a person's existence to "a body, and the occurrence of a series of thoughts, experiences, and other mental and physical events."[64] They differ, however, in what elements fall within the scope of each one's reductionist thrust. Identifying Reductionism involves a complete description in a way that no conceptual or empirical distinction can be made between a person and the series of events that constitute his body. It is, as Parfit says, "hyper-reductionist." Thus the statement "Persons just *are* bodies" reduces persons to bodies in so strong a way that it does not even distinguish between them. Eliminative Reductionism, on the other hand, attempts to make sense of Identifying Reductionism's lack of a distinction between a person and series of bodily events, by means of a downright rejection of any further use of the term "person." As Parfit describes it: "There really aren't such things as persons: there are only brains and bodies, and thoughts, and other experiences."[65]

Three quotes from Appendix J, of *Reasons and Persons*, will show why Parfit sees Eliminative Reductionism as the type operative in the Buddhist no-self view:

(i) A sentient being does exist, you think, O Mara? You are misled by a false conception. This bundle of elements is void of Self. In it there is no

sentient being. Just a set of wooden parts, receives the name of carriage, so do we give to elements, the name of fancied being.
(ii) The mental and the material are really here. But here there is no human being to be found. For it is void and merely fashioned like a doll. Just suffering piled up like grass and sticks.
(iii) Buddha has spoken thus: O Brethren, actions do exist, and also their consequences, but the person that acts does not. There is no one to cast away this set of elements and no one to assume a new set of them. There exists no Individual, it is only a conventional name given to a set of elements.[66]

This kind of reductionism, Parfit holds, is sometimes justified.[67] However, he also says that such kinds of reductionism about some kinds of entities is not often well expressed with the claim that there are no such entities. Contrary to these two kinds of reductionist views, therefore, he argues that "we should admit that there are nations, and that we, who are persons, exist."[68]

Since he does not subscribe to the total elimination of existing entities, e.g., persons, he offers his own form of reductionist theory, which he terms Constitutive Reductionism. Against nonreductionist views, he argues that the notion of persons as entities separable from their minds and bodies is untenable. But unlike the Buddhistic no-self view of Eliminative Reductionism, or the hyper-reductive thrust of Identifying Reductionism, he upholds the reality of persons. He also defends the meaningfulness of maintaining a distinction between a person and his body as well as any series of thoughts and experiences.[69] This leaves him with the position that a person's existence "just consists" in his body as well as his thoughts and experiences, in much the same way that a wax figure just consists in the wax out of which it was made. The figure is in no way beyond the wax or separate from it. However, neither are they one and the same thing, since if it were melted, the wax would remain but the figure would not.[70]

Constitutive Reductionism does not bar us from speaking of a person as a distinct entity. But it does hold that we cannot think of this distinct entity as existing independently of or separately from its body and series of mental events. It prevents us from positing the existence of something like a Cartesian Ego or any such separately existing immaterial substance.[71] In short, there is nothing more to being a person than the series of mental and physical events that are constitutive of it. Personhood is no further fact.[72] A person is no more than a series of physical and mental events, in much the same way that a nation, for example, is no more distinct from its citizens and its territory.[73]

The unimportance of identity and liberation from the "self"

Most of us regard personal identity to be a determinate fact. Someone who is trying to finish an article for an academic journal is either oneself or is somebody else. Personal identity, as we ordinarily understand it, is a matter of all-or-nothing which will not allow the possibility that a future individual is only partly oneself. There has to be a one-to-one correspondence between oneself now and oneself at any point in either the past or the future, such that if one were to ask the question "Am *I* going to die?" there is no other possible answer than a simple "yes" or a simple "no."[74] Parfit calls this ordinary belief into question. He disagrees that personal identity requires a simple and direct continuity between two selves that are simply the same at two distinct points in time.

Consider, he says, the example of a club which after having ceased to exist for several years is revived by some former members who decide to use the same name and go by the same rules of the old organization. Did these people reconvene the same club? Or is it another club which is exactly similar to the old one? To answer our question, we could inquire whether the old club's rules contained a stipulation to the effect that should it cease to exist, it could be revived after a period of time. We could also inquire about how its members conduct their meetings, and we could ask other questions which we may consider pertinent. But what if no stipulations about the club's revival exist? And what if there were no legal facts to support either of our answers to the question? There would then be no answer to our question. In which case, "the claim 'This is the same club' would be *neither true nor false*." However, even if there were no answer to our question, we may in fact—through our inquiries—have come to know everything that needs to be known about the club and its members. Should this happen, we would no longer be puzzled when we cannot answer the question "Is this the very same club?" When this becomes true of some question, Parfit says the question becomes "empty."[75]

There is no reason, according to Parfit, to take a different view with regard to personal identity. He argues that there are many situations in which we should simply admit that there is no answer to the question about personal identity. It too is an empty question on account of the fact that a determinate question must always be decidable. Personal identity in many instances is not. For not only is it a matter of degree, but it also does not entail a one-to-one relation between oneself now and oneself at another point in time. Parfit considers the two most commonly held criteria of personal identity: the bodily criterion, and the psychological criterion. In the imaginary case of a teletransported human being, the psychological criterion is fully satisfied, but not the physical criterion. The duplicate on Mars, while qualitatively identical with the original on Earth, remains numerically different. On the other hand, suppose there were a case in which the physical criterion were satisfied but not the psychological criterion, the two would be numerically, but not qualitatively, identical.[76]

According to Parfit, it would not be possible in either case to have certainty that the resulting person would be the original one.[77] From this he concludes that personal identity is undecidable if the criterion used were either the bodily or psychological criterion. But what if we were to use both criteria? Would such a combination give us a greater determinateness? Parfit calls this the Combined Spectrum, which includes in its scope all the different degrees of both physical and psychological connectedness.[78] He tests the plausibility of this Combined Spectrum by imagining a case in which a person undergoes several operations. With each operation, some cells of his brain and body as well as elements of his memory and character are replaced one at a time, not with exact duplicates. As Parfit notes, the greater the proportion of the person's body that would be replaced, the less like the original one would the resulting person be. At that end where nothing would be done, the person would still be himself; while on the other end, his whole body having been destroyed and his entire store of memory and character replaced, the resulting person would have no connection whatsoever with the original.[79]

The problem arises when we consider that each operation moves farther and farther away from the original person and closer to the new one. Since the difference of each operation with its successors or predecessors is slight, we are faced with the question of where and how to locate that line by which we can say that once crossed, the original ceases to exist and is definitely replaced by the new one. Since we have no real facts to base any clear demarcation, it appears that only an arbitrary decision on our part can provide such a line. But this unclarity problematizes our original notion of personal identity as a determinate fact. This problem, Parfit holds, should be enough to alert us to the reality that personal identity is not an all-or-nothing affair, but a matter of degree. As changes continuously happen along the spectrum, the original person's continuity with his successors is a matter of degree, as each progressively more extensive operation brings him farther and farther away from where he started and closer to the resulting person who would no longer be him at all.[80]

This view has repercussions far beyond the imaginary cases that Parfit suggests. For if we were to admit that personal identity is a matter of degree in such cases as illustrated using the Combined Spectrum, we would likewise have to give up our ordinary way of regarding personal identity as a determinate fact. In which case, we would also have to admit that the physical and psychological continuity of human life does not provide enough support to the ordinary idea of an identical "I" that continues throughout a person's entire life. There is nothing wrong with presupposing the existence of this "I." Hence he would not dispute the importance of such questions that have to do with whether loved ones suffering from Alzheimer's or amnesia are still the same persons. The concern we have for them, strong or otherwise, does reveal a presupposition on our part with regard to the continuance of personal identity. We would want to believe that they remain the same individuals. Parfit sees no problem in acknowledging this presupposition. But he stresses that we must not lose sight of the fact that such presupposition of an unchanging and self-identical "I" is a matter of convention rather than necessity.[81] Moreover, this for him only serves to corroborate his view that what we value, in ourselves and others, is not the continued existence of the same particular brains and bodies. A grandmother's memory may have been completely wiped out by disease, such that she can no longer remember her grandchild or the happy moments their family used to have, but we would hardly agree to the proposition that she no longer is that child's grandmother. For as Parfit says, "what we value are the various relations between ourselves and others, whom and what we love, our ambitions, achievements, commitments, emotions, memories, and several other psychological features."[82]

From self-concern to other-concern

As the very notion of a static and self-identical person becomes unintelligible within the Parfitian scheme, the self gradually disappears. One is, according to Parfit, but a passing phase in a constant flux with which one's present self will have an ever-diminishing connection. The only thing that Relation R secures is a certain type of psychological connectedness and/or continuity, even if this were brought about in such a manner that physical continuity is destroyed.[83] Because of this Parfit suggests that since it is unlikely that one will be very connected with oneself in 30-year's time, one has no reason to have undue concern for what will happen then.[84] Since personal identity is "no further fact," I have no reason to worry about my own future, and every reason to regard it with detachment.[85] And because I can regard my personal fortunes in such way, I allow myself to be more open and concerned for the fortunes of others.

This liberation from the self, Parfit claims, will enable us to reduce the undue emphasis that has been given to a self-interest theory.[86] Self-centeredness cannot be the basis of rational human action as it cannot be more rationally compelling than any moral principle.[87] Furthermore, "it becomes more plausible, when thinking morally to focus less upon the person, the subject of experiences, and instead focus more upon the experiences themselves."[88] Consequently, Parfit adds that "it becomes more plausible to claim that, just as we are right to ignore whether people come from the same or different nations, we are right to ignore whether experiences come from within the same or different lives."[89]

There is much to be admired in Parfit's claim that each person's supreme concern should never be himself or herself, but others. And as he emphasizes, a diminished concern for one's own fortunes—which is the underlying motive of his theory of the unimportance of personal identity—leads to an increased concern and involvement with other people, thereby removing the glass wall that separates oneself from the other.[90] However, as some critics have pointed out, there seems implicit in Parfit's account the idea that concern for the problem of personal identity, because one finds it important, is an indication of egotism or crass self-centeredness. Personal identity, these critics insist, is a problem of ontology, and to make such a leap—as they believe Parfit does—from considering the ontological question because it is ultimately unimportant for matters pertaining to morals is to play a dangerous game of founding moral principles on grounds made precarious by the absence of personal identity.[91]

If Parfit were indeed equating self-interest with egoism, then his account of personal identity would indeed be problematic. For even the great religions enjoin their adherents to be responsible and accountable for themselves and to "work out their own salvation in fear and trembling"[92]—a command which hardly passes as an endorsement of egoism and an encouragement to have no concern whatsoever for one's fellowmen. As Shalom, points out, "The knowledge of what religious thinking implies would have to have sunk to an incredible level if this kind of 'my responsibility is primarily myself' were equated with 'egotism.' The merest whisper of understanding of what most religions imply should at least lead to *some* understanding that their implications are usually the reverse of this curious identification between 'self-interest' and egotism."[93] However, such crass identification is not Parfit's intention. Granted that it may be regarded as one possible consequence of his theory of personal identity, his point nevertheless is that the notion of a substantial, monadlike self is ultimately unimportant.

Parfit is not arguing for the unreality of personal identity, nor the unreality of selfhood. He grants that in ordinary situations of everyday living our judgments concerning personal identity are relatively straightforward, flowing as they do from strong physical and psychological connectednesss on a one-to-one basis. Indeed, the persons we are acquainted with and whom we meet occasionally, change very little from the last time we saw them. They do not divide into persons equally continuous with themselves. They are numerically identical with themselves and are for the most part qualitatively the same as well. Hence, there is no reason to discard our normal way of judging personal identity whenever possible and when it suits our purposes; such kind of continuity is important.[94] However, although personal identity in most cases coincides with what matters, i.e., with such continuity, this should not be regarded as sufficient to make personal identity that which matters.[95] This brings us to the second point, namely, that Parfit's claim is consistent with his theory of Constitutive Reductionism, according to which personal identity just consists in certain other facts about physical and psychological continuity. Now if one fact consists merely in certain other facts, it can only be these other facts which are important. It is the constituent facts, not the "constituted" one that matters; the former are the ones that are morally and rationally significant, the latter, on account of them.[96]

Two unacceptable views

There are basically two views which Parfit is combating. On the one hand, there is the undue emphasis given to self-centered versions of utilitarianism. And although his theory remains utilitarian to some extent—not only because his endorsement of our normal judgments about personal identity is based on how useful our ordinary way of understanding it is, but also because he does not deny that basic human need to promote well-being and avoid suffering—these, for him, must be considered in themselves without any consideration for the entity who might be experiencing them. What we are thus freed from is not the necessity of owning these experiences as *ours*, nor of using these in order to identify our selves. Rather what we find ourselves freed from is a possible tyranny of the self which, because it is able to attribute and appropriate judgments and experiences to itself, is also able to erect dividing lines between a domain it calls its own, and one that is other to it. For Parfit, the boundaries between lives, or the separateness of persons must be overcome.[97]

The other view that Parfit seeks to overcome is the almost desperate skepticism about the self which, in Hume's words, is "the most deplorable condition imaginable, environed with the deepest darkness."[98] Total skepticism, he maintains, only brings darkness and utter loneliness.[99] Instead, it is a lessening, even a weakening, of that deeply ingrained idea of an invincible and impermeable selfhood that he attacks. A lessened importance given to the unity of life does not cause despair; it is in fact liberating and consoling, for not only does it coincide with a lessened importance given to the separateness of lives, but it also represents a *widening* of one's concern.[100] It makes one a citizen of the universe, as it were, an entity possessing kinship with the rest of what exists. This, for Parfit is what matters—a feature that we share both with mere animals and with mere physical objects, for it is this that makes us persons.[101]

While it is not difficult to see in Parfit's interpretation of personal identity as ultimately unimportant a broadening of the boundaries of concern by blurring the divisions between the self and its others, the jump that he makes from constituting facts to widened concern is much too quick. It leaves a great deal of perplexities unresolved. The plurality of constituting facts cannot provide a force strong enough to allow for that unity from which perspective alone talk of a broadening of concern becomes possible. The obscuring of the boundaries of self does not necessarily lead to an enlargement of its concern— i.e., notwithstanding Parfit's protest that his notion rids the self of the glass wall separating it from others. The even more insidious egotism which has no respect for the boundaries of others, because it does not know how to respect its own is a danger far greater than the individualism and concern for self that Parfit rejects. In this we echo the question posed by Ricoeur to the Parfitian account: "If my identity were to lose all importance in every respect, would not the question of others also cease to matter?"[102]

Selfhood, like reality itself, is neither an undifferentiated continuum nor pure growth and change. The plurality of constituting facts of which Parfit speaks, when further analyzed, would become sheer flux or chaos unless there were something that can be regarded as unified. This is precisely what the self is, a unity of identity and diversity. Hence, the defense of selfhood will depend upon showing that there can be something that is both a one and a many, together at the same time. Parfit's reductive analysis claims to show that the self is not necessary or that everything can be said about its reality without having recourse to the idea of selfhood. But an examination of this claim makes it clear that some substitute for the self is always brought in. His description of the problem of personal identity in terms of the relation of constitutive psychological and physical facts is inadequate. Such a description is only possible through an identification of these facts as belonging to some entity that can claim them as its own.

This is why in Hartshorne's philosophy, as will be shown later on, the bits of experience from and through which the self is understood are regarded as able to recognize each other, acknowledge, and appreciate, compare and apprehend, different degrees of relationship.[103] These bits of experience are, in short, already selves or aspects of selves. Yet even here in Hartshorne's appropriation of the idea of selfhood and his translation of it into his scheme, the idea of an entity sufficiently unified is presupposed. Even if we were to translate the self into a way of functioning—thus avoiding a Cartesian *ego*—or as a way of relating states to one another, we still eventually have to acknowledge that this manner of functioning or relating can only be performed by a self. In this regard, the self seems an unavoidable category.

Locke and Parfit are in basic agreement on the untenability of a Cartesian *ego*-like substrate as the foundation of personal identity. The notion of an "I" that remains self-identical throughout the vicissitudes of its career leads to the unfortunate duality between an identity which underlies change without participating in it and a realm of constantly changing physical or psychological states which are, at best, encrustations that neither enter into nor contribute to the constitution of this "I." Genuine organic development which encompasses novelty and creativity must not be neglected, much less denied. For in such case, the self becomes regarded as a completed blueprint or a finished scroll whose becoming is no more than the unfolding of necessary and eternal principles. This is the "self as substance"; a monadlike entity, a "Newtonian atom," existing in splendid isolation from its others whose existence, although recognized, possess no ultimate bearing upon the self's nature and coming-to-be.[104] On the other hand, the self can be identified with the bare unity of rational consciousness, and its concrete and changing states are left unconnected with any center of unity that provides its identity. This represents the dissolution of the self into its empirical states of consciousness or actual awareness as is evidenced in Locke, and more thoroughly in Parfit.[105]

The primary difficulty with this view is that without the unity of the self being understood as *in* and *through* its identifiable states and experiences, these latter are disclosed as a mere plurality or collection. In this regard, it is the strength of the substantialistic perspective that it affords selfhood with a ground for its unity and identity.[106] Its overemphasis on an *ego* notwithstanding, its insistence on the fact that this third term, because it is irreducible to its components, provides a unifying element that must not be glossed over in an adequate and defensible theory of the nature of selfhood. But with views such as Parfit's especially, this unifying element is nowhere to be found except perhaps in the manner of a belief that though useful remains unimportant in the long run.

The error of the substantialistic view of the self

In considering the concept of person in Hume's account, we can note that the error of the substantialist view does not in fact lie in its assertion of the unity of the self, but rather in its inability to show how this unity is *in* selfhood and permeates the states that constitute it. It is mainly this failure that led Hume and other empiricists to react by dissolving the self into its physical or psychological states. However, once the idea of a unifying term is repudiated, it becomes impossible to account not only for the unity of the discrete perceptions but also for their existence.[107] As a matter of fact, it is this kind of predicament that has led thinkers such as Parfit to hold that the only datum there can be is expressed by the impersonal statement, "there are thoughts," and nothing more.[108] Notwithstanding this, however, the fundamental error of theories representing strong reactions to the substantialist view is an almost vehement insistence that the identity must be associated with an object persisting without change. In the case of Hume, what we discover is that in the end he is led to presuppose the very entity whose existence he had originally denied. This is because his explanation of how we come to think of our successive perceptions as constituting a single entity in the absence of a self leans heavily upon the notion of a subject of experience.[109] This criticism of course should not be taken to mean that Hume is positing straight off the existence of an inner self.[110] What it points to rather is the fact that his explanation does require the concept of a subject.[111]

There is a sense of selfhood that need not require the notion of "same" or "self-identically enduring" substrate to which thinkers such as Hume and Parfit find themselves reacting. It may be true, as some commentators point out, that in Hume's case, the situation is more understandable. He was more concerned with the delineation of the psychological grounds of our belief in the abiding self, rather than with a possible definition of the nature of personhood or selfhood or even the notion of person in terms of numerical identity.[112] The fact remains nonetheless that in his "science of man," the assumption that Hume is rejecting, i.e., the underlying notion of what he takes to be the ordinary understanding of person, is that of a self-identical subject that remains the same throughout change. And while he attempts to dislodge this 'fictitious belief', it nevertheless remains, the specter that haunts his entire philosophical analysis of personal identity.[113]

Hume's is a situation not too different from Parfit's, as the latter also finds himself reacting to what he believes is one of our most deep-seated assumptions.[114] There is a difference, however. Parfit's thesis evolves into an attempt to justify the unimportance of the ongoingness of identity by claiming that a lessened emphasis on it enlarges its concern for others. Hume's thesis, in contrast, dissolves into failure to give cogent reasons for whatever it is that unifies the self's atomistic states.[115] In the end, even in Hume's skeptical philosophy, the centrality or ineradicability of the idea of self comes to the fore. According to Stround, Hume "absolutely needs a prior notion of a self or mind within which the fundamental principles or dispositions of human nature operate."[116] However, given that he had already totally repudiated the possibility of perceptions inhering in some substancelike reality or of perceptions being connected with certain others, there was no way to recuperate the loss. Thus the poignancy of his lament,[117] and the "darkness" of his "deplorable condition," assuaged only by "a game of back-gammon, merriment with his friends, and three or four hours of amusement."[118]

Although the skepticism of Hume contrasts with the much brighter outlook that Parfit says his theory of the person had effected in him,[119] and though Parfit's ethics of "broadened" or "enlarged" personhood could certainly find support in the Humean dissolution of the substantial self,[120] the fact remains that in considering both, one cannot help but have the impression that Albert Shalom alludes to. The real problem seems to be simply evaded by the creation of a new one. It focuses one's attention on another problem, which, however related to the original question, remains a secondary one. In fact, there are no adequate answers because the real questions pertaining to the original issue are merely swept under the rug.[121] The real problem is the question of the ontology of person, the anthropology that underlies both the idea to which Hume and Parfit find themselves reacting against, the specter which both endeavor to exorcise, and the account of personal identity that results from the analyses that they undertake.

The major difficulty with their views is not simply the failure to provide a center of unity for the various states and experiences of a "self" or to recognize that the very substitution of discrete states is only truly intelligible if we already presuppose that something like a "self" exists. Rather, the most serious difficulty is the inability to look into the possibility that the notion of personal identity that is being repudiated may not in fact exhaust all options. This is perhaps most intimated by the fact that Parfit's claim to provide an alternative to personal identity turns out to be, not an alternative *to* but an alternative *way* of dealing with personal identity. This, however, merely leaves the core problem unresolved, namely, the problem concerning the idea of what really constitutes a person or self. Parfit's position, as well as Hume's merely "leaves a gap," to use Penelhum's phrase, within an overall theory of personal identity. For however hard one attempts to dissociate one's theory from it, there does not seem to be a way of escaping the matrix of ideas which the concept of person or self secures: unity, continuity, and a point of reference both for oneself and for others.

It does seem that an adequate account of personal identity can be found only when that reality is found which is capable of holding together a unity and a diversity of constitutive contents as well as the more encompassing unity of these two features. A person or self cannot be a bare undifferentiated unity that excludes diversity and change, but neither can it be simply the constitutive states themselves. What is therefore required is a unified center which could be indicated by the *nominative* "I," together with a plurality or set of its determinant states expressed by the *accusative* "me," plus the union of both in a recognition that what constitutes the "I" extends to and is most intimately present throughout the entire succession of "me"s. This overarching unity between the "I" and the "me" could then be indicated by the *genitive* "mine," indicative of ownership, possession, appropriation, and concern. A complete account of personal identity must recognize that a person or self is the intertwinement of the *nominative* and the *accusative*, under the *genitive* umbrella. Substantialist theories grasp the center of unity but do not provide for an understanding of its inherent diversity save as an ineluctable unfolding of implicit contents. Empiricist theories, on the other hand, grasp the diversity but make little or no room for unity, thus ending up by attempting to show that there is no need to attribute the diverse states to anything. The truth of the matter must lie somewhere in between, i.e., in a concept of person or self that not only provides a way of understanding what it means to be a centered unity nor simply makes room for the diversity of constitutive states but also, and most importantly, serves as the proper locus for *appropriation* and *concern*. This brings us back to the two interrelated dimensions of personal identity: the question of selfhood or *ipse*-identity and the issue of sameness, *idem*-identity.

Paul Ricoeur's distinction between *idem*- and *ipse*-identity

In *Oneself as Another*, Paul Ricoeur provides an analysis of the nature of the person or the self in terms of identity. Like Locke, Parfit, and, to some extent, Hume, Ricoeur understands the necessity of taking into account the social and moral perspectives—i.e., the viewpoint of appropriation and concern— in his analysis of the nature of the self. (In this regard we can say that personal identity is treated as an axiological issue, albeit in varying degrees, within the four frameworks we are considering.) Ricoeur's work commences with an exposition of selfhood from the perspective of linguistics,[122] claiming that personal identity is better understood as *ipse*-identity (the "identity of the self") rather than *idem*-identity (the "identity of the same").[123] While *idem*-identity concerns numerical sameness, *ipse*-identity pertains to the person as the "who" of living and acting. Ricoeur holds that attempts—such as Parfit's—to establish an individual's *idem*-identity involves the reduction of this 'who' question to a question concerning the 'what' of personhood.[124] Ricoeur understands the Parfitian account—which he refers to as the most formidable adversary of his thesis—as grounded on an *idem*-identity or a "what" approach.[125]

According to Ricoeur, *idem*-identity focuses on the objective or objectivized features of a person.[126] Its primary concern is the establishment of clear criteria identifying the *sort* of entity a person is. Now while this represents a very real and undeniable dimension of a person, it remains nonetheless but an aspect, and therefore cannot provide an exhaustive account of personhood.[127] Ricoeur quotes from Heidegger's *Being and Time*, and mentions the Heideggerian distinction between the "permanence of substance" and "self-subsistence" (*Selbst-Ständigkeit*) in order to drive home his point that a person understood from the viewpoint of a "who" differs from a person understood from the perspective of a "what." The former coincides with the Heideggerian notion of *Dasein*, which ontologically is "in principle different from everything that is present-at-hand or Real. Its 'subsistence' [*Bestand*] is not based on the substantiality of a substance but on the '*Self-subsistence*' [*Selbst-Ständigkeit*] of the existing Self, whose being has been conceived as care."[128]

Ricoeur has two objections to Parfit. First, he criticizes Parfit on an issue already intimated earlier, namely, the latent presupposition of the self which Ricoeur says is also found in Hume:[129] Ricoeur notes that the central phenomenon of personhood upon which the entire problematic hinges, and which Parfit's theory reduces, is thereby eluded. How indeed, Ricoeur asks, can we even talk of thoughts without something or someone thinking? "Can what is *one's own* be a particular case of the impersonal?"[130] In asking these questions, he is voicing his objection to the substitution of such impersonal expressions as "thought is occurring" for "I think."

In the reductionist view of Parfit (as well as Hume), the thinker is no more than its thoughts; the "I" is no more than its constitutive psychological and physical states. In accounts such as Parfit's and Hume's, rejection of the Cartesian ego becomes tantamount to the *nominative, accusative,* and *genitive* dimensions being dissociated and rejected *in toto*, without even having recognized that within the repudiated notion, a diversity of aspects first requires recognition. This, albeit in a slightly different vein, constitutes Ricoeur's second objection to the Parfitian thesis. It is slightly different because Ricoeur does not use the same distinctions that we are making here. However, his criticism is essentially the same as ours in that he faults Parfit with neglecting to recognize the distinction that holds within the idea of personal identity; this being the distinction between *ipse*-identity and *idem*-identity, or the phenomenon of *mineness* and the factual character of personal identity.[131]

The recalcitrance of the self

In spite of his affirmation of the need to search for an objective view of what constitutes personhood—manifested in the respect he shows for the analytic tradition and the interest he displays in the conceptual challenges it raises, Ricoeur nevertheless sees his engagement in the thought of such thinkers as Locke, Hume, and Parfit, as no more than a useful "detour." He believes that the "what" question can and should eventually lead to the "who" question.[132] While Ricoeur certainly respects the thrust toward objectivity that the Parfitian and Humean analyses bring into the whole discussion of the problem of personal identity, he believes nonetheless that this approach fails to do full justice to the matter. He cannot see, he says, how the question "who?" can simply disappear in analyses of the problematic, and finally remain without an answer. The point that Ricoeur wants to drive home is the recalcitrance of selfhood. The "who," he says, continues to reassert itself after every attempt to tone down its force by turning it into a "what"; it resists its elimination in an impersonal description.[133] We must note here that despite his emphasis on the inescapability of the perspective of the self, Ricoeur is not returning to a Cartesian-ego position. There is, he says, "a gap that separates the hermeneutics of the self from the philosophies of the cogito. To say *self* is not to say *I*."[134]

Ricoeur's distinction between *ipse*-identity and *idem*-identity draws attention to the fact that it is very difficult and highly problematic to attempt to clearly define a fixed sense of what a person or self is. There is a shifting sense to the "I" that is involved in a person or self, which must be recognized and utilized in an adequate account of personal identity. What we find in the analysis of personal identity which he offers is a recognition—not easily found in either Parfit or Hume, and only tangentially in Locke—that the "I" is not simply a term of indication or reference that can be used by any number of speakers. Instead, it also has the function of fixing the "who" of speech. This anchoring is disclosed especially by the fact that the utterance of the word "I" creates an ambiguity, perhaps even an *aporia* between the "I" as subject and the "I" as object.[135] Indeed the very anchoring of the "I" suggests a privileged point of view, i.e., the vantage point of a subject which is in a very real sense a part of the world, while at the same time is more than simply another content of the world, but rather represents a limit to this world.[136]

This noncoincidence finds a resolution of sorts in a conjunction between person as subject and person as object brought about by the inscription of the "I" in the records of a community.[137] This noncoincidence and some kind of resolution in the objectification of the "I" is already found in Parfit, although in an attenuted form. In his desire to call our attention to "the egotism that nourishes the thesis of self interest,"[138] Parfit has managed to provoke a "crisis"—to use Ricoeur's own term—within the very concept of personal identity. It is a crisis that alerts us to the complexity and ambiguity of the idea, brings to the fore its multifaceted character, and highlights the fact that—as Locke had noted long before—personal identity is inseparable from, and is in fact founded upon the even more complex notion of person or self. This leads us to the second point Ricoeur makes which is most significant for our discussion, namely, that the bleached-out conception and search for an objective standpoint in dealing with personal identity is but one side of the coin. To make it the overarching concern and final aim of the search for an answer to the question of personal identity is not only inadequate but also ultimately futile.

The uniqueness of the self

The uniqueness of the person or the self, intimated by the different facets of a speaker's use of "I," reveals both the privileged perspective of the "I" as well as the fact that it is in a genuine sense immersed in the world as a constituent of it. No objective account can embrace within its scope the various dimensions of the identity it seeks to describe. Something will inevitably be lost if we try to understand personal identity merely from an objective vantage point distinct and isolated from the subjective pole of experience. This leads us therefore to the question that appears to be the one most germane to the whole discussion: *Which identity is important—identity in which sense of the term?* If it is not simply the sameness that Hume sought but ultimately failed to find, if it is not simply the isolated "self" at the core of the nonreductionist thesis, if it is not the identity of an impersonal self that Parfit offers, which identity is it? What kind of identity matters?

It is this question that underlies the search that Charles Hartshorne undertakes with regard to the issue of personal identity. Unlike the previous philosophers we discussed, Hartshorne seems more keenly aware of the interwovenness of the objective and the subjective points of view. In this he profits from the oversights of the perspectives we have surveyed. In making the organic, i.e., life, as a fundamental paradigm of his philosophy, Hartshorne is able to relate the self immediately with the ideas of process, growth, and development. Moreover, since he regards these realities as holding true of all entities in the universe, he is able to avoid the tendency of the substantialist view which regards the self merely as the necessary unfolding of a previously given essence, fixed, unchanging, and thereby susceptible to being localized within a clearly defined and objective framework. On the other hand, neither does he accept the narrow empiricist conception of the person as a mere aggregate of atomistic facts, i.e., physical and/or mental states. In repudiating this conception, he is able to expose the error of seeking to find the unity of the self in the content of a momentary datum, unconnected to any other.

Personal identity in the thought of Hartshorne is a unified pattern that characterizes the historic route of successive occasions of experience, distinct from each other, but nonisolable from one another or from the whole. In his philosophy, he is able to avoid the many difficulties of theories, which identify a person or self solely with the mind or with its physical states. Nor does he identify selfhood solely with self-consciousness. Instead, he regards thought, reflection, and self-consciousness as activities that take place within the unified locus, the total environment of an organism, without the self being simply identified with or reduced to any of these activities. The question of personal identity in this perspective is therefore inseparable from the question of person. The question "What kind of identity?" cannot be given an adequate answer if the question "What constitutes a person?" is not first given a complete response.

Like Ricoeur, Hartshorne is convinced that the "what" of personal identity is inseparable from its "who." Hence, Hartshorne's analysis of the problematic begins with a look into the notion that he believes lies at the bottom of the reduction of the "who"-question and its limitation to the "what"-question. This is the concept of substance. Unlike Ricoeur, however, Hartshorne does not see his dialogue with philosophies that seek to reduce personal identity to its objective dimension as a mere detour which will eventually lead to the more important question of the "who." In this regard, Hartshorne's theory represents a much more sober approach to the notions of person, self, and subjectivity. And thus, as we shall find out, although not too far himself from the concerns and reservations that Ricoeur (and in some respects nonreductionist thinkers) expresses concerning a search for the objective dimension of personal identity, Hartshorne appears to lean more toward the views expressed by Hume, Parfit, and the reductionists. For Hartshorne, unlike Ricoeur, the *who* of personal identity is much more intimately bound with its *what*.

3

Charles Hartshorne's Critique of the Ontology of Substance

Personal identity and the substantialistic framework

At one point or another, every human person finds himself or herself asking the question at the heart of the problem of personal identity: *What am I?* Of course, certain experiences, e.g., religious or mystical ones that seem to "enlarge" the "I," do more than others to awaken occasions for posing such question. A little less frequent perhaps is the question: *What relationship do I have with my body?* Physical pain wrought by accidents or bodily illnesses, especially severe ones, usually trigger such questioning. Here the relationship of the "I" to the "thing" one calls one's "body" is shown to be just as important as the question about one's identity.

These two sets of experiences seem diametrically opposed in terms of the feelings they elicit. The first enlarges the "I," making it feel a certain intimacy with a larger whole; the second reduces and alienates the "I" even from that which is usually most intimate to it. There is a third question, however: *What is the relationship of this "I" with the innumerable others, themselves "I"s, which it encounters in its lifetime?* The "I" can feel itself enlarged as it experiences itself sustained, held aloft by the power of its relationships. But it can also experience itself alienated, reduced, and crushed when these relationships turn sour and hurtful.

The three questions are intertwined, as are the experiences that give rise to them. The different theories as well as the relation between one's identity and those of others are grounded in what constitutes the identity of a person. The first level of reflection—the level of common sense—revolves around transtemporal identity: an account of the conditions necessary for a person identified at one moment in time to be the same person at another moment. As indicated in Chapter 1, there are at present a good number of theories about the constitutive criteria of identity. Different systematizations are offered which, wholly or in part, run into conflict with each other. To recall, these are theories which argue from either a physical or a psychological position (nonstrict theories) or theories which reject both and insist that personal identity is irreducible to either of these two parts (strict theories). However, there are also those which reject these either-or approaches and hold that the two criteria must be taken together in order to arrive at an adequate account of personal identity. Here as well, there are several variations though they would roughly fall under what we could call complementarity or interactionist paradigms which at bottom recognize the irreducibility of one of the components to the other.

These perspectives run into conflict with each other, and will continue to do so, not only because of their fragmentary approaches to the question, but more importantly, because of their basis on a substantialistic ontology. Nor for the very same reason can they arrive at a resolution of the difficulties that attend discussion regarding the criteria. Strict identity theories close the discussion by locating identity in a third term not simply irreducible to but isolatable from the constituent parts of a person. Nonstrict approaches, which take either the physiological or psychological criterion, being largely reductionistic, fragment the reality they are attempting to describe. They dichotomize and then ultimately limit the reality of identity to one of its two components. Interactionist and complementarity approaches, for their part, also remain fragmentary. For although they take into account both criteria in mapping out the nature of personal identity, they still fail to make sense of the fact that there is a real interaction that holds between the two factors being mapped out by each criterion. The interaction of body and mind is recognized, and this makes for a more sufficient analysis of the matter than the nonreductionist and reductionist approaches, but the interaction is itself left without a suitable philosophical explanation. What is common to all of them is the presupposition of an unchanging substrate, be this person, mind, or body, which serves to underpin each particular theory of personal identity.

An account of personal identity which simply spells out data regarding its components, the enumeration of which is considered necessary and sufficient, would be philosophically inadequate. For an important ingredient remains missing. The discussion of personal identity using two criteria may be made possible by the fact that the self is experienced as constituted by two components, body and mind. This duality notwithstanding, the experience of one's identity remains one and nonfragmentary. In illness both the experience of pain as well as the pain-wracked body which the "I" is capable of observing are immersed in a unified reality, viz., the experience in which both the "I" as well as its body are together is suffered by an integral individual who can say, "My back hurts," or "I am sick." However, the unified character of the narrating "I" notwithstanding, we hold that this unity cannot be seen as a reason for positing the "I" as a third term distinct from its components.

Our main criticism of strict-identity accounts is that their approach to the problem is anchored onto a substantialistic metaphysics. Although they have overcome a dichotomization between thinking substance and extended substance bequeathed by Cartesian thinking, they still remain embedded in the notion of identity that signifies an underlying, constant substantial self. Change, in this perspective, is limited to the various "encrustations," accidents that are predicated of a substantial subject, whose real nature is one of stasis. This seems to water down the reality of becoming and the historical character of the subject. For their part, nonstrict or reductionistic accounts merely locate the unchanging in either one of the components of person.

Approaches that look at the physical and psychological components as merely complementing each other are mapping two independently enduring substances, mind and body, whose constant interaction results in a subject's experiences. This too is an inadequate view of the nature of personal identity. While neither of the two components of the subject are explained away or reduced to the other, it misses the total experience itself which is neither simply the mind nor simply the body. It also ignores the simple fact that their interaction results in the experience of a third party, viz., the self-identical subject. For the very locus of this interaction is not the subject *simply* but the very subject-now who owns the experience by the very fact that he/she can appropriate it in a way no one else can. This is the uniqueness of the momentary subject; namely, that neither the past subjects belonging to his/her own sequence nor the other subjects with whom he/she interacts possess his/her own experiences in the degree and intensity by which he/she experiences them. His/her past sequence of "selves" provides but a vague outline, paving the way for his/her present experience. Other selves are limited in their participation in what is happening to him/her now. Going back to the example of pain, a simple interactionist approach may recognize both the mind, which identifies the pain, as well as the body, which is its immediate location. However, it cannot yield a complete account of the nature of the individual self, who, in saying "My back hurts," is disclosed as neither simply mind nor body. How we characterize the identity of this self that appropriates *its own* pain is the key factor to an adequate account of personal identity.

Substantialistic ontologies are inherently uncongenial to an account of personal identity. Even in ordinary discourse, we tend to resist attributions to ourselves that indicate a fixed constitution. A wrongdoer may be prepared to say, "I did this or that act," but will resist saying "I am a thief" or "I am a murderer." The ordinary person on the street will be generally inclined to see himself and his doings in nonsubstantialistic terms. He would rather consider himself as an agent, i.e., as someone whose acts and experiences aim at satisfying his needs and desires, as they are disclosed to him at the moment. While there is considerable difficulty in answering the question "What exactly am I?," there appears no comparable difficulty in experiencing "what I do." What characterizes "mineness," i.e., genuine ownership, in the self that can own and speak of its pain is not some peculiar qualitative characteristic which the pain exhibits. Instead, such possession is constituted by the fact that one's experience forms part of an overall ongoing process. Only "I now" yields concrete and definite identity. It accomplishes this through perceptual observation, not of the bare identity of an enduring subject but of a definite sequence of events of the personal kind.

Once the core identity of a person is conceptualized as a unified manifold of the actual and potential processes (both physical and psychical), then we can obtain a concept of personhood that renders the nature of its identity experientially accessible. Personal identity resides neither in the body as such nor in an individual's psychic unity simply, but in the synoptic unity of both, which is disclosed in its character as a historic event. What is involved here is a reorientation, a shift from the fixed language of substance to the fluid language of event, from a substantive unity of machinery to a processual unity of mode of functioning. The unity of a person is a narrative unity that is characterized not by stasis but by an appeal to be brought to life through an account portraying a coherent story. The identity of an individual *is* an event embedded in that individual's life history. And just as the events making up an individual's life history cannot be isolated from the entire temporal series, so the story of one's life cannot be isolated from the particular events which are the concrete loci of the individual's identity. Apart from the concrete events making up the temporal seriality of personhood, the history of an individual is nothing more than an abstraction. Identity is the uniqueness of an individual's career, not something given once for all at the beginning of this career, which then proceeds to unroll like a ball of yarn that is unwound. Personal identity is an event embedded in history, and it is by actively creating this history that an individual creates his own identity.

Hartshorne criticizes substance ontology as ultimately falling short of its own goal of capturing the truly real. This shortcoming has had a tremendous negative impact on our ways of conceiving the identity of persons. We have argued that it is an inadequate foundation for a theory of identity. It is also (as we shall show later on in the work) harmful when used as a basis for a theory of relations. According to Hartshorne, such ontologies lie at the bottom of a great many ethical theories that hold the "self" as an ultimate category. With regard to the distinction between numerical and qualitative identity, it is the latter that is his concern. It is this mixture of qualitative uniqueness and overlapping in relation to other persons and the world in general that he is interested in. Substance ontologies fail precisely not because they maintain that there is an element of identity through change but because they obscure the fact that there is also nonidentity involved in an equally literal and numerical sense. Personal identity is thus literally partial identity and partial nonidentity, with the nonidentity referring to the complete reality and simple identity referring to but a constituent of the whole.

It is event rather than substance, which, for Hartshorne, captures the complete reality of what is truly real. The language of event recognizes the reality of both stability and change which substance-language fails to accomplish. The concept of substance has always been associated with fixity, and although the category of becoming is recognized, this recognition is accomplished by holding that becoming itself is subject to analysis into compositions of ultimate individual realities themselves devoid of process. But this is not doing justice to the reality of becoming. The conception of an eternally enduring subject of change denies change and becoming, the kind of reality conferred upon changelessness. But Hartshorne's language of event does not propose to solve the problem by simply reversing the situation and making becoming the only reality. Mere process devoid of individualities is just as incoherent a theory as mere individualities bereft of processual character.

Hartshorne's metaphysical system

Metaphysical systems throughout history have tried to present what their formulators have conceived as the basic *descriptum*, i.e., the most fundamental unit of reality. In this sense, Charles Hartshorne's metaphysical system is no different from the many others that preceded it. For he also proposes that we consider the primordial building blocks of reality. Hartshorne calls his metaphysical system "neoclassical,"[1] since his thought represents an attempt to go into dialogue with earlier as well as contemporary thought systems. There is a dual aspect to the neoclassical label, a double relation of dialogue and critique, as well as overcoming and synthesis.[2] This point is important in understanding his metaphysics; otherwise, it would be viewed as simply being yet another system, set in opposition to earlier ones and destined like them to contribute to the discussion. The term "neoclassical" is intended to set his thought in clear contrast to either the great traditions or the perennial philosophy, on the one hand, while on the other, it is meant to emphasize his ideal that mere personal whim or contemporary fashion should be avoided in matters philosophical.[3]

Hartshorne endeavors to take into account traditional metaphysical formulations. This involves a critical appraisal of these systems, as well as an appropriation of their elements that measure up to the requirements of consistency imposed by the system of process thought.[4] He also takes into serious consideration developments in the field of science, which he holds to be an ally rather than a rival in his attempt to grapple with the nature of reality.[5] The natural sciences, it is held, provide an access to the world which can only be overlooked by metaphysical thinking, at the expense of a thoroughgoing understanding of this same world.[6] There can be no adequate accounting of experience, without an attendant and equally adequate grasp of what constitutes the world. Further, paying heed to the voice of science also provides a way of surmounting the danger of enclosure which constantly threatens any overarching systematization of thought.[7]

On account of this dual anchoring onto classical and contemporary modes of thinking, Hartshorne's metaphysics is different from the other systems with which he dialogues. Our presentation of his ontology of event will be done within his overall attempt to overcome the contradictions of substance metaphysics, especially in terms of the effect this has had on the notion of personal identity. We shall show that the definiteness of identity is due not to an underlying substance that remains fixed throughout change, but to the full definiteness of event.[8] Admittedly, at the most immediate and commonsense level identity rests on identifiability. Individuation always requires some element of reaction manifested in the real presence of causal interaction between entities. Being present throughout, this interaction involves the possibility of one entity being identified over and against another. To deny that there is a subject untouched by change is not to deny the reality of uniqueness and the possibility of identifying one entity from another. Our point rather is that identity, always and unavoidably, has the character of process – a character which is fundamental, relative to entities in the conceptual order of understanding.

Identity and the ontology of substance

With reference to a concrete individual Hartshorne holds that identity does not connote sameness. To understand Hartshorne's criticism of this traditional idea, we have to consider his concern to seek out the most definite or determinate unit of reality. This concern reflects the concern of Alfred North Whitehead, whose philosophy Hartshorne not only comments upon but also adopts to a considerable extent, as his own.[9] Whitehead has summed up in terms of the ultimate metaphysical problem the conception of a "complete (*panteles*) fact."[10]

What Whitehead's notion of "complete fact" means, according to Ivor Leclerc, is precisely what Aristotle meant to signify by the term *ousia* and which is rendered "being" or "existence" in the fullest and most primary sense of the term.[11] Hartshorne is also referring to this specific sense of existence when he speaks of the most definite or determinate unit of reality. This puts him (as well as Whitehead) within the great philosophical tradition traceable to the ancient Greek fascination with what ultimately constitutes reality and, in particular, to Aristotle's own way of conceiving this problem.[12] Central to Hartshorne's thought as well as Whitehead's is being or existence, but not being or existence as such. Instead it is the *existence of a particular*, a concrete entity, or distinct ontological unit[13] which, says Hartshorne, exists now.[14]

According to Hartshorne, Aristotle's answer to the question *What is the most determinate unit of reality?* is at the core of the traditional notion of a self-identical entity that remains untouched by change.[15] There is a double meaning to Aristotle's concept of substance,[16] which itself requires some elucidation in order to have a complete grasp of the flow of Hartshorne's critique. For Hartshorne's treatment of the concept itself moves somewhat back and forth from the more overarching concern for the most determinate unit of reality to his concern to treat the two senses by which this basic unit is understood. The two basic senses of Aristotle's concept of substance are (a) as an independently existing entity, a *res*; and (b) as an unchanging substrate of change, the *arche* or principle that makes an entity to be what it is.[17] These two fundamental notions can then be further subdivided into at least five characterizations, which woven into each other provide a much fuller comprehension of the notion. (Again, it must be noted that this breaking down of the concept is necessary in order to have an exhaustive view of the entire orbit of the Hartshornean critique.)

A first definition is to be found in the *Categories* (2a, 11), where substance is defined as "that which is neither predicable of a subject nor present in a subject." A comparable conceptualization can be found in *Metaphysics*: "All these are called substances because they are not predicated of a subject but everything else is predicated of them."[18] Substance in this sense can be regarded as the concrete individual thing, as in the individual man or horse. Aristotle regards this as the truest and primary and most definite sense of the word.

A secondary sense of the term is found shortly after this line in the *Categories*, in which Aristotle holds that things called "substances" are those "within which, as species, the primary substances are included; also those which, as genera, include the species."[19] These secondary substances, he points out, are predicable of a subject. Hence "man," for instance, is predicated of the individual man.[20] Aristotle seems to have the idea here of the essences or natures as substances; hence, the more qualities they comprise, the more substantial they really are.[21] This intimation suggests that being a substance is not a matter of all or nothing but one of degree. Moreover, it also hints at the way of thinking onto which Hartshorne latches an important move in his critique, namely, on the idea of probing the notion of determinateness by moving from the least to the most definite concept: in Aristotle, roughly, from genus to species to individual; in Hartshorne, from genus to species to individual to event-state. It appears that Aristotle's purpose expressed in the first and second characterizations is primarily to contrast the independent way of existence of substances, as opposed to the dependence of qualities and relations.[22]

The third characterization of substance is that which is capable of independent existence. Although Aristotle himself does not seem to develop this characterization further in either the *Metaphysics* or the *Categories*, the notion of independent existence, which was simply meant to *differentiate* it from the parasitic mode of existence of qualities, evolves in later philosophy into the notion of substance as "that which can exist by itself, without the aid of any other substance." There is a very short step from the idea of independent existence, used as a means of differentiation and emphasis, to the idea of self-enclosure and nonrelationality. This step, however, as both Hartshorne and Whitehead correctly observe, was indeed taken. Furthermore, some authors are quick to point out that though this may have been done by thinkers such as Descartes,[23] the most we can say about this particular Aristotelian characterization of substance is that the fact that Aristotle did not develop it himself has led to its being susceptible to stretches in interpretation. We cannot, they would argue—without distorting the fundamental Aristotelian impulse or intention—interpret the dictum of independence in any other way.[24] In fact, some would even go so far as to hold that what the Cartesian characterization itself meant was no more than that individual substances exist without either being predicated of or existing in anything else.[25] But this suggests that the Cartesian characterization of substance is very much the same as Aristotle's notion—that Descartes' notion too was a matter of differentiation, of emphasis, not of a downright suggestion of nonrelationality among substances.

Whitehead's interpretation of the Aristotelian idea of independent existence of substance, for instance, has been criticized as a "stretching" and thus a misinterpretation of the basic thrust of Aristotle's dictum. The criticism is that Whitehead's objection to Aristotle rests on a mistaken reading of the phrase "present in" and that the inference from "that which is neither asserted of a subject nor present in a subject" to "that which requires nothing but itself to exist" is uncalled for. What the dictum of independence shows *primarily* is that "substance does not have the relation of accident to another substance."[26] This observation is certainly acknowledged, and not even Whitehead would deny this primary intent on Aristotle's part. But it is incorrect to base the criticism of Whitehead on the same ground which has enabled the latter to subject Aristotle's notion to criticism. For it is only *primarily* that Aristotle's dictum works in a way that distinguishes the mode of existence of substance and accidents. That this is not the only way the dictum can be interpreted is shown by the very fact that it *has* in fact been interpreted so as to make the inference to nonrelationality possible. Descartes has done it. By declaring in the *Principia* that substance has no need of any other thing in order to exist(in a manner that went beyond Aristotle's original intent), Descartes opened the way for the Aristotelian dictum to be interpreted to mean nonrelationality. He also largely obscured the concept of substance even more, since his definition involved a negative determination which really does not say anything positively what it is *to be a substance*. Moreover, he has drawn attention, although obliquely, to the ambiguity and inadequacy of the Aristotelian conception—which has in fact made the Whiteheadian criticism not only possible but necessary.

If the second Cartesian characterization of substance shows anything clearly, it is that an obvious difficulty is truly present in germinal form in the Aristotelian notion. For once we introduce the idea of relations involving other substances, not only is a clear restriction placed on independent existence but the very notion of independence is also made problematic.[27] It is therefore incorrect to criticize Whitehead for pointing to Aristotle as the root of the difficulty, since the dictum of independence was inherent in Aristotle's theory itself.[28]

The fourth sense by which substance is understood—which Aristotle also calls its most distinctive mark—is that "while remaining numerically one and the same, it is capable of admitting contrary qualities."[29] This notion will also undergo evolution in the hands of later philosophers who will develop it into the idea of a center of change, a substrate supporting its attributes and qualities.

This fourth characterization of substance is linked with a fifth one— substance as "that which is not predicated of a stratum, but of which all else is predicated."[30] This fifth sense, which has also been called the logical criterion of substance, has been criticized as making the notion of substance dependent upon the structure of Greek as well as some other Indo-European languages, in which sentences with a subject-predicate structure are standard forms of expression.[31] It is also criticized as founded on a now outmoded view of logic in which all statements canonically expressed are structured in such a way that a predicate is affirmed of a subject.[32]

The question of determinateness

Hartshorne's discussion of the difficulties with the substance-concept begins with his treatment of determinateness. He considers notions which are of less determinate character and then proceeds to a consideration of those which are more determinate, until he finally arrives at that concept which he takes to be expressive of the full definiteness of truth. We could call what drives his analysis from the less to the most definite notion, a logic of determinateness, which proceeds from considering what is unique to genus, then species, then individual. Unlike Aristotle though, Hartshorne does not stop at this point. Instead he asks: could there be a concept that would be more expressive of a greater and fuller sense of determinateness than "individual"? Furthermore, he finds the answer, not in substance or enduring individual, but in the concept of "event," for as he points out: "To know all events in the history of an individual is incomparably more than simply to know which individual it is."[33] The concrete momentary state has, according to him, the character of genus, and species, and the individual identity. But it has more. For it includes not only these but all the arbitrary additions that make up the entity at every moment of its existence provide the richest determination and give fully definite and concrete reality. The question of determinateness is therefore the question regarding the final real things of which the world is made up.[34] According to Hartshorne, substance or enduring individual cannot be this final real thing. These concepts merely represent a simplification or shorthand, convenient approximations for the more adequate and yet more complex reality that is above and beyond substance and enduring individual in the scale of concreteness (this being a term synonymous with definiteness and determinateness).

To see what Hartshorne means, let us make this observation. For everyday purposes the entities we generally encounter are rightly conceived as self-identical, enduring substances.[35] Chairs, tables, trees, individual men and women—these are singulars to which we can not only point as occupying a definite portion of space but also identify as the same chair, table, tree, or person that we have known for a definite period of time. If, for instance, we were to inquire of any individual on the street what makes a tree which has stood on a certain plot, the same tree, today, yesterday, or a year ago, it would be difficult to imagine him failing to give an answer that was not founded on the idea of an unchanging *something that he knows to be* the same at the different periods mentioned. Likewise, asked about one of his friends, he will most likely find it strange if we were to doubt his ability to identify his friend as the same individual he has known for some time. He will not argue that his friend has changed in many ways: a few more strands of gray hair perhaps or even a few more lines on his forehead. But that *this* person in question *is* his friend, basically unchanged from the day they were first introduced up to this very moment, is something he would simply take for granted.

Spatial and temporal considerations are commonly regarded in this way. The law of contradiction after all only states that the same thing cannot have contradictory predicates *at the same time*. This renders spatial divisions substantial, and temporal ones adjectival, for "while what is *here* must be one thing and what is *there* another, what is earlier and what is later can be the same thing."[36] Concerning space, two different things occupying two different spatial loci can have identical qualities; with regard to time, *the same subject* can have contradictory predicates.

Hartshorne, however, finds this law to be problematic since both space and time are characterized in merely symmetrical terms. He says: "A thing can be red and not red either at different times, or in different spatial parts; any one-way order among the parts or the times seem, in so far, irrelevant. Diversity of times, diversity of places, suffice for the law of contradiction. So far, space and time are on the same footing."[37] Space and time, he insists, are not the same, and what distinguishes the latter from the former is not so much that the same object can have contradictory predicates but that the earlier members of a sequence of events only contain a more or less indefinite specification of their successors, while the latter are essentially successors of the very entities which they follow. The temporal order in Hartshorne's philosophy is at bottom asymmetrical: "The past comes into the present; the present cannot go back into the past."[38] This is time's distinctive character.[39] And if contradictory predicates are to be reconciled with the unity of a single subject throughout a specified period of time, it must be in terms of this asymmetry.

Common sense tells us that the friend to whom one was introduced as a teenager and the friend of whom one now speaks many years later are basically *the same*. Indeed a great deal of substance ontology's appeal is its agreement with common sense. Hartshorne, however, says that such agreement is only apparent.[40] As we have already pointed out, commonsense ways of viewing things work quite well in ordinary everyday life. They enable us to simplify the complexities of life and the universe. However, as Hartshorne correctly observes, such simplifications do not describe human thought in its full range and can deny as "unreal" some aspects of experience.[41] The self-identical, enduring individual is a prime example of such simplification. The concept of substance understood as insusceptible to any further analysis works quite well for ordinary purposes. However, it is exactly in those purposes that make the very notion important that it is shown to be inadequate.

Moreover, the full definiteness of the friend's identity is not as simple as what the earlier statement expresses. One's adult friend now, Hartshorne would insist, is *more determinate*, possessed of more determinations, qualities, and relations, than the young friend one knew then. He has had more experiences, seen more things, been to more places, known more people, etc. Who he is now not only encompasses who he was but also surpasses it. As Hartshorne puts it, "The more can contain the less, the less cannot contain the more."[42] Hence, the subject which really possesses the contradictory predicates is only the latter.[43] It is neither the earlier one, nor an abstract *something one knows not what* which self-identically endures throughout the changes that take place. The earlier entity as well as the later one belong to the same ordered sequence, but they are not simply one identical concrete entity. Thus Hartshorne argues that "the spatial diversity of parts can be *possessed together* by the individual, but the temporal diversity is so possessed, if at all, only in the later phase. Hence the genuinely concrete or inclusive unity, the determinate subject, is a new creation each moment. Consequently, the self-identical entity is not the truly concrete and determinate, for its reality is embraced by the entity that is new at every moment. Given that there is real novelty of qualities at each moment, "the contrast of B to A includes A."[44] The present or latest in the series belonging to the career of a particular entity is therefore the total concrete reality containing the former elements of the series.[45] The entity as numerically the same is but an abstraction from this series which is constantly being renewed.[46]

For Hartshorne thus—contrary to the Aristotelian fourth characterization of substance, as noted above—there can be no numerically identical subject that *simply* endures through time. The subject which can admit contradictory predicates[47] is not merely something here, in contrast to something there; it is rather, something here-now, in contrast to something there-then. And this something here-now is a new entity at every moment, an event in a continuous process of becoming. Change in a single thing is thus a "shorthand for the *succession* of a number of contrasting events, where the sequence of events has some connectedness and continuity of character which lead us to verbalize it as the history of a single enduring 'individual.'"[48] This is why Hartshorne insists that traditional ways of predication are inherently ambiguous. For in certain cases, what is being predicated could be an abstract (or more logically weak) characterization, and what it is describing could be less abstract. For instance, what makes the statement "Birds are animals" true is that the more abstract idea—animals—is included in the comprehension of the more definite concept, viz., birds, as one of the latter's determinations. However, in other instances, e.g., if we take the statement, "John is ill," the case is entirely different. For the mere identity of John is of less determinate character than his present actual state, i.e., of being ill. And unless John has never been well in his life, his simple identity *as* John, cannot be said to include the actual state of his illness. Instead, it is the other way around. Thus, in this instance, Hartshorne contends that "the 'subject' fails to perform its primary function of furnishing the definiteness of truth" adding that "Only 'so and so now' yields the required definiteness; but it does this not by virtue of a date on a calendar, but by virtue of perceptual observation, and observation not just of so and so, but of a definite event-sequence (not implicated by X's being so and so plus the date), which we observe to occur."[49]

The ascription of definiteness is therefore possible only because there is an entity, i.e., a subject, whose definiteness embraces the less determinate predicates ascribed to it. Nonetheless, this definite entity of which things are predicated is not the enduring individual which Aristotle and the subsequent ontologists of substance have proposed. This self-identical entity is in fact much less determinate, much more abstract and general. This is why Hartshorne insists on the ambiguity involved in the old language of essence and accidents among predicates. For there is a reversal of meaning that takes place concerning predication itself. This reversal is illustrated by the fact that we can predicate a particular quality to an entity in much the same way that we can say that this predicate in question is "in" the entity. Nevertheless, the more determinate, i.e., the logical subject, is not the entity which is said to have a certain quality, but more properly, that whose very determinateness embraces the predicates in question, namely, the event.[50] The locus of the full definiteness of reality, the actual entity—understood in terms of the real signification of *ousia*—cannot be the enduring entity that remains self-same in the midst of change. As Hartshorne says: "one must see that the subjects 'in' which predicates finally inhere are not individual substances but their successive states."[51] Moreover, the ascription of definiteness to the enduring individual relegates the processual aspect of the stability-change relation to a lower level reality—hence, a surreptitious reversal to a bifurcation of reality, albeit of a more sophisticated sort.

Hartshorne also criticizes another ambiguity inherent in the Aristotelian description of substance. For he says that Aristotle's notion of substance as the entity which all true characterizations correctly describe is rendered problematic by the suggestion that "the knowable truth is truth, not about the individual, but about the species or form."[52] Although he rejected the Platonic bifurcation of reality into two realms, one more real than the other, Aristotle concurred with the Platonic notion that the universal form is not simply a subjective idea. The universal in the mind corresponds to an object's specific essence—though such essence does not exist in a separate state outside the mind. Only in the mind and through the mind's analyzing activity are these two made separate. This universal, according to Aristotle, is the object of science, not the individual object to which this universal corresponds as the latter's form, for "without the universal it is not possible to get knowledge."[53] Science, in Aristotle's thinking, directs itself to the universal element in things. It concerns itself with those essential characteristics which individuals of a certain class have in common for it is in this way that definition, which is of the universal, and the form can come about.[54] According to this line of thinking then, a scientist would not be interested in individual entities, say individual human beings, but with "humanity" or the form common to all human beings.

In the *Categories*, however, we have seen that Aristotle also calls individuals *protai ousiai*, "primary substances," in contradistinction to the species "man" and the genus "animal," which he terms *deuterai ousiai*, "secondary substances." Species and genus are substances only in a secondary and derived sense. The individual alone, the primary substance, is the subject of predication and is itself not predicable of another. The ambiguity lies in the fact that species and genus, although substances only in the secondary sense, have a higher reality than the individual *qua* individual. They are in fact the object of science, the source of true knowledge. It is this apparent contradiction that is a target of Hartshorne's criticism of the Aristotelian notion concerning the determinateness of substance or the enduring individual (the second of the Aristotelian characterizations of substance mentioned above). Hartshorne's criticism is that if only the individual is primarily and thus truly substance, and if science is concerned with the *ousia*, it follows that the individual is the true object of science. But this is the opposite of what Aristotle teaches, namely that science is "of universals."[55] Put in simpler terms, Aristotle, on the one hand, holds that science is concerned with substance and that the individual is substance in the primary sense. On the other hand, he argues that the universal is of superior quality and is the true object of science.

Hartshorne points to this particular ambiguity in Aristotle in the very first paragraph of the chapter on "event," in *Creative Synthesis*. Although parts of it have already been mentioned earlier in other contexts, it serves us well now to quote the passage in full:

> A statement capable of being true or false, correctly describes or characterizes something. Philosophies may differ in the class of entities which they suppose to be the basic *descripta*, those which all true characterizations correctly, and at least indirectly describe. Aristotle codified one answer: what is described is the substance or enduring individual. However, since he also held that only the species, not the individual is truly knowable, his answer was somewhat ambiguous; for it seems that the knowable truth is not about the individual but about the species or form, even though this is real only in individual cases.[56]

If we regard the order of determinateness under which "individual," "species," and "genus" fall, we notice that "individual" is more determinate than "species"; "species" is more determinate than "genus"; "genus" is the most universal term. If this is the case, Hartshorne asks, why not say that the genus, rather than the species is the truly knowable? Individuals, after all, are special (and more determinate) cases of the species, but are not species special cases of the genus? Secondly, if "individual" is substance—*ousia*, in the primary sense of the term—because it is more determinate than the secondary term "species," our inquiry into the most determinate unit of reality should stop only at that entity which clearly possesses the greatest degree of definiteness. This most definite unit Hartshorne calls an "event."[57]

Now with regard to identity, we can either define it in terms of everything that happens in a person's life from the moment of birth to the day he dies. Or we could define it in terms of the Aristotelian notion of essential as opposed to contingent determinations or accidents. In the first instance, a problem arises for we really cannot say we know the person until his death. This view would open the floodgates to determinism, for "it would be contradiction to say that a person could have acted and experienced otherwise than he has."[58] However, the second case is not without its perplexities either. For the accidental state of an entity at any given moment is by far richer in definiteness than that which the entity *is* by *simply* being itself. The accidental state, Hartshorne insists, includes both essential as well as the contingent properties.

The relation between individual and event is compared to that of individual, species, and genus. The species possesses what is essential to the genus, *plus* some other determination particular to the species itself, while the individual possesses what is essential to the species, *plus* some other determination particular to the individual itself. Now if this were the case, Hartshorne stresses, the event which possesses the character of genus, species, individual, *plus* some other arbitrary additions at each moment—such as one's typing these very words, for instance—is therefore, much more determinate than any of the earlier-mentioned categories. Hence, his criticism is not of the notion of substance *simply*. Instead it is of the fact that the logic which drove the Aristotelian analysis from genus to species to individual—a logic in function of the search for the fully definite unit of reality—should have led Aristotle to the event or momentary state.[59] And what underpins this logic that lies behind the search for definiteness? It is that truth is finally about the individual instead of species, or species instead of genus, precisely because the individual is more definite than species, and species more definite than genus. In short, it is the quest for determinateness itself. Substance-language is therefore shown to be—as Hartshorne insists—a shorthand for event-language. The very reasons that have led Aristotle to say that species rather than individual is really known are the same reasons which point to the use of substance-language instead of event-language.

In this regard, one could not really claim that Aristotle was wrong in holding the more abstract and universal category, and not the individual, to be the object of scientific knowledge. Substance-language, as we have already noted, is shorthand for the more complex language of event, which is expressive of genuine concreteness. An individual that endures through change, an entity that we can identify as being within a given spatiotemporal locus, is more easily susceptible to our grasp, to our comprehension, to our ways of dealing with reality, than what constantly fluctuates. Thus, for instance, Hartshorne observes: "If the human 'present' has as its maximal length 1/10 of a second, then obviously we must normally think together in a few bundles the hundreds of thousands of events in each person's experience in a single day."[60] Species, being too general and complex, must be simplified; this simplification is accomplished by the notion of individual substance. In a similar vein, event sequences are too complex to deal with without the requisite simplification; we must think together in a few bundles, or better still, a single bundle. The Aristotelian impulse, i.e., the motive behind the ascription of ultimate reality to the enduring individual, which is regarded as the truly knowable, is therefore understandable. However, to concede that because the more complex necessitates simplification (as happens with species and individual) is not the same as saying that the end result, i.e., the simple concept (substance or the enduring individual) that is meant to render our grasp of the complex more manageable is acceptable.

In this regard, even Aristotle's notion that the more abstract species is the true object of science is not indefensible, and the charge of self-contradiction that is sometimes leveled against the idea can be answered. Thus Hartshorne himself does not charge the Aristotelian notion with incorrectness, but only of ambiguity. For Aristotle, the individual alone is a substance in the true sense. However, the individual sensible thing is complex. The intellect in scientific knowledge proceeds right to the universal element which is really there, albeit existing only concretely, as an element of the individual.

Hence, individual men and women perish while the nature of human beings remains the same in the succession of men and women. And thus for Aristotle, it is the nature of man that the scientist considers and not merely John or Mary. In regard to both ordinary and scientific knowledge, thus, it is the fact that the complex needs simplification *for us* that stands out. Thus, when Aristotle speaks of primary and secondary substances, he does not mean primary and secondary in nature, dignity, or time, but primary and secondary with regard to us. This is why we can argue that Aristotle does not contradict himself even with regard to terminology insofar as he makes a distinction between the two meanings of *ousia*. Substance in the primary sense, as we have seen, is the individual substance, the *res*, made up of matter and form. In the secondary sense, substance is the formal element or specific essence corresponding to the universal concept. *Protai ousiai* are objects nonpredicable of another but of which something else is predicated, namely, the accident. *Deuterai ousiai*, on the other hand, refers to the nature, in the sense of the specific essence, that which corresponds to the universal element or the form of the thing which makes the individual truly a substance, and which the mind abstracts and conceives in its formal universality. When Aristotle says that the universal is the object of science he is not denying objective reality to the universal; instead what he denies is the notion of its separate existence.

Strawson's defense of substance

The complexity and richness of reality requires simplification for us. Thus the notion of "substance" or "enduring individual" is meant to facilitate our identification of particular entities. The overwhelming power of flux necessitates the search for a locus of stability thereby rendering change itself bearable. The claim has been made that these observations lie at the very foundation of the ancients' response to the question regarding the basic *descripta* of reality. This need for a stable locus is given much attention in P.F. Strawson's book *Individuals: An Essay in Descriptive Metaphysics*,[61] in which another element is introduced to further the search for stability, namely, the element of spatiotemporal localizability. In this work, Strawson first of all decries the propensity of what he calls *revisionary metaphysical systems* toward reconstructing what they believe to be the real behind the appearance. This impulse, he points out, has resulted in the reduction of much of speculative philosophy to a sequence of incompatible and conflicting systems.[62]

Strawson's work is relevant to our criticism of substance ontology. First, he holds that the method of metaphysics must be limited to disclosing the latent structures of thought. Metaphysics for Strawson should be consigned to describing a "massive central core of human thinking which has no history."[63] Second, this core is composed of categories and concepts that are unchangeable in their fundamental character. Although he admits the changeable nature of the critical and analytical idiom of philosophy, he also insists that the central subject matter of metaphysics, as he conceives it, is beyond change.[64] And while acknowledging that metaphysics *per se* is a means of furthering new directions or styles of thought, he nevertheless insists that metaphysics must not be thought of simply in this historical style for there are categories and concepts which simply do not change in their most fundamental character. Contained in this central core of human thinking are the elements which on the one hand are the most ordinary, "the commonplaces of the least refined thinking," while, on the other hand, are also the "indispensable core of the conceptual equipment of the most sophisticated human beings."[65]

Hartshorne's thinking runs contrary to this idea. "The history of philosophy should be viewed as exhibiting progress but also regression,"[66] says Hartshorne. The recognition of this dual movement is opposite to Strawson's view that it is "unlikely that there are any new truths to be discovered," and that "if there are no new truths to be discovered, there are old truths to be rediscovered"—as if the object of the philosophical quest is a mere recapitulation of what has been forever fixed. The static element is inextricably woven into Strawson's view of reality itself, central to which is an undeniable aspect of fixity. "Particular identification in general," he points out, "rests ultimately on the possibility of locating particular things we speak of in a single unified spatio-temporal system."[67]

In line with his notion of what metaphysics should be, Strawson asks two further questions that are important to this discussion. The first is whether it can be claimed that there is a single scheme of relations in which every particular can be directly located. This is a conceptual scheme, and every entity can be plotted onto a specific point in it—as for instance in a system whereby a thing can be spatialized by referring to its place using x and y coordinates. This is due to his major concern in the work; namely, the identification of particulars. This allows for the postponement of any consideration of an identification that would be dependent upon the particular entity's immersion in a subjective matrix. Since a common point of reference is what Hartshorne seeks, there is a clear need to eliminate relative identification. The speaker's general picture in which a particular is inserted has to be bracketed by enabling the hearer to identify the particular through sensible discrimination of a particular within a certain range of particulars. Nothing is to be outside this range. The hearer must be able to directly locate the particular being referred to. The identification of particulars is therefore tied to the interchange which takes place between a speaker making the identification and the hearer who may or may not be able to identify the speaker's particular referent. By identifying a particular, one should be able to make apparent to another that individual thing of which he intends to speak, within a range of particulars of the same kind.

The second question Strawson considers is whether there is any distinguishable class of particulars which is basic from the viewpoint of particular identification. He gives an affirmative answer, explaining that material bodies are the most basic particulars. They best satisfy the criteria of localization in a common point of reference. They "secure to us one single common and continuously extendible framework of reference, any constituent of which can be identifyingly referred to without reference to any particular of any other type."[68] Having argued that the basic particulars are material bodies, Strawson points out that the case with regard to the scheme and the particulars embedded in it is "not that on the one hand we have a conceptual scheme which presents us with a certain problem of particular-identification; while on the other hand there exist material objects in sufficient richness and strength to make possible the solution of such problems."[69] He notes that it is only because the solution is possible that the problem exists. It is obvious that the criterion of localization and the entity suggested as satisfying it are so well suited to one another that one may say that what provides a solution to the problem is also that which opens the possibility for posing it.

Strawson rightly argues that the particular fit between problem and solution characterizes all transcendental arguments. And, in this case, the mutuality between spatiotemporal scheme and material bodies could very well be construed as falling within such classification. However, it is one thing to argue that such fit must exist in a transcendental argument. It is another thing to claim that such sort of mutuality is the kind that is obtained in the particular pair which he has in mind. The first is an accurate observation; the second seems more like a question-begging maneuver.

Another instance in the work can perhaps serve to clarify our point. In the chapter on "bodies," Strawson, intent on according pre-eminence to physical particulars over events and processes, picks out instances of the latter which are carefully calculated to produce the result he aims at. This aim is to illustrate how mere sequences of events are insufficient to make up a world that is characterized by intersubjective agreement about a particular referent of linguistic exchange. Now since the sorts of events he picks out as examples are naturally insufficient to assure this, his argument against events and processes would then appear to hold.

This, in fact, is Hartshorne's first major criticism of Strawson's thesis. Hartshorne agrees that spatiotemporal orientation requires more than events. However, he quickly adds that what is needed is more than the sort of events Strawson's discussion takes into account.[70] Strawson's choice of examples obviously derives from the conclusion he has already decided upon. His methodology serves to call attention to the static element that appears inextricably woven into his view of reality. Indeed, central to this view is an undeniable aspect of fixity, both of the conceptual scheme[71] as well as the particulars that are both completely localizable and hence stable.[72] The arrival at both a fixed conceptual scheme and self-identical particulars is due to an inadequacy in method.

A more rigorous consideration of the matter, i.e., a method that is more open and processive in nature—would have yielded quite different results. It certainly would not produce a scheme and (using Hartshorne's term to describe the basic units of reality) a "descriptum" that are both unchanging. Here we are brought back to the very first point made regarding Strawson's assertion of the task and character of metaphysics as simply descriptive and his disavowal of "revisionary" systems. For if "descriptive" means that there are no more new truths to be discovered, then a metaphysics of this sort cannot but arrive at the point where his inquiry leads. An inquiry based on a presupposition of fixity will yield a scheme and descriptum which are likewise fixed. But metaphysics cannot be merely descriptive. It must be exploratory and critical. Of course, "revisionary" must not be equated either with some sort of iconoclastic tendency that does characterize certain systems. Both descriptive and revisionist impulses must thus be reconciled in a metaphysical system that seeks to be a more faithful interpretation of reality. A stable element as well as an authentic openness to the creative impulse and the genuinely eruptive character of the givenness and disclosure of the real must be accommodated within a metaphysical system seeking to be adequate to the reality it maps out. Such metaphysical systems must be tentatively descriptive of what they continuously discover and what is unceasingly given or disclosed to them.

The real and the manner of its appearance are so intimately woven into each other that any distancing would be the product of a high abstraction. This abstraction locates the real in the wrong place, neither in what is given nor in what lies at the foundation of the given but in the process of separating the two. Consequently, the abstraction process becomes more real than the reality being described. But it is the given that is real; it is the locus of concreteness, not the distancing process. The real behind appearance is not reconstructed by revisionary metaphysics if reconstruction is understood to mean the creation of an artificial construct to be imposed upon reality. This is yet another instance of something to which is ascribed more reality than the really real or its manifestation. It is, of course, an undeniable fact that a metaphysical system can deteriorate into such a kind. However, to say that this has been the lot of certain revisionary metaphysical systems is not to say that all revisionary metaphysics is of such a kind, nor will such be their inevitable lot. In both cases a grave error is found in the localizing of the real in the wrong place: in the first instance, in the distancing of the real from appearance; in the second case, in the theoretical construct that results from such distancing. In both, the locus of the real is an abstraction.

Strawson gives pre-eminence to physical particulars, i.e., material bodies, because these are eminently subject to identification and reidentification, without having to fall back on speaker-relative identification. Physical particulars, being directly locatable on a spatiotemporal matrix, can be "identified without a mediating reference to any particular type or category other than its own."[73] Strawson then defines "relative identification" as identification relative only to a range of particulars, which is itself identified only as the range of particulars being talked about by the speaker. Apart from a statement that could qualify the identification made, the hearer will not be able to identify the particular being referred to by the speaker. This then makes the hearer's identification of the object dependent on the account of the story in which the object is inserted, i.e., the speaker's story.

It is this relative identification that Strawson wants eliminated. And rightly so, for if the speaker's general picture were allowed to determine the totality of the identification, there would be no way to say that the hearer is able to directly locate the particular in question. This, it must be recalled, is of paramount importance for Strawson's thesis since at the very outset of his treatment of particular-identification, he makes it clear that a hearer either is or is not able to identify the particular referred to by the speaker. He sets out to expound the criteria which would allow us to say that the hearer does identify the referent, "for it is not merely a happy accident that we are often able as speakers and hearers, to identify the particulars which enter into our discourse."[74]

The difficulty arises not so much with what he intends to accomplish but with the means by which he proposes we do it. Moreover, the manner by which such tools are regarded also results in serious difficulties. For instance, there can be no question as to the need for a conceptual scheme which would allow for a lessening of relative identification. The importance of an objective consideration of a particular in question must not be watered down. Speaker-relative descriptions carry with them the disadvantage of being ultimately private rather than public descriptions. Their lot, as belonging specifically to particulars called selves, must be postponed. Without such postponement, it would be difficult to pry ourselves free from a subjectivist idealism that ascribes to private particulars the dominant position of ultimate reference. However, the need for a high degree of objectivity does not translate into a need for fixity and stasis with regard to scheme construction.

"Objectively identifiable" must not be equated with "unchanging" or "completed." However, it does become equated with such when there is an underlying assumption concerning what is supposed to express the most concrete aspect of nature, i.e., the basic particulars. This assumption is that these most basic particulars can simply be located in a definite portion of space and time. It is an objection that can be made against substantialistic ontological schemes, including Strawson's. For a common feature of both space and time is that an entity can be said to be in a definite locus in space and time, identifiable by both speaker and hearer, in a sense that is perfectly isolable from any reference to other regions. But this is exactly the point of Strawson's discussion, viz., that an item be directly locatable and identified without referring to any other particular at all.[75] Part One of his book, as a matter of fact (pp. 2–133), especially Chapter 1.3: "Basic Particulars" (pp. 27–49), is devoted to the argument that material bodies fit well into the category of particular things that are locatable in a single unitary spatiotemporal framework. And even in Chapter 3.1–7: "Persons" (pp. 81–113), in which he delves into the issue of distinguishing oneself from states of that self and distinguishing oneself and its states from selves other to it as well as the states these others are in, a great deal of stress is given to the idea of identification of particulars via localization in a unified spatiotemporal scheme.

Strawson's thesis does not work well with an account of personal identity. Implicit in his proposed metaphysical scheme is a view of reality—a cosmology—which epitomizes the atomistic mechanism so characteristic of the modern mind. In this worldview the fundamental notions are that of matter, space, and time. The main concern is an objective disclosure of the characteristics of material particles and the formulation of descriptions of the principles (in as exact a mathematical way as possible) that are held to govern the motion of physical particulars within the spatiotemporal continuum. This kind of perspective on reality, which holds a fixed matrix of fragmentary particulars has become increasingly difficult to uphold especially with a number of significant developments in both the human and natural sciences, which tend to reveal a far more connected, organic, and dynamically evolving reality. The concept of a fixed metaphysical scheme and the idea that its ultimate components are simply located bits of matter has become increasingly problematic.

4

The Fallacy of Simple Location and the Ontologies of Substance and Event

The fallacy of simple location

The term "simple location" was coined by Alfred North Whitehead, in his book *Science and the Modern World*.[1] It is a fallacy of simple location to attempt to locate concrete particulars in definite portions of space and time. According to Whitehead, there are three characteristics of space and time.[2] First, entities are separated in space and separated in time. He calls this the "separative" character of space-time. Second, entities are also together in space and together in time, even if they are not contemporaneous. This is space-time's "prehensive" character. Third, each entity in space has a definite limitation, which is why it has its own peculiar shape and none other and why it is in its specific locus and in none other's. The temporal analogue of such characteristic is that an entity is said to endure through a defined period and in no other. This third characteristic of space-time, taken by itself, gives rise to the idea of simple location, which then holds that each bit of matter is individually independent. Hence, it is regarded as fully describable, apart from any reference to any other portion of matter. An entity could very well be the sole occupant of uniform space; but it would nonetheless remain the entity that it is. Any relation that may be held between itself and any of the other entities, should these other entities in fact exist, becomes of secondary importance and cannot constitute an explanation for its internal constitution.[3] What is true of space is likewise true of time. Thus, any bit of matter could be adequately described without any reference to the past or the future. The bit of matter in question is fully itself in any subperiod, however short, and is equally itself at any instant of time. However, as Whitehead likewise points out: "This gives no more than an accidental character to the passage of time, as the bit of matter in question is itself indifferent to the division of time. Temporality cannot thus constitute the essence of the entity; it has nothing to do with the character of the material."[4]

When we look into the intellectual foundations of the fallacy of simple location, especially as it has evolved in history, we discover that the fallacy itself is heir to the centuries-old presupposition concerning the atomistic character of nature, first proposed by the ancient Greek atomists. In fact, the term "simple location" is but a new label for the ancient notion concerning the atomic structure of nature. But whether considered in its ancient or modern form, the underlying idea remains the same: nature is comprised of discontinuous material particles that move about in homogeneous space, and at any particular moment, each of these atomic entities occupies a definite spatial slice with a clearly delineated boundary. Whitehead traces the roots of the fallacy to the question that the ancient Ionians posed regarding the final constituents of nature. "Simplylocated" particles became, as it were, the *definitive* answer that the metaphysics of the 17th and 18th centuries gave to this ancient question as well as every subsequent question concerning the matter. Between these two periods lies an entire epoch of intellectual activity that gradually built up a perspective of reality founded on the idea of simple location.

Whitehead singles out three main factors in the evolution of thought, leading up to modernity. Its offshoot is the fallacy of simple location that has become a chief presupposition of subsequent metaphysical thinking. These factors are: the resurgence of mathematics, an instinctive confidence in a detailed order of nature, and the unbridled rationalism of the late Middle Ages—all inherited, to a greater or lesser extent, from ancient Greek thinking.[5] On the one hand, the work of the translators of the 12th and of the early part of the 13th century made Aristotle's thought largely available to Christian thinkers in Western Europe. Most of Aristotle's works as well as a number of commentaries on them were already available in translation early in the 13th century.[6] This eventually spurred what during the late Middle Ages (and the Renaissance) became a revival of ancient Greek modes of thinking. On the other hand, the recovery of higher Greek mathematics (especially pronounced in the influence Euclid had on mathematicians of the Renaissance and after),[7] as well as the gradual spread of knowledge and influence of Islamic achievements in mathematics and astronomy,[8] reawakened interest in simplicity and certainty, which characterized the work of the ancient mathematicians. As a result the sciences that arose at the end of the medieval era began distinguishing themselves from other disciplines, in their fusion of experimental observation with mathematical reasoning.[9]

The resurgence of mathematics

Whitehead points to the union of passionate interest in detailed facts with equal devotion to abstract generalization as forming the novelty in our modern way of thinking.[10] Mathematics is an important element in the history of thought, especially thought which values simplicity, precision, and certainty. What is peculiar here though, is that these values are arrived at through a progressive movement toward the highest possible generalization or abstraction from concrete experience. Certainty in mathematics hinges on complete abstract generality.[11] This totality of general abstract conditions is then applicable to the relationships among the entities of any one concrete occasion.[12] With mathematics one manages to do away with the particular instance and even any particular entity in that regard. Its realm is that of the completely general.[13]

Such a description of mathematics, however, is not meant to limit it to a one-dimensional reality. Abstraction is but one of the two distinct but interconnected dimensions in mathematics. It represents, as it were, the ascending trajectory of mathematical thought, which is complemented by a descending movement embodying a progressive effectiveness in the analysis of concrete particulars. An interesting relationship of mutual "tempering," so to speak, exists between the two, since as Whitehead argues, "too large a generalization leads to mere barrenness. It is the large generalization, limited by a happy particularity, which is the fruitful conception."[14] The upward movement toward progressive and higher abstraction is tempered by a downward trajectory which then discloses a sustained increase in the importance of the upward movement in analyzing concrete facts, a phenomenon which is truly remarkable. "Nothing is more impressive," he says, "than the fact that as mathematics withdrew increasingly into the upper regions of ever greater extremes of abstract thought, it returned back to earth with a corresponding growth of importance for the analysis of concrete fact."[15]

This is a rather paradoxical situation wherein the utmost abstractions are what truly enable us to control our thought of concrete fact.[16] This paradox indicates that the two movements are mutually sustaining. Furthemore, they are unified by a third dimension which unifies them both and which is already intimated by Whitehead's term "control." Mathematics, at least in the second movement, functions as an effective tool of manipulation. The more its flight takes it to higher abstraction and generalization, the more its downward plunge increases its usefulness in controlling the ground of the concrete and particular. Underlying this effectiveness is the idea of its "functionality," which, beginning in the abstract sphere, is then "reflected in the order of nature under the guise of mathematically expressed laws."[17] It is precisely in this function that mathematical abstraction has served as the background of imaginative though, appropriated by science in its understanding of nature.

A particular example of this would be the effect the abstract development of mathematics had on the sciences of the 16th and 17th centuries. Whitehead refers to the notion of periodicity. Recurrence is a common enough experience. Apart from it, it would not be possible to connect present experience with past ones, thus making knowledge itself impossible. Measurement would likewise be impossible as recurrence is fundamental to our experience of exactness. Hence, from the ordinary and concrete experiences that we have everyday, we gain the abstract notion of periodicity which took a central position in the newly emerging sciences of the 16th and 17th centuries:

> Kepler divined a law connecting the major axes of the planetary orbits: Galileo observed the periodic vibrations of pendulums: Newton explained sound as being due to disturbance of air by the passage through it of period waves of condensation and rarefaction: Huyghens explained light as being due to the transverse waves of vibration of a subtle ether: Mersenne connected the period of the vibration of a violin string with its density, tension and length.[18]

These examples, he argues, point to the fact that the birth of modern physics would not have come about if a way had not been found to apply the abstract idea of periodicity to a variety of concrete instances—something which would have likewise been impossible had mathematics not already been able to work out in the abstract the different abstract ideas connected to the idea of periodicity.

The utility of abstraction

We have seen how mathematics served as the background of thought that spurred the development of the modern sciences. The historical developments, for their part, i.e., the concrete events which show the usefulness of mathematics, correspond to the foreground of the image we are painting. Background and foreground complement each other, and the harmony and discord that has existed in the continuous interweaving of both has resulted in a particular mode of viewing reality that has become deeply ingrained in modern thought. Today this mode is found particularly in the worldview of the sciences.

Whitehead delineates two great periods in the growing influence of mathematics upon general thought, with both periods lasting for about 200 years.[19] The first period lasted from Pythagoras to Plato, when the possibility of science and its general character first dawned upon thinkers of ancient Greece, and the second comprised of the 17th and 18th centuries, of the modern era. The ancient Pythagoreans maintained the deeply rooted mathematical structure of the world. Pythagoras, Whitehead argues, insisted on "the importance of the utmost generality in reasoning and divined the importance of number as an aid to the construction of any representation of the conditions involved in the order of nature."[20] It is with these absolutely general conditions that the exercise of logical reason is concerned, i.e., with the disclosure of an entire range of general conditions that make up the pattern drawn from the selected set of conditions that are exemplified by an entity.

By asking the question regarding the status of numbers in the realm of things, Pythagoras intuitively drew out the future importance of mathematics in the formation of science. Although exempt from temporal flux and spatial location, numbers are nonetheless involved in the real world. And while the notion that numbers lie at the base of the real world seems rather crude, it has proven to be a philosophical notion of immense importance in the development of science and its worldview, i.e., the expression of quality in terms of numerically determined quantity.[21] Plato took over the Pythagorean program and applied it to his theory of matter, arguing that the four elements are reducible to regular geometrical solids, which are reducible in turn to triangles. For Plato thus, the fundamental building blocks of the visible world were not material, but geometrical. His world of ideas can therefore be regarded as a refined version of the Pythagorean doctrine of number at the base of the world.[22]

With the arrival of Aristotle, there was a lull in the importance given to mathematics. Whitehead believes that Plato and Pythagoras, rather than Aristotle, stand nearer to modern physical science.[23] Indeed, the Copernican exaltation of the beauty of a smaller number of concentric circles, in the explanation of the revolution of the earth around the sun was very much in line with the Pythagorean belief in the harmony of numbers. In the absence of new data the nature of the support that Copernicus received was largely philosophical. By then the revival of Platonism was beginning to challenge the dominance of Aristotle's authority.[24] Moreover, as the historian of science Alexander Koyré points out, Galileo constituted classical mechanics within the framework of a loosely "Platonic" metaphysics. The strategies and practices of scientific research always follow from one's metaphysics, and Galileo succeeded in founding the first version of classical mechanics because he worked, perceived, and argued within the correct sort of metaphysical framework. It was a sort of nonmystical Platonism—a belief that at the base of the world are mathematical objects, which move according to simple and symmetrical mathematical laws. Koyré further holds that such a Platonic metaphysics was the only viable framework for scientific advance. Other frameworks, e.g., the Aristotelian, may have had their merits but were not scientific. Aristotle's natural philosophy and cosmology, for instance, were themselves coherent as a categoreal framework. But they could never structure experience and reason so as to produce modern mathematical physics since they were too closely enmeshed with the categories of natural language and everyday life.[25]

Mathematical abstractions

Whitehead observes that the stress that Aristotelian logic placed on classification over measurement, as well as its popularity, retarded the advance of physical science throughout the Middle Ages. Classification is necessary, but it remains a midway point between the immediate concreteness of a particular and the complete abstraction of mathematical concepts. Reason itself becomes limited unless progress can be made from classification to mathematics.[26] Moreover, Aristotelian thought is whole oriented. This resulted in an ambivalent attitude to using mathematics in science—an ambivalence that continued in the Aristotelian tradition of the Middle Ages.[27] On the one hand, Aristotle was certainly mathematically informed and utilized mathematics in his investigations. He regarded geometry, for instance, as the paradigm for a demonstrative science. And in the *Posterior Analytics*, there is even an implicit recognition of the superiority of the mathematician over the observationalist.[28] On the other hand, he seemed to shy away from fusing the more physical branches of mathematics into his overall metaphysical scheme.[29] He likewise pointed out that while physics considers natural things in their entirety, i.e., as sensible and changing bodies, mathematics simply strips away all sensible qualities and then concentrates on what remains.[30]

Between Pythagoras and the radical developments of modernity, mathematics made considerable but silent leaps in growth.[31] This, however, was rather limited along technical lines. Whitehead argues that its influence in the formation of philosophic and scientific thought within this almost 2000-year period significantly failed to recover from its "*deposition* in the hands of Aristotle."[32] This view, however, must be understood in relation to Aristotle's general ambivalence toward mathematics. The negative influence which may seem to be portrayed as coming from Aristotle with regard to the decline of mathematics until the late Middle Ages cannot be traced to a particular inadequacy of Aristotelian thought on the subject. He was, however, convinced that there was a real difference between mathematics and natural science or physics. But it did lead him to seek a middle road concerning the question of the applicability of mathematics to the study of nature. The "deposition" then, of which Whitehead speaks, concerns this very distinction Aristotle makes regarding brute fact and abstract reason, with an emphasis placed on the latter. In this regard, the influence mathematics may have on considerations of brute fact would indeed suffer. This is why the steady "fusion" of experimental observation with mathematics, which took place from the late Middle Ages until the 18th century, becomes more significant. For it shows that the gradual overcoming of the hardened demarcation between ways of considering brute fact was slowly being overcome. Whereas Aristotle sought a middle ground separating physics and mathematics, modern science overcame the difference by fusing the two.

This situation was to undergo an unprecedented change, almost a reversal in the fortunes of mathematics itself from the 16th to the 18th century. Aristotle's influence was at its lowest point in this era. Prior to this time of course, there already was an erosion of his influence. During the period immediately preceding the scientific revolution, Aristotelianism was still deeply entrenched and made up the bulk of the education received by men who had any serious concern for natural philosophy. In the late 16th to early 17th centuries, for instance, Scholastic Aristotelianism found new lease on life in the then rigidifying academic curricula of the Protestant Churches and of the Catholic Church of the Counter Reformation period. However, the Aristotelian system found itself under increasing attack from many angles. The greatest challenge came from the Copernican system, which was largely regarded as having cosmological truth. Still, the challenge remained largely dormant way up to the last stages of the 16th century. It was only during the time spanned by Galileo's career and afterwards that the scientific challenge to Aristotle's system gained considerable momentum. Galileo was, after all, anti-Aristotelian himself and was the first to successfully combine mathematics with experimentation. He was convinced that the task of science was to reduce the complexity of the observable to mathematical structures. The combination of theory and experiment can certainly be traced back to earlier centuries. But it was specifically in Galileo that the distinctive features of the new methodology was given its explicit formulation and was fruitfully applied.[33]

Mathematics had also gradually regained its importance. It was, as Whitehead says, "an age of great physicists and great philosophers; and the physicists and philosophers were alike mathematicians."[34] In this age of Galileo, Descartes, Spinoza, Newton, and Leibniz, mathematics became a driving force in the formation of thought. There had already been a transformation going on during that rather quiet period between the two epochs we have just delineated. The seed that had lain dormant was silently germinating, gradually being formed and energized by the technical developments we had alluded to earlier, until such point when something new was ready to emerge. The bud that came out in this second phase, however, was very different from the mathematics of the earlier age. For one, it had gained more strength in its power of generality. It had also begun "its almost incredible modern career of piling subtlety of generalization upon subtlety of generalization."[35]

Throughout the changes that were taking place, however, one thing remained constant: with each growth of complexity, some new application either to physical science or to philosophical thought was being achieved. The functionality and use of mathematics grew by leaps and bounds. And to a considerable extent, this is not surprising. For one, there were very important developments in the way human beings in general, and the more sensitive thinkers and observers of human nature in particular, were viewing the world about them.[36] In both epochs alike, a state of general disintegration of traditional modes of thinking was taking place. The overall hold and attraction of unbending doctrinal formulations and arcane rites—pagan in the earlier age, Christian in the latter, formerly held without question—were being increasingly subjected to intense scrutiny and critique.[37] Modes of thought and ways of relating with the world were passing into a new phase characterized by a decline of the old, as well as a desire to penetrate more into the hidden depths of reality and ultimate meaning. What was hoped would be achieved was direct enlightenment, on the one hand, and an awakening of analytical thought that was both critical and dispassionate, on the other.[38]

If we look back and consider the inspiration of mathematics in both epochs, we will discover that it is precisely these two goals—although in different degrees in both eras—that propelled thought to the heights of discovery. What is disclosed here is further support of the point already made regarding the trajectories traversed by the thinking inspired by the push toward increasing generality in mathematics. Whitehead likens this movement to the flight of an aeroplane which "starts from the ground of particular observation, makes a flight in the thin air of imaginative generalization, and again lands for renewed observation rendered acute by rational interpretation."[39] Such flights of thought originate in generalizations from particularities discerned in specific human interests such as physics, psychology, physiology, aesthetics, ethics, etc. Their power, however, lies not only with the upward movement of abstraction, but more, in fact, in the return that abstract thought makes as it sheds a new and more vibrant light on the particularities from which it began its flight. This likewise is what gives assurance that there will in fact be some important application which is a greater manipulation of concrete fact.[40] Mathematics, because it is the highest exemplification of the flight of abstract thinking may, as Whitehead says, lay claim to be the most original creation of the human spirit. Its originality consists "in the fact that in mathematical science connections between things are exhibited which, apart from the agency of human reason, are extremely unobvious."[41] It is this trust in the power of human reason that lay behind the strength of the sciences in the 16th and 17th centuries.[42]

Reason and order

Medieval thought had placed a tremendous amount of confidence in the capacity of reason to discover the reality of existences and the activity and function of things through metaphysical analysis.[43] There are two sources of such confidence in reason: Greek rationalism and the Judeo-Christian tradition's trust in an ultimate reasonableness of creation on account of its belief in a rational Creator.[44] They are two strands woven into each other and formed the backbone of the power of mediaeval speculation. We shall now consider the relation of these two and the important ideas within each, as these are pointed out by Whitehead, with a view to trace their points of intersection.

The ancient Greeks were very theoretical; science for them was an offshoot of philosophical speculation. They believed that by pushing reason to its utmost boundaries, while paying careful attention to the meanderings of thought, they could divine the nature of things. This was, moreover, bolstered by an ultimate, often unarticulated, trust in the general orderliness of the universe. The world made sense; things did not come together nor fly apart for no reason at all. This confidence in such orderliness is illustrated, for instance, by the essentially dramatic cosmology which the Greeks transmitted to later ages—an imaginative background implicit in the way they viewed the world. Whitehead observes out that the Greek view of nature was akin to that of a drama. He meant that the Greeks conceived nature in terms of a dramatic work of art, each element of which converged toward its proper end.[45]

The ancient Greeks' vision of the world was that of a dramatic tragedy. There was a remorselessness to the workings of the cosmos, coupled by its indifference to human existence. Fate was the operative view, which, according to Whitehead, is what ultimately lies at the foundation of the modern-day scientific vision couched in our conception of the ultimacy of physical laws.[46] Whitehead makes it clear though that this is not necessarily the view to which Aristotle would have subscribed without great reservations. Nevertheless, this is the view that subsequent Greek thought, taking its inspiration from Aristotle, passed on to the Middle Ages.[47]

The idea of order, which their observation of the cosmos impressed itself so deeply in the Greek imagination, was coupled and thereby strengthened by the conception of a moral order. In Plato's philosophy, for instance, cosmology and anthropology are closely connected. He attached a deep ethical significance to the study of the cosmos. He believed that the human soul was connected to the "world soul." Only when the human soul comes to know of its connection with the world soul—whose movements are characterized by perfection and beauty—will it become perfect and beautiful itself. Morality, for the ancient Greeks, was founded on cosmic order. This connection also found expression in Stoic philosophy, which regarded ethical life as somehow founded on the movement of the planets and actually caused by this movement. Stoicism held that the ordered motion of the cosmos was the very source of morality. Whitehead quotes Lecky's *History of European Morals*, where the latter speaks of Seneca's notion concerning the determination of all things by laws that are inexorable and divine, decrees which Divinity itself obeys. Having been adopted by the Romans, this Stoic idea was then passed on. It later influenced medieval thinkers on account of that sense of order which resulted from the notion of law that arose from the Roman empire.[48]

What we see here is a gradual interweaving of the elements that lie at the foundation of medieval thinking. The notion of order, both cosmic and moral, which Greek thinking held dear was eventually to inform the minds of medieval thinkers—but not without having first been mingled with elements belonging to the Judeo-Christian view of reality. The result was a marriage of worldviews which then became the imaginative backdrop of the medieval worldview. Whitehead calls attention to the formation of thought that the Middle Ages provided, for instance, with regard to the sense of law and order: "The Middle Ages formed one long training of the intellect of Western Europe in the sense of order. There may have been some deficiency in respect to practice. But the idea never for a moment lost its grip. It was pre-eminently an epoch of orderly thought, rationalistic through and through."[49] That the world is intelligible is a result of a deeper conviction that real connections can be made between things and events that recur. And based on these connections, certain general ideas governing recurrences can be derived.

Faith in reason then, as well as in the intelligible nature of reality, lies at the base of both medieval and modern scientific thought. Both held that there is a reason and meaning to be divined in the ceaseless workings of nature that has the proper place and end for all things. Both trusted in the harmony which characterized the ultimate natures of things and excluded mere arbitrariness. But there is a difference in their views on how the nature of things was to be discovered. While medieval thought trusted reason and metaphysical speculation, the new sciences insisted on an active interest in the simple occurrences of life *for their own sake* and put their trust in direct observation and inspection of stubborn fact.

In a way, the scientific revolution was an anti-intellectualist movement through and through, seeking to free itself from medieval intellectual presuppositions and conceptual categories as well as its rigid intellectualism. The scientific upheaval from Copernicus onwards, resulted in the dislodging of notions that were deeply entrenched in the medieval worldview. It was Isaac Newton (1642–1727), however, who brought to fulfillment the alliance of general principle and stubborn fact. Newton's monumental discoveries were themselves the product of the confluence of genius that had been building up prior to his time. The cumulative process from Copernicus to Newton unified in a set of mathematical laws all previous efforts with respect to the mathematical determination of motion. Galileo was concerned with terrestrial motion; Kepler, with the lawlike patterns evident in celestial motion. In Newton both interests found unification. Laws covered both heavenly and terrestrial spheres.[50] By the turn of the 18th century, Newton's scientific work had subsumed and solidified Copernican astronomy and had unified the terrestrial and celestial mechanics deriving directly from Galileo and Kepler.

In this way the mechanistic imagery was gradually brought to life in the consciousness of modern individuals. It was an image in which the very laws of nature are determined by some kind of mechanistic structure. For instance, the laws that govern the movement of bodies, it was learned, applied to all objects from the smallest particle in the laboratory to the farthest planet. The harmonious order of Greek and medieval thought had been gradually replaced by a harmonious structure of forces and masses, an intricate machine obeying immutable laws, with every detail precisely predictable. This image of the machine led, for instance, to Laplace's notion of determinism, which was an extrapolation from Newton's mechanics. Laplace argued that if a being knew at one instant the positions and motions of every particle in the universe, he would have at his disposal all the information necessary to compute the entire past and future history of the universe.[51]

The impact of such mechanistic view is demonstrated by the fact that it has paved the way for a completely new approach to the analysis of the physical world. This mechanistic view of the world comes to the fore right into the 20th century. Up until the late 19th to the early part of the last century, the deepest core of reality was viewed as strictly machinelike. So pervasive was this paradigm that it spread into other sciences and into almost all fields of human endeavor and has held sway over the minds of modern thinkers.[52] There are at least three characteristics of atomistic mechanism which immediately stand out.[53] First, the world is reduced, as far as possible, to a set of basic elements, or physical particulars. Second, these physical particulars are external to each other not only in terms of being separate in space and time but also because the fundamental nature of each is independent of the other. These particulars are not related to each other, as parts of an organism relate to other parts. Instead, they are like components of a machine whose forms are determined externally by the machine's structure. Thirdly, interaction between the elements happens mechanically. They relate to each other only through forces of interaction that do not affect their inner natures.

It is this particular view upholding the fragmentary nature of basic particulars and the externality of their relations that Whitehead says underlies the whole philosophy of nature during the modern period. This is the fallacy of simple location. And to say that a basic particular, e.g., a bit of matter, has simple location "means that, in expressing its spatio-temporal relations, it is adequate to state that it is where it is, in a definite region of space, and throughout a definite finite duration of time, apart from any essential reference to the relations of that bit of matter to other regions of space and other durations of time."[54] This presupposition of individual independence, Whitehead holds, is the very foundation upon which is built much of modern metaphysical speculation.[55] Without it, the entire modern scientific worldview would crumble for it would be incapable of expression.

Developments in physics and psychology, and the erosion of the Newtonian worldview

The critique of simple location which found its most lucid expression in Whitehead represents a kind of culmination to a much bigger movement and transformation of thought that began taking shape during the last century. Milič Čapek in his book *The Philosophical Impact of Contemporary Physics* discusses the significant shifts that took place in the physical sciences and the effects of the "contemporary storm in physics" on philosophical ideas concerning the world.[56] Our analysis and further clarification of the ideas contained in Hartshorne's own exposition of the parallel developments in physics and psychology draw from Čapek's conclusions in this work. At the very outset, however, we must point out that our adoption of Čapek's ideas does not preclude our keeping a critical eye on the limitations of philosophical discussion with regard to alleged implications of developments in physical science or, even in this regard, psychology.[57]

Since the last century at least, convergences in terms of views of reality were gradually becoming noticeable—although in a piecemeal fashion—in the physical sciences as well as psychology. Movement away from the mechanistic model happened more slowly in the biological sciences. However, as Joseph Needham points out, this was not on account of a satisfaction on the biologist's part with the "seventeenth century statistical picture of the fortuitous concourse of particles, each with a momentary defined position in space."[58] But there was yet no alternative scheme by the help of which the biologist could proceed with the causal analysis of biological phenomena. The mechanistic conception of the universe was being subjected to intensifying critique almost simultaneously, especially within the two widely divergent fields of physics and psychology. Eventually, such criticism led to the breakdown of the very cosmology that had supported both these fields. The account of this breakdown spans an entire century. Ideas were slowly accumulating into a body of thought that would be found inconsistent with the dominant Newtonian ideas which were themselves the shapers of prevailing modes of expression.

The highlighting of the *contrast* between the most general ideas which respectively underpin the atomistic cosmology and the newly-emerging non-corpuscular paradigm is of paramount importance, for it points to the ferment of ideas that had taken hold. Whitehead's critique of simple location arose out of such ferment. His criticism gave a coherent and systematic articulation to what could have otherwise been no more than an intuitive insight which may have found expression, but in a piecemeal and fragmentary manner.

The Newtonian insight in physics, which worked very well for several centuries was slowly being shown to lead to unclear results when it extended to the domain of the very big and the very small. In order to account for these spheres of reality, new insights were gradually being formed, which would in the 20th century propose a radically different picture of the world from that of 17th-century mechanics, although the latter, of course, remained valid within a limited region.[59] In psychology, for example, the theory of the *Gestalt* was a result of a reaction against the atomistic view of psychological processes. Its main slogan, "The whole is more than the sum of its parts," was chiefly directed against the explanation of perceptual experience in terms of a "bricks and mortar" account of the combination of simple sensations.[60] Granted that like all revolutionary theories it exaggerated the difference between its peculiar doctrines and traditional notions, nevertheless it makes a contribution in terms of an increased emphasis on theories concerning the properties of total fields of activity contrasted with the properties of isolated units. This becomes even more true as one takes into account the fact that its entry into the arena of thought roughly coincides with Whitehead's critique as well as the monumental developments in physics during our century.

The dominance of mechanistic corpuscularianism among the natural sciences since the 16th century was far reaching. Up until the early part of the last century, it remained the well-established, if not unquestioned, view of reality. The three earlier characterizations mentioned above rightly belonged to the atomism of the scientific revolution of the 17th century. Throughout the course of the centuries that followed, the idea underwent further sophistication and complexification. The characteristics that we shall now be considering are thus characteristics of the later kind of atomism. Čapek outlines five major characteristics of the mechanical scheme.[61] First, matter is regarded as discontinuous. It is made of absolutely rigid and compact units that move about in space in accordance with the laws of mechanics. Second, the qualitative differences that are observed in nature are only apparent and are simply the result of differences in configuration or motion of the basic units. Third, qualitative changes are also only apparent. They are simply the surface effects of the displacement of the elementary units and their aggregates. Fourth, direct impact among the basic particulars is the sole explanation of whatever interaction exists among them. Fifth, qualitative variety and transformation do not belong to the nature of things. Rather, they are merely psychic additions that are cloaked upon the basic corpuscles by the perceiving human mind. Simple location is the thread that runs through all five propositions. And since it was basically the same fallacy which had colored the development of both physics (from the 17th to the late 19th century) and psychology (during most of the 19th century), it does not come as a surprise that the critical reaction against this fallacy in both the areas has some analogous features.[62] Čapek captures the significance of the almost simultaneous developments in physics and psychology by asking the question: "Was it really a sheer coincidence? Or was it rather a symptom that the human mind began to become increasingly sensitive to certain inadequacies of traditional modes of thought?"[63]

Hartshorne himself discusses these convergences and their implications for philosophic thought in "The Parallel Development of Method in Physics and Psychology."[64] In this article, Hartshorne discusses similarities in certain shifts that were then taking place in these two disciplines. The underlying argument is the existence of a clear commonality between the two in terms of the gradual movement away from an atomistic paradigm. Among the most dramatic developments during the 19th century were certain newly emerging theoretical programmes which had as an imaginative background, the idea that physical forces are but manifestations of a fundamental conserved force. There was a clear movement away from the simple and rigid corpuscularianism of early centuries toward a more relational outlook which bore a clear commitment to the unity of all natural powers.[65] In some respects, these newly emerging theories found particularly consistent expression in German *Naturphilosophie* and other related idealist schemes. This school of thought held an organismic and dynamical cosmology, which was associated with German Romanticism and found expression most especially in the writings of F.W.J. Schelling (1775–1854). The classical atomistic view regarded force as the external relation that is held between these atomic entities. By contrast, *Naturphilosophie* made force—as a natural power—the essential reality and matter its phenomenal manifestation. Those who supported the old corpuscularianism held the vacuumlike character of space, while adherents of *Naturphilosophie* regarded it as a plenum of force. Within such matrix an entity that had simple location could possess only geometrical significance; it was merely a center of a distribution of force.[66]

The work of individuals like Michael Faraday (1791–1867), who, in studying energy and its conservation, adopted definitions of force which went against the grain of the prevailing mechanistic corpuscularianism, represents a watershed in the march toward what was becoming a gradual increase in sensitivity to certain inadequacies of the classical atomistic theory. Faraday's most important contribution to physics is the notion of lines of force, which represents the beginning of the development of the field theory. Up until his time, the generally accepted approach to electrodynamics was the description of forces in terms of mathematically direct actions at a distance.[67] It must be noted, however, that Faraday was not trained in the mathematics necessary for this tradition in physics. In fact, coming from a rather hard-up family background, he had no formal schooling beyond the elementary level. And it was while working as an apprentice in a bookbinding shop that he first became interested in chemistry and electricity. This interest led him to attend the lectures given by Humphry Davy, the leading British chemist at the time. Faraday eventually became Davy's laboratory assistant at the Royal Institution in London. His lack of mathematical techniques may have been, to a certain extent, behind the fact that he never attempted to measure exact conversion equivalents. He insisted on utilizing relative mechanical measures; his notion of force, which, being nonmechanical, was not subject to quantification. His use of a geometric-intuitive representation however, should not obscure the clear quantitative nature to his researches.[68]

Faraday noted the artificiality of the usual distinction that is made between solid material particles and the forces that supposedly flow from these particles. Matter, he argued, is known through its dynamic manifestation, further pointing out that the two properties of matter, viz., gravitational and electromagnetic action, pervade the whole space. The atom, he argued, is a point center of force. This notion was already suggested in the 18th century by Ruggiero Boscovich (1711–87). In his work *Theoria Philosophiae Naturalis,* Boscovich (who while holding the Leibnizian principle of continuity disagreed with Leibniz's insistence that the principle excludes the possibility of space void of mechanical matter) made use of the principle in creating a theory of continuous force functions. He also rejected the entire notion of the discreteness and extension of matter. The individuality of these pure centers of force is constituted by the point at which the indefinite lines of force cross, thereby radiating throughout space. The extension of the atom, therefore, may be identified with the extent of these lines so that all atoms would be mutually penetrable and each would occupy all space. Hartshorne himself alludes to this notion of the universality of continuity when he says that "all matter is one and in a sense continuous throughout space, and an individual thing is merely a knot of intersecting spatio-temporal world lines, merely the one world-process drawn to a particular focus."[69]

Faraday saw something which many of his colleagues at the time failed to see clearly. The difference between the two perspectives and the subsequent shift away from the corpuscular model is already intimated in this paragraph from a work by James Clerk Maxwell:

> We are accustomed to consider the universe as made up of parts, and mathematicians usually begin by considering a single particle, and conceiving its relation to another particle, and so on. This has generally been supposed the most natural method. To conceive a particle, requires a process of abstraction, since all our perceptions are related to extended bodies, so that the idea of all that is present in our consciousness is perhaps as primitive an idea as that of any individual thing. Hence there may be a mathematical method in which we proceed from the whole to the parts instead of from the parts to the whole.[70]

There did seem, at least for a time, to be a possibility of saving the principle of simply located particles of matter. For even if the inseparability of particle from electric field was admitted, certain quarters held that the field remained granular in structure. Faraday's conclusions concerning physical field theory were themselves met with opposition from scientists doing work on electrodynamics on the continent. Wilhelm Weber, for instance, in 1846 rejected Faraday's lines of force concept and in its stead developed a theory of the action of forces at a distance, between charges which included electromagnetic induction. Faraday's notion of such lines, however, found eventual vindication in the works of William Thomson and Clerk Maxwell who put Faraday's ideas into mathematical notation. Clerk Maxwell points to this more specific contrast between Faraday's method and those which prevailed during his time: "Faraday, in his mind's eye, saw lines of force traversing all space where the mathematicians saw centres of force attracting at a distance. Faraday saw a medium where they say nothing but distance. Faraday sought the seat of the phenomena in real actions going on in the medium, they were satisfied that they had found it in a power of action at a distance impressed on the electric fluids."[71]

Of course, Maxwell himself did try on several occasions to provide a model which would show that the energetic field was itself made of ultimate minute particles. This would have preserved the basic atomistic idea. The failures of such and similar attempts to arrive at a mechanical explanation of the field are sufficiently known. However, we must refer to the most significant transformations to which the classical concept of the simply located corpuscle was subjected. The significance of these changes, which were brought about to a great extent by Faraday's discoveries, is made even more evident by the fact that Whitehead specifically points to it in *The Concept of Nature*, in a way that anticipates what was to be his future criticism of simple location.[72] These transformations fall roughly under two headings; namely, the untenability of the notion of solidity simply understood and the impossibility of precise spatiotemporal localization due to the ambiguity inherent in boundary definitions.[73]

The classical atomistic theory which held sway from Democritus to Lorentz characterized the ultimate *descripta* of reality as solid, impenetrable, constant, indestructible, and uncreatable particles that moved about in homogeneous Euclidean space. These characterizations no longer hold when it is the particles of contemporary microphysics that we are dealing with. As Čapek points out:

> We know today that mass is not constant, but a function of its velocity; we know that even the nuclei, in which practically all mass of the atom is concentrated, are under certain conditions lacking impenetrability, being "transparent" to the slowly moving electrons (Ramsauer's effect); we know since Anderson's discovery of positive electrons in 1932 that the microphysical particles are not permanent as they can be either created or annihilated. Even if it is true that the corresponding "creation" is not "creatio ex nihilo" as a particle in question is a result of "materialization" of electromagnetic radiation into which it may be reconverted in the converse process of "dematerialization."[74]

Being no longer possessed of the eternal solidity that characterized the classical Lucretian atom, the so-called particle of contemporary microphysics no longer lends itself to precise localization in a defined spatiotemporal matrix. Its boundaries are no longer as definite as that of a particle of classical physics. Newton defined inertial mass in terms of a force that resides within the definite location occupied by a particle. Such localization of force *here* and *now*, constituted the entity's substantial nucleus, which was externally related to all other particles. In this scheme, resistance to external influence coming from other well-defined localizations of force constituted the essence of a specific particle.

However, as Čapek notes, the situation changes when the whole scheme is considered vis-à-vis Newton's third law, which deals with the complementary nature of action and reaction. Every force, according to this law, is met by an opposite force of the same magnitude, which shows that both forces are merely two partial aspects of one and the same dynamic phenomenon.[75] The idea of a particle isolated from this whole dynamic context is thus an artificial construct. Considered from this perspective, even the Newtonian idea of residing force is shown to be an abstraction from the dynamic matrix to which the individual particle is related and to be a result of our substantializing habits of thought.[76] The idea of a particular, understood as an isolated bit of material which is simply located in a fixed spatiotemporal region, is an abstraction. A concrete particular is in fact produced by the entire universe to which it belongs and it pervades this whole cosmic context as well. A simply located particular is the creation of an artificial process of abstraction. It is just not possible—if one does not intend an impoverished treatment of a particular—to localize an entity within the bounds of a well-defined, fixed, and unchanging coordinate system.

Associationism

The monumental changes in physics are paralleled by the equally significant shifts that took place in psychology, particularly with regard to the status of the old notion of associationism which, as Hartshorne points out, was a "quasi-mechanical affair," in which "ideas cohered to one another like Newtonian bodies in space."[77] Under the influence of atomistic mechanism psychological processes themselves were regarded as atomistic in structure. Intimations of the modern theory of association are already found among the ancient Greek thinkers. In Plato's *Phaedo*, we find him pointing to the association that a lover, for instance, makes between the object of his affection and the things that are connected, i.e., *associated* with his beloved. In particular, he cites the mere sight of a lover's lyre or gown, which Plato says brings thoughts and feelings similar to those that are caused by the lover herself.[78] Aristotle in his work, *On Memory and Reminiscence*, argues that the recollection of a particular object can be seen as due to the fact that it is either similar or dissimilar to the object of one's present thought or because he originally perceived the two objects as being close in space and time. He likewise held that repetition, emotion, attention, and certain forms and shapes of objects influence the formation of the associations we make between things. In its modern garb, however, the idea of association was given a far more sophisticated and complex expression. For in this era, theories concerning the nature and origin of knowledge, thoughts, images and ideas were confronted and in many ways affected by the atomism that had been revived by Newtonian physics. Descartes could very well be designated as the thinker mainly responsible for the introduction of the idea of simple location in psychology. His notion of the *substantia cogitans* as an entity which had no need of anything other than its own existence (*res quae ita existit, ut nulla alia re indigeat ad existendum*), was at the origin (or the inspiration) of the later Humean characterization of the independence of impressions from any relational matrix. Thus, the Cartesian substantial soul, which Hume attacked vigorously,[79] was merely cut into smaller fragments which remained nonetheless as substantial as the Cartesian *substantia*. In its contemporary form, however, the doctrine of associationism can be traced not only to Hume but also to Hobbes, Locke, Hartley, Wundt, Taine, Mills, and Bain, among many others.[80]

Consciousness as understood by associationism has *sensations* as its most fundamental elements. The richness of psychological life was reduced to a mere product of the various forms in which sensations are associated, and thought itself was regarded as simply a more complex collection of less vivid sensations. It is true that there were different terms employed in the specification of the various elements: *sensations, impressions, mental states, elements, etc.* However, this variety notwithstanding, all the elements retained as a commonality a quasi-atomistic character. As they were elements that were psychological in nature, they were not regarded as existing in space—something which should have very well been the case given that they resembled physical atoms in so many ways. For instance, like physical atoms they were well-defined entities, mutually external and permanent in time. Granted that the resemblance of these "atomic" ideas to Newtonian particulars in space is merely metaphorical, it remains the case that the simply located particulars of classical physics served as the imaginative background out of which the spatial metaphors were derived.

Reaction to associationism came in the form of an anti-atomistic trend in psychology. There were several significant moments in the critique that was then developing. As early as 1874, Franz Brentano was rejecting the notion of the mind as essentially a machine that automatically elaborated material that was provided. He insisted that judgment is a primary indivisible act irreducible to a simple aggregation of ideas.[81] Experience, according to him, does not disclose an inert content of sensations and their combinations but mental acts. While the existence of sensations is not denied, he nevertheless did not regard them as mental. What is mental is instead the very activity that occurs when an individual sees a color, hears a sound, or smells an odor.[82] In 1884, James Ward in his article "On Some Omissions of Introspective Psychology," published in the British journal *Mind*, argued that what is usually called "complexity of mind" stems from a gradual differentiation of a primary unity rather than a simple conglomeration of various elementary units akin to the Humean "atomic" impressions.

In 1886, the publication of Ward's article, "Psychology," in the ninth edition of *Encyclopedia Britannica* created a considerable amount of sensation. It represented, first of all, the first time that psychology was treated by the Encyclopedia as a science recognized for its importance in its own right. Prior to this, it was treated under the heading of "Metaphysics." Furthermore, Ward's article put associationism in its place by pointing to both its importance as well as its limitations. It was, according to Ward, important as a "mechanism," a *method* of investigation, but was far from adequate when dealing with questions on the unity and creativeness of the mind. In dealing with these two, the undivided subject was an indispensable element. The complexity of mind, he argued, was the result of a gradual differentiation of a primary unity and not of the simple combining or re-combining of diverse primary elements.[83]

Henri Bergson, in his *Essai sur les données immédiates de la conscience*, published in 1889, emphasized the successive continuity of consciousness and rejected the idea of arithmetical multiplicity as wholly inadequate for psychology. He argued that plurality of mental states does not correspond to the type of plurality that holds with physical bodies. The former do not have fixed boundaries separating them from each other in the way that the latter are separated. Mental states, he argued, pervade each other. William James' *Principles of Psychology* came out in 1890. In it he laid stress on the continuity of the "stream of consciousness" and criticized psychological atomism under the name "mind-stuff theory."[84]

Gestalt theory

Also in 1890 Christian von Ehrenfels published the article "Über Gestaltqualitäten," in which the term "Gestalt" makes its first appearance.[85] Von Ehrenfels observed that to appreciate a melody, we need to be aware not of a single tone in isolation but of a succession of tones which combine in a particular way. If notes of the same pitch as those of the original melody are presented in a different temporal order, there will be a completely different effect, whereas the same melody played in a different key is immediately recognizable, even though the notes are different in pitch from the original ones. The melody as a whole, according to von Ehrenfels, had a *Gestaltqualität* which was independent of the qualities of the separate notes. Three years after the publication of von Ehrenfels' work, Wilhelm Dilthey, in *Ideen über eine beschreibende und zergliedernde Psychologie*, criticized the atomistic and fragmentary approach of associationism and contrasted this with what he regarded as the necessary comprehensive approach to psychology.[86] It was out of such ferment of ideas that Gestalt-Psychology arose. Its founders, the German psychologists Max Wertheimer,[87] Wolfgang Köhler,[88] and Kurt Koffka,[89] were concerned to apply the concept of Gestalt over a wide area and thus give a new direction to psychological research.

There are two characteristics of the anti-atomistic character of Gestalt Psychology that are significant for our discussion. Here, we once again adopt Čapek's analysis.[90] The first is its radically empirical character. The theory of associationism claimed to be more empirical than Descartes' notion of the *substantia cogitans*. Hume, for instance, argued that no such entity as a substantial soul is ever an object of our introspective experience. Instead, it is a particular impression, feeling, or idea that is revealed in introspection. The Gestaltists on the other hand, insisted that these so-called "impressions," "feelings," "mental states," etc.—the psychological atoms of associationism— are no more than methodological fictions, carved out of the continuity of the "stream of consciousness." Through the manipulation of these psychological entities, we obtain merely an inadequate and clumsy imitation of concrete reality. We see thus that although Humean associationism is really more empirical than the rationalistic psychology of Descartes, Gestalt theory shows an even more radical attentiveness to experience, in particular, to the more elusive and non-sensory aspects.

Gestalt theory in its application to time also poses a serious challenge to the idea of simple location. Applied to temporality, simple location holds that a particular event is where it is, in one particular moment, and nowhere else. Its presence is hence confined to that narrow moment which, when gone, causes the particular event to be irrevocably lost. Moreover, the application of the fallacy to time requires that a past event be past; that is to say, whatever relation it may have to a present or future event is totally external. Just as action at a distance is impossible in space, application of the same principle makes it likewise impossible in terms of time. However, as those who criticize psychological atomism have argued, this is not what is disclosed by our experiences. Going back to Von Ehrenfels' ideas concerning melody, we can say that superficially considered our awareness of melody appears as a mere aggregate of successive individual tones. In this sense, our awareness of melody would be constituted by the gradual addition of successive auditory sensations, each of which would be temporally external to each other. But this would effectively prevent any awareness of melody from ever arising since nothing would in fact be present to consciousness, save a single tone perduring for one single moment.

In reality though, it is not only a preceding moment but also the entire antecedent musical phrase which, in spite of its pastness, is undefinably manifest in the present tone. This tone acquires a peculiar coloration within its antecedent musical *context*, without having to lose its musical individuality. Apart from this *context*, our very consciousness of melody would disappear. Or it would be replaced by the sensation of the individual, within the context of the antecedent silence, which is yet another temporal Gestalt. This *context* can be likened to a matrix, whose contents interpenetrate. This interpenetration in turn constitutes the very basis of their relationships. These contents are not sharply separated from each other, and the degree of their relative distinctness is quite unstable.[91] Deceived by language and simple location unconsciously applied, however, we speak of one and the same tone no matter if it were embedded in a melody or preceded by a silence. It is not, however, one and the same tone although it is a similar one. The differentiating features introduced by different temporal contexts are very elusive, so elusive that it was possible to ignore them for such a long time. (This in fact accounts for the very plausibility of associationistic psychology.) However, by claiming a complete self-identity and self-sufficiency of the individual sensations, the continuity of our experiences as well as our experience of immediate memory and the reality of temporal Gestalten can never be adequately explained.

Whitehead's critique

In view of these widespread developments, we can see how it became possible for Whitehead to insist that the concept of the basic particulars as simply located material particles is mired in inconsistency. For, the very ideas of motion, velocity, and momentum—which simply located entities are supposed to be able to explain—are themselves rendered problematic. As such, he holds that there is a fatal contradiction inherent in the corpuscular view of reality.[92] For even from the perspective of classical physics itself, the assumption of self-identical material particles in motion, changing their spatial relations at successive times, involves serious difficulties. The ultimate concern of Newtonian physics is not a material particle in motion or the plethora of physical particulars that make up the world as in motion. Instead its real concern is with the precise mathematical expression of the *transitions* of a particle or of their configurations. But in order for this to happen, Newtonian physics has to take the relative spatial positions of the particles at one durationless instant of time, and then at a later instant. In such a scheme, the ultimate fact is none other than the configuration of material particles at a durationless instant of time. And while there may be a succession of such facts, each at a durationless instant, there is nevertheless no real particle in a state of change as an ultimate fact.[93] A state of change at a durationless instant of time is self-contradictory since the notions of motion, velocity, momentum, etc., are themselves impossible to define apart from a past or future reference.[94] The repudiation of simple location becomes even more acute when we consider that contemporary physics has, for all intents and purposes and despite the continued employment of scientists of the older terminology, moved to a new mode of conceptualization. Whitehead refers to this shift in *Adventures of Ideas*:

> Modern physics has abandoned the doctrine of Simple Location: the physical things which we term stars, planets, lumps of matter, molecules, electrons, protons, quanta of energy, are each to be conceived as

modifications of conditions within space-time, extending throughout its whole range. There is a focal region, which in common speech is where the thing is. But its influence streams away from it with finite velocity throughout the utmost recesses of space and time. Of course, it is natural, and for certain purposes entirely proper, to speak of the focal region, thus modified, as the thing itself situated there. But difficulties arise if we press this way of thought too far.[95]

Simple location, Whitehead says, is itself a corollary of a more insidious fallacy, the roots of which have already been intimated in the earlier treatment of mathematics. This is the fallacy of "Misplaced Concreteness," which is, "the accidental error of mistaking the abstract for the concrete."[96] Simple location—as an expression of the attempt to directly locate particulars within a defined matrix—is, according to Whitehead, to be found in no element of nature whatsoever apprehended in immediate experience.[97] To insist on this, however, is not to assert that the science of the 17th century, for instance, was wrong. Similarly, to argue that a metaphysical theory such as Strawson's attempts to locate physical particulars within fixed spatiotemporal loci is not to say that it is wrong. For by means of a process of progressive abstraction, it is indeed possible to arrive at abstractions that are simply located. And there are genuine advantages to the confinement of attention to a definite group of abstractions.[98] Thought, first of all, is confined to clear-cut things that are constituted by clear-cut relations. Such definiteness can facilitate deduction of a host of conclusions about the relations that are obtained between these abstract entities.

This advantage, however, is in the long run far outweighed by the disadvantages. To focus one's attention solely on a cluster of abstractions—however well founded they may be—means that one has, for all intents and purposes, abstracted from the remainder of things. Moreover, insofar as concrete particulars have already been excluded, one's mode of thinking is no longer suited to deal with the richness and density that characterizes them. The murkiness of thought immersed in concrete particularity is cleansed with the antiseptic of abstract generality. The resulting inability to think without abstractions creates a view of reality deficient in its vision of depth. The loss of richness in our encounter with reality is the price we pay for the power of control we obtain through sanitized thought. Abstract thought eventually finds itself too narrow for the analysis of concrete fact.

In this regard, simple location cannot be an intrinsic feature of reality but an offshoot of distorting abstraction and conceptualization. No element of nature possesses this characteristic. And hence, attempts to construct a paradigm which represents nature as an arithmetical sum of discontinuous and mutually external entities are a result of an artificial procedure which dissects the inherent continuity of reality into discrete, self-identical units and overlooks the dynamic interwovenness of these entities. This is not to deny discrete particularity. What is denied, however, is the attempt to make a dogma of such discreteness. It is but one aspect of nature. The dynamic relatedness of each concrete particular with the rest of the universe is just as essential an aspect of a description of reality. As such, it can be ignored only at the expense of an adequate description of the same reality. To simply neglect this fact because of an erroneous application of simple location leads to the error of misplaced concreteness, the reification of an abstraction. For no matter how valid and justified an abstraction may be, it remains an abstraction which ought not to be confused with the fullness and fecundity of concrete fact.

Substances versus events

The main difficulty with ontologies of substance is that, being founded on the fallacy of simple location and misplaced concreteness, what they offer is more of an impoverished view of reality than a way of ensuring the inter-subjective agreement in the identification of particulars which they are supposedly aiming for. The notion of physical particulars identifiable in a definite portion of space and time is a convenient approximation of the concrete totality of a particular. As such, in regard to the aim of eliminating speaker-dependent accounts of a particular, the simple location of an entity does appear to open the way for intersubjective agreement. After all, objective particulars (units that are directly locatable, entities that can be pointed to, which have mass, size, shape, and hardness), it seems, cannot be trifled with. They are *what* they are, *where* they are, and *when* they occur: individuals enduring in a self-identity untouched by the temporal flux and whatever change of description they are subjected to by those who regard them.

But the existence of such a sovereign isolated particle, as Whitehead says, is a myth[99]—one, however, that lies at the foundation and provides coherence to the structure of substantialistic ontologies. It is therefore this myth that required exploding, in order for us to comprehend Hartshorne's rejection of the idea of substance and his insistence that event is in fact, the more fundamental and concrete reality and the real key to understanding our experience of identity. As we have seen, the three major points of theses such as Strawson's, namely, (i) the notion of metaphysics as merely descriptive, (ii) a fixed theoretical framework and objective particulars, and (iii) the rejection of events in favor of bodies, are founded on the idea of a simply located entity. The presupposition that such an entity can be found—and is in fact found—is what creates the possibility of a merely descriptive metaphysics. On account of the fact that the basic units of such scheme are simply located, the scheme itself can be understood as a complete and well-defined grid of fixed spatiotemporal relations. Any change which might take place within this grid will be finally constituted by the changes in position of the basic elements that occur within its confines. Aggregation is then transformed into the ultimate category of explanation in such an ontology, and change and becoming are rendered superficial.

This is the bottom-line argument of Hartshorne against substance ontologies, viz., that a self-identical substance enduring through space and time cannot give a sufficient explanation of the nature and continued existence of an entity (which is precisely what substance metaphysics seeks to uphold in the first place). The continuity of an entity does not consist in the mere endurance of a selfsame unit through a definite spatiotemporal slice. Furthermore, the real continuity in an entity's existence presupposes a non-symmetrical interpenetration of its past, present, and future—spheres of its existence that are related to each other both internally and externally. It is only in this way that the reality of determinacy and freedom, as well as endurance and novelty, can be reconciled in an adequate and non-contradictory manner. For an individual is, in a very real and intimate way, dependent upon—except for a final and very small degree of self-determination—the past which it's present inherits. The individual, Hartshorne points out, is a creation, the concrete making of which is not *by* the "individual" itself but by the other "individuals" that it had been, up to its present moment. Hence, the notion of individual, as a completed and static entity, cannot be the final term of analysis, for "the individual who now acts creatively is not simply I, or you, but I now, or you now. I yesterday, you yesterday, did not enact and can never enact our today's actions; only today's selves can do that. ... At any given moment, we are *almost* entirely a product, not a producer. And what productive power we have would be totally vacuous without inheritance from past actions, our own and those of countless others."[100]

Moreover, the putting forward of "body" as a primitive notion reinforces the primacy of the category of sameness. Physical particulars are indeed eminently identifiable as being the same. And indeed in the most readily recognizable but superficial manner by which we understand identity, sameness would be the first thing to come to mind. The equation of identity with sameness, however, represents but one aspect of the global reality of self-identity for "the self as numerically the same is an abstraction."[101] And it is precisely the identity of a self, not self-identity *simply*, that is the more primordial notion with which we are concerned. The question is thus not so much "What makes one the same entity, or the same self?" but "What makes one a 'self' which is not only the unity of its past, present, and future, components gathered in one enduring totality, but also a 'self,' capable of recognizing itself as 'composed' and at the same time realizing itself as the unity of these components."

5

Methodological Considerations in Hartshorne's Event Ontology

Hartshorne's methodology

Hartshorne holds that the overcoming of the inconsistencies and contradictions that arise out of a metaphysics of substance can only be achieved by means of a shift from the concept of substance as the basic unit of reality to the notion of event. Event as the basic descriptum, in his view, opens the way for an adequate understanding of the nature of an entity in terms of both its aspects of continuity and change, individuality and relatedness. It is dipolar; that is to say, it incorporates both domains of stability and flux, uniqueness and sociality. Event ontology accomplishes this by recognizing the reality of both spheres while at the same time asserting the primacy of our experience of becoming and relationality.

In contrast, the kind of continuity that a metaphysics of substance offers is not only one-sided but is also guilty of the fallacy of misplaced concreteness. It is one-sided because it either dismisses the aspect of change or waters it down by holding stability to be more real. In either case, the more concrete experience of change is eclipsed by the quest for stability. It is guilty of the fallacy of misplaced concreteness because it brings in a third element, which is supposed to unite stability and change in a simple conjunction—an "and"—while in reality it locates the real in an abstraction. This abstraction is a substance which may be undergoing accidental changes but is nonetheless possessed of an unchanging core, a singular that is in itself. Hartshorne holds that this idea is meaningless and is the real error at the bottom of dualism.[1]

The concrete and the abstract, as basic or a priori concepts that express dualities, "need not be a third entity, but may be the concrete as containing the abstract."[2] Hartshorne calls the idea that the real must be found within the totality of the changing-unchanging pair itself, the principle of inclusive contrast. It is the comprehension of both terms in an inclusive form of reality—neither in one taken simply, nor in a third concept that supposedly unites both. He explains the principle by first stating that all ideas, even the most general ones such as "reality," express contrasts, i.e., "nonreality."[3] Secondly, he holds that all such dyadic relations that make up ultimate contraries can be characterized in two ways: as *pure abstractions* (their relation is that of mutual implication; each is internal to the other's definition) and as *exemplified*, the relation that obtains is both internal and external, i.e., asymmetrically internal to the constitution of one pole and external to the other.

Hartshorne is able to make such characterization because his rejection of Bradley's insistence on the internality of all relations does not lead him to accept the Humean blanket characterization of relations as simply external conjunctions.[4] He believes that there must be both internal and external relations.[5] An external relation is only nominally a relation of the term to which it is external. This is because external relations are subject to two conditions; namely, that "every relation is internal to *something*, either to one at least of its terms or to some entity additional to these," and that "the entity to which the relation is internal is a *concrete* whole of which the externally related entities are *abstract* aspects."[6] Hence, certain relations have terms in such a way that some of them do not really have the relations.[7] Not every term is therefore constituted by the relations which it is in; only the term to which the relation is internal possesses the other term as a constituent.[8] Hartshorne recalls Bradley's argument against external relations saying, "if *A* is not, in its very being or identity, related to *B*, then we must relate *A* to the relation to *B* to get *A* really related. And this leads to a series of relations to relations to relations … a series which is vicious not only because it is infinite but because it can never arrive at a relation to *B* which is really *A*'s."[9] He does not accept Bradley's insistence that this argument must lead to the rejection of any relation external to any of the terms. He holds that it proves that relations cannot simply be external to all their terms. If the relation constituted no term, then the relatedness that does exist is an additional element to all the terms which must hence be related to them by a further term *ad infinitum*.[10]

External and internal relations, like any other pair of metaphysical contraries must therefore be held together by an inclusive reality of which the terms are aspects or dimensions which cannot be taken in simple isolation from each other or simply made to coincide.[11] Although dualism distinguishes categorially or a priori into certain ultimate dualities, such as concrete-abstract, relative-absolute, dependent-independent, subject-object, it errs in taking the relation between them as a mere conjunction, forgetting that one contrast could very well be the inclusive term.[12] This unity is an all-inclusive form of reality within which every contrast falls. As such, neither of the two poles, he contends, is simply to be denied or explained away, or called "unreal." If either pole is real the contrast itself, including both poles, is so.[13] To explain this assertion, Hartshorne adopts Morris Cohen's Principle of Polarity.[14] These ultimate contraries are correlatives, mutually interdependent such that "nothing can be described by the wholly one-sided assertion of ultimate categories such as simplicity, being, actuality and the like, each in a "pure" form, devoid and independent of complexity, becoming, potentiality and related categories."[15] However, in spite of the ultimate character of such metaphysical contraries, Hartshorne likewise holds that there is no strict equality of status between the poles. As correlatives, each requires the other in order to have meaning. But as applied to reality itself, one pole includes its contrary within its scope.[16] A basic asymmetry is therefore involved. The whole reality is expressed by the entire truth, not simply by one or the other of the two contraries. Further, this truth is not arrived at by means of a simple denial or negation of one of the two contraries but by seeing that the referents of one can be found in the referents of the other. For instance, while there is no such thing as a purely concrete or purely abstract entity, that which is concrete is inclusive of that which is abstract. The converse inclusion does not obtain. Hartshorne calls this a two-way, yet asymmetrical, necessity.

There exists a mutual dependency of sense in the contrast of these terms taken as abstract concepts. Each pole taken simply, i.e., apart from its contrary, is devoid of content, empty of ostensive reference.[17] Hence, even the term "particular" can be taken to mean any particular whatsoever, including each particular instantiation of a universal; and "concreteness" itself is an extreme abstraction, denoting everything and nothing. Considered abstractly therefore, the terms are dialectically symmetrical and independent. By laying the contraries out in this way, Hartshorne calls attention to the necessary place of symmetric conceptions of relations. For considered in their exemplifications, what is disclosed is something far less symmetrical. It is this manner of consideration that will comprise his reorientation of the symmetrical concept through the doctrine of metaphysical asymmetry.[18]

Asymmetrical relations

What we are seeing here is the gradual unfolding of Hartshorne's theory of relations. As already noted, taken simply by themselves, metaphysical contraries are symmetrically related. However, this binary relation is itself contained in a triad, namely, the relation between the two terms and the proposition produced by their combination. To understand what Hartshorne means, one has to consider not only relations of comparison such as equality, likeness, and difference but also relations of existential connectedness such as effect and cause, experience and object experienced, succeeding events and their predecessors. Relations of comparison are directionless and hence symmetrical. With regard to relations of existential and dynamic connectedness, however, the basic idea is directional. The mere juxtaposition of contrary concepts, i.e., their simple comprehension in terms of equality, puts them in no ordered relation to each other. This renders their defining power negligible since a relation which expresses mere equivalence yields no more than an idle symmetrical tautology.[19]

On the other hand, a symmetrical relation which is comprehended within an overall asymmetry possesses the highest defining power. For although two propositions taken as equivalent are related symmetrically, taken as a triad (the two propositions *plus* the compound proposition which results from their combination), the conjunction is less symmetrical. Now if negation were added to the conjunction, what results is a proposition with the highest defining power. In order to illustrate what he means, Hartshorne gives the example of knowledge of words (in a foreign language) which express nonsymmetrical relations, e.g., "greater than." If one knew this word, he says, he would have no need of knowing the term for the corresponding symmetrical concept, i.e., "equal to." The combination of "greater than" with a negative will readily yield the notion "equal to" in a way that "equal to" combined with a negative will not yield the notion "greater than." Hence, X is "equal to" Y if X is *not* "greater than" Y, or if Y is *not* "greater than" X, while X is *not* "equal to" Y—or the reverse for that matter—will not (as easily) tell us which of the two is "greater than" the other.[20]

Symmetry within an overall asymmetry, Hartshorne believes, is a paradigm for metaphysics. Thus comprehensive asymmetry, i.e., directional order which embraces symmetry as its subordinate concept, is what we must look for in basic concepts. He therefore decries the fact that philosophy has, for so long, regarded symmetry as the basic concept. For instance, he criticizes Hume's dictum, "What is distinguishable is separable," as a blurring together of a nondirectional relation of comparison with an asymmetric relation of existential dependence. Two terms X and XY (a whole containing X plus an additional factor) are distinguishable. However, while X may in some cases be separable from XY, the latter term can never be separated from X. The dependence is not bidirectional. If we had a term X, we will not necessarily have a term XY; but if we had XY, there is simply no way that we will not have X. Symmetrical separability by no means follows from distinguishability.

Hartshorne does grant that Hume was right in holding that an X separable from XY, which in this case denotes X plus something additional, is simpler than XY. And indeed Hume assumes that the entities to which his maxim is to be applied are equally simple. Successive "impressions" or events are not related as X and XY.[21] Impressions for Hume are either simple or complex. If the first, then no other ideas can be entailed by them; if the second, however, they are distinguishable into parts.[22] Thus, to be distinct means to be separable. However, Hartshorne argues that there are basically two types of separabilities and only the disjunction of the two coincides with distinguishability:

> Suppose event E' follows event E; they are then not identical, not one but two events. However, in which of two very different senses are they separable? (a) One of the two, say E, could have occurred alone, but not

vice versa (not E' without E); or (b) either event could have occurred alone. A whole, say XY, is inseparable from either one of its parts, X or Y, but X might occur though XY did not. This illustrates separability in sense (a). Similarly, a set of premises is in its truth inseparable from that of an entailed consequence, but the latter could be true though the conjunct of the premises were false. Here again we have one-way inseparability, together with distinguishability. (For the truth of the conclusion is not identical with that of the set of premises).[23]

A later event is related to its predecessor by its inseparability from the earlier event, while a preceding event is related to its successor by its separability from this successor event.[24] The later event had obviously not yet been actualized when the earlier one occurred; this makes for the independence of the predecessor event. When the second event comes to pass, however, the earlier one being already in existence, the synthesis of earlier and later can no longer be undone. There is thus no possibility of separation—and no empirical proof of such, at least not in this direction. The observation of an event as it takes place happens in a proper temporal order. The future cannot be observed as already completed; this is the realm of the past. The future is the domain of events anticipated, a realm influenced by the past in a way far stronger than the influence going in the reverse direction.[25] This, according to Hartshorne, is especially evident in the case of memory.[26] For what is shown, contrary to the Humean maxim, is that later experiences refer back to and are complicated by experiences which have come before, in a way unmatched by the forward reference that characterizes anticipation. What is future is merely a rough blueprint, while what is past is made up of events irrevocable to the last item.[27]

Symmetry discloses a lack of order; its simplicity is deceptive.[28] X simply equal to Y puts neither X nor Y in a definite order relative to each other.[29] Even human beings, he holds, are not all strictly equal in any factual sense. Concreteness always means contrast. To know *simply* that Frankie and Charlie are friends does not *ipso facto* disclose anything as to who is the friendlier, kinder, or more understanding one. And this contrast cannot but exist. For they cannot be equal in terms of friendliness nor in other aspects, such as intelligence, looks, creativity, etc. The contrast is concrete, but the contrast of Frankie with Charlie cannot be same as the contrast of Charlie with Frankie, as this can only be the case in the limiting and scarcely realizable instance of perfect balance. It is only by means of abstraction that this symmetrical notion can be obtained. Hartshorne's intention is not to depreciate the value of symmetry. Indeed, he says it has its indispensable place.[30] But given the witness of both ordinary human experience as well as formal logic, he holds that symmetry is, in a certain technical sense, secondary to asymmetry and is indeed contained in it. Symmetrical cases are derivatives of asymmetrical ones and are therefore inexplicable solely on their own terms.[31] Symmetry is a special case, not the general principle.[32]

Defining characteristic

Hartshorne sums up the arguments of those who reject events as the basic descripta of reality: events are only genuinely identifiable with reference to substance (e.g., "minds" are known through "bodies"; the unobservable particulars of physics through larger, observable bodies), and any allowance made for events or event sequences in metaphysics holds only insofar as they are secondary realities to substances. He rejects this claim, pointing out that the fact that the knowability of the microworld presupposes the knowability of the macroworld is not an argument against event metaphysics.[33] The identification of events cannot be the result of grosser bodies—substances—that merely move about or internally alter from one state to another. An event is not merely the collective career of an aggregate of substances. It may seem so on the macroscopic level, for do we not call the changes that take place in respect to a particular entity or in respect to a group of entities, "events"? However, on the ultramicroscopic level—the level of the unobservable particulars—there is no strict applicability of the category of substance. Even on the macroscopic level itself, the idea of an event that happens ultimately to a self-identically enduring substance is a misconception. An identifiable substance that merely changes its locus is itself a convenient approximation. On both these levels, identity "is not, in any perceptual or pragmatic way, distinguishable from an identity of form in an unbroken or quasi-continuous event-sequence."[34]

Hartshorne accepts that communication would be impossible if events did not form some relatively unbroken sequence with recognizable identical spatial and qualitative structures persisting from one event to the next through more or less long periods of time.[35] This, however, does not amount to asserting that an event is not susceptible to explanation apart from substance or that that which changes can only be explained in terms of that which does not. In this pair of contrary notions a basic asymmetry of relation is involved and explained in terms of a continuity of form. It is what is constant, not something additional such as thinghood or substance. In this view, there is no fixed and unchanging substance. Rather, what is fixed is simply the limit of alternative possibilities confronted at each moment by an individual event-sequence, which ensures that an object A at time 1 will be the same object at a later time 2 or at an even later time *n*.

This limit of alternative possibilities is determined by an entity's defining characteristic. It is a recognizable sameness of form belonging to a sequence of events, sufficiently unbroken, thereby enabling us to *perceive* an entity as enduring. As Hartshorne points out: "Happenings are discerned perceptually; persistence of quality and pattern is also observed, as are changes of quality and pattern, and persistence of past events in subsequent ones; but persistence of something additional, that is, thinghood or substance, who has observed that?"[36] It is true that events are not ordinarily conceived as having a spatial shape in the way that things such as trees or human beings are conceived. And it is *of* such things as trees and human beings that we ordinarily say that events happen. However, Hartshorne argues that "man-at-the-present-moment" has a shape that is at least imperceptibly different with each new present (even if the distance between the two temporal points were a mere fraction of a second). Moreover, "man-now" remains the same as the set of mental and bodily events that prolong its sequence at the present moment. This means that events can have shape. Hence, that events happen to someone does not necessarily mean that events happen to an entity that does not change. It simply means (in the event-language which Hartshorne espouses) that these events usually fit into well-ordered and unbroken sequences which are ordinarily called things or persons.[37]

Now what differentiates events belonging to the sequence "human being" from events belonging to any other sequence, e.g., "tree," can be understood in terms of the principle of process itself. It is the congruence that exists between the *manner* (process) by which a particular sequence becomes and the *kind* (essence) of sequence it is. Whitehead states it in terms of the harmony between the "how" and the "what" of an entity: "how an actual entity becomes constitutes what the actual entity is; so that the two descriptions of an actual entity are not independent. Its 'being' is constituted by its 'becoming.'"[38] On the one hand, an entity in the process of coming-to-be is intimately *dependent* to a considerable extent upon events belonging to its sequence, which are temporally prior to its present self. On the other hand, it is *free* in terms of the act of bringing together of the previous events in its sequence, thereby producing a novel whole. However, the self-identically enduring, i.e., changeless, individual cannot be the most concrete term of analysis. For, according to Hartshorne, "the 'individual' is indeed a product, something made, and the concrete making is not *by* 'the individual' itself but by *de facto* members of individual sequences."[39] "I simply" or "you simply" is not the locus of the congruence of the *manner* of my coming-to-be nor the *kind* of being that I am or that you are. I simply or you simply are abstractions. The concrete is the entity situated in a present temporal locus, as Hartshorne observes; it is the I or you that inhabits the present temporal slice—I-now, you-now.

An entity's defining characteristic is therefore constituted by the continuous process of synthesizing past events, which are the data upon which a sequence's present feeds.[40] This activity of feeding upon past events as data has a twofold composition. First, there is the activity, i.e., synthesizing previous data, an activity which brings about the novel whole, namely, the thing-now. Second, there can be no such activity without some aim, purpose, or direction to it. This fundamental aim which induces the activity of synthesis is an entity's self-creation. Purpose is already an intimation of an aim, and aim is itself an indication of an end. This end is the entity inhabiting the present temporal slice.[41] The thing-now can therefore be likened to the *final cause* which operates in the coming-to-be of an entity. The data (previous events in an entity's own sequence) are then the entity's *efficient cause*. Both causes therefore are factors within the constitution of an entity in the process of becoming.[42] (It will be shown later how this constitution is also a derivative from other event sequences.) Since an entity is a process of self-creation, it must have its final cause as an inherent element within it. This can be expressed by saying that an entity is an activity of self-causation. Hartshorne uses the phrase "creative synthesis" to describe this insight.[43] The phrase brings out the twofold character of each entity—novelty (creativity) and partial determinateness (synthesis), the former being the new aspect, and the latter, the old aspect of every event sequence. The old is basically constituted by previous events which give rise to and persist in the new entity. Justice is therefore done to both permanence as well as change for in each new coming-to-be, in each new synthesis, previous data are held together and preserved.[44]

The kind of ontology that Hartshorne criticizes locates something like the defining characteristic of an entity in a substance unaffected by change. In a person for instance, character would, in classical substance metaphysics, be defined in terms of a hypothetical—or abstract—substrate which has attributes peculiar to it. The attributes may change, but the character, the underlying substrate, stays the same. For Hartshorne, on the contrary, character itself is no more than a vague outline, a "label for the pervasive quality of a person's past actions."[45] What is true of his idea of character is true of all entities whatsoever. In Hartshorne's mind, the defining characteristic of a particular entity is fixed only in so far as there is permanence in the holding together of previous data by present synthesis.[46] There is no unchanging substance. Each event is a perpetual unification of a pluralistic reality which, as soon as it achieves integration in its synthesis of events belonging to its past, becomes immersed in plurality once again. Here we can recall Whitehead's phrase, "the many become one and are increased by one."

The *manner* by which an event sequence continues its career not only constitutes the *kind* of event sequence that it is, it likewise distinguishes it from every other type of event sequence. The event sequence "man" will synthesize, as data for its present coming-to-be, events which primarily belong to the sequence "man." This holds true for any other kind of entity. Through such analysis Hartshorne shows that substance—understood in terms of a fixed reality untouched by change—is not so unproblematic as many would hold. Thus, he successfully moves the discussion from the mere notion of substance or literal thinghood to the question of signification. For indeed, if by substance is meant the classical definition given to it by substantialistic ontologies, then as he says, we lock ourselves up in an intellectual prison. However, if substance is understood to mean simply those everyday things to which we refer and which we manipulate (which of course are also regarded—legitimately and correctly—as self-identically enduring entities), then Hartshorne would find that acceptable. The same would be true if it meant the permanent aspect of an event in the process of coming-to-be, i.e., the character that defines the *kind* of event sequence that an entity is (what shall later on be defined in terms of the Whiteheadian "subject-superject" structure of becoming). In fact, he is even willing to call an event a substance, i.e., provided this does not imply that the schema (identical subject with *changing* qualities) is equally correct.[47]

Descriptive Theories of Events

Although identity does rest on identifiability, and interaction requires that one entity be identifiable from another, identification still has always and unavoidably the character of process, which is fundamental to entities. However, even if process were taken to be fundamental, it is possible to distinguish between a stronger and a weaker view of the metaphysics of event.[48] The stronger view, which can be termed the causal or strict ontological view, holds that processes are causally or existentially fundamental relative to actual entities. This perspective regards substance as that correlate of process usually taken to be a thing.[49] The weaker (or conceptual or explanatory) view still holds that processes are fundamental with regard to things. But instead of being existentially fundamental, processes are basic only to the conceptual order of understanding. This point of view has close links with perspectives such as Donald Davidson's, who admits the category of event along with that of substance on the grounds that such admission best suits the language used to describe the world. Davidson holds that it is not possible to "give a cogent account of action, of explanation, of causality, or of the relation between the mental and the physical, unless we accept events as individuals."[50] This basically means that processes are fundamental, since the explanatory characterizations of what an entity *is* always involves recourse to an account of what the thing *does*. Moreover, the identification of any particular entity always involves reference to various processes.[51]

This represents a divergence from the view held by Strawson concerning the relation between events and substances. Strawson claims that events are conceptually dependent upon physical particulars since events are not capable of providing a single, comprehensive, and continuously usable framework of reference provided by physical objects.[52] Davidson agrees with Strawson that for the greater part events are understood as occurrences in a more or less stable object. He even argues that it does seem likely that the notion of event depends in every case on the notion of change in a substance. This is in spite of the fact that there are certain events of which it is difficult to say what substance undergoes the change.[53] However, he criticizes Strawon's understanding of the relation between events and substances in terms of the absence of a two-way dependence between these two categories.[54]

The sympathetic hearing given by Davidson to events is motivated by his belief in their utility in our descriptions of reality. And although Strawson refuses to admit events into his substance-based ontology, his motivation is quite the same as Davidson's. Strawson rejects events as basic particulars because they represent a category that can be done away with for the most part in description. Unlike Davidson, he does not ascribe the same necessity to events with regard to our ordinary ways of description. Physical particulars are more useful than events in ordinary discourse precisely because the events always refer to substances.[55]

The tie that binds both of their ontologies, however, is the attempt to describe, in as faithful a manner as possible, the fundamental concepts by which the world is normally thought about. Strawson terms this endeavor "descriptive metaphysics." The most basic question it asks, relative to our ways of approaching the real, is, *What are the structures of the way we talk about reality?* A corollary to this question is, *What do these structures disclose, relative to the class of entities that are fundamental to our way of describing reality?* The emphasis is clearly on the reliability of already existing or established modes of conceptualization. Hence, an analysis of ordinary ways of expressing our ideas about the real takes center stage, and the attempt to construct new metaphysical theories that may be more adequate is avoided. It is, as Strawson says, an approach that seeks to "produce a systematic account of the general *conceptual structure* of which our daily practice shows us to have a tacit and unconscious mastery."[56] Donald Davidson captures the essence of descriptive metaphysics when he expresses his interest in how English and languages like it (i.e., all languages) work, but is not concerned to improve on or change it. As he puts it, "I don't believe in alternative conceptual schemes, and so I attach a good deal of importance to whatever we can learn about how we put the world together from how we talk about it."[57]

Revisionary theories of events

The descriptive approach is clearly different from that which attempts to radically revise our common sense conceptual frameworks, i.e., our ordinary view of the world. Strawson terms this alternative way "revisionary metaphysics" and defines it as the attempt to construct a better structure by which our worldview is expressed.[58] This definition, however, already represents a further step in the characterization of this kind of metaphysical endeavor. For even before the attempt to build a new structure, the first concern is with the question regarding the nature of reality, which our common and ordinary ways of speaking may not always faithfully and adequately describe. Unlike descriptive metaphysics therefore, its primary question is, *Do our common ways of describing the real do justice to the nature of this reality?* The question betrays a suspicion that somehow ordinary talk falls short of a faithful grasp of reality.[59] It may be true that abstract concepts embedded in the structure of ordinary description have proven their pragmatic worth, offering us a relatively secure way of managing our commonsense world,[60] however, ordinary language does not do justice to the generalities, profundities, and complexities of life.[61] For instance, not all sensed phenomena are embraced within such simplified classificatory criteria.[62] Thus, a certain violence is done by ordinary modes of conceptualization to the richness, complexity, subtlety, and concreteness of the real.[63] This is another observation in the revisionary metaphysician's question. Words tend to distract our attention from concrete facts. Moreover, an even greater danger is that the apparent simplicity of a verbal formula—which may very well be correct as far as it goes—may actually hide a far more vast and complex matrix of facts to which such formula refers. Thus for instance, the Hegelian and Marxist interpretations of history only go so far before actually distorting the reality they originally intended to describe with all faithfulness. And this is but the tip of the iceberg. For really, the supreme danger embedded deep in our use of words is a kind of intoxication wrought by an excess of devotion to the pragmatic dimension of word use. As A.H. Johnson observes, "men become bemused by the rhetorical flow of their own unimpeded verbosity," thereby giving rise to what Whitehead calls the "triviality of quick-witted people."[64]

Hartshorne's theory of events

Where does Hartshorne's ontology of event fall within this descriptive-revisionary distinction? In his "Preface" to *Creative Synthesis*, Hartshorne acknowledges the revisionary character of his metaphysics, immediately pointing out, however, that the characterization would only be correct if it were not taken to mean that those who fall under this label are merely adding superfluous metaphysical baggage to our ways of conceiving reality.[65] It is true, he says, that our common everyday approaches to what is real, e.g., our ordinary modes of conceptualization, enable us to simplify the often overwhelmingly complex vicissitudes of life and the universe. We are subjected to a constant bombardment of data which we ourselves contrive. We are also subject to experiences beyond our control and which we therefore cannot but regard as "givens." The structures, linguistic and otherwise, which we impose upon these realities enable us to cope with their richness and complexity. Paradoxically though, these very same structures can, and eventually do, become straightjackets which constrict and confine our ways of appropriating and making sense of what is real. Hartshorne therefore sounds a *caveat*. He insists that the faithful description of the basic concepts by which we normally think about the world must not lead us to denigrate or deny the reality of those aspects of experience which are not normally included in ordinary discourse.

Hartshorne does say that the ontology of event is a way of speaking.[66] This could very well be interpreted to mean that although avowedly revisionist in approach, his concept of event can still be exempted from the strict ontological view, as Rescher terms it. The description of an event as a way of speaking or *mode* of conceptualization—instead of a conceptual framework, for instance—can certainly be interpreted to mean that Hartshorne's view falls under the explanatory kind. From this perspective, an event would be understood as a concept which although expendable would nevertheless facilitate an even more faithful description of reality. It may be dispensable for metaphysics, but we can certainly concede its usefulness for epistemo-logical purposes. Thus for instance, although it may actually have a very mar-ginal role to play in our notions of causality, action, or the relation of mind and body, it is still useful to hold on to it as a conceptuality in order that our descriptions of these phenomena may be made easier and our overall world-view less susceptible to the charge of being truncated. From this vantage point, event-language is needed as a complement to substance-language.

This complementary view of substance and event is how Davidson, for instance, has come to admit the idea of event into his philosophy.[67] And although this perspective which tolerates events appears far less inimical to Hartshorne's metaphysics than the downright rejection of the concept, it still remains contrary to Hartshorne's view.[68] For this perspective still con-cedes too much to the doctrine of substance. While it may appear to be more acceptable than an unqualified rejection of events, it remains but a more subtle form of the conception that events ultimately refer to substan-tive particulars. Hartshorne considers this as unacceptable. He insists that one cannot demonstrate the invalidity of the event-philosophy by consid-ering it only in extremely weak formulations.[69] Flashes, bangs, births, deaths, and battles, Hartshorne says, are inadequate examples of concrete event units precisely because they are events tied to, and hence incompre-hensible apart from, substantive particulars.[70] As such, they are not the kinds of events that would make an event ontology plausible.

A weak or conceptual label fails to capture the full radical nature of his ontology, for Hartshorne does not simply hold a view of substances and events as symmetrically related concepts, one being a necessary correlate of the other. Neither does he accept a rather cash-value perspective on events as admissible in our discourse only because we cannot make full sense of what substances *are*, without recourse to what substances *do*. Rather, in argu-ing that the universal category is event, not substance,[71] he is dispensing with substance altogether in favor of a pure ontology of event. He clearly does not merely intend to provide a more useful tool to grasp reality. Even more importantly, his notion of event reverses the very ontological priority of the commonsense conceptual scheme put forward by substantialistic ontologies.

Hartshorne's nondualistic theory

In the whole of his philosophy Hartshorne rejects any ultimate fragmenta-tion of reality as well as any dichotomization in any of its levels. This has significant repercussions on three important and interrelated areas of his thought: his cosmological notions, ethical and religious considerations, and his psychology and theory of perception. In the area of cosmology, on the level of the relation that holds between human beings and the cosmos, he argues that there can be no absolute break between human and nonhuman reality. There is, as it were, only a continuous spectrum of complexity in organisms, from the hypothetical superhuman to human beings, down to the one-celled amoeba and even further. This view he shares with a number of authors who also endorse the evolutionary viewpoint which regards human reality as continuous with that reality out of which it has evolved.[72] In the area of ethics and religion, on the level of the relations that are obtained between human beings, he has radicalized the scriptural dictum to "love one's neighbor as oneself." He calls attention to the inadequacy of a regard for the other which seeks to find its origin and justification in a love for oneself and offers a fresh insight into the dictum.[73] He arrives at this novel understanding by looking deeper into the command and discovering in it what he believes is a message whose subtlety shows why it is often overlooked. Interest in others is basically altruistic, self-love and love of others being alike.[74] The most fundamental principle is love *plain and simple.*[75] The love-of-neighbor command means, not so much that one must be concerned for the other in the same way that one shows concern for one's self, but that one is concerned for the other as oneself because one's self is first and foremost an other. Hartshorne thus gives no privileged metaphysical basis for self-interest in his philosophy.[76] In the area of psychology and his theory of perception, Hartshorne refuses to admit any dichotomization which effectively endorses quantitative entities to the neglect of important features of experience and perception. He likewise rejects the bifurcation of nature into matter and mind which results from the attempt to explain nature regarded as mere matter in terms of something, i.e., mind, that is held to transcend its very order. In place of these he argues first of all that no *percepta* lie outside the boundaries of nature.[77] He also argues that no concrete entity, no actual existent, can be regarded as incapable of even the most primitive type of experience.[78] Thus, in opposition to fragmentary conceptualizations, Hartshorne endorses a view of reality as an unbroken and seamless whole.[79] This viewpoint regards actualities of the universe as objects of external experience which in turn become data in the subjective occasion of experiencing. Here, as in the attempt to solve the problem concerning the relationship between physical particulars and events, a simple view of complementarity will not do. Merely correlating experienced object to experiencing subject is inadequate to provide a viable solution to the difficulties that arise on account of the bifurcation of nature and the disconnectedness of experience. Hence, there is an appeal once again to the method of regarding metaphysical contraries as asymmetrical concepts.

Generalizing beyond human experience

The application of the asymmetrical method is most evident in Hartshorne's adoption of the Whiteheadian metaphor of reality as an "ocean of feeling"[80] which is really an extrapolation from the basic structure of human experience, a move from lesser parts to larger wholes. In Hartshorne's cosmology, the whole of the universe cannot be characterized as having either physical components only or psychical components only. This is classical materialism and spiritualism which are both reductionistic; the first reducing all things to matter, the latter reducing all things to mind. These views are regarded as strictly unipolar or one-sided. However, neither can the universe be characterized simply as having both a physical as well as a psychical domain, each having nothing to do with the other. This is classical dualism which he likewise rejects. Neither can the characterization be that of both physical and psychical components which merely complement each other, juxtaposed one to another in the conceptual order of understanding. This is the view of complementarity offered by descriptive metaphysics which, together with the dualistic model, is regarded by Hartshorne to be characterized by symmetry. And though these last two are more tenable than the one-sided views, Hartshorne holds that they fail to capture the full reality which is disclosed not by symmetry but by asymmetry. Unipolarity is too exclusive whereas mere symmetry is too inclusive. The truth must lie somewhere in between.

Instead of these perspectives of fragmentation which he finds inadequate, Hartshorne proposes that we look at the evidence of experience in order to discern its structure. For he holds that this will provide the conceptual tool necessary to understand the structure of reality itself.[81] This recall to a heedfulness of what experience discloses in order to arrive at a fuller understanding of reality bears witness to a mirroring between human experience and experience in general. Hartshorne's ontology is marked by a recognition of the constant interplay of these two elements which, at an even deeper level, is revelatory of the unity of reality. Existential reflection on the structure of experience as such begins and, in many ways, culminates in a clarification of the structure of human experience. And against a possible charge of anthropomorphism, his response would be that there is no other starting point, no other way to proceed.[82] For the question is not whether a notion is anthropomorphic or not; rather, it is how reasonable such anthropomorphism is.[83] Furthermore, the question is not that of discovering the difference that exists between the two categories. There can be no question with regard to this. Rather, it is that of discovering the *degree* of such difference. It is a difference inscribed within a larger domain of similarity which makes the very talk of difference possible. This means that all the variables of reality, whatever else these may be, must be variables of human experience. There must be more than one value satisfied by that experience. As Hartshorne insists, "it is just not possible to conceive any mode of difference *from* human experience which is not in some degree also a mode of difference *between* these experiences."[84] Hence, using human experience as a point of departure in the investigation of experience in general can only be done through a generalization of experience beyond the strictly human sort. There can be no experiential meaning to a distinction between what is experienced and what is simply not, but only to the distinction between what is experienced by a given individual and what is not so experienced.[85]

One of the first things noticed with regard to experience is its *ecstatic* or *transcendent* character, i.e., its outward directedness. Experience is always experience of something other than itself.[86] As Hartshorne says, it is essentially *of* something.[87] Thus, in the act of experiencing of conscious beings, for instance, there is always an other-than-oneself that forms a significant part of the overall picture. It is significant because experience would not be experience in the absence of this factor. As Hocking explains in his "Foreword" to Hartshorne's book, this other-directedness of experience constitutes an important part of the Hartshornean cosmology.[88] There is, however, a corollary to this notion, one that is no less important. This is the *universality* of the ecstatic nature of experience. Such concept is arrived at by means of a generalization of the transcendent character observed in human experience. The other-directedness primarily observed in human experience is transformed by Hartshorne into an ultimate category. The whole of reality and not just conscious reality displays it.[89] It is what he calls the "social conception of reality."[90] This is another most important fact disclosed by our observation of experience, the universality of which is an important notion in Hartshorne's metaphysics. All reality experiences, or to use a more technical Hartshornean and Whiteheadian term, "feels." What exactly does this statement signify? And how did Hartshorne arrive at such conceptualization or description of experience? These are the questions that we shall turn to now.

The unity of the real and the pervasiveness of mind

Hartshorne maintains "that all things, so far as they are individuals rather than aggregates, fall upon a single scale (allowing for parallel branches such as the races of man), running from the least particle of inorganic matter to the great universe itself."[91] Indeed, when one observes the make-up of the world, he immediately notices three kinds of entities: (i) those entities which are below him and yet akin to himself, e.g., nonhuman animals; (ii) entities which are farther below him, and yet like the first kind, are also similar to himself, albeit in a remote way, e.g., plant life; and (iii) entities that are so different from human beings that they seem not relatively but absolutely nonhuman. On the one hand, there are the inorganic objects, which a human being can hardly think of as being of equal status with himself—objects which nonetheless seem more alien than inferior to him. On the other hand, there is the entire universe regarded as a "whole" which is made up of both organic and inorganic entities. As such, it is manifested as the greatest of all realities, but which can nevertheless be regarded as more than simply the sum of all its individual components.

These kinds of organisms may be classified as follows: (i) and (ii) can be regarded as belonging to class *A*, which we designate as the category of organisms forming a scale from low to high, while (iii) can be regarded as another class *B*, one that cannot be situated on the scale with the same ease with which organisms are. Hartshorne argues that although class *B* entities cannot be readily called organisms, they could very well be composed of finer, more minute entities. Their behavior can be analogically compared with class *A* entities. He says a pile of sand is an example, "for when we come to individual molecules, atoms or electrons, the lack of dynamic integrity characteristic of many larger objects can no longer be confidently asserted."[92] Hence, he argues that the components of inorganic masses can be regarded as belonging to the scale of organic beings after all. But it is clear that they come way below what would ordinarily be described as organisms.[93] Concerning plant life, he points out that although these lack the same integrity as is shown by nonhuman animals, a plant is really a colony of cells. Each of these cells possesses an integrity analogous to that found in humans and nonhuman animals. A tree, he notes, is more of a pseudo-organism.[94]

We need to see beyond the particularities of these analogies, however, to the possible reactions elicited by such conceptions of atoms, molecules, or cells being relational entities, i.e., having "feelings," or even plants being pseudo-organisms having no "ruling member," as Hartshorne calls it. This conceptualization begins with the recognition of the need to generalize beyond human experience in order to arrive at an adequate and coherent description of experience in general. Only in this way can the meaning of experience-in-general be understood. But this means first and foremost that our starting point is none other than human experience itself.[95] By asking whether the other-directed orientation can be said to characterize experience-in-general, other-directedness is itself universalized, and the possibility of making this characteristic applicable to all entities on the scale is opened.[96]

Hartshorne's generalized comparative psychology

Here we come upon what Hartshorne calls a "generalized comparative psychology" in which certain variables of human reality have their meaning expanded in order to cover the whole of reality. "Feeling" and "experience," for instance, are technical terms in process thought. They are terms which, though most primordially referring to human beings, are expanded in the scheme of the generalized comparative psychology in order to refer to any entity whatsoever that exhibits a reaction to stimuli. In such a scheme, consciousness and thought become secondary. "Conscious mentality," as Whitehead calls it, is made to refer primarily to those entities on the scale whose reactive character are of a much more subtle and complex sort, e.g., human beings.[97] Hence, feeling and experience mean, first and foremost, that all concrete entities react to their constituents if they have these, to their environment if they have such, or to both if they possess both.

The universality of experience is therefore the universality of response to environmental stimuli.[98] All concrete entities respond to what in effect are stimuli, and having done so become themselves stimuli for other entities.[99] Going back to the analogy of the scale of entities, if one considers the so-called organic parts of nature, one would most willingly concede that experience can be detected, at least among the higher animals. Hartshorne, however, goes further, arguing that reactive behavior can be followed far down the animal scale, perhaps even to the very bottom.[100] He points out that we can only go so far in arguing that the farther an entity is from human beings in the scale, the less definite must our conception be of its reactive nature. We cannot hold that it does not react at all.[101] Further, the same situation holds for both the lowest-grade entities as well as the most complex one, the whole of the cosmos.[102]

Hartshorne does admit, of course, that there is very little benefit for the generalized comparative psychology to consider the joys and sorrows of single-celled or low-grade organisms, and perhaps even of the cosmic whole. Still, this does not constitute an evidence that these do not possess feeling or experience.[103] And while he grants that the notion of the ubiquity of feeling or experience is subject to factual falsification, he also warns against failing to give sufficient generality to the psychic variables. This would be tantamount to leaving certain portions of the analogical scale of entities impenetrable mysteries.[104]

The idea of the whole of reality as an "ocean of feeling" represents an attempt to close the chasm between nature as mere matter and mind. Human being, which emerged from nonconscious nature stands out of nature as either something little less than a god,[105] to use an expression from Christian scripture, or a freak accident. The positing of an absolute break remains problematic in that no adequate causal explanation can be given to the rise of the higher level reality of conscious mentality. Without the positing of its existence, albeit in a germinal or primitive form in non-human (or more properly perhaps, prehuman) reality, the mentality which in human beings becomes conscious would not be explainable except as an anomaly of nature.

The notion of emergence employed here is actually regarded by Hartshorne with a certain degree of reservation.[106] He says that any analogy between emergence—as for instance, the emergence of life from lifeless matter ("lifeless" here requiring qualification)—and the so-called emergence of mind from mere matter, is tenuous to the extreme. In a very real sense, the conscious mentality of human beings really is a break with nature. Hartshorne admits this. Nevertheless, this so-called break cannot be construed to mean the total absence of mind in mere matter out of which mind emerged. Hartshorne is unimpressed with this fashionable notion, for indeed, mere matter has been understood to mean the total absence of mentality.[107] However, as he insists, "before we can talk scientifically about experience arising from mere material stuff or process, devoid of experience, we must be able to specify the sort of observations which would falsify the statement, 'mind or experience in some form is everywhere.'"[108] This sort of observation, Hartshorne says, is not available, nor are the criteria which could make such observations useful.[109] All we are capable of observing are cases in which mind meets mind, feeling of feeling. And only absolute introspective clarity is capable of observing mere non-feeling, the zero presence of mind or experience. Only the positive instantiations—experience in what could be its germinal form—are accessible to us, not the absolute negative, but the total absence of experience.[110]

This rudimentary form of mentality, experience sufficiently generalized, is responsiveness to environmental stimuli. The universality of this primitive form of mentality constitutes the core of the Hartshornean doctrine of pansychism (or psychicalism), or panentheism.[111] Nature—which in classical dualistic conceptualizations is regarded as primarily matter—is, according to Hartshorne, "mind-like, if not actually some form of mind."[112] This is how he proposes to resolve the ultimate bifurcation of nature into matter (completely devoid of mentality) and mind (completely transcendent of and breaking completely free from its origins in lifeless, material nature).

The unity of the real and the transformation of the subject-object distinction

The rejection of the ultimate fragmentation of nature has significant repercussions for Hartshorne's views regarding the subject-object structure of experience. Experience or feeling, which is the most basic unit of his cosmology—the ultimate *descriptum* of his metaphysics—transforms the classical subject-that-experiences and object-that-is-experienced categorization of the real into an account of subjects-experiencing-other-subjects. In short, it is a metaphysics in the idealistic mold which Hartshorne defines as "the belief that reality can be explained in terms of mind."[113] All actual entities react or respond to received stimuli. Hartshorne admits that his theory is indeed a subtle form of interactionism. "Interaction," "responsiveness," "reciprocation" are kindred concepts used to describe what he means by "feeling," "experience," as well as the presence of "mentality."[114] How is such interactionism or reciprocation explained? And how does it transform the subject-object relation, basic to the structure of all experience, into a relation of subjects- experiencing-other-subjects?

The manner by which Whitehead explains his understanding of experience is relevant, as it parallels the Hartshornean explanation of the relational character of feeling. In *Adventures of Ideas*, Whitehead speaks of the emotional basis of experience and points out that "the basic fact is the rise of an affective tone originating from the things whose relevance is given."[115] Relevance is a key concept to the explanation of the relation between a subject that knows and an object that is known. It is the line of influence proceeding from the object to the subject. Simply stated, a subject knows an object—or gets to know it—because the latter discloses itself as relevant for it. On the other hand, the line proceeding from the subject to the object can be described as a line of concern.[116] An actual entity has a concern for its object whose relevance it has experienced. "Concernedness" as Whitehead terms it, belongs to the very nature of a subject.[117]

This relevance-concern structure which is obtained between subject and object is a way of understanding what Whitehead means by the term "prehension"[118] (from the Latin *prehendere*), which has the literal meaning of "grasping" and "seizing." It is his answer to the question: *How can other actual entities, each with its own formal existence, also enter objectively into the perceptive constitution of another actual entity?* Among higher entities, i.e., those possessing consciousness and the power of speech, such relevance-concern is manifested in the use of signs by which they interpret, verbalize, theorize, and make more or less educated guesses about what is experienced. However, even among lower entities and, for that matter, in all experience whatsoever, such relevance-concern dynamic is not absent.[119] The relevance an object has for a subject is therefore due to the fact that an object functions as a datum for the subject to synthesize, i.e., make part of its internal constitution. Thus any entity is a subject insofar as it has a special activity concerning an object. Any entity is an object in respect to its provocation of some special activity within a subject. What this perspective does is to relativize the otherwise fixed categorizations of subject as simply that which prehends, and object as simply that which is prehended. It loosens, if not unbinds, the all-too-easy and unqualified equation of the subject-object relation with that of the knower and the known. By doing so, a way is opened to a reconsideration of the rigid demarcation between the two. It is a move that is consistent with the perspective of unity and nonfragmentariness. Thus even if the subject-object relation is the fundamental structural pattern of experience, this presupposition must not, without qualification, simply be identified with the knower-known relation.[120]

Experience—fully generalized to mean the universality of interaction—is coextensive with reality itself. Hartshorne relates how, when pondering at some point the question whether there is a basis for the dualism of mind and mere matter, he was reminded of Santayana's phrase "beauty is objectified pleasure." This, he says, led him to the realization that what is experienced—for instance, in the human manifestation of the pheno-menon of experience—are not bare and neutral data. Rather, the world as experienced is constitutive of experience itself, a part of its living unity. How is the non-neutrality of sense data explained? Hartshorne holds that the most direct contact that holds between ourselves and physical reality is with what happens inside our bodies. What occurs in sensation is a par-ticipation by human individuals in the experiences of the subhuman indi-viduals that constitute their bodies. In the experience of physical pain or pleasure, Hartshorne contends that we participate or share in the pleasure or pain experienced by the minute constituents of our bodies. "Our feel-ing," he says, "is a comprehensive pooling of, or participation in, their feelings."[121]

The emotional basis of experience

The most immediate contact or approach that an experiencing entity has with reality is spontaneous. It is preconceptual, precategorical, preinterpre-tative, and prereflective. It is not only prior to any interpretation, but is even prior to conscious apprehension.[122] Knowledge, Whitehead says, is itself already the result of an abstraction. As he puts it: "I contend that the notion of mere knowledge is a high abstraction, and that conscious dis-crimination itself is a variable factor only present in the more elaborate examples of occasions of experience. The basis of experience is emo-tional."[123] Experience at its originary core, i.e., our most direct approach and immediate appropriation of the real is emotional. Moreover, the real which is given to be prehended is itself characterized, as being itself emotional. In his essay defending William Wordsworth's idealistic view of nature, Hartshorne quotes the former's poem, "The Simplon Pass."[124] We can, says Hartshorne, dismiss the poem as mere indulgence in "crazy metaphysics" or "charming poetic fancy and no more." However, to do so would be to miss the point. For the question is not, whether the winds, for instance, are lit-erally bewildered or forlorn. It is not the description of meteorological con-ditions that primarily concerns the poet. Instead, in Hartshorne's view, "the question concerns our experience of winds and other natural phenomena. As what are they given to us? The poet is describing our experience of nature as the basis for any knowledge of it."[125] The experience of bewildered winds and muttering rocks are revelatory of the fact that our initial encounter with such entities as winds, rocks, peals of thunder, throbs of pain, appear in our experiences as primordially emotional, even if for the most part, we are quite unaware of the feelings themselves.[126]

That our most direct approach to reality is preinterpretative does not mean that one already knows what is approached in this preinterpreted state or can tell oneself just what it is. The situation rather is that one senses, or more properly intuits, without the conscious categorizing which is properly termed "knowing." Consciousness, Hartshorne says, is already interpretation. The role of the data of experience is the facilitation of judgement, not about the datum itself, but about the context which its presence enables us to know. Data cannot simply be inaccessible to introspection for it would be a contradiction to insist on the concealed character of the features of experience while holding the notion that the nature of experience is to be made manifest.[127] The data of experience cannot simply be defined as items consciously noted unless the experience being defined is that of an entity possessing an absolute capacity for self-awareness or consciousness. And concerning such entity, only deity in Hartshorne's philosophy will fit the bill.[128]

Putting these two considerations together leads to the qualifications that "data are accessible or inaccessible to inspection just insofar as the capacity for such inspection is great or little in the experiencing subject" and that "data are accessible or inaccessible to conscious noting so far as they are or are not prominent, striking, important, obvious, or intense."[129] What unifies these two qualifications is the inaccessibility of some data to human consciousness. Some data, as Hartshorne says, are in experience; but their presence there is not subject to observation. But is this not a contradiction? How can data be in experience which is manifest and yet remain concealed to inspection? Would this not for all purposes mean that the data are not actually present? Hartshorne responds by saying that an experience would in fact not be itself if the data constitutive of that experience were absent. The datum—whether subject to inspection or not—is essential to the experience as the latter's *sine qua non*. An experience would not be itself without its constituting datum.[130] Thus he says that "while the experience requires the datum, the datum does not require the particular interpretative use to which it is put. In short, the given is the independent variable relative to experience, that which influences but is not influenced by it."[131]

What this conceptualization discloses is that any independent condition must be a datum of experience, whether or not this be reportable by means of introspection. This is on the part of the object experienced, the datum upon which experience feeds. On the part of the subject, this means that its concern for the object is an essential part of the experience.[132] It values the object, value here having the same meaning as concern stripped of its implications of conscious mentality. Thus, Hartshorne states that "valuation is not an adjunct to experience, it is experience. All organisms are seeking, and to some extent finding, satisfaction in whatever they do. Valuation is not something we can take or leave; to live *is* to value. ... Neutrality is for machines, not living beings!"[133]

The localization of feeling

Feeling is concern or intuitive valuation. This characterization of feeling, Hartshorne says, is basically one with sensation which is a kind of localized feeling in neural activity. In contradistinction to associationistic theories which dichotomize between sensation and feeling, Hartshorne argues that affective tone is the primitive component of all human experience.[134] It is true that a distinction can be made between sense qualities and feeling tones. However, aside from the fact that this distinction is simply a logical one, we should not confuse such logical distinctions with the manner by which the world of sensory experience operates.[135] There can be no qualitative gulf between feeling and sensation.[136] In fact, they are so intimately related that one cannot be understood without the other. Hartshorne calls the sensory characters of the world structural and qualitative icons of feeling. He treats the difference between sensation and feeling "as specific difference within a genus that is more suitably termed feeling than anything else."[137] However, while this relationship is one of mutual implication, feeling remains the more primary, being more primitive and fundamental, with the sensory factor being a localization of the affective.[138]

How is such localization of feeling explained? Hartshorne turns to a phenomenological analysis of the experience of pain. Of all sensory experiences, pain appears as a centerpiece illustration of his notion that the fundamental defining character of a sensation is affectional. For him, pain, more than any other sensory experience, discloses the primacy of the affective. Pain is rarely, if ever, disclosed as neutral.[139] While there are circumstances in which pain and suffering—whether mental or physical—can in fact be enjoyed,[140] it remains the case that it has intrinsic reference to negative reactions of avoidance or rejection.[141] Wayne Viney puts it in terms of the fact that the notion of disinterested pain is a contradiction in terms, or at the very least, a paradox.[142] Hartshorne explains such localization by using a phenomenological analysis of tolerance for pain. An individual who struggles not to give in to physical pain stands in contrast, spatially at least, with that part of his body which is in pain. There is a definite contrast between himself as struggling subject and the pain as objectified in his lacerated flesh. Thus he can say, "My thigh was cut by broken glass and it hurts." And yet at the same time, pain as an object experienced is not an individual clearly differentiated from the self experiencing the pain. The pain one feels down in one's wounded thigh is *one's own* like no one else's. He is *the one* in pain. Hartshorne explains the intertwinement of sameness and difference that stands out in this analysis of pain in terms of his analogy of the body.

Subjects-experiencing-subjects: the analogy of the body

Hartshorne's notion of the human body bears an analogy with a monarchical society in which there is a regnant member that directs—though in a relative fashion—the actions of the lesser members over which it has control. The regnant member is also affected by these members which are themselves unified and integral individuals possessing the same capacity for a unified response to stimuli that the entire society—monarch and member—possesses.[143] This does not mean that one, for instance, is in control of his limbs and their actions. Limbs, though part of the body of which the self—understood in its totality—can be considered the regnant member, are still not individual terms for Hartshorne. This is because arms and legs do not possess the same unity of functioning and the capacity to react as a whole to stimuli which cells (or the even more minute molecules or atoms of which they are composed) possess. Limbs, according to Hartshorne, are simply not natural individuals. The I (the self in its concrete totality) is the regnant member of the entire society, made up of itself plus the constituent individual-members because it draws together in a unified way the individual functions, actions, aspirations, and reactions of the lesser parts. In this way it is both immanent in the societal whole as well as transcendent to it. Translating this into the language of the experience of pain, "I am in pain" means both "I—the regnant, transcendent member capable of observing what is taking place in my body—am in pain," as well as "My body—whichever part it is that is actually hurting, so long as this is understood to mean not only the limb but the natural individuals that make it up—hurts." We can say that the first statement is "involved," the second, "observational." The former shows a subject immersed in the situation it is narrating; the latter, a subject narrating a situation that it observes as being over and against himself.

This analogy which Hartshorne utilizes is meant to bridge the gap between the sameness of the individual (subject) experiencing and the pain (object) experienced, and the difference[144] is disclosed in the fact that one can observe one's pain. He holds that the minute constituents of the human body, the cells that make up one's flesh, are the individual terms, not the pain itself. Hence, he states that "the pain is at one and the same time a part of ourselves, or we should not suffer it, and yet also in some way involves some other agency or agencies, some other feeler or feelers, or we should not have to struggle against it."[145] The pain one feels down there in one's thighs is an abstraction from the pain individually experienced by the cells that constitute that part of one's body that had been wounded. There is not but one self that is the "feeler"; there are many. And the individual who speaks of "his pain" is not speaking of "his" pain alone, but the pain experienced by himself, and the numerous other individuals (cells) that are themselves in pain.[146] The struggle that athletes for instance put up with in order to build increased levels of tolerance of pain is a clear indication of the fact that the totality of one's experience cannot be understood in isolation from the reality of otherness inserted into the experience itself.[147]

This analysis of pain discloses two concepts which are central to Hartshorne's philosophical analysis of the subject-object structure of experience. First, what is experienced is itself an occasion of experience; or in Whitehead's phrase, it is sympathy or feeling *of* feeling.[148] The concrete

actualities of nature—e.g., our bodies—as we experience them are themselves drops of experience. If being a subject therefore means primarily to
experience or to be an occasion of experience, then the objects we
encounter—being drops of experience as well—are themselves subjects in
their own right. What we come upon are not objects *simply*, i.e., entities
devoid of feeling and therefore of subjectivity, but objects which themselves feel and experience. Thus, Hartshorne argues that our experiences
are participatory experiences (of the human type) of certain feelings. These
feelings are possessed primarily by our bodily constituents, perhaps cells,
possibly cell nuclei, possibly other units which are themselves centers of
subhuman feelings.[149] Second—and the more significant one—what is traditionally understood as the object-pole of an experience is therefore
transformed by Hartshorne into another experiencing subject. That subject becomes an object for another experient entity because it falls within
the latter's domain of concern and is therefore relevant to it. The phrase
"feeling of feeling" then comes to mean that feeling becomes a bridge
mediating the subject-end (or "pole," using Hartshornean terminology)
and the object-end of every experience. And it does this by being on both
sides of the relation. This discloses feeling as possessing a Janus-like character, presenting "an obvious dual aspect of being which is at once subjective and yet a content or object of consciousness, once a mode and a
datum of experience."[150]

The data of experience

To appreciate the conception of the data of experience as feeling, it is necessary to understand Hartshorne's further conception of the pastness of
data. The transformation of the simple subject-object designation is accomplished because the object with which a present subject is concerned was
once a subject itself.[151] The antecedence of an object together with affective
tone belongs to the intrinsic character of the prehended entity. The character of data as emotional, i.e., as genuine cases exemplifying responsiveness
to stimuli, is shown by the fact that there is a transference of feeling that
occurs from the already completed entity to the newly emerging one. The
feeling from one actual entity being integrated into another as feeling
within the object is reproduced in the new subject. What is given in any
experience is always already in the past. This in fact, according to
Hartshorne, is what prehension means in its primary or concrete form: "it is
the experience of past events, these being necessary conditions of the experience."[152] The very term "datum" (derived from Latin) implies a pastness. It
is founded on the fact that what is given already is; it is already there. This
means that an entity can only serve as a datum of experience if it is already
complete and therefore susceptible to being taken into the coming-to-be of
yet another entity.[153] Now it belongs to the very character of a datum of

experience that it is of the past. As Hartshorne observes, the very concept of prehension which suggests a "grasping" implies that what is grasped already *is*, for one cannot grasp what is not in being.[154]

What is given therefore is the necessary past condition of an entity in the process of coming to be. However many be these data as necessary conditions for the coming into being of a new entity, they nevertheless still do not constitute a sufficient reason in the strong sense of this word. Thus, Hartshorne rejects any deterministic notion concerning the relation of the data of experience to the actual coming into being of an entity. All experiences are the result of past conditions themselves experiences, which are then synthesized by the new entity in the process of coming-to-be. This notion concerning the pastness of the data of experience represents the cornerstone, as it were, of the Hartshornean panpsychic edifice. It is a perspective concerning the unified character of reality disclosed by the pervasive character of mentality and spelled out in terms of the transformation of the categorization of subject-object into that of subject-*experiencing*-other-subjects or subject-*experienced-by*-other-subjects.

Experiencing is constituted by the active concern of entities presently in the process of coming into being for other entities whose being is antecedent to that very process. It is these antecedent entities which are commonly termed "objects." An object is thus that entity that has already come-into-being, which is related to later entities in a manner which makes these later ones dependent on the former already having become. In regard to this perspective, the object primarily signifies a relational function, not a thing.[155] This primary signification means that an object must be finished and completed so that it can be genuinely related, pastness being the very basis of relationality and dependence.[156] Furthermore, an object is itself Janus-like. On the one hand, it looks back to a completed past. On the other hand, its very nature as an object requires that it be taken into account in the present coming-to-be of a subject which itself faces a future yet unborn. This double-faced nature, however, is only possible because an object, though over and done with, is never obliterated. It is rather immortal in the subject whose present coming-into-being requires an already completed (and therefore "*object*-ified") subject to synthesize as datum in its present experience.

The past according to Hartshorne, is immortal.[157] It is immortal because what has become can never be undone.[158] What has happened, happened; it can no longer be blotted out from the fabric of existence. Thomas Aquinas says as much. As he states in the *Summa Theologica*, with regard to the question whether God can undo the past, "if the past thing is considered as past, that it should not have been is impossible, not only in itself, but absolutely since it implies a contradiction."[159] And he states further that to undo what has happened, "is more impossible than the raising of the dead."[160] For Hartshorne the past is also immortal and cannot be undone because it is given a "home" in the coming-to-be of present actuality.[161] These two notions are inseparable for to become past, says Hartshorne, "only means a new entity becomes which feels the previous entity."[162]

Subjective and objective immortality

Before proceeding to a discussion of the concepts which the irrevocable nature of the past entails, it is necessary to distinguish two senses of immortality: "objective" and "subjective" immortality. Both of these senses are found in Hartshorne's discussion. But while one—objective immortality— is clearly favored, and in fact necessitated, by his metaphysics, the other is detected in his writings only elliptically, and cannot be separated from his particular view of death and the value of human life. Thus, for instance, at the beginning of his treatment of "Time, Death, and Everlasting Life" in *The Logic of Perfection*, he quotes a line from Shakespeare's *The Tempest*[163] which provides an intuitive feel for the beauty and brevity of life (whose end, shrouded in a cloud of unknowing, is captured by the metaphor of "sleep"). Using this quote, Hartshorne manages to encapsulate with peculiar poignancy the evanescent and yet valuable character of life—an evanescence that is yet not tantamount to an ultimate nihilation, and a value that does not require an eternal continuation of an already completed earthly career.

The basic position espoused by Hartshorne with regard to the question of immortality is that although death represents a necessary limit to our fragmentary existence,[164] death is neither the end, understood as the annihilation of all that had been, nor the beginning of yet another form of existence in continuation of what had in fact come to an end. The first represents the transformation of being into nonbeing; the second, the belief in personal or subjective immortality. Subjective immortality concerns the belief, enshrined in numerous religions, in the everlasting life of mortals, the continuation or prolongation of one's career halted by death and, as Hartshorne puts it "the unexpressed but felt anticipation of living virtually forever."[165] While these basic intuitions enshrined in the religious beliefs of humankind embrace certain truths, Hartshorne nevertheless insists that such truth is mixed with error. Intellectual and spiritual effort is required in order to purify these concepts of error and thereby arrive at a closer approximation of the truth they contain.[166] Thus, our experience as creatures involves a continuous losing of life—the realization of which is salved by the *hope* which some religions offer, viz., that death is not the end. But the larger context of hopefulness in which the experience of death is situated does not necessarily require that it be the individual himself who will continue existing.[167]

One can detect in Hartshorne's writings a certain harshness toward those who espouse the idea of personal immortality, especially when tied with the notion of a divine justice which metes out postmortem rewards and punishments.[168] He says that one can find in such beliefs irrational elements not in the sense of doctrines that transcend reason, but "doctrines below and contrary to it."[169] This seems to be a pointed rebuke of those who refuse to accept the inevitability of death and obstinately hold onto the continuity of their earthly careers by refusing to accept that God alone is subjectively immortal.[170] However, he also criticizes those who for some reason or another believe death as an end which signifies *annihilation*. A two-fold rejection therefore becomes quite evident. On the one hand, he does not subscribe to the traditional belief in immortality; on the other hand, he rejects the idea that death means the becoming-nothing of what was once being. For instance, in his brief intellectual autobiography in the volume of *The Library of Living Philosophers*, dedicated to his thought, he states: "Everywhere there are those who believe they can accept death as the nullification of our earthly careers (apart from our influences on posterity) and those who hope for the continuation of our individualities in posthumous careers on earth or in some supernatural heaven."[171] The desire for a continuation of one's personal career is regarded as an immature stage of spiritual development. It is a stage which has yet to fully assimilate and integrate the truth that for one who has realized that "we are called to love God first and foremost" and that because "we find our own fulfillment in loving God," a life of virtue and love is its own reward.[172] Thus he writes: "The time and place to look for the rewards of virtue is now and here. If you cannot on earth find good in being good and ill in being or doing ill, then I doubt whether you will find it in any heaven or hell."[173]

Subjective immortality therefore, if understood to mean the simple continuation of one's career, is rejected by Hartshorne although in some of his writings, he appears at least not to be completely averse to the idea. In Chapter Ten of *The Logic of Perfection* for instance, one can glean a certain receptivity to it. Here Hartshorne says that death cannot be regarded as the destruction or fading of the book of one's life, only "the fixing of its concluding page." Now he argues that while this means that nothing more can be added nor subtracted to what has been written in the book, he also says that subtracting from the writing appears more impossible than the adding to it. Then he makes a statement which is quite suggestive, if not revealing: "Perhaps personal existence without a body is indeed impossible, yet the analogy to a butterfly with its succession of bodies, while remote and implausible, is not necessarily strictly inapplicable."[174] What these lines disclose is a particular distinction that can be discerned in Hartshorne's understanding of survival after death, i.e., between, on the one hand, continuation-in-*transformation*, and on the other, simple *continuation*.[175] The first opens the possibility for us to say that death is not the end in the sense that the book will have further chapters; the second, which says simply that there will be no end and that the chapters will be infinite is, according to Hartshorne himself, a genuine impossibility.[176] These thoughts, however, while seeming to open the possibility of other ways of reinterpreting the traditional notion of immortality remain largely unexplored by him.[177] But judging from Hartshorne's own words in *The Logic of Perfection* concerning the butterfly with its succession of bodies, while there is a downright rejection of the classical religious notion of immortality, he appears largely indifferent (or perhaps noncommittal), as to how the particular details of "whatever may or may not happen upon or after our death" are to be played out. Why? Because on the one hand, he is only concerned that immortality is not understood to mean the mere continuation of existence entailing an infinite series. On the other hand, the question of subjective immortality is subsumed and assimilated into what is for him the more important issue that, if fully understood and appreciated, sheds clearer light even on the traditional conceptualization. This is the issue of objective immortality in whose compass the subjective immediacy of the entities so retained is embraced.[178]

The reasons Hartshorne has for rejecting immortality as a career after death are very much the same reasons—structure-wise—that he has for rejecting the notion that the death or perishing of entities signifies the simple becoming *nothing* of what was once *being*. "Death," he says, "is not sheer destruction, the turning of being into non-being."[179] It is not the destruction of the reality we have achieved.[180] He asks, "If death means that the careers we have had become nothing, or a heap of dust, what is history about, or biography? And what is autobiography, if the past experiences and actions are now reduced to mere faint and partial recollections and a few records, photographs and the like?"[181] It is here that the notion of "objective immortality" comes in. For Hartshorne takes it to be the *middle ground* between the downright rejection of immortality and the almost vulgar holding-onto-existence which insists on the continuation of one's life on earth or in some supernatural heaven.[182] This idea of a middle way is also spelled out in the book, *Omnipotence and Other Theological Mistakes*, in which he regards as the fifth mistake among the six that he enumerates,[183] the notion of immortality as a career after death. Here he juxtaposes the two extreme assumptions of a mere corpse, on the one hand, and survival in a new mode of heavenly or hellish existence, on the other.

The concept of the objective immortality of actual entities is built on the idea of the imperishability of the past in the mind and memory of God.[184] The manner by which an entity—whose becoming already lies in the past—is taken into the present coming-into-being of another entity is analogous to the doctrine of the becoming of the divine reality which everlastingly synthesizes the data provided by all of creation.[185] Creatures are not subjectively immortal; they do not prolong their careers after death. However, creatures do not become nothing either when they die. That they once were is a fact that cannot be obliterated. But this cannot be because posterity will keep their memory alive, since by all indications a time will come when there will scarcely be anyone left to remember anybody.[186] Rather, Hartshorne's solution is that God alone is subjectively immortal. God alone is ultimately and literally deathless.[187] Creatures are given a share in this immortality by their contribution to the divine life which, because it is forever creative of novelty, will continuously need to synthesize the data provided to it by creation's past experiences.[188]

The entire past, from its largest to its smallest detail, is objectively immortal, not because it is subject to recollection of the human kind[189] but because all the joys, sorrows, triumphs, and defeats of every actuality that has ever been or will ever be will be remembered in the everlasting "treasure house of all fact and attained value" which is the mind of God.[190] In *The Logic of Perfection*, Hartshorne quotes from Richard Hovey's *More Songs from Vagabondia*, which neatly sums up in a few brief lines his thought on the matter:

> God has said, ye shall fail and perish
> But the thrill ye have felt tonight
> I shall keep in my heart and cherish
> When the worlds have passed in night.[191]

Creatures are objectively immortal. They and their past experiences become objects for the knowledge and contemplation of God.[192] They are imperishable because God who lives everlastingly will forever hold them in his gaze as "a picture which forever will hang in the divine mansion."[193] However, preservation is not the only point of such remembrance; there is the equally important dimension of valuing. The lines above speak of God not merely "keeping" the feelings of the creature that has perished, but of "cherishing" these as well. The ultimate value of life rests not in finite and limited valuation that creatures bestow upon the past, but because in God and in his appreciation alone does all that had been "add up to anything."[194]

What stands out most in this description is that the doctrine of objective immortality is in fact a "theistic yet non-conventional view of immortality."[195] The question of immortality, in Hartshorne's mind, presses us toward the theistic solution which views God as the overarching source of the "final integrative unity of reality."[196] The foregoing treatment of Hartshorne's notion of the objective immortality of concrete actualities cannot be adequately comprehended outside the context of his concept of God.

6
The Structure of an Event as Creative Synthesis

The creative impulse

It is first and foremost in the human being that the questionable claim that there is nothing new under the sun is disclosed. Even a rather superficial reflection on human existence will show this. Hartshorne gives an example. If someone were to hit me in the face, it is possible that I would react with anger. The situation seems rather simple: stimulus—being hit on the face; response—anger. In fact, an observer can say that my reaction was expected, as it would be normal for anyone in my situation to react in such manner. And depending on what the observer believes to be my perception of the assailant's motive, as well as the severity of the blow and the pain it has caused me, he could predict the intensity of my anger and perhaps even, with some degree of certainty, the manner by which I shall respond. Even here, we see that the simple prediction of a specific response to a specific stimulus is not as easy as it may seem. For two contributing factors are already mentioned, my possible perception of the other's motive, and the severity of the blow and the pain it has induced. There are, Hartshorne observes, as many forms and qualities in an experience of anger as there are cases.[1] And what an observer can articulate are only more or less rough and crude descriptions of my specific reaction. In fact, he cannot even be sure that anger will indeed be my reaction.

Let us take another example. A human person is necessarily a product of one's past: culture (in all its dimensions), ancestry, upbringing, education, past experiences, etc. Such factors mold an individual's character and personality. To some extent—more so in some individuals than in others—one's actions and reactions can be traced and predicted accordingly. They are givens which one needs to accept as part and parcel of who he is. There is no escaping the possibilities or the obstacles which they present. The human individual is a subject bound to the world. However, such circumscription is but half of the story. There is also the "transcending" half. For an individual is not a powerless captive of her former life nor of the factors that have shaped her present reality. Rather, he/she is a free agent, capable of overcoming to a considerable degree the limitations such factors impose on him/her. The stimuli which shape any particular experience or any specific person are numerous. And yet this multitude of factors do not add up to a precisely predictable response or an absolutely determined individual. Thus Hartshorne notes that "the many stimuli are given, and certainly they tell us much about the response. But it is a logical impossibility that they should tell us all."[2] The human being, he says, is a clear instance of "the coexistence of life and law in the same object."[3] And it is indeed in the delicate and complex fabric of human existence that the intimate wovenness of vitality and order stands out most. For the human being is as much a creature of volition and spontaneity as he/she is of law and regularity. He/she is as much a product of the world as he/she is a producer of this very same world.[4]

This particular condition is not limited to human reality. In Hartshorne's view, the intertwinement of freedom and determinism is a universal reality; cases of both are discernible throughout the cosmos. This situation, like that of mind and matter, can again lead to dualistic and fragmentary analyses and ontologies, reductionistic accounts, as well as simple complementarity theses. Here once more, Hartshorne's view is that such dualism is only apparent and that fragmentary, reductionistic and complementarity accounts result in inadequate portrayals of reality. But if in fact no dualism holds, which of the two categories is more ultimate? Which of the two is the more general instance of which the other is but a specific and limited case? Hartshorne's response is that creativity is the fundamental principle applicable to all reality.[5] It is the ultimate category. In this view, freedom is the more general and all-embracing concept under which is subsumed, lawlikeness, order, and regularity.

This universal and ultimate character of creativity is explained in terms of two related concepts: emergence and synthesis. The first dislodges the traditionally held notion of absolute determinism. Recognizing the reality of unpredictability and novelty, it acknowledges their more fundamental metaphysical nature vis-à-vis permanence and constancy. The second sheds light on the complex inner structure of emergence. On the one hand, it is a dynamic process of unification and integration and, on the other hand, an enshrining of the irrevocable character of past actuality and its relative necessity with regard to present acts of becoming.

Emergence

Hartshorne regards chance as a real aspect of worldly occurrences.[6] As he puts it, "Do what you will, it is an odd world from end to end, full of stupendous variety of items *not a single one* of which could have been anticipated by the mere exercise of reason."[7] On the other hand, he holds the view that law and order are genuinely discernible aspects of existence.

Things do not fall apart because the ordered and permanent are just as real dimensions of existence as are the spontaneous and the unexpected. But the very reality of law in fact demands its nonabsoluteness.[8]

Both chance and orderliness are inescapable realities in Hartshorne's philosophy. Instances of both pervade the becoming of things.[9] Hartshorne asks: "Shall we suppose that the world as a whole is one vast throw of the dice, and yet within this we not rather say that the whole is irrational, lacking 'sufficient reason', because each part of it is devoid of such reason and incapable of furnishing it to any other part?"[10] He puts forward the idea that there is no mutual exclusivity between the two categories.[11] While neither category can be dismissed, they are not on an equal footing. Instances of law dominate in some systems, instances of spontaneity in others.[12] Hartshorne, however, is also of the opinion that the spontaneous remains the more comprehensive concept; freedom is thus the more inclusive reality.

Every experience integrates in a relatively predictable manner the various data which are temporally prior to the particular act in question. These previous data upon which an experience in the process of coming-to-be feeds determine to some extent the "what" or the "ingredients" that would be available for the experience to integrate. For as Hartshorne observes: "Content has to be furnished by other experiences, we can't simply experience our present experience—of what?"[13] Experience cannot but have content. It is in a sense necessarily parasitic on prior experiences, feeding on its own previous products, and on nothing else whatsoever. Creativity itself is nothing other than responding to prior stimuli. Nonetheless, however dependent creativity may be on prior data, and however numerous such data may be, a present experience in the process of becoming cannot, in its comprehensive totality, be deducible from such myriad factors. Each experience, Hartshorne emphasizes, is a free act, for there can be no logic to the derivation of the *experience* of *a, b, c, d* from the antecedent data *a ,b, c, d*. However strong the influence data may have on the experience in question, this influence does not suffice to explain the total reality of "the *experience* of *a, b, c, d.*"[14]

No experience in its full concreteness is susceptible to being given a complete description by means of a specification of the factors that have brought it into being, however lengthy the inventory of data may be. Perceiving or remembering are instances in which the form that a present experience takes hinges on the data perceived or remembered. Hartshorne stresses that even here the plurality of antecedent factors do not fully determine the resulting character of the experience. The strict causal account misses something important to a complete description of an experience; namely, the unity of all these factors and aspects into one comprehensive totality whose very nature is that of novelty. Furthermore, the novel whole that emerges from the unification of data also possesses a uniqueness and particularity irreducible to the plurality which has constituted its present existence.[15] From the experience of several data, what has to be derived is not just any experience of these data, but precisely *this* particular experience in question. This specificity signifies, in Hartshorne's thought, a uniqueness and value that can be found in no other. The absence of any clear logical derivation of present experience from past data discloses the purely gratuitous nature of present actuality and the real nature of chance, as the relation between actuality and unrealized possibility.[16] There is a clear asymmetry that is involved here, i.e., between what has already become actual (the component data which belong to a fully settled past) and what is yet to become actualized (a partly open or unsettled future). Hence, although in its component parts, actuality is permeated by order, constancy, and permanence, it remains suffused by spontaneity and chance in its global reality.

Synthesis

Although the inescapability of chance is a genuine aspect of the real, no less so are lawlikeness and regularity. The indeterminism which Hartshorne espouses with regards presently becoming actualities does not give a *carte blanche* to sheer chaos. It does not imply that *anything* could simply happen in a particular situation. In fact, he is careful to point out that "many things will be impossible in a given situation, according to any reasonable indeterminism."[17] It is only with regard to the extremes of absolute order and sheer chaos that Hartshorne sees difficulties. Between these two, there is a vast room of moderate positions.[18]

Hartshorne's concept of indeterminism rules out sheer chaos because the becoming of novel wholes is itself oriented toward integration. Creativity is not the eruption of chance and randomness, plain and simple; creativity is also, and more properly, an act of synthesis. Thus, creativity involves a synthesis of data coming from past experiences. Becoming is the putting together of antecedent factors into a new unitary reality. However, what is put together is not created but the new inclusive togetherness that is the novel creation. The past—under which domain, are the data of experience that have already become and as such are determining factors for new instances of becoming—is that which is housed in the present. Freedom in Hartshorne's thought means the transition from the experienced antecedent many to the new unit-experience.

There is thus no such thing as absolute freedom. Each entity possesses only such freedom as is possible within limits, and those limits are set by the antecedent events that make up its actual world, or imposed by the free decisions of other event-individuals.[19] The coming-to-be of an event, i.e., its actuality, and the limit set upon individual acts of freedom by what, for Hartshorne, is the supreme exemplification of freedom, i.e., the freedom of God, means that freedom cannot be absolute. For Hartshorne, divine freedom is that which gives direction to these lesser forms thereby preventing unlimited disagreement and conflict.[20] The creativity/novelty that characterizes the coming-to-be of actual entities is not chaotic precisely on account of the ordering that the supreme form of freedom brings about. This, he says, is why God is at all introduced into the scheme.[21]

A genetic analysis of an event actuality

Classical attempts to reconcile change and stability have always posited the existence of an entity that does not change. In contrast to the classical way, process thought considers the abandonment of an unchanging subject of change as a fundamental tenet of its metaphysical system. Furthermore, it holds that the only way to consistently and coherently arrive at a reconciliation of change and stability, of being and becoming, is by conceiving process as essential to the nature of an actual entity. The question that arises of course is *how?* How do we conceive process as essential to the nature of an actual entity?

In dealing with this problem it is important to remember that an actual entity, the *res vera* of process philosophy, is an entity that *exists* in the fullest sense of the term, beyond which there is no other.[22] Now if an actual entity is not to be conceived as an unchanging subject but rather an entity in process, then existence and process are somehow interrelated concepts. In fact, Whitehead says that these two notions presuppose each other.[23] This of course means that if *becoming* is to be given a real place and not merely paid lip service in a metaphysical system, there has to be an "actual entity" that is "in process." For, to recognize the genuineness of becoming is to recognize that "becoming exists." But process in itself is not an actual entity. Hence, its existence requires derivation from the fullness of existence of an actual entity.[24] In this way, process presupposes existence in the full sense of the existence of actual entities, while actual existence presupposes process. Without the intrinsic involvement of process in the existence of an actual entity, we could not coherently and consistently admit process in any form.

An actual entity therefore cannot exist completely devoid of becoming; process is an essential dimension of its nature. As Whitehead states: "The process itself is the constitution of the actual entity; in Locke's phrase, it is the 'real internal constitution' of the actual entity. In the old phraseology employed by Descartes, the process is what the actual entity is in itself, *formaliter.*"[25] Process therefore is constitutive of the very nature of an actual entity. This represents the heart of process philosophy's consistent and thoroughgoing rejection of the idea of an actual entity as the unchanging subject of change.[26] Substance speaking, as Hartshorne stressed, is no more than a shorthand or simplification of the language of process.[27] For his part, Whitehead argues that "an actual entity is a process ... not describable in terms of the morphology of a 'stuff.'"[28] There is no unchanging entity that *is* or *exists* antecedently to its process of coming-to-be, just as there is no subject that is already given and presupposed by its experiences, as it is in traditional conceptualizations of the subject as a self-contained static substance. In like manner, an event cannot be conceived as "brought into being" by its process and thereafter, having "fully become," exists as a "finished" or "completed" being. This would again imply the conception of an actual entity as some kind of "stuff." An event *is* (i.e., exists) only in its process of coming-to-be.

Such mode of conceptualization is of course open to some disconcerting questions. If process were fundamental to the nature of an actual entity, does this not completely repudiate the notion of stability as genuinely belonging to the character of an event? Since an oft-repeated critique in process philosophy is that changelessness cannot account for real change, does not the claim that "an event *is*, only in its process of becoming" involve the very same difficulty—this time, change being unable to account for the reality of stability? And is the abandonment of this latter idea not tantamount to an abandonment of individuality, with its related concepts of unity and self-identity? For does the notion of individual not involve the idea of a completed unity? If it does, how can there be a unified individual if actuality exists only "in process," and when, at the end of such process, there simply is no existent at all?[29]

The discreteness of becoming

Hartshorne recognizes the difficulties that these questions represent, and he readily admits that "one of the subtlest problems which event pluralism has to face [is] the apparent continuity of process, its apparent lack of distinct units."[30] Nevertheless, he maintains that these questions arise if process is regarded as continuous, i.e., as some kind of Heraclitean flux. Against this view, he holds, with Whitehead, that the notion of a continuous process is a misconception. He considers a number of difficulties that are involved in the idea. One of these—which he dismisses as a poor argument—is the Bergsonian idea of the interpenetration of mental states.[31] He objects to Bergson's use of "inter" as yet another instance of the prejudice of symmetry,[32] and insists that the passage of becoming may involve the penetration of past states into present ones, but never present ones into past.[33] Some authors have attempted to reconcile the discreteness of becoming, as in Whitehead, and Bergson's insistence on the continuity of the flow of immediate experience.[34] The proposed reconciliation hinges on the argument that whereas the Bergsonian idea of continuity is intuitive,[35] the discrete view of becoming, in Whitehead and Hartshorne, is a result of "intelligence [making] conceptual blueprints, intellectual snapshots of experience" which ultimately divests process of its real continuity which only intuition can disclose.[36] There are two difficulties with this position. The first is a reversion to "*something like* a new substance-type metaphysics," although not necessarily involving "a substratum *underlying* the experience itself."[37]

The second, which is more significant for our discussion, is reflected in the question: "Why do we not notice the successiveness of the multiplicity of actual entities required by the theory for even the shortest of ordinary human experiences?"[38] The first proposal goes totally against the basic intuitions of process philosophy. Hartshorne considers the second. Thus, he asks: "If there are discrete events, why are they not experienced? If there are atoms and molecules in matter, why are they not perceived?"[39] The answer he gives is intimated in his question, to preface his treatment of the objection: "Is process given as continuous or is it merely not given as discrete?" Instead of seeing the problem as deleterious in any final sense to the theory of the atomicity of process, Hartshorne points out that "direct human perception reveals only certain of the gross outlines, vague in every spatial and temporal way as to exact details, of the world."[40] Perception only goes up to a certain point, after which it becomes in large part, noncommittal, neutral, indefinite, or vague. Once this threshold is crossed, much is left to an overwhelming urge to interpret. It is such an urge that Hartshorne suspects is behind the allegedly experienced continuity of becoming. Experience at its best is simply vague with regard to any discreteness that may be there. This vagueness, Hartshorne insists, is misread as a revelation of actual continuity. And thus he concludes:

> Experience is at most quasi-continuous, or pseudo-continuous. To say more implies a fundamental error in theory of perception, of what it could possibly accomplish. ... Obviously there is something wrong with the notion that continuity, in any strict sense, is given. Yet definite discreteness is also not given. The third possibility, which seems to fit the hard facts, is that a real discreteness is vaguely or approximately given.[41]

Process is therefore regarded as "subtly discontinuous or quantized."[42] It is constituted by discrete actualities, drops of experience[43] which Hartshorne terms events.[44] Becoming is itself not continuous but discrete, or in Whiteheadian terms, epochal.

The idea of becoming as continuous is inadmissible in process philosophy because it involves two notions, the combination of which results in a vicious regress. These are the concepts of process and continuity.[45] Whitehead takes into account the point of Zeno's paradox which would entail that if process were continuous, then any portion B, would supersede an earlier portion A. However since B itself is a continuous process, the tail end of B, say B_2 would have superseded an earlier portion B_1. Now what applies to B, also applies to B_1, and so on and so forth.[46] The vicious regress involved here only goes to show that there is something amiss in the notion of a continuous process. The discreteness of process is the conclusion that is drawn from this consideration. As Whitehead states: "if we admit that 'something becomes,' it is easy, by employing Zeno's method, to prove that there can be no continuity of becoming. The actual occasions are the creatures which become, and they constitute a continuously extensive world. In other words, extensiveness becomes, but 'becoming' is not itself extensive."[47] Actual entities in process philosophy are therefore considered as discrete or atomic units of becoming. There is a real plurality in terms of real countable units, and there is the creation of a new unit of definite reality with each particular unit.[48] This means that there is no single continuous process of becoming. Continuity therefore "comes to be" through the succession of unit becomings, but there is no such thing as a continuous process of becoming. Rather it is constituted by the coming-to-be of individual events. The succession of these atomic events is what gives rise to the extensive continuity of the universe.[49]

The structure of an actual entity

If, as Whitehead holds, the ultimate metaphysical truth is atomism,[50] and if each "atomic" actual entity is itself a "process of becoming," are we not confronted with an infinite regress, since the latter portion A_2 of an actual entity A supersedes the earlier portion A_1, and so on and so forth? The problem, it seems, cannot be solved simply by means of further and further atomization. The extensive character of an actual entity cannot preclude its also being a unified *whole*, for it is as characterized by such wholeness that entities are in fact given to us in experience. For instance, Whitehead quotes William James who says: "Either your experience is of no content, of no change, or it is a perceptible amount of content or change. Your acquaintance with reality grows literally by *buds or drops of perception*. Intellectually and on reflection you can divide these into components, but as immediately given, they come *totally or not at all*."[51]

Here as well, Zeno's argument must be made to bear. For a serious difficulty does arise if each actual entity, i.e., each process of becoming, is conceived as itself a continuous process of one portion of becoming superseding another, and another *ad infinitum*. Zeno's argument, Whitehead notes, " so far as it is valid, elicits a contradiction from the two premises: (i) that in a becoming something (*res vera*) becomes, and (ii) that every act of becoming is *divisible into earlier and later sections* which are themselves acts of becoming."[52] Whitehead argues that the contradiction can be avoided by rejecting the latter of the two premises. This would entail that we cannot validly regard the atomic process of becoming as a continuous process of simple succession if we must likewise hold that becoming is the coming-to-be of an actual entity. And the latter is the more important notion to uphold, i.e., if "process" is to be given room at all in our metaphysical system. Otherwise, there would simply be "nothing which becomes."

The notion of process as atomistic provides for an adequate means of resolving some of the problems involved in conceiving the relationship of stability and change, of being and becoming, of the one and the many, of selfhood and otherness. For so long a time, because of the seemingly insuperable difficulties involved in reconciling it with unity and individuality, change has been denied as belonging to the very nature of an actual entity. For much of classical philosophy, for an entity "to be" meant that it had to be what it is. No room was allowed for the possibility of change, for to do so entails that the entity would have to cease being what it is and thereby become *something other than* what it is. Thus, for instance, Étienne Gilson, in his book *Being and Some Philosophers*, notes:

> it is one and the same to be *a* thing and to be a *thing*. In other words, the "really real" is *free from otherness*, because what we could ascribe to it as other than what it is would actually be "another being." For the same reason, being as such is free from change. In a doctrine where *to be* is *to be the same*, otherness is the very negation of being. Thus, in virtue of its self-identity, which forbids it to change unless indeed it ceased to be, true being is immutable in its own right.[53]

The kind of change implicated in neoclassical metaphysics is one of a process whose very nature is the coming-into-existence of an actual entity understood as extensive and at the same time a unified *whole*. "Process" cannot be conceived simply as being devoid of such discrete individualities. Rather, there is a relation of mutual requirement between process and individuality.[54] An event as an atomic entity is an indivisible whole. This means that conceived as a "bud" or "drop" of becoming, an event is an individual unit that *becomes as a whole*. In this way it changes in the sense of involving a process in its becoming. But since at the point of completion of its own process of becoming, its existence necessarily ceases, an actual entity can also be said to remain *changeless*.[55] This last statement represents the oft-misunderstood Whiteheadian concept of the "perishing" of actual entities.[56] This notion brings us to the core of our analysis of the nature of an event actuality, namely, the structure of an actual entity itself as both a "subject" and a "superject."

Hartshorne himself admits to being "puzzled ... by talk of 'earlier' and 'later' phases in the becoming of entities said to be devoid of actual succession."[57] Furthermore, he expresses a certain degree of reservation with regard to the Whiteheadian notion of the "perishing" of actual entities.[58] In fact, in another place, he calls the idea "a metaphor which has sadly misled many."[59] At the same time, however, he does seem to implicitly adopt it in his conception of the relation of pastness to the becoming of an event—a relation that is of paramount importance to the overall scheme of Hartshorne's metaphysics and his understanding of the nature of actuality. In *Creative Synthesis*, he writes that "actuality is pastness, since presentness is a becoming actual rather than a being actual ... They (*event-actualities*) 'perish yet live for evermore' is the final word of *Process and Reality*, and to this I adhere."[60]

An event is a process of concrescence, i.e., the coming together of the antecedent data prehended into a unified and novel whole. Concrescence signifies the process of becoming that is constitutive of a novel actuality. According to Whitehead, "it is a derivative from the familiar [L]atin verb meaning 'growing together.' It has the advantage that the participle 'concrete' is familiarly used for the notion of complete physical feeling. Thus Concrescence is useful to convey the notion of many things acquiring complex unity."[61] Every novel whole is therefore concrete and actual by virtue of its process of concrescence. Whitehead further analyzes this "growing together," into its constitutive phases. Thus the initial phase in which the innumerable antecedents are prehended is followed by further phases of activity whereby the diverse physical prehensions are unified into one complete and integrated prehension. He explains: "An actual entity is a process in the course of which *many operations* with incomplete subjective unity terminate in a completed unity of operation, termed the '*satisfaction*.' The 'satisfaction' is the contentment of the creative urge by the fulfillment of its categoreal demands."[62] Whitehead thus speaks of two termini to each actual entity's process of becoming. The first is its components in their disjunctive diversity. These pass into the second point, which is their concrete togetherness.[63] Now each *terminus* or phase is itself complex—the first is made such by the plethora of data; the second, by the fact that the integration achieved by the innumerable "givens" presupposes a complex activity, akin to that of a "subject" that has recognized the mutual incompatibilities that characterize the data, and has worked with such incompatibilities in order to produce a novel entity.

These divisions and further subdivisions into more and more atomic conceptualizations that Whitehead embarks upon disclose that an actual entity is by its very nature a highly complex "concrescence of prehensions." Hence, although a unified and integrated whole, each actual entity remains nevertheless susceptible to an analysis that distinguishes the various factors that make up its complex unity.[64] This is what Whitehead means when he says that while being in fact undivided, an event still is divisible.[65] And its divisibility is precisely due to the fact that various factors enter into, and make up its complex character as a unified and integrated whole.[66] However, it must be recognized that the divisibility of an actual entity is no more than an abstraction from the entity's concrete totality.[67] As such, these abstract divisions require constant and consistent reconnection with the concrete reality, whose nature we are attempting to discover in the first place. Furthermore, as Hartshorne likes to stress, however many the antecedents that enter into the make-up of an event, however innumerable the prehensions implicated in the coming-to-be of an event, the resulting novel entity remains but one unitary whole, an integrated "subject" of feeling.

As a concrescence of prehensions therefore, an event is a subject of experience. Whitehead points out that although he retains the term "subject," because in this sense it is familiar in philosophy, it remains nonetheless mis-leading,[68] primarily due to the insurmountable difficulties involved in try-ing to dissociate it from the idea of an unchanging subject of change. It is on account of this latter reservation that Whitehead accords a double aspect to the notion. He insists that it must always be understood as possessing this duality of description. He says, "It is fundamental to the metaphysical doc-trine of the philosophy of organism, that the notion of an actual entity as the unchanging subject of change is completely abandoned. An actual entity is at once *the subject experiencing* and *the superject of its experiences.*"[69] The subject is not that which is already given and presupposed by its expe-riences, as was the case in classical conceptions of a self-contained and static substance. While the numerous prehensions of data require a subject, this latter concept cannot be conceived as already in being prior to the process of prehending. For to say that it is so nullifies the foundational idea of process; namely, that the being of an actual entity is in its becoming.

However, the subject *strictly speaking* is not that which finally emerges from the feelings or experiences of the actual entity. Although it is emergent from the process of becoming, it is not an entity that exists *after the fact* of becoming. This is what Whitehead calls the superject. Although it may seem confusing at first, Whitehead's distinctions and the reasons he has for mak-ing them are understandable. An actual entity understood in its reality as an integral whole is neither simply the "given" nor simply the "result" of process. A subject does not exist simply before or simply after its own process of coming-to-be. Its locus is neither simply *anterior* nor simply *pos-terior* to its becoming because it is actually *in both*. This is why Whitehead makes use of the term "subject-superject" to describe the complete reality that the notion of subject is supposed to convey. Hence, the subject under-stood as an integral whole is: "the subject-superject and neither half of this description can for a moment be lost sight of. The term 'subject' will be mostly employed when the actual entity is considered in respect to its own real internal constitution. But 'subject' is always to be construed as an abbre-viation of 'subject-superject.'"[70] A subject becomes as a whole. It is not given as a datum to which experiences are merely superadded as "accidental" qual-ities are added to a thing. A subject arises in the fundamental process of becoming which aims at satisfaction and achievement of unity. Upon achievement of this satisfaction, however, the actual entity in its aspect as "subject in the process of becoming" reaches what Whitehead calls its own "absolute self-attainment" and is then transcended. At this juncture, the actual entity is then describable in its aspect as "superject." At this point its subjective immediacy comes to an end—perishes and becomes objectively immortal—thus becoming available as a completed datum for further influ-ence in the future.[71]

To understand an event in the fullest sense of the term is to understand it in terms of these two particular aspects. And to discuss it in either of these aspects as subject or as superject alone is a conceptual abstraction. It must be noted of course that Whitehead himself does not ordinarily identify which aspect of the actual entity his statement is referring to. This can create some confusion if one did not supply the intended differentiation. Thus, for instance, his statement that "an actual entity does not become" can be easily misunderstood. Or "every actual entity is what it is, and is, with its definite status in the universe, determined by its internal relations to other actual entities."[72] Lines such as these seem to imply a denial of creative freedom to actual entities, which Whitehead stresses in many other parts of his work. Here, however, the term "actual entity" is being used to describe the entity in its total nature as subject and superject, wherein it is indeed completed. Having already achieved satisfaction, it becomes a novel datum to be synthesized by further acts of becoming. But it remains important to realize that this satisfaction is achieved only through an *initial* self-creative process of the actual entity in its aspect as subject.

In its aspect as superject, the actual entity *is*, as the actual entity as subject *is not*. It is completely determined within itself, and is devoid of all indecision and process. In its guise as superject, the actual entity will serve as data for prehensions for future actual entities and will, in such function, be objectively immortal and unchanging.[73] In this concrete finality, the actual entity is "nothing else than a decision referent beyond itself."[74] An event actuality in its guise as superject is thus the actual entity that has lost its subjective immediacy but has acquired definiteness and objectivity.[75] As it becomes a permanently completed being,[76] however, it perishes, but in doing so, assumes the role in a transcendent future.[77] "Perishing" is not the reduction to simple nonbeing. It is rather, the transformation of process into a fully objective datum for further, i.e., future, creative acts of synthesis. For as Whitehead emphasizes, "it belongs to the nature of every 'being' that it is a potential for every 'becoming.'"[78] This is "how the past lives in the present. It is causation. It is memory. It is perception of derivation. It is emotional conformation to a given situation, an emotional continuity of past with present. It is a basic element from which springs the self-creation of each temporal occasion. Thus perishing is the initiation of becoming. How the past perishes is how the future becomes."[79]

Perishing

Hartshorne expresses a number of reservations with regard to this Whiteheadian notion, however. "Perishing" is too suggestive of death and lifelessness.[80] Whitehead does in fact quote from the prophet Ezekiel, who beheld a field of dried bones and skeletons which God had commanded him to raise from the dead: "So I prophesied as he commanded me, and the breath came into them, and they lived, and stood up upon their feet, an exceeding great army."[81] Indeed, Whitehead calls this "the miracle of creation." And yet, the very quotation from Scriptures suggests that the materials out of which the "exceeding great army" is raised, are, in Whitehead's words, "dry bones"[82] of the dead. This Hartshorne takes to run contrary to Whitehead's final word in *Process and Reality*, where the latter stresses that events "perish and yet live for evermore." Hartshorne notes further that there seems to be a contradiction between Whitehead's saying that actual entities do not change and the idea implicit in the notion of perishing that an actual entity's subjective immediacy "dries up"—thereby connoting change.[83] The most significant difference between Whitehead and Hartshorne, however, is that for the latter, there is no absolute loss of subjective immediacy in the actual entity. An entity's subjective immediacy is never lost, for it is retained in their objective immortality in God. As Marjorie Hewitt Suchocki points out: "In Hartshorne's view, objective immortality within the life of God includes the subjective immediacy of the occasion so retained."[84]

Of course, we could argue with some authors that by "perishing," Whitehead meant no more than "being inherited," and that his intention in utilizing this term was clear and precise. Hartshorne himself recognizes this in some of his works.[85] William Christian, in his book *An Interpretation of Whitehead's Metaphysics*, has argued that although there is that element in Whitehead's notion of perishing that is suggestive of death and the "drying up of subjective immediacy"—as in the case of the field of dried bones and skeletons in Ezekiel—this should be taken to mean simply that an entity must perish with regard to its subjective immediacy before it can be objectified, i.e., taken into as datum of experience, by another entity.[86] This notion has in fact, its variant in Scriptures as well: "Unless a grain of wheat falls to the earth and dies, it remains just a grain of wheat. But if it dies, it produces much fruit."[87] As Christian suggests, this is a valid way by which Whitehead's concept of immediacy can be understood.[88] It is what needs to perish upon attainment of satisfaction in order that the fully completed entity may become a datum for further becoming. It is most likely the case that Hartshorne's chief complaint against this idea centers around what he sees as an inconsistency in Whitehead's insistence that, on the one hand, there is no loss or obstruction in the consequent nature of deity, and, on the other hand, the idea that subjective immediacy vanishes leaving only the objectively immortal and abstract superject.[89] Hartshorne argues that Whitehead seems to waver between these two positions.[90]

Hartshorne's complaint is not unjustifiable given that for him, the Whiteheadian dictum that "nothing is lost in God," is the far weightier concept.[91] And given the particularly Hartshornean conception of God as the locus of all creativity, it is far more consistent for him to hold the notion that finite entities do not lose their subjective immediacy (especially not before these are objectified) but retain this in their objective immortality in God, than to hold for instance that a finite entity is present in God only *objectively* but not in its subjective immediacy.[92] This of course does not mean, as Hewitt Suchocki noted, that Hartshorne admits subjective immortality. Indeed he admits this only as somehow "inserted" into the objective immortality in God.[93] For Whitehead, on the contrary, the process of becoming is not prehendable since it is not determinate. Thus, what cannot be saved by God's prehension is the event's subjectivity inherent in its process of coming-to-be. Deity does prehend all occasions in the full immediacy of their being. However, there is still the "perishing of becoming," because the process of becoming—as not prehendable—is not prehendable by God either.[94] But as Hartshorne stresses in *Philosophers Speak of God*, this would create difficulties for a view of God's supereminent character. He asks, "If abstractness or limitation affects even divine prehensions, in what is their 'supreme' quality?"[95] Hartshorne has rejected a literal interpretation of the two perplexing points in Whitehead as is found for instance in Christian's book. For as Griffin notes, Hartshorne's rejection of this type of interpretation hinges on his desire to bring them into harmony with the apparent affirmations in Part V of *Process and Reality*, where Whitehead insists that "nothing is lost."[96]

Thus, there can likewise be no inconsistency or contradiction in the Whiteheadian thesis—Hartshorne himself recognizes this.[97] But here once again, the differences point us back to that fundamental difference in concern we have spoken of earlier. The loss of subjective immediacy, which for Whitehead is inherent in an event that has arrived at its completion, is for Hartshorne attributable only to the finitude and inherent limitation of the capacity for prehension of nondivine prehenders. Unlike God, "they have to abstract from things so much that they are no longer conscious of their immediacy."[98] The line that distinguishes the two views is hair-thin. But it makes all the difference when it is the "ultimate concern" of each metaphysical system that we are dealing with. Hartshorne's theistic concerns are of primary importance in his philosophizing. (This has led him to put greater emphasis on the retention by God of the subjective immediacy of objectified occasions.) Unlike him, Whitehead seems to have kept a cautious but still well-thought-of distance.

God and Creativity

The description of actual entities, i.e., in terms of their constitutive structure as well as their careers, is so intimately bound up in the Hartshornean scheme with what he takes to be their supreme exemplification: deity itself. God, for Hartshorne, represents the summit of what in nondivine entities are lesser experiential characteristics.[99] This is consistent with the generalization of experience that characterizes the methodology of neoclassical metaphysics. It represents an extrapolation, as it were, from the limited characteristics of our experience, to what Hartshorne believes to be the highest conceivable limit.[100] If, as he argues, freedom is a universal princi-ple, then "the only solution to the problem of order, or of mutual adapta-tion, is in the idea of a supreme form of freedom that issues directives to all lesser forms, directives that cannot be ignored."[101] Hartshorne affirms the genuineness of the creativity and freedom of nondivine entities and the guidance and direction that divine creativity and freedom provide to crea-turely freedom, thereby bringing these lesser forms into an ongoing cosmic order. This affirmation highlights the pervasiveness of the creative impulse but at the same time draws its boundaries. It also lays stress on the gen-uineness of novelty while emphasizing that order is just as real and explain-ing its ultimate source.

Like Whitehead, Hartshorne calls creativity, "the category of the ulti-mate."[102] There is no absolute contrast between God and the world when it comes to creativity.[103] For Hartshorne each act of creation is also an act of *self-creation.*[104] As such, the Creator is not merely creator, but in some ways also created, primarily by itself, and secondarily by the contribution its crea-tures make to its very life.[105] The divine *fiat* that had created the world is a contingent fact that, like the world, was brought into being, but within the creator himself. Hartshorne objects to the traditional view according to which an absolute gulf exists between a totally creative God and a totally created but uncreative world. Neat and definitive as this doctrine may seem, Hartshorne insists that the truth is much less simple. For even if God decided to refrain from creating the world—in which case no world would exist—God nevertheless would have created something else, namely, the decision itself.[106]

Since freedom is an ultimate principle, a final explanatory concept, this means that not only the Creator but also the creatures themselves are free and creative agents. All reality, down to the minutest entity, is creative; there is no such thing as a zero-instance of freedom and creativity. For as Hartshorne points out, "Causality is a matter of degree, and there is no one degree which fits all cases."[107] Moroever, creatures, which for Hartshorne are the effects of divine *fiat*, cannot but express the nature of its cause in one way or another. "God," he says, "being both self-creative and creative of others, produces crea-tures which likewise, though in radically inferior ways, are self-determining, and also productive of effects beyond themselves."[108] The variables that char-acterize beings on the uppermost levels of the scale of being cannot be totally absent from beings on the lowermost levels. Creativity is not the sole prerog-ative of higher entities, rather as one goes down the scale of entities, one dis-covers that all of these as well are self-creative creators, self-determining and creative of others even if this be in some slight or trivial way.

Self-creation or self-determination for Hartshorne is inseparably linked with other-creation or other-determination. As he puts it, "A free agent deter-mines not only himself, in some aspect, but also all those who know him."[109] Knowledge and awareness in a most generalized form are constitutive of an actual entity. For Hartshorne, it is in the God-world relation that this consideration applies most strictly. God is eminently knowledgeable because he is most eminently aware and is most affected by the free decisions, choices, and acts of his creatures.[110] All a creature needs to do then is determine something in himself, and he determines something in God as well.[111] For as Hartshorne insists, "either we determine the divine knowing, in some degree, or we determine nothing at all."[112] This is why John Cobb describes the divine perfection as it is conceived by Hartshorne as God perfectly receiving all that happens in the world and perfectly responding to it.[113]

The eminent openness of God to the influence of his creatures represents but one side of the coin which is universal creativity itself,[114] the other side being the eminent and supreme influence that he exerts on all lesser creative agents.[115] A supreme form of freedom is necessary in order to secure the freedom of the lesser forms.[116] Using Whiteheadian terms, we can say that God is the "aboriginal condition"[117] which qualifies each and every instance of creativity by supplying each event with "that initial aim from which its self-causation starts."[118] As Whitehead would put it: "His particular relevance to each creative act, as it arises from its own conditioned standpoint in the world, constitutes him as the 'initial object of desire' establishing the initial phase of each subjective aim."[119] And since the process of self-creativity is governed by the subject's own "ideal of itself," God being the provider of this "ideal," is the sure foundation and ultimate reason of creaturely creativity and self-creativity. God and the world *together* act in concert in the creation of each new occasion of experience. God provides the entity in the process of becoming with an initial aim that affords the best resolution to an *impasse* created by the limitations of the actual world.[120] It could of course be asked if God would not in effect be the one ultimately responsible for the outcome of any creative process. If the actual world determines the realm of real potentiality for an entity, and if God provides it with its initial aim, wherein does an entity's freedom actually lie? This is a question we need to explore further in the next section.

Divine prehension of the past

According to Hartshorne, what God prehends is the previous situation, i.e., the realm supplied by the actual world, of entities-already-become. God interprets this realm in such a way that he gives the entity its initial subjective aim. However, out of this subjective aim, the entity alone creates its final and fully concrete subjective aim. And only when the entity has done so does God prehend what has been fully created. According to Hartshorne, "God waits to see what you or I may decide."[121] An actual entity is not created by God's prehending it. The divine creative influence upon a present event does not result from the divine prehension of that event, but of the divine prehension of a past actual situation from which the present event has arisen. The event actualities that God prehends are presuppositions of the particular divine prehension, not vice versa. Hence, God does not make an event by prehending it.

By providing the initial subjective aim, however, God is indeed exerting influence upon the actual processes of the world. This influence is disclosed by the fact that embedded in the subjective aim is the limit set by God to creaturely freedom. God sets boundaries to the freedom of creation by establishing a general order. Hartshorne is thus refuting the view that the various forms of experience scattered through nature miraculously restrain or control themselves and each other and thus preserve a measure of harmony or mutual compatibility.[122] The difference between the Hartshornean view and that of classical theism is that God's influence is not of a deity who is completely in charge and absolutely omnipotent without qualification. For Hartshorne there is nothing contradictory in the notion that the "greatest possible power (which by definition is *perfect power*) may not be the same as 'all the power that exists united into one individual power.' For such union of all power may be impossible. Had God 'all the power there is', he must be responsible for all that happens."[123] There is a division of powers, and as such, a division of responsibilities as well. Allurement and persuasion, not tyranny and coercion are the paradigm notions which articulate the divine reality's relation with the world.[124] God sets the best or optimal limits to creaturely freedom.[125] The initial subjective aim simply provides the entity with a range of possibilities to be realized. It remains up to the entity to select, as it were, from this realm of possibilities whatever it wants to realize. The divine action serves merely to guide the process of becoming.[126] It sets up lines of demarcation stemming disorder and confusion.[127] Throughout this process, moreover, the subjective aim continues to undergo development, specification, and definition. "The lure for feeling," as Whitehead remarks, "develops with the concrescent phases of the subject in question."[128] Thus, what began with a range of conditioned alternatives provided by past occasions of becoming is directed toward greater coherence and definition through the successive decisions made by the event-in-process. This renders the actual entity, the autonomous master of its own becoming.[129] It also makes of the event's own aim the final locus of freedom within the limitations presented by the causal influence of the already-settled past and the principle of order provided by the divine lure.

A particularly significant question to ask, however, is: What lies behind the possibility of an event to follow the ideal aim? If freedom dwells in the actual entity's own aim, we must ask if the exercise of this freedom would lie in the event's ability to perhaps modify its initial aim, i.e., in its ability to ratify or deviate from it. Is the locus of freedom in the ability to modify the aim or does it lie in *something else*? If it were in the ability to modify the aim, does this not result in the initial aim's degradation? John Cobb saw this as a possible difficulty and said that the Whiteheadian notion of "graded relevance" might solve the problem.[130] But this is exactly the problem. For if the locus of freedom is in the entity's ability to modify its aim, then there is a degradation.

There are two possibilities to avoid this problem. First, we can say that God does not specify a possibility as the ideal toward which an event is lured, but that the lure is of a more general character leading the event toward an exhaustive range of possibilities for realization. The difficulty with this suggestion is that it renders vacuous the meaning of divine persuasion. In leading an event toward the widest range of possibilities for realization, God would for all intents and purposes be luring the event toward nothing. While this secures the divine activity in terms of an efficient causality, it eliminates it in terms of final causality. The second possibility is to say that God's persuasive activity leads an event only toward some indeterminate ideal or particular type of realization. In this way, the initial aim may be said to undergo some sort of modification; but instead of its being degraded, we can say that the divine ideal which was in fact initially indefinite, simply becomes progressively more distinct.[131]

Notwithstanding these perplexities that arise from the suggestion that freedom dwells in an entity's ability to modify, deviate from, or ratify its initial aim, what seems to be suggested is that there is a distinction between a positive conception and a negative conception of freedom. The positive conception of freedom is a *freedom for*, a positive power of self-realization, or the ability to develop one's own innate capacities to the full. Within this positive conception, the ideal aim is that possibility which enables the event in the process of becoming to realize its own potentialities. To be free in the positive sense is to be "free in the service of God," and hence to be truly oneself.[132] After all, God always aims for the good as such—this aim being but a vague outline, the particularization of which is left to creatures.[133] To choose a different aim therefore is not merely to deviate from the ideal, it is no less than a diminution of genuine freedom. Negative freedom on the other hand is *freedom from*. It is simply the absence of coercive constraints—being able to do *this* rather than *that*. It appears that such negative conception of freedom is what underlies questions concerning whether freedom should be understood as lying in the ability to modify or deviate from the ideal supplied by God. It is certainly true that freedom lies in the ability of an entity to modify or deviate from the divine ideal; but this is freedom in the negative sense, the ability to say no and the freedom from all constraints. But it is just as true, and more significant for both Whitehead and Hartshorne, that freedom lies in the ability to say yes, to affirm the outline of good which God wills, vague and indeterminate as it may be.

To the question whether the locus of freedom is in the ability to modify the aim or whether it lies in *something else*, the answer would have to be that it lies in both, i.e., in the negative conception of freedom presupposed by the first alternative and in the positive conception of freedom which underlies the second. They are not mutually exclusive. However, the first alternative is of lesser significance, not only for the reasons already mentioned, but more so because of the proviso that God does not coerce.[134] And in this regard, an entity may indeed choose to deviate from the ideal, but divine power will not force it to do otherwise if this is what the entity so desires.[135] The second alternative is more important for our discussion and for clarifying Hartshorne's own position as well as the relation of his theory of divine causality in relation to the Whiteheadian doctrine of eternal objects.

Eternal objects

The gulf separating Hartshorne's thought from that of Whitehead appears the widest in regard to the doctrine of eternal objects.[136] Whitehead's eternal object is that in virtue of which an actual entity has its form of definiteness. The notion of eternal objects represents Whitehead's adoption of the Platonic forms, the Platonic ideas, or the medieval universals.[137] Each actual entity, according to Whitehead, is an individualization of the creative process; its constitution is that of ultimate creativity taking a particular form. Ivor Leclerc observes: "Just as for Aristotle there is no 'matter' purely as such, so for Whitehead there is no 'activity' purely as such; the concept of activity as such is an abstraction. There are only the concrete individual acts, which are the concrete individual actual entities."[138] The being of an act, however, depends upon having a determinate form or character.[139]

Whitehead holds that there are many eternal realities.[140] However, while the forms do exist, they do not exist as themselves actual. Rather they exist merely as the forms of definiteness for actual entities. They are "components" or "ingredients" of actual entities. But they are not simply forms of *particular* entities for different actual entities can have the same form.[141] Thus Leclerc remarks that "in the forms we have to recognize a unique kind of entity which, in certain respects, stands in an extreme contrast to 'actual' entities."[142]

Unlike actual entities, however, whose being is constituted by their process of becoming,[143] the being of eternal objects—the Whiteheadian forms—is not constituted by a process of becoming. As process is irrelevant to their nature, they truly are eternal.[144] However, process and change still form undeniable constituents of the fact of their existence. This is because they *come into existence* in that they "inform" the actualities in the process of becoming, but not in the sense that they are novel entities. This informing of entities-in-process by the eternal objects is what Whitehead terms "ingression"[145] or the "participation of other things which constitute the potentialities of definiteness for any actual existence."[146] Actual entities, according to him, arise by their participation in the things which are eternal. While suggesting a certain antecedence on the part of the eternal objects vis-à-vis the actualities in which they have ingression, we must be careful not to understand this antecedence in terms of the eternal objects existing in some sort of Platonic world of forms. Whitehead maintains that "it is mere phantasy to impute to them any sort of 'absolute reality', which is devoid of implications beyond itself."[147]

The notion of eternal objects is that Whiteheadian doctrine with which Hartshorne most explicitly takes issue.[148] In *Creative Synthesis*, Hartshorne says: "The doctrine of 'eternal objects' has always seemed to me ... an extravagant kind of Platonism, a needless complication in the philosophy of process."[149] However, as David Griffin notes, Hartshorne does not reject the notion in its entirety.[150] Hartshorne holds that we must distinguish between two radically different levels of potentialities: (i) metaphysical universals, i.e., the completely general dimensions of reality without which nothing can be genuinely conceived; and (ii) specific qualities, i.e., those which need not be instantiated in every experience, and from which one can abstract and still have meaning.[151] And he insists that only the metaphysical universals are eternal,[152] adding that he cannot accept that specific qualities, such as a determinate color "haunts reality from all eternity, as it were, begging for instantiation, nor that God primordially envisages a complete set of such qualities."[153]

At any rate, it appears that Hartshorne's main objection to the doctrine of eternal objects is restricted primarily to no. (ii). He regards it a mistake to speak of this qualitative possibility as a plurality of eternally distinct, determinate entities possessing individual identities. Instead, he says that general qualitative possibility should be considered as an "affective continuum" in which subdivisions are susceptible to being inexhaustibly created, and which is therefore "beyond multitude." The actual as concrete is finite and atomic; the possible or abstract, an infinite continuum. "Feeling is a determinable of infinite range, not a vast sum of determinates. ... Possible qualities of feeling form a continuum without definite parts."[154] There is thus no ground for supposing that besides numbers or similarly abstract entities—including metaphysical categories—every quality of sensation or feeling that occurs in experience has an eternal duplicate. As Hartshorne puts it, "Feeling as such, quality as such, yes, but not red, sweet, as determinate qualities identical with those we enjoy in experience."[155]

The divine dipolarity and identity

Despite his rejection of Whitehead's doctrine of eternal object as an unnecessary complication of the philosophy of process, Hartshorne maintains that the divine essence is an eternal object. This divine essence which is the embodiment of and constituting factor behind the ultimate dimensions of variables makes up pure possibility as a continuum of possible states of divine experience. He explains that "the necessary or eternal aspect of deity is *the only eternal object*. ... This eternal entity is not a multitude, but in the language of classical theism, is 'simple.' (Not that God is simple, but that this *aspect* of him is so)."[156] In order to fully understand this particular Hartshornean statement, we must look into the peculiar view of deity that is found in his metaphysical system, namely, the dipolar character of God.

Hartshorne's neoclassical theism is an attempt to reconcile diverse currents in traditional conceptions of God—as this was articulated in religion and philosophy—with contemporary developments in the sciences and progress in the metaphysical enterprise.[157] Underlying his monumental enterprise, reflected for instance in one of his major works co-authored with William Reese, *Philosophers Speak of God*, is the belief that no single religious or philosophical system has a corner on truth when it comes to describing the divine reality. Elements of truth as well as error are to be found in all of them. One of the areas in the philosophico-religious discussion to which Hartshorne gives much attention is the attempt to make sense of, and thereby to reconcile, the notions of divine immanence and transcendence. God in both religion and philosophy is held to be both *other-than* the world, and *present-to* the world, both absolute and relational, both "dwelling in unapproachable light," as Scripture holds, and "the one more intimate than one's most intimate thoughts," as Augustine puts it. Hartshorne believes that the "both-and" here involved is much more complex than it first appears and requires further elaboration.

As reality is dipolar, God who is the supreme exemplification of the real is also dipolar. He has an abstract pole as well as a concrete pole, an absolute aspect as well as a relational aspect, a transcendent state as well as an immanent one. The abstract aspect of deity is his absoluteness. This does not mean that absoluteness is his entire character. God is more than an abstraction and consequently, his absoluteness is but one side or pole of the totality of his being. The other pole of the divine reality is God's concrete relational side. God is both supremely relative as well as supremely nonrelative. These two, according to Hartshorne, constitute the two aspects of divine perfection, which is an excellence such that its possessor surpasses all conceivable beings.[158]

There are two ways of understanding perfection. There is that type of perfection in the Platonic-Aristotelian sense of excluding change and the possibility of being surpassed by another. It is this kind of perfection that Hartshorne believes is a most appropriate description of the divine essence, i.e., on account of its fully abstract nature.[159] This is absolute perfection. However, the belief that the idea of an absolute maximum gives us an exhaustive definition of perfection holds only on the assumption that what cannot be surpassed by another must likewise be unsurpassable by itself. Hence, Hartshorne argues that we should understand the word "perfect" not to mean that which *in no respect* can conceivably be greater, but as that "than which no other individual being could conceivably be greater, but which itself in another 'state', could become greater."[160] A perfect being on this understanding, would then be "the self-surpassing surpasser of all." This is the second way of understanding perfection, which Hartshorne calls "relative perfection." In this manner of conception, the divine reality is not self-surpassing in every way, as its abstract pole is absolutely perfect. In his concrete pole, however, God surpasses even itself as a new totality is constituted at every moment of the creative advance. This reflects Hartshorne's rejection of the classical view of God as fully abstract and completely outside the realm of all change and becoming. He notes that what lies beneath this view is the idea that a being that can change could therefore decrease in value and deteriorate. But he objects to it, arguing that decay cannot be inferred from the idea of change.[161] Although in ordinary experience, the changeable is also the corruptible, we must consider that not every data of experience we encounter is applicable to God, but rather any characteristic must be confronted with the question, Is it supremely excellent, or is it an eminent form unique to God? And with regard to the characteristic of change, since what we are talking about is change in the context of unsurpassability, the idea of corruption needs to be ruled out.[162] God cannot be held to decrease in value as this would render his unsurpassability nonsensical. For if he were subject to degeneration, there would conceivably be another being superior to God, i.e., an incorruptible being. Now this would obviously conflict with God's unsurpassability.[163] Thus, God can only increase; he cannot be inferior, even to himself. But he can, and endlessly does, surpass himself as well as others. This constitutes Hartshorne's definition of relative perfection: God is not absolutely perfect, but he is strictly all-surpassing.

The two poles of the divine reality, taken together, constitute the totality of God's being. He is neither simply one nor simply the other. However, the concrete pole is properly understood as inclusive of the absolute aspect of the divine reality. There is thus an asymmetrical relation that holds between the two poles. The abstract aspect of deity is externally related to the concrete aspect, while the concrete pole is internally related to the abstract. This latter is then externally related to all things, whereas the concrete pole is internally related.[164] As the absolute, God is the object-for-all-subjects; as concrete, he is the subject-for-all-objects.[165]

Along this line Hartshorne talks of the unsurpassability of the divine power. It is, as Hartshorne says, "power adequate to cosmic need."[166] It does not determine completely what will happen in the world. A plurality of genuine powers makes it impossible for God to be *the only power*, but Hartshorne still maintains it to be the greatest power there is.[167] Power is a social reality for Hartshorne; it is social influence. As such, causal conditions, even if these be divine, do not determine the effect in its full particularity, but only require that there be some effect of a more or less general description. Causes merely limit the possibilities open for the realization of new entities. God, being the supreme cause, while remaining the supreme instance of social influence, cannot be totally different.[168] Divine power does not interfere with the freedom and creativity of the world. It is because of this that there is an unavoidable element of chaos and tragedy in the cosmos.[169] And the only reason why there is no ultimate chaos is the "primary inspiration of deity upon all." God, though he does not totally or absolutely determine everything, nevertheless orders the world, "making the best possible use of irrepressible part-chaos of free acts."[170]

God does not eliminate chance; he limits it. He does not abolish risk; he maximizes the opportunities that are part of it. Does he maximize it for good or for evil? The universality of creativity means that God wills only the *good as such*. How this is played out however, that is, how the worldly particulars are determined—whether good or bad will result—depends on the freedom of creatures.[171] Deity does not control in an absolute manner. As the supreme form of creative freedom, he only determines how the data of the past will be synthesized.[172] He moderates and harmonizes creaturely actions, because all that is done is done also to him, whose reaction to this action "absorbs and transmutes all influences into counter influence, integrative and harmonizing in tendency, discouraging excessive factors and encouraging insufficient ones."[173]

How does God limit and optimize what would otherwise be pure chaos and randomness? As a causal agent, the successive states of his concrete pole impose restrictions upon lesser agents. Self-causation, for God as for nondivine entities, also entails the partial determination of others. As such, and in this function, God is an *efficient cause*.[174] God as efficient cause, says Hartshorne, is past.[175] "The reality of past events taken into the ever-developing and ever-growing concrete pole of the divine reality enables there to be a *de facto* totality of genuinely successive events."[176] It is thus the concrete pole of the divine reality, that as past, is an efficient cause. The absolute pole on the other hand, is the only final and supreme cause. God's essence which embodies and constitutes the ultimate dimensions of variables, is what makes up pure possibility as a continuum of possible states of divine experience.[177] From out of this continuum of possibility, qualities emerge which are only relatively indeterminate and time-independent universals. The only wholly determinate qualities are those which emerge in actualities.[178] The abstract pole of deity is the *final cause* which "informs" the actualities in the process of coming-to-be, not in terms of their particularities. The absolute pole, though "universally required by all other things, itself requires only that the class of other things be not null."[179] As the eternal final cause, the absolute pole of God's reality is abstract.[180] And it is in the prehension of this abstract aspect of the divine reality that an entity's subjective aim originates. God's absolute pole supplies each entity in the process of becoming with that initial aim from which its self-causation starts.[181]

The subjective aim, universally required by the process of becoming,[182] finds its ultimate source, not in any particular concrete state of God's being, but in the wholly abstract essence of God, the absolute, the Cause of all things and the effect of none. It is the final cause which, although immanent in the world, is nevertheless not the total concreteness of this world. For this latter is God as having actually created and now possessing all previous worlds. The concrete pole of deity embraces the abstract pole within its scope. But it is the latter which establishes God as the everlasting One and the eternal final cause which persuades the world toward the all-inclusive divine end. This immanent teleology renders creativity genuinely universal and efficacious vis-à-vis the becoming of all entities, and at the same time, renders the divine activity as the primordial limitation of freedom and creativity whose locus is the very constitution of each actual entity. At the heart of every event therefore, one finds the intertwinement of creativity and the divine *telos* which is the optimization of this very creativity.[183] It is the mingling of freedom and the divine element of limitation/optimization that discloses what can be—that which is beyond what is,[184] which according to Hartshorne, constitutes an irreducible aspect of the universe as the synthesis of the possible and the actual.[185] In this locus where freedom and its limitation/optimization are locked in embrace, the autonomous energy which is the creativity of the cosmos is unlocked, rendering the actual entity genuinely transcendent, uniting itself with the creativity of the world as it hurls itself beyond the bounds of the world.[186]

The divine essence—the defining character of God's identity—is utterly neutral to alternatives provided by creaturely becoming. Since God's concrete pole is characterized by genuine becoming, his essence or defining character can nevertheless find expression in a relational pattern while allowing God to still be himself, as it were.[187] This defining character, however, is abstract and *in itself* is nonrelational, "abstracted from its *commerce* with particulars."[188] In this sense God's essence or individuality would mean independence from others. In its essential individuality the divine reality is no less than the most neutral being, possessing an infinity of possibility on account of the utter abstractness of God's individual character.[189] Not only God's relationality, his love, care, and compassion for the world, but also his transcendent otherness, is required by the religious conception of God. In this way, the traditional philosophical and religious characteristics attributed to deity are truly safeguarded as they are eminently and invariably shown to be exhibited by God alone, independent of what the world does.[190]

This duality of aspect is in part the way Hartshorne understands the notion of an "individual." An individual exhibits self-identity through time, in as much the same way as certain abstract qualities remain the same in spite of changes in its environment. Personal identity *in itself* is an abstraction. But talk of identity isolated from the concrete minute-to-minute changes that take hold of an individual can never capture the full reality of a particular individual, "person" or otherwise. For there is another sense of identity implicated in Hartshorne's notion of the divine dipolarity. As Hartshorne insists, in God, as in all concrete realities, there are two grades of identity: "the abstract or outline individuality which the thing has indifferently at diverse times of its history, and the fullness of individuality which the thing has in a given present, as containing its history up to date an in outline foreshadowing its future."[191] This type of identity is not an abstract essence. Rather, it is a concrete reality. For even granting that the abstract form of deity is the only form of adequate or supreme personality as such, Hartshorne adds—rather emphatically—that personality is not in itself a person.[192] It is as a concrete reality that God is a person. And it is as comprehended within such concreteness that he can be said to think, will, act, and love.

In his book *The Goodness of God*, Peter Bertocci shows a clear appreciation of the fact that the idea concerning the "relational," i.e., concrete aspect of God, is important in safeguarding the religious conviction that God's character is personal. In lines of thought similar to Hartshorne's, Bertocci argues that such a God need not be conceived as self-sufficient, uninhibited by restraints other than those he imposes upon himself. Bertocci who regards his philosophy as "personalist," says that if personhood reaches its highest realization in interrelationship and communication, then God's perfection can only be enhanced—instead of weakened—by being genuinely responsive to his creation. Such a God, Bertocci adds, is like any of his creatures, exposed to risks, not far removed from those run into by human beings, in their efforts to arrive at the good. Bertocci calls this a "creative insecurity." He explains: "Insecurity inheres in the very nature of being a person whose actual freedom of personal choice is involved in the pursuit of truth and goodness. Intrinsic to the good for persons is the insecurity that can become creative, because values are compenetrating, and because persons themselves can choose orchestration-within-pattern as they change and grow."[193]

Finally, Hartshorne insists that the genetic identity of the divine personality is not a simple unity, but "an integration of a very real multiplicity of states and lives sympathetically participated in."[194] The analogy of the dipolar structure of the divine reality with the identity of human persons is unmistakable. Just as in the case of deity, so too with the identity of human persons, unchanging identity is sheer abstraction. Identity is thus an incurably abstract reality which represents the persistence of certain *defining characteristics* in a very complex reality which ceaselessly undergoes change.[195] The constitution of this complex reality, viz., a "person," in the neoclassical philosophy is drawn by Hartshorne, from his analysis of the causal structure of memory and his metaphysics of relationality.

7
Ethics and the Mnemonic Structure of Persons

Persons and personal identity

Like John Locke's and, to a considerably greater degree, Derek Parfit's, Charles Hartshorne's theory of personal identity is motivated by a moral and ethical agenda. It arises from his reflections upon concerns that underpin an exploration of a basis for a theory of ethics and social relations within process thought. For him, what constitutes the core of such theory is a repudiation of psychological egoism, i.e., the ultimacy of self-regard and self-centeredness in a theory of human concern. This view, according to Hartshorne, is founded on a misconception of the self as possessing an absolute identity. He holds that the conception of personal identity in terms of an unchanging substrate of change is an abstraction from the innumerable concrete experiences that together make up a sequence of experiences ordinarily called a "person." As we have already seen, Hartshorne regards a person as changing through time, never numerically the same from minute to minute and forever being influenced by what he has been in the past and influencing what he will be in the future.

Consequently, personal identity is understood by Hartshorne as an affair of difference along a continuous historic route of occasions whose identity with other members of the sequence is relative rather than absolute. This notion constitutes the cornerstone of ethical and social discourse within neoclassical philosophy as well. Since each person is made up of numerous other individualities that form the continuous sequence of his/her life, and since these innumerable others are not simply reducible to himself/herself as the same individual, a person is defined as genuinely *other-constituted*. His/her life is not akin to a single unchanging substance to which the experiences along the historic route of his/her career are merely attached in an external way. There is no underlying substrate of change which is the self-identical individual. Instead, what is there is a defining characteristic, an outline of possibilities for realization which confers a kind of continuity of form to a person's life. In this regard, personal identity for Hartshorne is an abstraction from the stream of atomic events in the process of coming-to-be. It is the persistence of certain defining characteristics in a very complex and orderly society possessing a pre-eminent pattern of unity and integration.

Hartshorne defines a person as a society of events connected to one another in an unbroken sequence of atomic processes of becoming. The integral unity and continuity of this society is secured by the internality of the relationships that characterize each of these minute moments. The *otherness* at the heart of each member of the stream, i.e., each event's difference from every other event in the unified series, is constituted by the externality of the actual entities' relationships. These two modes of relatedness, far from being mutually exclusive, are dynamically entwined in the very nature of the connections that hold between the billions upon billions of events that make up the "personal society." Furthermore, these two modes of relatedness are, for Hartshorne, explanatory of the genuineness of causality in the universe. In this he rejects the skeptical thesis of Hume, which regards causal relations as mere constant conjunctions. At the same time, he rejects the deterministic thesis that holds all relations to be simply internal and as such, that every entity is necessarily implicated by every other entity, thereby constituting a person as a closed system of relations.

Hartshorne arrives at his conclusions by means of an analysis of the experience of memory. He believes, contrary to Hume, that it is possible to derive from such analysis an understanding of causality that embraces both the internal and the external forms of relatedness. He argues that the structure of causality at the base of memory is asymmetrical and cumulative. A later event belonging to a particular sequence of events does not simply *inherit from* former events of the same sequence, it also *enlarges upon* the bequest of its forebears. On the other hand, former events *bequeath* to its successors the fullness that it has managed to come upon by creatively synthesizing data that had come even earlier on in the stream of atomic becomings of which it is part. This fullness which it gives is nothing other than its very self, objectively immortalized in its descendant events. There is, consequently, no room for a selfsame "I" in neoclassical philosophy, no unchanging "person." This does not amount to a denial of its reality; it is rather an affirmation of its reality as it is encompassed within something far richer in determination than itself, namely, the "I *here* and *now*," the subject in its full concreteness.

The existential foundations: ethical and relational concerns

In the final chapter of *The Logic of Perfection*, Hartshorne quotes from Albert Schweitzer's *Kultur und Ethik*, as a way of opening a discussion of the basis of ethical concern in neoclassical philosophy. "Ethics," Schweitzer points out, "is the *infinitely extended responsibility* toward all life."[1] This idea, which encapsulates Hartshorne's ethical theory, is also the point of departure in an investigation into his notion of what constitutes the identity of persons.

For it is as embedded in his ethics and social theory that his anthropological views must be considered. It is in turn within this specific domain that his account of what constitutes personal identity must be sought. This is consistent with Hartshorne's insistence that his metaphysical thinking is anchored upon genuinely existential concerns. And as we have seen for Locke and Parfit, concerns dealing with guilt, reward, and blame are integral components that shape their theories of persons and personal identity.

These concerns figure prominently in Hartshorne's thesis as well. They are also sources of reflection on the nature of this entity that can impute to itself responsibility and blame, that can hold itself accountable and can own or disown its past thoughts, deeds, and experiences, as well as anticipate future ones.[2] But in contrast to both Locke and Parfit, Hartshorne not only has a more well thought-out theory of person, he also founds his ethical and anthropological reflections upon a much more solid and well spelled-out theoretical scheme, namely, the ontology of event. It is this ontology that underpins his critique of what he terms the "illusions of egoism."[3] This critique is an important component of Hartshorne's ethical theory. For it is upon reflection on what he takes as the errors of egoistic theories of concern that he comes upon his notion of a widened concern at the basis of ethics.[4]

Hartshorne argues that the notion of a static selfhood in the midst of change lies at the very heart of egoistic theories of motivation. In "Beyond Enlightened Self-Interest," he enumerates and discusses what he calls the five illusions of egoism:

1. The notion that motivation depends basically upon the mere spatiotemporal continuity of organic careers

Hartshorne admits that there is a real difference between our awareness of our own bodily and mental continuity and that of others in that the former is much more pronounced and obvious than the latter. At the same time, he insists that this difference is one of degree. It is not absolute, and as such should not be made a reason for absolutizing one's interest in oneself over one's interest in others. "To value oneself rationally is to value oneself for the same reasons, and by the same criteria, as are used in valuing others."[5] He likewise admits that one has far greater control over the value one gives to one's own life over those of others. We understand our lives more easily, and as such it is also our greatest single responsibility.[6]

He would therefore not dispute the idea, standard in the science of psychology, that self-love and love for others are inseparable. Some psychologists, most especially those dealing with interpersonal theories, would agree with Hartshorne that our own life is our greatest single responsibility, with the proviso that we understand it to be inextricably linked with our responsibility toward the other.[7] Love for oneself and the quest for personal growth are of the utmost importance, for without these one will never discover that individuals matter.[8] But as Hartshorne insists, these are important for the very same reason that makes anyone else's life important, not just to himself, but to any rational spectator.[9] Reason requires that we value ourselves for the same reasons that we value others and vice versa.[10] It also requires that the extension of interest embrace not only oneself but others as well.

2. The unexpressed but felt anticipation of living virtually forever

Like Parfit, Hartshorne criticizes the commonly held belief that it is one's own future that matters. What is not usually asked, however, is the question, What future? To what does the term "future" refer? Is it one's own future before he dies? Or is it one's "whole future" altogether in a way that connotes personal immortality? What is common to both cases, however, is that either way our future is to become "heaps of dust." But we banish this thought from our minds rather easily. We go about our daily tasks oblivious to such ultimate possibility, facing everyday things as though we would always be there to reap what we have sown. The illusion of invincibility is not always articulated nor even recognized, but it is in many ways what powers a large segment of humankind. Youth, most especially, seems more beguiled by the idea. For its opposite does indeed seem ridiculous: How could I not be there to harvest what I have sown?

Hartshorne regards this as an illusion, and insists that what ultimately matters is not so much one's own future, but "any future as such which one can influence, sympathize with, and understand as good or bad for someone."[11] Now obviously, one's own future is included in this. But it is not the only one that matters or even that it is what matters most. "The rational aim," Hartshorne points out, "is the future good that we can help to bring about and take an interest in, now whether or not it will do us good in the future and whether or not we shall be there to share in the good. We share it now, and that is all that present motivation requires."[12]

3. The misconception of the meaning of death and the real problem of immortality

The third "illusion" is closely related to the second. Allied to the commonly held belief that it is one's own future that matters is the belief that death is either the complete nihilation of one's existence and all that it means or the simple continuation of this existence in some other state where one shall have further experiences of a scarcely imaginable kind. We have already discussed how Hartshorne rejects both these possibilities and instead tries to reconcile, via his theory of objective immortality, the truths that each possibility seeks to secure. He says that "death is merely the definitive form of a lack of permanence which pervades our entire lives."[13]

The transience of reality, he says, is not something that we encounter only at the moment of our death, but is what happens at every moment to what we were the previous moment. It is a constant element in our lives, the apparent continuity of which is actually "punctuated" by billions upon billions of deaths to what is old and births to what is new. If there is to be an existential basis to his theory of the discreteness of process, it is this: that it enables us to make better sense of the ultimate transitoriness of all existence which we encounter at the end of our lives. The notion that becoming is "in drops" enables us to have a better grasp of the minute "deaths" that occur throughout our lifetime, the coming-to-be and the coming-to-pass of the minute experiences that constitute an entire life. Each atomic unit of experience embraces in itself both the element of becoming and that of passing away, thereby holding within the bounds of its actuality genuine change as well as genuine stability.

Death is not something we encounter once-and-for-all; rather, it is something for which we are prepared by our "small deaths" at every passing moment. But it does not only prepare us for the ultimate and final encounter with our transitoriness. It also enables us to see, as Hartshorne says, that the complete rational aim cannot therefore be anything less than the service of God, whose future alone is endless and who alone fully appropriates and adequately appreciates our ephemeral good.[14] Our mortality, Hartshorne claims, should make us aware there is much more than merely our own future advantage.[15] The ultimate recipient of value is beyond any of us, individually and collectively. In this alone can the idea of immortality be reconciled with the demands of rationality.

4. The misconception of God as immutable and immune to influence of any kind

Hartshorne believes that the desire for a kind of immortality that entails the simple continuation of one's earthly career in some radically different state is underpinned by the belief that God is immutable and uninfluenced in every way by his creation. Classical theistic views have regarded God as totally different, the "wholly other." Consequently, nothing that we ever do really has any ultimate effect on him. They matter ultimately only for us and for our being assured of our own immortality and reward or punishment. Hartshorne suggests that the fear of death and the desire for personal immortality tied with the "most disgusting morality" of God meting out rewards and punishments can be overcome by the notion that what we do does affect the divine reality and has ultimate value for God. Because it does have such value, it will be taken up as a further ingredient in the divine life itself. In short, it will be "immortalized" and made continuous use of in the ever-advancing and growing concrete nature of deity.

The desire for subjective immortality is grounded on the suspicion that nothing we do will ultimately matter unless we ourselves are there to reap the fruits of our deeds, be these good or evil. Hartshorne seeks to dispel this "theological mistake." The question, what would all our experiences, good and bad, amount to if we could not be there to enjoy them? is anchored on the fear that after death, we become totally and utterly nothing. Because of this, we seem to be haunted by a nagging suspicion that nothing we do matters. For Hartshorne this fear is unnecessary if we hold that God were genuinely affected by what we do, i.e., if he took these into account and made these acts immortal by making use of them. Only such a doctrine can free us from simply equating what makes a person himself with what actually happens to him.

5. The failure to recognize the radical abstractness of personal identity

Of the five so-called "illusions" which Hartshorne enumerates, the misconception concerning the abstract character of personal identity is the one that is most pertinent for understanding his critique of egoistic motives of concern. Hartshorne makes it clear what he sees to be the foundational principle of an ethics of self-concern. He says: "That each of us is always the same human individual is true; but that each of us is always simply the same thing, the same reality, is false. We are identical through life as human individuals, but we are not identical as concrete actualities. The identity is abstract, the nonidentity is concrete. Without this distinction the language of self-identity is a conceptual trap."[16] Personal identity is an abstract aspect of life; it is not life in its concreteness. For concretely, each individual is a numerically new reality every fraction of a second. A 'person' is many different things throughout his lifetime. He is an infant, scarcely passing for a rational animal; an adult in full possession of his rational faculties, a senile individual barely different from an infant in regard to his thoughts; an individual in dreamless sleep, in a state of intoxication, perhaps delirium induced by some drug, amnesia, insanity, etc. Personal identity, argues Hartshorne, must span all these differences. And since they are not slight, personal identity must abstract from the innumerable nuances involved in each of them.

Hartshorne does not dispute that each individual is distinguishable from another. Otherness is real. And nowhere perhaps is this more true than in bodily continuity—which he admits to a significant extent. But he adds that bodily continuity is an extremely abstract feature of one's existence. It allows for very radical transformations in quality from a nearly mindless infant to the full maturity of an adult, from dreamless sleep to waking states, from states as diverse as anger to jubilation, etc. Here already otherness is implied. Hartshorne also says that many minute portions of one's body were once part of the environment, and vice versa. As far as such portions are concerned, spatiotemporal continuity connects an individual not with oneself simply, whether such "self" be in the past or the future. It also connects one with the environment, i.e., other individuals, both in the past and in the future. Indeed one's very own genetic map is a bequest of an entire past history extending as far back into the mists of time as one's earliest ancestor. And barring any vow of lifelong celibacy, which precludes bearing offspring, such genetic map will be handed on further, unto the most extreme point the yet-to-be-lived history of humankind. Physical continuity is suffused with otherness.

But what of mental continuity? Hartshorne says that our thoughts are constituted of bits that also go back to thought or knowledge not simply our own, but some of which, in the future, will be part of the knowledge of others. He explains, "If I am influenced now by what I have been in the past, I am as genuinely influenced by what others have been in the past."[17] Apart from the already-granted abstract physical distinguishability, Hartshorne asks where then lies any absolute distinction between relation to self through time and relation to others? His answer is that it lies in nothing concrete for it is an abstraction. It is when we forget this partial and abstract nature of personal identity that we run the risk of adopting a self-interest theory of motivation. In such an instance, one cares about one's future because it is first and foremost one's own. And though one may care for another's future, one does so not primarily on account of the other, but because the other's well-being will ultimately redound to one's own. One's own future advantage is then the end, while contributing to the other's advantage is but a means—the ethics of egoism.

Ethics: the self transcending and the self transcended

There are two senses by which we can say that egoism traps an individual within himself. First, since the perspective of genuine otherness is eclipsed, the social factor is not allowed to contribute its own complexity to the process by which an individual's concrete identity is established. One is oneself no matter if one were the last and only entity that existed in the entire cosmos.[18] The other may add something to one's nature, but such addition is ultimately superfluous to one's own constitution. Second, the trajectory of growth and development which is the nature of all actuality is stifled, leaving the person languishing in sterility and decay. Whitehead refers to such individuals trapped in their egoistic shells as "good people of narrow sympathies,"[19] who, after having arrived at some point of progress, refuse to move any further. They thus languish in what little goodness they have achieved, thereby nullifying any ultimate good that can yet be accomplished. "Their case on a higher level," Whitehead remarks with an uncharacteristic sarcasm, "is analogous to that of a man completely degraded to a hog."[20]

The vocation of all reality is to go beyond itself, to extend itself as far as it can, beyond its heretofore-arrived-at boundaries. This is yet another important constitutive element of the point of departure of Hartshorne's understanding of person. Jan Smuts, a thinker sympathetic to process thought writes that activity, which for him is the nature of cosmic entities, does not stop in its structures, but remains in action. Smuts remarks that "there is more in bodies, things, and events than is contained in their structures or material forms. All things overflow their structural limits, the inner action transcends the outer structure, and there is thus a trend in things beyond themselves." He adds, "A thing does not stop at its boundaries or bounding surfaces. It is overflowing action, it passes beyond its bounds, and its surrounding "field" is therefore essential not only to its correct appreciation as a thing, but also to a correct understanding of things in general, and especially of the ways in which they affect each other."[21]

The vocation of what exists is to be more, to expand and reach out. Actual entities are not locked up in that small portion of space and time where they are ordinarily understood to be located. Rather, the nature of an event is that of a constant struggle with its past "for objective existence beyond itself."[22] Thus, while there may be a focal region—a concentration of activity—which we ordinarily refer to as a thing, this thing does not merely sit there. Rather, it transcends itself, its "influence streaming away from it with finite velocity throughout the utmost recesses of time and space."[23] There is no separating the entity from this divergent stream overflowing its known limits.

The idea that the vocation of event actualities is always toward a "more" is enshrined by both Hartshorne and Whitehead in their ethical theory, the essence of which is captured by the terms "optimization," "generalization," "widened concern," and "enlargement."[24] Ethical anthropology for both thinkers is therefore ultimately founded on a metaphysics of relationality and the nature of all entities as endlessly self-transcending.[25] Such "ethics of enlargement" moreover requires a view of the event as somehow unbounded in terms of its other-regarding reach.[26] It is an unboundedness that Hartshorne intimates by saying that the moment a limit is decided upon, one "shall already have come in sight of passing beyond that limit."[27]

With human individuals especially, such unboundedness takes on a much greater significance. For as Hartshorne says: "Thinking on the scale that goes with language produces a change so drastic, it is only quibbling to argue whether it is a difference of kind or of degree. ... To speak is to be at home with universals."[28] For Hartshorne, thinking on a scale that goes with language carries with it the burden of being either ethical or unethical; neutrality not being an option at all. A similar sentiment is echoed by Henry Nelson Wieman, for whom linguistic communication signifies a point in the emergence of a high level of organic life which becomes capable of further expanding its range of qualitative meaning.[29] Thinking extends the scope of an entity's domain of concern and influence indefinitely, if not infinitely. Thus, it is the vocation of rational creatures, to generalize, to go beyond themselves. Hartshorne believes that to be able to think is a privilege that brings with it the demand to have a goal that is both all-embracing and eternal. Because of this, he calls man "the obligated animal"[30] for whom being ethical cannot but entail "the generalization of instinctive concern, which in principle transcends the immediate state of the self and even the long-run career of the self, and embraces the ongoing communal process of life as such."[31]

Hartshorne says that he is in basic agreement with Kant in maintaining that the ethical will is the rational will and that this is the only form of will appropriate to a thinking animal. "Conscience," Hartshorne adds, "is practical reason."[32] And he contends that the only end that can be said to make an absolute claim on the rational will is "the maximizing of the value-content of the universe."[33] Such, he admits, is a metaphysical as well as a theological principle. This represents a clear restatement on Hartshorne's part of the point of contact between the ethical, metaphysical, and theological sciences that have become fragmented by the critique of what John Cobb calls a "victorious modernity"[34] and pushed even further by the voice of postmodern deconstructionist modes of thinking. Hartshorne's thought, mirroring much of process philosophy itself, recognizes the validity of the modern and deconstructionist critiques. The unquestioning use of reason and an uncritical regard for its power to give a unified voice to the diverse disciplines of thought which characterized premodern modes of thought is also rejected by Hartshorne, Whitehead, and other process thinkers. However, their thoughts diverge from the deconstructionist tendency of postmodernity in that they allow for the possibility of a constructive postmodern thought. The latter rejects modernity's ideas of individualism, materialistic atomism, anthropocentrism, and its fragmentation of knowledge into academic disciplines[35] and at the same time retains modernity's self-critical stance, its concern for the personal, commitment to human freedom and the freedom of inquiry. On the other hand, it attempts a recovery of certain premodern elements such as the unity of more organic traditions that were obscured and ridiculed by the triumphant march of modern thought. In regard to such, Cobb notes that "the mood is not so much to recover and renew earlier stages of Western thought as to search globally for insight and wisdom and for points of contact with new speculations arising from contemporary sciences."[36]

The supreme ethical principle is no less than the contribution to the creation of beauty, of intense and harmonious experience in ourselves, in and for others, to life in general, and ultimately, to the life of deity as the supreme goal of all moral action.[37] We are called, as Cobb points out, "to appropriate as broadly, as inclusively, as possible from the past. The freshness and originality of our present being correlates positively with this inclusiveness. The task is to take elements that seem in themselves mutually opposed and mutually exclusive and to transform them into a novel contrast that gains richness and intensity through inclusion of the best of both."[38] This statement amply captures what Hartshorne calls the aesthetic basis of value theory in process philosophy. Its primary notion is that "aesthetic experience heightens the sense of subjective individuality through the intensity of enjoyment ... evoking the awareness of compelling entities other than ourselves which lay their grip on us in such experiences."[39] For Hartshorne thus, the question, What is good? is inseparable from considerations that deal with what in experience is beautiful. "Goodness, truth and beauty," he says, "overlap in important ways."[40] Eugene Freeman discusses this overlapping of moral and aesthetic values.[41] He cautions against regarding these grades of value as simply separated from each other by clear-cut lines of demarcation. Instead, he suggests that what differentiates them are relatively arbitrary divisions with intrinsically vague boundaries separating the continuum of value into areas proper to each. Thus, when an object under scrutiny consists of a human action or character of institution which may be judged morally, then the moral and aesthetic responses of the observer are so inter-related that either will elicit the other. He gives the example of an observer in our own culture, whose moral and aesthetic sensibilities are reasonably well developed. Such an individual would have responses on the ethical scale which would parallel his responses on the aesthetic scale. "For if this observer evaluates the action he is observing as having positive moral value (i.e., as being 'good' in the moral sense) then his contemplation of that action will produce in him a corresponding degree of delight; while if he evaluates the action as having negative moral value (as being 'evil') then his contemplation of the action will produce in him a corresponding degree of aversion."[42]

Ethics leans upon aesthetics.[43] In order to understand this association, it must first be noted that, according to Hartshorne, all qualities directly given in experience are aesthetic or emotional.[44] This is an echo of Whitehead, for whom all feelings are rooted in aesthetic experience.[45] For Hartshorne, sensing is not so much like cognition (knowing), but is emotional (feeling) "in its utter immediacy and non-inferential character."[46] The immediately given is felt, for "there is no independent faculty of cognition which includes a neutral way of sensing qualities. ... The given world is the enjoyed or suffered world."[47] What is felt is thus a component in the becoming of actual entities—the primary data in fact. Hartshorne explains: "Before we 'know' anything about an extremely bitter or foul-smelling substance we have begun to reject it. This built-in relation to feeling and action is the primitive substratum of all experience. ... The primitive facts are value-facts already."[48] The given, which is felt, is productive of the process leading to the event's satisfaction. But it is also determined by what the individual ultimately takes as important in actualizing its subjective aim. Since value depends upon the entity's subjective interest, satisfaction is understood as dependent upon the achievement of harmony and intensity in the overall outline or pattern created by the event's process of becoming. It is such intensity and harmony "arising not only from visual or auditory stimuli as in painting or music, but in experience of whatever sort," that give life its value.[49] Hence, in *Reality as Social Process*, Hartshorne is able to articulate the relationship between ethics and aesthetics in such manner:

> If experience is the source of meanings, then the basic traits of experience must somehow correspond to the basic possible meanings, and these to

the basic structure of any world that can be meant. Now all experience is concerned with value. Experience is an act; and every act at least strives to realize a value. What basically is value? It cannot be ethical value that is basic; for ethics is concerned with consequences or with justice to others; and the goodness or badness of these consequences, or the good and bad that is to be justly distributed, must be measured by a criterion other than the ethical. Moreover, infants and animals experience and enjoy value, but are not ethical beings. The study that concerns itself with value in its universal character is aesthetics, taken in the broadest sense. Aesthetic value is immediate value, and this all experience must present, and to this all mediate value must lead.[50]

The good and the aesthetic matrix

The good, according to Hartshorne, is inseparable from this aesthetic matrix. In some places in fact, he goes as far as saying that in certain ways aesthetic values are more ultimate than ethical ones.[51] An ethically good act is one that brings about an increase or enlargement of this "good." An individual optimizes it, not only for herself, but also for her environment, her community.[52] Optimization of experience for oneself involves a widening of concern and an opting for the higher experience in place of a lower one. And according to Whitehead's rather strong indictment of the latter, to choose it over the higher form is a kind of "destructive evil, purely self-regarding."[53] This type of evil decried by Whitehead is that stable goodness that refuses to broaden one's outlook through a willingness to respond in a sympathetic way to an ever-widening range of elements, inharmonious as they may at first seem. Instead, one narrows one's field of attention, if only to block fear-inducing and stressful elements of discord. Whitehead refers to this as the choice for "perfection at a low level" which "ranks below imperfection with higher aim."[54] The dynamicity of human life, as Schroeder remarks, is inseparable from "self-determination informed by excellence."[55] Arrival at a stable and static goodness that refuses to press forward only serves to deaden the soul which "cries aloud for release into change," and "suffers the agonies of claustrophobia."[56]

Optimization of experience for the community on the other hand involves not merely striving toward the good for others, but also aiming at that which is better. The concrete embodiment of this first level of optimization is social progress, and its key concept is adventure. In *The Function of Reason*, Whitehead describes the art of life as the impetus "to live, to live well, to live better."[57] To be ethical in this regard is to seek to contribute to the realization of a society's ideal of itself, concretely embodied for instance in its churches, governments, educational system, and whatever else constitutes a society's overall structure.[58] He warns of the danger of an individual's arrival at a static form of goodness. He likewise calls attention to the danger to a society of what he calls the "Gospel of Uniformity" which quells the urge toward betterment by a conformation to established ideals leading to nothing more than static repetition and the gradual but certain slide toward minor forms of experience. The need for adventure in the maintenance of the freshness of the human spirit is captured by Whitehead in these words:

> When man ceases to wander, he will cease to ascend the scale of being. Physical wandering is still important, but greater still is the power of man's spiritual adventures—adventures of thought, adventures of passionate feeling, adventures of aesthetic experience. A diversification among human communities is essential for the provision of the incentive and material for the Odyssey of the human spirit. Other nations of different habits are not enemies: they are godsends. Men require of their neighbours something sufficiently akin to be understood, something sufficiently different to provoke attention, and something great enough to command admiration.[59]

A second dimension of the call to optimize experience for the community is an extension and enlargement upon the first. It is founded upon the widest possible generalization from what Hartshorne takes to be the most fundamental principle of other-regarding concern, namely, "the appeal of life for life, of feeling for feeling, experience for experience, consciousness for consciousness."[60] And for him, it is the contribution of individual creatures to the life of deity that serves as the ultimate motive for good action. Thus, he says that we are "co-workers with God, in that we add nuances of feeling to the ocean of feeling" which is the richness of his ever-growing experience.[61] And for Hartshorne, there is no simple "and" between God and the world—the latter being included in the all-embracing nature of the former. Thus, the raising of one's goal from a purely local, i.e., individual concern, to a universal one, i.e., one that seeks to contribute to the ongoing growth of God's relational pole, renders one a true citizen of the world in the sense that the ultimate value is cosmic citizenship.[62] It is a belongingness that entails a willingness to contribute to the ongoing life and development of the whole. On the cosmic level this is the essence of the universal fellowship of all creatures; and on the human level, the notion of human brotherhood.[63]

Contrast, memory and imagination

The "movement" toward ever-widening circles of concern and influence is at the center of the reflections on ethics and social relations in both Hartshorne and Whitehead. As has already been noted, a morally good act has, as its ultimate foundation, the contribution of richness and intensity of experience, to oneself but also, and more importantly, to other selves, both now and in the future. Hartshorne therefore emphasizes that without such an aim "beyond self, and even beyond any merely human good, life on this temporary planet seems as absurd as Sartre says it is."[64] Harmony and intensity are two significantly entwined elements of the optimization of aesthetic experience.[65] Both of these elements depend upon a concept that is integral to our attempt at understanding Hartshorne's concept of personhood and personal identity. This is the notion of contrast which is given an important niche in Hartshorne's theory of aesthetic value,[66] and which he defines as "the amount of diversity integrated into an experience."[67] Beauty for Hartshorne is a "balance," a harmonization of unity and variety.[68] In this he follows the old Aristotelian ideal of the golden mean which regards the mean as the desirable quality between the two undesirable extremes of the hopelessly monotonous, arrived at when there is too little contrast, and the hopelessly chaotic, which results when there is too little similarity. In this regard, harmony is first and foremost "a kind of relation between things such that though they are felt to be different from each other ... are yet felt to be not merely different."[69] It is the harmonization of elements otherwise diverse and contrasting that makes something beautiful. This harmonization is achieved only through the interweaving of pronounced unlikeness with pronounced likeness. Hartshorne sums it up: "Contrast is essential to maintaining the vitality of life's harmonies."[70]

Harmony, however, according to Hartshorne, also involves the interweaving of expectation and fulfillment as well as the ingression of "that unforeseen novelty [which is] as essential as the realization of the foreseen."[71] This constitutes the temporal aspect of the contrast involved in harmony which Hartshorne tries to explain by giving several examples. He asks us first to consider what sometimes happens when we listen to a beautiful piece of music. The point comes when, because of our having become too familiar with it, its magic disappears; and it becomes possible for us to anticipate its future passages in great detail. At such moment, we begin to get tired of it. Excitement has died down, and we may decide that it is time to listen to something else and not to listen to the familiar piece for some time. We become bored when what was new becomes old. Moreover, the excitement that powers the scientific enterprise is also an illustration of the role the new and the different play in the realization of harmony. Science, being a romantic adventure, is a means of widening the horizons of beauty.[72]

The more one knows about the past, the more likely it is that one becomes less capable of being satisfied with its mere repetition.[73] One would want something new, something different.[74] And this is perfectly consistent with the reconciliation of order and novelty at which process philosophy strives to arrive.[75] Hartshorne calls our attention also to the phenomenon that "in highly civilized communities fashions succeed each other in rapid succession in spite of the protests of those who are able to avoid discord between past and present only by avoiding all vital contrast between them."[76] The entrance of what is new and different is an integral part of our experience as human beings.[77] Hence, while being ethical, as Whitehead says, requires of us the "control of process so as to maximize importance,"[78] it is likewise an ethical demand—and for both thinkers, a much bigger one at that—to save process from decay and deterioration through the welcoming of novelty which is additionally creative and which alone can further the value of experience.[79] Moreover, since time is change through and through, the genuineness and freshness of harmony can only be maintained with the bold use of contrast.[80] Pronounced contrast is thus the essence of intensity; it is what gives strength and vitality to art, to nature, and to life itself.[81] As experience arrives at the point of culmination, and teeters on the brink of staleness, the introduction of elements of stronger contrast serves to further intensify the harmony already achieved, bringing it to an even higher level of value.

The experiential basis of contrast is memory. Hartshorne makes use of the experience of memory, fully generalized, in order to unearth the innermost structure of the upward trajectory of growth at the heart of all reality. He does the same to articulate, using an experience so readily accessible to all of us, his notion of what constitutes the identity of a person as an ethical and relational being. Memory is, Hartshorne says, central to high-level experiences, a way of understanding an important mode of contrast between the new elements and the remembered old ones in experience.[82] What exactly does he mean by this?

In order to answer the question, let us take a concrete and vivid, perhaps even radical, instance of contrast, namely, the experience of conversion. The conversion of Paul the Apostle is a clear example. Saul the Pharisee who actively sought to persecute the early Christian church, who witnessed and approved the stoning of Stephen the first Christian martyr and who was on his way to destroy the young community in Damascus, contrasts in so vivid a manner with the Paul of later years under whose leadership, the church spread to a considerable part of the ancient world. For Hartshorne, change on such drastic and conscious a scale is possible only for human beings; inanimate objects, plants and animals are not capable of it. It does not mean that these latter entities are not susceptible to radical changes; but unlike human beings, they are capable neither of consciously initiating it (or in some cases, of feeling it coming beforehand) nor of observing and articulating it afterwards. This is why radical as the contrast may be, there is no absolute break between Saul the Pharisee and Paul the Christian; somehow, a continuity exists in the midst of the transformation from the earlier to the later individual. This "somehow"—this manner by which such continuity amidst change can be made sense of—is explained by Hartshorne in terms of memory. One knows there has been a change—in oneself or in someone/something else—because one can see the difference between a present experience and an old one that one remembers. Memory witnesses to the temporal aspect of harmony which involves, on the one hand, a genuine (and sometimes even radical) contrast between the old and the new[83] and, on the other hand, a real continuity between the old and the new. For as Hartshorne says, what persists from the past into the present is the past itself.[84]

Memory is able to disclose contrast-in-continuity because it is the paradigm of realistic experiencing.[85] Hartshorne's treatment of memory belongs to the complex and intriguing phenomenological aspect of his neoclassical metaphysics. On the one hand, he maintains that the roots of all abstract ideas are to be sought in concrete experience of various kinds.[86] In this regard his use of memory is perfectly consistent with his method, which we have already enunciated as being rooted in concrete everyday experience.[87] On the other hand, he also says that human experience is to be divested of its contingent specificities in order to eliminate those limitations that do not seem inherent in its meaning.[88] Thus, while insisting on the existential character of metaphysics, Hartshorne also stresses that they are necessary existential statements, meaning that they cannot be otherwise. That is to say, insofar as they are necessary, they cannot be opposed by facts but are instead illustrated and confirmed by any such fact whatsoever.[89] The point is perhaps better clarified by contrasting the generalizations of metaphysics with those made by natural science. Hartshorne says that the latter, just like metaphysics, focuses on the details of experience and then generalizes these in order to arrive at the total system of details which distinguish the actual world from merely conceivable ones. Metaphysics, for its part, turns to the generic traits of human experience which are then generalized so as to arrive at the generic traits of both actual and possible experiences, and from here moves on to discover the abiding features of the whole of reality.[90]

It is the search for these generic traits that underpins Hartshorne's discussion of the role of experience in his philosophy and his focusing on the experiences of memory, perception, and imagination. He holds that these are three obvious aspects of concrete experience, and that a philosopher needs to make a careful examination of all three in their essential or generic aspects.[91] He analyzes these experiences by looking for the generic traits they have in common, comparing and assimilating cases, and then generalizing their properties to infer notions which are applicable to concrete actualities.

At first instance, Hartshorne's treatment of imagination appears rather cursory. In some places, he treats it in relation to the inductive aspect of metaphysical reasoning. Induction, he says, is reasoning from samples. In ordinary cases of induction, these are taken from perceptual experiences. However, in metaphysics, these samples are drawn from perception and imagination—what he calls an ideal experiment. In science, he remarks, such imaginative samples prove nothing apart from pure mathematics.[92] In other places, he treats imagination in relation to motivation, saying that it is imagined experiences that chiefly motivate us. This line has to be understood vis-à-vis his critique of the self-interest theory. He admits that the experiences that one imagines will be undergone by one's own "self" can be more interesting to oneself than the other experiences one imagines. Nevertheless, Hartshorne adds that "imagination may, yet need not, be preoccupied with one's own future weal or woe." Furthermore, to "canonize the former is a sad but common misuse of speculative reason."[93] Finally, he also treats imagination in relation to dreams. He discusses imagination and dreaming in order to refute the misconception that since in dreams, the mind seems to create its own content, and since there is no absolute difference between dreaming and waking states, the content of the latter may also be no more than the mind's creation. Here he mentions Descartes' use of dreams in order to cast doubt on the reality of the physical world as an example of this misconception. It could certainly be argued that the nonobjectivity of dreams does not imply the same of waking states. But Hartshorne goes farther than that, arguing that to assert the complete nonobjectivity of dreams is arbitrary, if not absurd.

Against the skeptic who uses the apparent nonobjectivity of dreams in order to cast doubt on the veracity of the physical world, Hartshorne says that since our bodies are "as truly part of the physical worlds as sticks and stones,"[94] there is no reason to believe that every experience, dreaming included, does not in its own way and degree disclose something of the physical world. Elsewhere, Hartshorne argues that even granting that the things we apprehend or interpret in dreams are in fact nonexistent, it does not follow that nothing is in there which is sheerly given. To conclude thus is arbitrary; for although in dreaming of a person, for instance, no person is in fact genuinely given, the array of sense qualities is. It is not merely an image, our own mental state, or a mere sense datum, either physical or psychical.[95] In other passages, Hartshorne stresses that there can be no final inseparability of experience with the things experienced. For "if our experiences are in their over-all characters as syntheses, self-creative, they are also in part created (or at least made possible, caused) by the things experienced."[96]

Moreover, since what is directly given in experience is cellular feelings as we feel it,[97] there can be no absolute separability of the "inside" and the "outside." Hence, Hartshorne states in another place that "the external object as immediately given is not the object which we "see" or "hear" and handle, but the body as actually in a state which is in a "unity of meaning" with what we are immediately aware of as potentialities of existence which, through the bodily state, are mediately perceived or known (probably) to exist in actual form outside the body."[98] It is not the object outside the body that is the thing most directly prehended; rather, it is the neural process itself which is the absolutely possessed item in experience.[99] It is this latter which is given to experience, and it has an independent existence, not simply constituted by the mind, nor simply existing apart from it.

What this discussion of imagination and dreaming draws attention to is the givenness of the data of experience. No absolute dichotomy holds between the mind and the physical world.[100] Mind is not the sovereign creator of its data, for the physical world is always and immediately implicated in human experience, the physical object being more than any real ingredient of the stream of consciousness.[101] Hartshorne gives three examples to illustrate this point. Consider, he says, the experience of dreaming of being cold then waking up only to find out that it is indeed cold and more blankets are needed. Here obviously an actual physical situation was reported in one's sensory experience. Or consider, he says, the experience of dreaming about hearing a noise only to wake up and hear an actual noise—here as well, one's auditory process and not merely one's mental state was involved.[102] At the same time, however, experience does not depend simply on the physical world for it is feeling which is immediately given in experience. Feeling is first and foremost mental, and even sensation is itself localized feeling.[103]

What this discloses is the relativity of experience, which is an important concept for Hartshorne.[104] "No experience is merely 'of' that very experience, nor even merely of an earlier moment in the same stream of experiences, nor can merely 'intending' an object which may not exist constitute the 'of' relation in 'experience of.'"[105] According to Hartshorne, experience is in principle relative because it is logically dependent upon given concrete entities whose existence in turn is necessary to, and independent of, the given experience. The experience of something implies a one-way dependence.

Hartshorne's analysis of the object of dreams calls attention to his argument that imagination, which is usually regarded to be of the same structure as dreams, is more than a "purely immanent affair, the mind exploring or utilizing its own states."[106] There is always, even in imagination, an object which is given and which is independent of the mind which regards it. For experience can only accept; it does not generate its own data.[107] As he puts it, "Always there is the givenness of the other and antecedent experiences, without which nothing could be either intended or given."[108] This having been said, Hartshorne has three conclusions. First, imagination should be regarded as a form of sign usage, in which the signs physically exist as given, albeit as events belonging to the nervous system.[109] Second, what is given, i.e., the object or datum of any experience is always the independent term. Third, as given, the data of experience belong wholly to the past.[110]

The relativity of experience, according to Hartshorne, has two main forms: memory and perception. Memory "makes experience logically dependent upon previous phases of the same 'stream' or personal sequence," while perception "makes experience dependent upon previous phases of other processes."[111] Hartshorne moreover, holds that memory and perception have a common structure[112]—this being the fact that both have past experiences as data.[113] In this he has found the generic trait common to imagination, memory and perception, namely, the pastness of what is given to these three dimensions of experience.[114] "What we experience," he says, "is actual past occurrences of 'experient occasions.' Nothing can ever undo the fact that they have occurred."[115]

Every experience therefore is, to a very large extent, the effect of conditions that belong wholly to the past. And both memory and perception provide clues to this thesis. Perception, Hartshorne holds, is "always and necessarily of the past of the world, not its contemporary state";[116] its confinement to the present being only apparent.[117] The objects we perceive in the present are really wholly in the past. For the objects that are given to perception require a being that is already settled, i.e., given as definite.[118] This is because there is a time lapse between the moment when a stimulus reaches the body and the moment when perception takes place. "Experience," he says, "is never simultaneous with its concrete objects but always subsequent."[119] Sound is a very clear example of this lapse between occurrence and perception. Light is another. Hartshorne notes that astronomers take it for granted that in seeing the starry heavens we are seeing events that occurred long ago.[120]

Furthermore, Hartshorne also rejects the strict simultaneity between an event—even if perceived inside the body—and our perceptual experience of it.[121] In *Insights and Oversights*, he says that rather than there being a simultaneous relation between an effect and its cause, there is actually a very rapid interaction between these.[122] He further mentions Karl Popper and John Eccles, who he says partially support the idea. And indeed, in their book *The Self and Its Brain*, these two authors criticize the theory of perception, which holds a simple one-to-one correspondence between stimulus and response, as well as between input and output.[123] Thus, even that which is perceived within the boundaries of the body—which should be our initial sample of perception[124]—belongs to past. This is founded on the notion that all experience—perception included—is social in structure.[125] To use the example of pain once again, the suffering that I endure from a cut in my arm is not merely my feeling of my own feeling. Rather, it is my experiencing, i.e., my participation in a suffering that is not simply my own. It does not have merely a subjective form, but an objective one as well. It is directly given as there, as more or less sharply localized. Thus, pain is always down there, over against me.[126] The point is not that the bodily process is there in my arm in the same way that I can say that a bee has landed there on my shoulder. It is rather that pain is a bodily process not simply identical with one's awareness of it. It does not have the identical localization.[127] "Human sensations," Hartshorne insists, "are our participatory human experiences of certain feelings possessed, in the first instance, by bodily constituents, perhaps cells, possibly cell-nuclei, possibly other units."[128] This represents the notion of experience as participation, which Wayne Viney explains in terms of the relation that exists between ourselves as feeling and the more minute parts of our bodies as themselves, feelers—a thesis which, he remarks further, can be attributed to the assumption of Hartshorne's philosophy and psychology of sensation concerning the fundamental continuity between molar (whole) and cellular processes.[129] The object of one's experience is thus always other-than simply the experience itself,[130] and whether outside or inside the body, the data of perception are given to it. Perception simply does not generate its own content.[131] And the only way by which an object can be given is when it has completed its coming-to-be, when it is, when it belongs wholly to the past. For only that which is past can persist into the present and thereby be prehended.[132]

It is on account of the foregoing conclusions that Hartshorne is led to observe that in some ways memory is a better key to the nature of experience than perception[133] and that "the paradigm of realistic awareness is rather memory than perception, since memory more obviously seems to be what perception after all also is: awareness of the past."[134] In *Creative Synthesis and Philosophic Method*, Hartshorne enumerates the reasons for this thesis.[135] First, by the time a datum of perception is used, it would have already been taken over by memory.[136] Second, there is much less ambiguity when it comes to discerning what it is that we are trying to know in memory than in perception. The object of memory is one's "own past experiences which are more or less closely similar to the experience doing the remembering."[137] With perception, on the other hand, when one perceives a stone, for example, there is a puzzling element that requires assimilation, i.e., the gulf that seems to separate human awareness from inanimate matter. Memory has a more obvious temporal structure than perception. Acts of remembering involve a clearer awareness that we are at least trying to know the past. By contrast, in perceiving we are more inclined to regard the present as that with which we are dealing. However, as Hartshorne stresses, "science tells us, what a sufficiently subtle philosophy could have inferred, that the events perceived, at least if outside our bodies, are in the past quite as truly as what we remember."[138]

Memory therefore in Hartshorne's philosophy is a key to understanding three distinct but interconnected ideas:[139] (i) that the structure of experience and realistic awareness is one of pastness, (ii) that, contra Hume, causality and givenness are really experienced, and not merely constant conjunctions, and finally (iii) that personal identity is no more than one prominent strand of the basic unity or continuity of becoming, and as such has no absolute priority.[140] In this regard, the relation implicated in memory, i.e., between new experiences and remembered old ones, is truly an important mode of contrast. For by showing that the relationship involves both creativity (in the sense that the new is not completely determined by remembered old experiences)[141] and continuity (that the old, i.e., that which has already become, will be an object for new experiences)[142] it also shows a way of reconciling contrast or difference and continuity. Such reconciliation belongs to the essential definition of the identity of persons in Hartshorne's philosophy.[143]

Hartshorne criticizes the view that what is given in memory is something merely temporally present but taken as a sign of something past.[144] There are basically two reasons, says Hartshorne, why memory is regarded as having data belonging wholly in the present. The first one is the idea, already discussed and criticized in the third chapter of this work, that what is past no longer exists. It is gone, and as such cannot be what is given in remembering. But this problematizes historical truth, which cannot be truth about nonentities. This kind of argument, Hartshorne says, proves too much. For he asks: "When we speak of the past, are we speaking about nothing? Or about the present only? If past events can influence present events at all, to say they cannot influence present experiences by becoming their data seems wholly arbitrary. And if past events cannot influence present events what is all our science?"[145] He therefore disagrees with the notion. Obviously, something is given as the object of memory.

The illusions and mistakes of memory constitute the second reason why it is usually held to have data existing solely in the present. For how can we be mistaken about something if it were absolutely given? And indeed, if we hold that the data of memory is the past as given, we have to hold that what is given is given as whole and complete. There cannot be something merely half or a quarter-given—this being a necessary implication of the theory of the absoluteness and immutability of the past. The only way that the mistakes and illusions of memory can be reasonably explained is by maintaining that—like perception, in which some objects we see turn out not to be there at all[146]—the data of memory are in fact not absolutely given. That is to say, they do not belong to the past, but are mere images, surrogates, or interpretations which stand for the past in the present. And these interpretations which secure the validity of memory are also the reasons why memory may, on occasion, be mistaken.[147]

This objection, Hartshorne counters, is founded on the notion that the given is everywhere mixed with thought, and hence, that memory must already be an interpretation of the given. For unless such were the case, the given could not become a permanently available item to be remembered. Insofar as it has been consciously reported upon, memory involves interpreting the given. Such interpretation is fallible.[148] Thus, Hartshorne says that the biggest error of this idea would be that of confusing the how with the what of remembering.[149] For the how is the locus of fallibility and the source of controversy, not memory simply.[150] It is certainly the case that in every experience—albeit in a much more negligible fashion on the lowest levels of nature—there is the admixture of interpretation and the sheer possession of data. This involves responding to signs, which are prehended in the ordinary perceptual way.[151] Furthermore, on the higher levels of the scale, this sign usage becomes what Whitehead terms "symbolic reference."[152] This represents the synthetic activity through which the two modes of direct perception—presentational immediacy and causal efficacy[153]—are fused into one perception. The resulting process is none other than "what the actual world is for us, as that datum in our experience productive of feelings, emotions, satisfactions, actions, and finally as the topic for conscious recognition when our mentality intervenes with its conceptual analysis."[154]

It is, however, erroneous to confuse the admixture of interpretation and the sheer possession of data in such a way that the latter is understood to be already constituted by what is most characteristic of the former, namely, consciousness. Consciousness may indeed be interpretation, as Hartshorne notes; but the sheer posession of data—perception in its most primitive form—is preconscious. He points out that the notion that experience has something given to it for interpretation does not imply that one knows this something in its preinterpreted state or can tell oneself just what it is. He explains, "Rather one simply senses or 'intuits' it without the conscious categorizing which should be termed knowledge. One has the given, and uses it in judging what things or event-chains are at hand."[155] Hence, to say that the preinterpretative data must already be consciously apprehended is to be involved in the contradiction that it must be interpreted before being interpreted. Memory does not involve right away the interpretation of the given. "One should not identify memory with conscious recollection, which is a good deal more than mere memory, this 'more' introducing various possibilities of error."[156] As such, the fallibility of interpretation cannot be used as an argument to discredit the idea that the data of memory are past. It does not, as Hartshorne argues, prove that the very pastness of the remembered is supplied by the interpreting process.[157] And although he admits that consciously reported memory does involve the interpretation of the given—an interpretation that is liable to error—this in no way proves that the past data of memory (its "what") is supplied by the interpreting process (its "how"). The given therefore need not be interpreted in order for it to be an available item for recollection.

Now with regard to the errors and illusions to which memory is subject, such fallibility, just like the overall fallibility of perception, does not lie in the interpretation simply. Rather, as Whitehead says, it lies in the synthetic activity by which the two modes of causal efficacy and presentational immediacy are fused into one perception.[158] Error is encountered neither in immediate experience nor in "primitive" memory. Instead, it is on that high-level of interpretation, coupled with conscious inspection and verbalization that numerous possibilities of error are introduced.[159] Thus, Hartshorne states: "Obviously the having of past experiences as given is itself nonverbal, except so far as it is itself mnemonically had. Consequently, to say what we remember involves all of the risks which verbalization always involves, not only of failing to communicate to another, but of self-confusion."[160] The errors and illusions of memory arise because the ties that connect the signs or surrogates used in a present act of recollection with the original experience being remembered become more and more tenuous and strained with the march of time. Hartshorne observes that "in two or many steps, usually many, the first experience becomes confused with other factors of imagining and inference, all of them past in relation to the case of memory under consideration."[161] In Whitehead's words, they become "blurred and confused by the intervening occasions of our personal existence."[162] On account of this, Hartshorne takes a cautious stand.[163]

What we have seen so far is that "past events do not exist, or are not present, in the same sense as they once did or were, but they may yet be, in a genuine sense, still real and still present."[164] There is no contradiction involved here. There would be if it were held that memory had nothing past as its datum. Hartshorne articulates his proposed theory as such:

> In conscious memory, e.g. verbally reported memory or recollection, certain real past happenings, now given ... are interpreted as signs affording more or less reliable information about still other, usually more remote, past happenings which are no longer given, at least not with the same degree of distinctness and vividness.[165]

This is conscious memory. It is memory "ordinarily so-called," long rather than short run.[166] It is memory that has an object belonging wholly to the past, but nonetheless mediated by a series of steps, going all the way from our present act of recollection to the actual experience located in our remote past. It is what Milič Čapek calls "mediate memory,"[167] as opposed to what Hartshorne calls "memory in its primary form,"[168] which alone is memory in its purity.[169]

Memory and the past

It is in his treatment and use of the concept of immediate memory as a way of explaining the identity of persons that Hartshorne differs most from other philosophers who have dealt with the question. Indeed, a great deal of past as well as contemporary literature on the subject—as we have seen in the first two chapters—has attempted to explain the problem of the continuity of personal identity based on memory "ordinarily so-called," i.e., "mediate" or "remote" memory. And as Hartshorne himself notes, echoing Whitehead, there is nothing unusual or surprising about this, given that philosophers have rarely given sufficient consideration to memory in its primary form. In contrast to this ordinary understanding of memory, memory in its primary form, is "awareness of the immediate past—less than a second ago"; it is "extremely short-run memory, where no intermediate case with the same past datum intervenes [and] scarcely leaves room for verbalization."[170] Whitehead describes this type of memory in these words: "[It does not refer] to our memories of a day past, or of an hour past, or of a minute past. ... But our immediate past is constituted by that occasion, or by that group of fused occasions, which enters into experience devoid of any perceptible medium intervening between it and the present immediate fact."[171]

The distinction between these two types of memory is not one of nature, but only of degree. They refer to two qualitatively different degrees of pastness, two recollections, one of which refers to the immediately preceding past, another to a more distant past. That which refers to a more distant past involves a mnemonic awareness of a multiplicity of successive phases. Čapek compares this to Husserl's notion of the 'temporal horizon' which involves a similar multiplicity of successive phases, and is also characterized by a synthesis of unity and diversity of elements which, to a simple perception, are nonetheless inseparable. The whole experience is from the outset, a unified one, though when considered from any standpoint outside of the origin, it can be distinguished as having a beginning different from its successive states. Čapek further notes that this distinction would not be possible if the original datum were completely homogeneous, i.e., if it were not qualitatively diversified into successive phases, not parts.[172]

This portrayal of the successive 'phases' involved in mnemonic awareness should not be understood in terms of an arithmetical multiplicity of mutually exclusive units externally related to one another. For the instants that constitute any one mnemonic succession are characterized by both external and internal relations, but in an asymmetrical way. The later events are internally related to earlier ones, while the earlier events are externally related to later ones. This type of memory is what is subject to interpretation and verbalization as well as all the errors and illusions that arise from them. Likewise, the language of "phases" should not be understood to mean that there are two distinct and clear-cut instants. Rather the past is prehended at the same instant it becomes a datum.[173] Hartshorne reiterates this unity of becoming by pointing out that the fleeting present comes into actuality as a whole, not bit by bit.[174]

On the other hand, that type of memory which refers to the just finished past scarcely leaves room for verbalization. Furthermore, it is such that no intermediate case with the same past datum intervenes.[175] It is extremely short-run memory, so brief that Hartshorne adopts the term "specious present" to capture its fleeting character.[176] But does this not collapse the present and the past by blurring the distinction between them? If the datum of present awareness is past, how do we know that the present is not already in the remote past? Hartshorne says that the first step is to take seriously the Whiteheadian doctrine that introspection is really memory used in a certain way[177] Introspection is really retrospection.[178] Elsewhere he says: "What is called introspection is not simultaneous experiencing of that very experience—which implies a vicious regress—but an experience of just preceding experiencing. It is memory."[179]

The prehended or known actuality is already past actuality. What is pre-hended by present awareness—even in perception—is not itself.[180] What it prehends is its past, not itself simply. This follows from the analysis of becoming, for until an actuality has become, it is not fully itself, not really there to be known. An event has to be, in order for it to be a datum for fur-ther experience; but when an event has in fact become, it is fully itself and the strife toward further becoming ceases. "Its 'decision' has once for all been made, and it is available in its entirety as material for a new deci-sion."[181] When that happens, the event "perishes," thereby becoming, on the one hand, a fully completed fact, a thing of the past, while, on the other hand, it lives forever more in the memory of God.

Of course, the more remote a certain section of the past is, the less vividly felt will its influence upon the present be. Still, the totality of the past is present, not as one monolithic and undifferentiated bloc, but in the form of a qualitative line characterized by varying degrees of vividness and complexity. The notion that the whole past—even its most remote ele-ments, as more or less faintly, unclearly, or unconsciously reremem-bered[182]—is immanent in the present follows from the doctrine of the immortality of the past and the inclusive (retrospective) unity of process.[183] The mind unifies in such a way that one's momentary unity of feeling is a new felt synthesis of the antecedent feelings or experiences in which one now participates.[184] Only in this way does the mnemonic influ-ence of the past—memory in its most general and psychological sense—become possible. It could be asked, of course, how much of the past is included? And why, if the whole past is truly immanent in the present, does one not remember one's entire personal past? What in human con-sciousness prevents the past in its totality from being integrally present to consciousness, thereby limiting the past's domain of influence? The answers lie both in the nature of the past as well as in the nature of human awareness itself.

Hartshorne's initial answer is that we are not divine.[185] Only in the divine memory is the totality of the past embraced in all its vividness and remem-bered with pristine clarity.[186] For all nondivine entities, however, the aware-ness of the immanence of the past within the present is not only limited, it is also subject to error. Hence, the influence exerted by the whole past upon the present of nondivine existents is characterized by gradation or diversifi-cation, such that the more remote an event is, the less intense will its effect be on the present. This is why we are not as affected as God is, and why our compassion is not as subtle and as all-embracing as his. The past fades, and as it is pushed ever backwards by newer presents, both its influence as well as one's awareness of it gradually dissipate. But it is never destroyed. Even for us, it remains a dim yet ever-present horizon of our existence, a shadow which we strive to leave behind us but which casts itself again and again upon our every departure.

The power and influence of the past is just as genuine as the freedom of present acts of becoming. Such power or influence is founded on the idea of the past's immanence in the present. Nancy Frankenberry calls attention to the importance of Whitehead's doctrine of immanence spelled out in his theory of the "power of the past" which holds that the creativity of past occasions are not "passive or static as though only inertly 'given' to the present."[187] She quotes Whitehead who says that although regarded abstractly the antecedent data of experience are passive, "viewed in conjunction (with the prehending occasion), they carry the creativity which drives the world."[188] And indeed, the language used by Whitehead to describe the data of experience gives the impression of vigorous activity. It is "the throbbing emotion of the past hurling itself into a new transcendent fact." It "provokes some special activity." It is "energizing in the present," "imposing ... on the novel particular in process of creation."[189] The present event is constituted by the influx of the other and as such does not simply emerge out of nothing. "Rather, the creativity which is internal to epochal occasions is partially inherited from the antecedent determining conditions, and partially spontaneous. The self-creativity of the nascent occasion, its spontaneous features, consist in 'how' it responds to 'what' it receives through physical prehensions of its past actual world."[190] The defects of conscious memory notwithstanding, one's entire past remains a reality, influencing the present moment and casting its shadow over every other subsequent present in the life of an individual.

It is interesting to note that Čapek mentions the phenomenon of hypermnesia in his article on memory. It is an experience usually reported by individuals who have been in situations of extreme danger, say death. In such an experience, as Čapek notes, "the totality or quasi-totality of the past is glimpsed 'at once', more accurately in a present moment which is contemporary with a very short interval of public time."[191] It is commonly described by the statement: "I saw my whole life flash before my very eyes." Moreover, as Čapek states, this was how Royce and Bergson conceived the divine consciousness and how Whitehead may in fact be understood when he says "that in God novelty is present without the fading of the past, without 'perpetual perishing.'"[192] Thus, although Hartshorne is correct in saying that it is because we are not divine that the past is never in full vividness available to our recollection,[193] it could very well be the case that even with regard to this point, there may actually be some experience which could provide us with a window into what Hartshorne believes the divine memory actually is.[194]

But even if such were not the case, the experience of hypermnesia still affords us with some experiential basis for holding the immortality of the past.[195] On account of this, Hartshorne appears to be correct in stating that "because future experiences must contain their unity with their predecessors (to some extent, remember them), and in this way, literally possess them, there are limits upon what the future, so far as it consists of experiences can be."[196] In a similar vein, the nature of the past as indestructible imposes limits on the conscious or verbalized reports of the events being reported. Interpretation is susceptible to deviating from the truth, more or less widely. Such deviation cannot be absolute for verbalization cannot proceed simply as though the given events were not given. They could not have been given had they not occurred. For givenness (no matter how interpretive) does not create its data, it merely accepts and uses them.[197]

8
The Social Structure of Persons

The causal structure of experience

That no phase of our past is ever destroyed is what makes the mnemonic influence of the past—memory in its most general and psychological sense—possible. That memory, both mediate and immediate, is *of the past* is what limits the freedom of experience.[1] No phase of experience can fail to possess relations to its previous phases. No present experience wholly transcends the influence of the data of its past. Insofar as this is the case, Hartshorne says, "we have causal necessity, the very thing Hume looked for and failed to find."[2] And thus a key to answering the latter's skepticism with regard to our experience of causal relations is to show that the way to form a positive conception of the causal interrelatedness of events is "to admit analogues of memory connecting subjects of feeling more radically distinct than present and past selves in one (human) stream of consciousness ('personally ordered society of experient occasions')."[3] Hume, we recall, denied that sense perception can disclose causal necessity and insisted that what is experienced are mere "constant conjunctions." What we experience in nature is the continual, and often repetitive, succession of events. While in agreement with Hume that we do not directly observe causal relations, Hartshorne nevertheless rejects Hume's thesis that causal relations are no more than constant conjunctions. In his view, it is still possible to grasp the principle that underlies causal relations if we are able to overcome "the habit of regarding psychical conceptions, such as *memory*, as secondary, merely special cases of something nonpsychical which is more fundamental."[4] This is why Hartshorne contends that rejecting Hume's skeptical thesis will necessitate a similar rejection of materialism and its corollary notion, viz., classical determinism.[5]

It is at this juncture that Hartshorne's notion of memory is called upon to provide a key to the causal problem.[6] As we have seen earlier on, the experience of memory affords us a way of understanding how the past exerts its influence upon the present. Such influence, moreover, happens not merely in terms of memory's presentation of the past in the present, it happens because the past itself plays a role in the modification of the present.[7] The creative-synthetic character of the process of becoming involves the creation of novel wholes through non-novel parts. The data of the past—the antecedent particulars which are the objects of memory "*impose* themselves on the novel particular in process of creation,"[8] thereby putting restrictions upon the newly emerging subject. They "preserve something of the ideas, emotional qualities, and valuations in prior experience, and the whole of the remembering experience, as one experience, must achieve integration of feeling and value because, or in spite of, what memory imports into it."[9]

Hartshorne argues that the reality of causal necessity can be defended if we give up some questionable assumptions—"pieces of confused ontology," he calls them.[10] The first is the idea that causal relations in order to be logical necessities, must concern the effected events in their full particularity. This is the strictly deterministic notion of causality. The second concerns the notion that our experience of causality is primarily physical causality.[11] This is the materialistic hypothesis. Contrary to the first, Hartshorne insists that causal necessities can be regarded as logical without being understood to connect events in their entire particular nature.[12] However, this would require that we reject the notion of classical determinism which has prevented us from seeing that the limitations to causal determination involve much more than simply the defects of human knowledge.[13] Hence, by dropping determinism, Hartshorne claims that "we are free to look for a species of logical necessity connecting events, not with subsequent events *in their exact particularity*, but with respect to certain limited aspects—approximate, statistical, or otherwise *outline* characters—only."[14]

With regard to causal connectedness, Hartshorne argues that memory, in one type of instance at least, constitutes for us a real connection of the present with the past and of effect with cause.[15] The type of memory of which Hartshorne speaks when dealing with causality is first and foremost immediate memory.[16] As has already been noted, the so-called "errors of memory" need not be regarded as deleterious to this view for it renders problematic, not the *givenness* itself of the past, especially the immediate past, but the *interpretation* that is done. It covers the intermediate phases between the present and the more remote past being recalled. What we have in the experience of memory, according to Hartshorne, is a retrospective relation between a remembering present and a remembered past. This can in turn be construed prospectively such that in terms of it *the present* can be understood as both a cause genuinely related with its future effect, and an effect really connected with its past cause. Similarly, *the future* can be regarded as that which will (even logically must) have retrospective relation to the present being experienced.

Two considerations follow. First, such prospectively valid retrospective relation, when adequately generalized to cover nonhuman and even nonanimal cases, affords us, in principle at least, with what we need by way of real causal connections. However, this will only be the case if we were to give up the supposition of merely physical causation (the materialistic thesis of relations).[17] Second, these relations likewise furnish a basis for the truth value of prediction since observed past conjunctions(or correlations) are held true also of the future.[18] But this will only be true if we were to give up the supposition of strict determinism and regard the causal influence of the present upon the future as having to do with "outlines." Although these *must* indeed be filled, they are nevertheless only to be filled *somehow*, i.e., in one way or the other, and in no one particular way alone.[19]

The best way of illustrating the first consideration, according to Hartshorne, is through *intra*-bodily instances of relatedness and not through *extra*-bodily ones.[20] This leads us to consider what he means by "memory being taken in a very broad sense," or the "generalization of memory."[21] This is consistent with his methodology of taking instances of human experience as points of departure for metaphysical reflection and generalizing beyond these instances. This allows for all sorts of levels and kinds of experiences other than the human, while at the same time looking for the variables that are common to all the entities implicated in the scale.[22] The clearest instance of direct influence of the past upon the present and the direct possession by the present of the immediately preceding past is what transpires in the nervous system.[23] There are two plausible candidates which can be regarded as providing us with instances of direct prehension of "foreign actualities": (i) physical processes outside the body, and (ii) physical processes inside the body.[24] To accept that it is physical processes outside the body that is most directly prehended is to fall into the error of naïve realism and would involve us in paradoxes.[25]

The more reasonable supposition therefore is that whatever visual or sensory experience one may have depends upon certain nerve cells being suitably stimulated.[26] In his analysis of sensation, for instance, Hartshorne states: "In all cases, I hold, the object outside the body is not the thing most directly prehended or sheerly given; rather, it is the neural process itself which forms the immediate content, the absolutely possessed item."[27] The rejection of any ultimate bifurcation of reality means first and foremost that feeling is present, not merely in the object pole of an experience, but also in the subject pole. And the moment we become aware of any quality, our feeling acquires it also as its own quality.[28] It is true that "experience of blue" qualifies both the subject as well as the object. It is a unitary experience—this is what Hartshorne terms the "synthesis of idealism and realism."[29] At the same time, however, the "experience of blue," which qualifies the subject does not merely entail the subject's awareness simply of its own quality (of experiencing blue), "but rather, or also, of *something not itself* nor *merely a quality of itself*."[30]

This something that is not merely a quality of itself is experience by the living cells of the body which are the primary experiencers, so to speak, of blue.[31] "The direct conditions of color sense," Hartshorne argues, "are living cells, entirely, by all established principles of comparative psychology, capable of feeling on their own."[32] Now concerning the possible objection that if "experience of blue" which the subject intuits is *of* the cells, why then do we all not know the truth of the cell theory intuitively? Hartshorne's reply is that such question assumes that direct intuition is bound to be clear and distinct. This is opposed to many facts of science,[33] not to mention philosophical principles ("for our intuition is not divine").[34] It is true, he says, that there are many questions of detail, as for instance, why we do not sense the cells *as such*, but rather must learn about cells from physiology. However, he retorts that "if the immediate object is the stimulus source—say, a blade of grass—and this also consists of cells, why do I not know about plant cells without benefit of botany? The reasoning is the same."[35] Moreover, Hartshorne compares the abstractions that science and sense experience come up with. Science, he points out, does not merely abstract from, it also omits and adds to the positive features of the perceived world. On the other hand, sense experience also works with abstractions, i.e., through an enormous simplification of the perceived world. From these observations concerning the abstract character of both science and perception, Hartshorne concludes that "direct perception cannot be the criterion for the existence or nonexistence of individuals other than those above the threshold of the resolving power of our vision and touch."[36]

The processes which we immediately experience are primarily somatic, belonging initially to human cells, not to human experiences or minds.[37] As such they are first and foremost, independent.[38] When one becomes aware of these members, one is not a self aware of that very self. At least at a given moment, one is a *single* individual while one's bodily members are a vast *multitude* of other (though only relatively independent) individuals. Hartshorne insists on this distinction between self as knower and the self's body to prevent confusion about the structure of perception.[39] Experience really does not create its own data, for these are given, primarily through immediate experience (which is immediate memory), and secondarily through successive interpretations of the originally given (which is also memory).

Now if the data of experience are independent, and if they are primarily bodily processes, it follows that the given somatic processes are independent of our awareness of them. Awareness is itself dependent upon the bodily processes. Sense data are primarily physiological.[40] This is why Hartshorne does not accept the theory of an unqualified interactionism between mind and body. He does not regard mind and body as two isolated components of the person which nonetheless relate to each other in a purely external manner—the mind *acting upon* the body, and the body being *acted upon* by the mind—as if the body were no more than a lifeless piece of matter. Instead of a simple interactionist theory between mind and body, he advocates what he calls a "cautious interactionism" which takes into account that there is no absolute and simple contrast between mechanical and nonmechanical processes. He adds that the only possible explanation of an influence of human experiences upon cellular processes is in the supposition that cellular processes are themselves experiences participating in our (antecedent) experiences.[41]

Hence, the relation that obtains between body and mind is also one of asymmetry.[42] The effect in human experience of any event in the nervous system is immediately subsequent; the effects in the nervous system of any event in human experience are also subsequent.[43] There is interaction, but it is one that is qualified by a temporal difference between cause and effect in either direction.[44] The mind is dependent upon its objects, the knower dependent upon the known. That which is an object known first and foremost by experience is the human body itself.[45] This one-way dependence of the mind upon its objects is, according to Hartshorne, the key to every and all the asymmetries.[46] This is what he means when he speaks of a one-way influence of bodily upon mental processes.[47]

It is this influence which enables Hartshorne to further speak of genuine causality since, as he says, to speak of influence of action is the same as saying that causes precede effects. The somatic conditions of givenness must precede the experiences in or to which they are given. It is a realistic conception of experiences that they must follow, rather than be simultaneous with, their data. Events asymmetrically include their predecessors as objectified data and as such are influenced by their forebears. However, these prehended events are not in the same way related to the successor events.[48] Instead, the predecessor events enter into the formation of their successors and as such are the latter's causes.[49] The data of experience are a "stimulus object, in its state in the near or remote past [which] is the beginning of *a chain of activities* the penultimate phases of which are certain events in the human nerves and brain cells."[50] In this regard, Hartshorne shows that causal influence is an experientiable reality and that a real connectedness holds between the past and the present. These two temporal points are neither totally independent nor isolated from one another. The phenomenon of temporal continuity and connectedness need no longer be an inexplicable mystery.

Having interpreted causality as a one-way, asymmetrical dependence, Hartshorne delves into the idea of necessary connections. He objects to the notion that for causal relations to be logical necessities, these have to cover the effected events in their full particularity. This means that for there to be real necessary relations, later events (effects) in their concrete totality must be deducible from their predecessor events (causes). They must be related to these in their entire particular nature. In place of this deterministic notion of logical necessity, Hartshorne proposes a way of looking at the relation in such a way that events can be connected with subsequent events, not in the latter's exact particularity but only in regard to certain limited, approximate, or statistical characters. It is a mere outline rather than a completed blue-print.[51] He notes that "Occurrences can implicate their exact predecessors without implicating any exact successors. This is merely the familiar logical schema of "p implying q and q implying r," and so forth, although r does not imply q, nor q, p."[52]

As was noted earlier, Hartshorne argues that since observed past conjunc-tions also apply to the future, certain prospectively valid retrospective rela-tions can provide a basis for the truth value of *prediction* provided the supposition of strict determinism were dropped. What is the meaning of "Is going to be?," What is meant by "true of the future?" This could mean either that the character of the future which renders a prediction true or false is somehow also a determinate aspect of the present or that it in no way is an aspect of that present. If the first case were correct, then the connections that hold between the present and the future are not only real but logical as well. The Janus-like character[53] of experience renders it possible for it to implicate both its past data, as well as its successors. The being of every actu-ality is its contribution to the future of life.[54] It could be granted that an event, when it occurs, is independent of all subsequent events, even those belonging to its own sequence or chain. Hartshorne nevertheless argues that "it is not independent of there coming to be *some* subsequent events or other, for which the given event will be past."[55]

The determinism that Hartshorne rejects is limited to that type which holds that to be is to be experienced by *this* or *that* particular experience or that to happen is to be followed by *this* or *that* particular subsequent event. It is perfectly acceptable within the canons of the metaphysics here enunci-ated that "*to be is to be destined to be experienced* by *some* suitable subsequent experiences, just as to happen is to be destined to be followed by some suit-able subsequent events."[56] The only requirement is that the subsequent event not be an empty class, although no member of the class is a necessity. Real relations are present between the events in question; that is to say, later events implicate their predecessors but implicate their successors only subject to some limitation. This is what Hartshorne's theory of relative indetermin-ism entails: not that some concrete events have no causes, but that the *exact* nature of succeeding events is left unspecified by the totality of their causal conditions.[57]

The alternative to this view is to hold that earlier events implicate their successors completely. This of course leads to the notion that causes deter-mine their *exact* effects, and further, to the paradox that events are already "there" even before they really are, i.e., before they have actually happened. Hartshorne rejects such deterministic thesis that leads to this paradoxical situation.[58] Statements of prediction cannot be understood to imply a reference to the future from the standpoint of a presently completed or fulfilled fact. It cannot be understood to mean as if the future were real now. For the assertion cannot be held true until the time reference is actually fixed and until the event predicted actually comes to pass.[59] Until such time, statements of prediction refer to the future as a realm of may-or-may-not-be's.[60] From the standpoint of the present therefore the future is determinable, not determinate.[61] It is the realm of possibility.[62] Hence, the truth of statements with regard to the future cannot mean that everything that the statement holds to its most minute detail is already determined or settled upon. If everything were already predetermined from all eternity, no order of derivation becomes possible. And prediction itself is rendered meaningless. For how can prediction even mean anything if what is being predicted were already real?

Since the character of the actual, says Hartshorne, is its potentiality for further determination, the future must be regarded as genuinely open.[63] And he explains this notion by means of an analysis of a statement concerning something one has thought of doing in the future.[64] Consider, he says, two statements: "I will write a letter tomorrow," and "I will not write a letter tomorrow." While it is certainly the case that only one of these can be true, it is likewise possible that both of them are false. For it may be the case that it is unsettled that I will write the letter, and equally unsettled that I will not. Thus, the statement "I will write the letter" is either true or false. However, to say that it is false is not to say that the statement "I will not write the letter" is true. For such statements as "I will do it" only means that the present state of affairs determinately excludes my *not* doing it, while the statement "I will not do it" means that the present state of affairs excludes my doing it. In between these two, however, there is the situation expressed by "I may or may not do it," signifying the indeterminacy of the present situation of myself and the world as a whole.

What we have here is another instance of what Hartshorne means when he says that we should think in three's instead of two's,[65] or what he refers to elsewhere as "exclusive and exhaustive triads."[66] In this case, any "will," 'will not," or "may or may not" statement, if not true, would be definitely false. It can only be right or wrong to say that *all*, or that only *some*, or that *none* of the possibilities at a specified present or past time for a later time include the deed or act in question. However, whichever of the three statements is true, the others are both false. This is how the volitional meaning of "will" behaves, according to Hartshorne. "It is untrue that he wills or intends to do it" does not imply "He wills not to do it," for the individual may be irresolute or neutral as to the deed. Abstracting from this, Hartshorne notes that what we are left with is the third case, i.e. simply that he may or may not do it. The outcome is still to be decided upon.[67]

Relative determinism therefore, says Hartshorne, means thinking in terms of no more than futuristic outlines of possibility and probability, with boundaries of necessity,[68] not fixed and completed actualities. Necessary relations do hold (for causal connections, regarded retrospectively are rigorous[69]); but not strictly necessary ones that run from causal conditions to ensuing events.[70] The future as the realm of possibility cannot be determined as to its most particular details.[71] For possibility means alternativeness.[72] Now if the future were already determined, say, of one's choosing a career, then the possibilities with regard to whatever choice one eventually makes is, for all intents and purposes, reduced to one, i.e., reduced to that choice that one eventually makes.[73] But this collapses the contrast between the possible and the necessary, a contrast upon which, as Hartshorne points out, both terms "possible" and "necessary," depend.[74] This, however, need not be the case, as there is a way of reconciling necessity and possibility without destroying the all-too-important contrast that exists between them.[75] Hartshorne suggests that, instead of regarding the future in terms of a domain of already actualized events, we consider the situation in terms of a range of possibilities which, however defined with regard to its limits, will necessarily have *common* factors which pervade the range. Now these factors, *considered within the range* will indeed brook no possible alternative. Necessity is understood as a common or invariant factor within a particular range of possibilities.[76]

The realm of the future encompasses a range of possibilities for actualization. What is yet to be is not predetermined. There is no such thing, says Hartshorne, as timeless truth.[77] Even the divine experience envisages the future as future, possibility as possibility.[78] At the same time, the range itself is not infinite, as it is "informed" and "influenced," to a very large extent, by the data of the past. If the range were simply unlimited, i.e., if there were in fact no room for the past to exert its influence on the becoming of events, absurdities would also result. An absolutely deterministic framework precludes any real becoming since the future would already be actual in the present. The framework of absolute freedom and indeterminism reduces becoming to sheer chaos, which is no becoming at all. In neither scheme are genuine necessity and succession given real room. Asymmetrical causality, which is the essence of temporality as well as memory, is likewise precluded in both. Hence, Hartshorne has sought the truth somewhere in between, i.e., in the notion that while the future is the realm of an indeterminate range of possibilities, this range is limited to those things which, in given conditions, *really could* happen.[79]

Neither causal connectedness nor necessary relations concern the effected events, i.e., later occasions, in their full particularity.[80] There is simply no need for every single detail of later events to be completely deducible from their causes. Causality can be thought of in terms of approximate or statistical regularity. But there is also no need to posit the existence of these latter events in complete isolation from the data of their pasts. Once again it is memory that serves as the key to this nonclassical way of understanding the causal structure of experience. It is first and foremost a key to its integration.[81] Memory is not constituted simply by the data of the past, nor the response of a present act of concrescence to these data, nor simply by the objective form of the response itself. Instead, and more importantly, it is constituted by the unity of these, which expresses the subjective form of the entire event sequence itself. This unity is the whole of the novel event which is logically richer in determinations than the mere data, and is not derivable from any predetermined combination of the previous data. Causality and givenness are genuine elements of experience; they are not merely constant conjunctions. The integration of experience witnessed to by the structure of mnemonic awareness has a principle which we find most vividly in aesthetic phenomena and most clearly formulated in writings on aesthetics. The briefest formula for this, according to Hartshorne is "identity in difference," or "unity in variety."[82] And the most concrete exemplification of this principle together with all its attendant dimensions is the person himself/herself.

Personal identity

The experienced structure of mnemonic awareness reveals the asymmetrical structure of causality which in turn discloses the character of personal identity as Hartshorne understands it.[83] He also makes the distinction between strict identity which involves a symmetrical/nondirectional relation and generic identity which implicates a nonsymmetrical one.[84] Strict identity (the identity of "the same," *idem*-identity) puts the two related entities A and B in no ordered relation to one another, $A=B$ being the same as $B=A$. Indeed, very little meaning is derived from such a perfectly symmetrical relation. Meaning requires contrast,[85] but the relation $A=B$ puts neither A nor B in a contrasting relation to the other. This is because the difference between the two would lie in no more than the symbols or the act of symbolization, not in the thing that is symbolized.[86] In which case all we would be saying is that A has no property which B does not have, and vice versa. And we really cannot say anything more than the statement of sameness.[87]

Personal identity requires not a simple juxtaposition, nor even unification of sameness and difference, with the sameness being explained through the conceptuality of substrate and the difference through the notion of changing external qualities. The question really is, "Is the identical in the different or the different in the identical?"[88] Here too it is not simple nondirectionality, but asymmetry that is the key. Strict personal identity implies a symmetrical relation between one's self at a particular point in time, with one's self at another point.[89] Genetic identity in contrast is "only some way of being identical and nonidentical: or to remove the contradiction, of being only partially identical."[90] Genetic identity, according to Hartshorne, involves (i) some "defining characteristic" continued through the members of a sequence of occasions and (ii) direct inheritance of this character from previous members. Both continuity as well as contrast are therefore involved in the definition of genetic identity; the continuous being the abstract pole, while the contrast being the concrete aspect. Personal identity for Hartshorne has these two dimensions or poles: the abstract and the concrete.

Personal identity is founded on the witness of the experience of persons, and as such, points to the issue of experience itself. Even the nonhuman variety, i.e., the identity of things which we do not regard as selves, is anchored onto the notion of experience.[91] The structure of experience is asymmetrical. The structure of mnemonic awareness, as we have seen, is a key witness to this fact. Experience involves a given *other*, as well as a causal structure that is cumulative. Who I was yesterday is immanent in who I am today, and who I am when I wrote the earlier half of this sentence is immanent in who I am as I finish writing this sentence.[92] Personal identity is inheritance of the past, which is why an adult is not simply the same as the child he/she had been. As an adult, he/she is more determinate; he/she possesses in a cumulative way the whole gamut of experiences had from childhood to the very present moment. Thus even Whitehead states that "we—as enduring objects with personal order—objectify the occasions of our past with peculiar completeness in our immediate present."[93]

Surely, a person endures, but such endurance does not encompass the whole reality of personal identity. It does not represent the whole story, as it were. Rather, it is a mere aspect of it, and an abstract one at that. For personal identity, in Hartshorne's words, is no more than "the persistence of certain defining characteristics in a very complex orderly society endowed with a *preeminent linear society* or 'soul.'"[94] There is no selfsame ego which endures since a person is defined as a society of event actualities possessing a defining characteristic or form, with this defining characteristic having no absolute meaning. For as Hartshorne says, not only is it the case that a person regarded as an entity enduring from birth to death, is "a very loose assemblage of things,"[95] this very characteristic also precludes any fixed and definite answer to the question, "When does one become himself?" Personal identity is an affair of difference along a continuous historic route of event experiences. What persists along this line of experient occasions is abstract, while the actual subject having these experiences is concrete.[96] Thus, no selfsame ego is required, this concept being no more than an abstraction from the concrete reality which is the person existing *here* and *now*.[97] It is this most concrete event which for Hartshorne, just like it is for the Buddhists and Whitehead, is the true locus of self.[98]

Hartshorne does not deny the reality of strict identity; he merely argues that it is abstract, and real within something far richer in determination than itself. As there is genuine novelty at each moment an event synthesizes the data of its past, and since this novel event is different from its predecessors, both immediate and remote, it is "the different self which is inclusive of the self that was there all along, not *vice versa*."[99] It is the contrast between one's present reality and one's past reality that contains the past reality, for "contrast of Y to X" includes X; but it is one's present which contrasts itself with one's past, not the other way around.[100]

To posit the existence of a third term, i.e., a selfsame ego that endures through the changes that take place between, for instance, E and E^1 does not really solve the problem of explaining how the earlier can relate itself to the latter.[101] For it is in E^1, i.e., in the present experience, that the relation between the two must obtain, not in the earlier one, for the earlier is (or was) unaware of the latter—hence, a one-way relation. This is an asymmetry that becomes inexplicable if both E and E^1 are related to the selfsame ego, and if this is how the latter is understood to be in fact related to the former.[102] E, the old reality, experienced no contrast whatsoever with whatever succeeded it. The cumulativeness of life ensures its basic asymmetrical relatedness, as it is always the latter event, or the latter self as new and concrete, that contains the reality of the former self. What connects these two is no more than an abstraction—whether this abstraction be understood in terms of an enduring *ego* or a preeminent linear society in a society of innumerable event occasions of experience. And as has been pointed out, the referent of 'I' is usually some limited part of that sequence of experiences. The question then is how to describe this limited part.

The self as a society of event experiences

The self according to Hartshorne is primarily a society of event actualities linked together across spatiotemporal lines. Our analysis of the causal structure of mnemonic awareness and how the past influences the present has shown how it becomes possible to hold that we are related, first to our more minute 'parts'—the cells that make up our bodies and which are genuine others to ourselves,[103] then to our past selves which are likewise real others to us.[104] What we experience *here* and *now* are not experiences we simply constitute ourselves; they are, rather, experiences of 'selves' truly different from us and whose experiences which we "house," *here* and *now*, belong completely to the past. A human self is thus a special type of society of selves, a personal society in which there is a nexus—to use a Whiteheadian term—forming a single line of inheritance of the defining characteristic.[105] 'Nexus' is a technical term used by Whitehead to describe the ultimate fact of the togetherness or unity of actual entities[106]—a unity that the older concept of an enduring substance intended, but ultimately failed, to articulate and safeguard.[107]

All the enduring entities encountered in everyday experience: persons, chairs, tables, books, etc., are societies of actual occasions.[108] They are, as

Hartshorne says, "changing persisting things."[109] They are complex societies, not simply because they are made up of more minute constituents—a block of ice is not simply a society because it is made up of ice molecules, nor simply because they are constituted by successive epochal actualities. Rather, they are societies because they are clusters or strings of superseding actualities which are unified by a particular defining characteristic.[110] This can be illustrated in terms of the concepts of modern physics. An ordinary physical object for instance, is made up of a multiplicity of atoms, with each atom being itself composed of more minute entities, e.g., protons, electrons, and so forth. Consider now a route of electronic actualities. According to the societal theory, this route constitutes a society in respect to its character as "electronic." Moreover, such character is inherited by each member of the route from the antecedent actuality of this same route.[111] Whitehead explains it thus:

> A nexus enjoys "social order" where (i) there is a common element of form illustrated in the definiteness of each of its included actual entities, and (ii) this common element of form arises in each member of the nexus by reason of the conditions imposed upon it by its prehension of some other members of the nexus, and (iii) these prehensions impose that condition of reproduction by reason of their inclusion of positive feelings of that common form.[112]

On account of this, the nexus of actualities constitutes a society. The very defining characteristic of that society takes on a serial form. And when it does, i.e., when the genetic relatedness of its members orders them "serially," what we have is a special type of society which is called a personal society or a person.

Hartshorne explains that there are basically two types of societies: (i) Linear societies or personally ordered societies, the familiar example being a "stream of consciousness" of a single person. (ii) Nonlinear societies such as a tree considered as a colony of cells, with each cell being personally ordered without the entire tree being itself ordered in the same unified manner. But there is a third type of society, which is a sort of combination of the first two. It is a form of nonlinear society that is at the same time accompanied by a linear society of "presiding occasions." A live human body with its "mind" or "soul" is the example nearest at hand.[113]

Hartshorne makes use of the same basic distinctions. He says there are societies which involve a "dominating" ("personal" or "regnant") unit; and societies which do not possess such a unifying thread, and are thus more like "democracies"—plants, for instance. These latter are individuals only in a slight degree for the reality is that their more minute constituents, their cells, are much more unified than the entire organism or society itself.[114] But the human being is not only a society of other-selves, which are the innumerable cells that make up his body; he is also—and for Hartshorne's theory of personal identity, even more importantly—a society of other-selves which are the innumerable past "selves" that constitute his life from birth up to the present moment. And just as a regnant member or dominating unit secures the integrity of his bodily (spatial) components (cells), so too a regnant member or defining character secures the integrity of his temporal constituents (past-selves).[115] For Hartshorne, thus, the defining characteristic of a personal society in linear temporal (personal) order is what comprises personality or individual selfhood. It is that which can be said to remain the same in the midst of change. But it still is "less concrete or particular than its expressions; it has certain abstractness or neutrality with respect to alternative possible experiences and acts."[116] Elsewhere, Hartshorne points out that the distinction between two meanings of personality or individual selfhood is often not clear enough, resulting in the two meanings being confused. On the one hand, it means that which is concrete and determinate, rather than abstract; on the other hand, it can also mean that which continues to exist through change of states of itself.[117] It is this latter which is often taken to define personal identity in its totality, when it is in fact but a special and abstract form of the former.[118] It is what makes one the same at 15 and a hundred years of age. It is what makes Philip who is drunk and Philip who is sober still Philip.[119]

Personal identity and the notion of the "receptacle"

It must be pointed out that even such defining characteristic which for both Whitehead and Hartshorne constitutes personal identity and which comes closest to the perspective of strict identity is still very different from the notion of a substantial self that remains intact, basically unchanged throughout the temporal meanderings of the series of event occasions that make it up. There is, to be sure, continuity in a personal society, secured by the character of the special genetic relations among the members of the nexus. And it is this nexus that sustains a character which is one of the meanings of the Latin word *persona*. And yet as Whitehead insists, person connotes much more than the mere sustenance of a particular character.[120] The serial inheritance of the events in a society which constitutes the society's form is indeed the cause of the continuity of that society. It is what produces the self-identity of the society. Thus, both Whitehead and Hartshorne use the terms "soul" and "receptacle" to explain this notion. But neither soul nor receptacle is a substance possessing an unchanging content.

The use of the notion of receptacle can most certainly be regarded as due to the need to introduce a third term to the relation between change and stability. Whitehead himself uses the terminology of a third term in speaking about personal identity as akin to the Platonic notion of the receptacle in the *Timaeus*.[121] Hartshorne also mentions the term and says that the Platonic notion brings Plato as close as possible to the Buddhistic conceptualization.

Hartshorne understands it in the same way as does Whitehead: "Plato's *Timaeus* is the nearest counterpart to Buddhism in the ancient West; for Plato's cosmos consisted of the universal and elusive 'receptacle' and its momentary qualifications, thus allowing for both mysterious ultimate unity and radical empirical plurality."[122] In fact, the theistic color of Hartshorne's philosophy brings him even closer to the Platonic understanding of the unity as somehow also the world soul and creative demiurge. In "Beyond Enlightened Self-Interest," for instance, Hartshorne, points to an ultimate receptacle of value which lies beyond any one human career, and even beyond human life as such—this of course being God himself.[123] Now such conceptualization can be regarded as a way by which Hartshorne and Whitehead saw the need to find an integrating notion for the discontinuous events that make up a series. Thus, for instance, Peter Bertocci, in his critique of Hartshorne's theory of personal identity, insists that the notion of a self different from the entire series, as well as the atomic selves that make it up, is necessary. Since at no point does one simply experience oneself as a succession of unit events, Bertocci suggests that Hartshorne should rather consider the need to posit an experient (a self, separate from the series as well as the unit events of becoming) who is a self-identifying unity without which there would be no meaning for either the succession or the entities that succeed one another.[124] A similar criticism is voiced by Albert Shalom and John Robertson who say, contrary to Hartshorne's account, that one is not aware of oneself as this person now, and now, and now, nor does one refer to oneself as a section of a person now and another and different section at each succeeding microsecond.[125]

These criticisms reflect the concern of some thinkers, otherwise sympathetic with the perspective taken by process thought with regard to the untenability of a substantial self, that the notion that subjectivity is atomic renders the idea of self as largely discontinuous. This notion, they hold, appears much less in line with our common sense experience of selfhood, namely, as much more of a continuity, than as a concatenation of discrete subjects (selves) related causally through inheritance of past experiences.[126] These authors have likewise criticized the notion of atomic successiveness as guilty of the fallacy of misplaced concreteness and that the atomic self as itself no more than an abstraction from our ordinary experience of self.[127]

The atomic theory of becoming

Čapek in an article on the notion of the self in the later philosophy of William James also discusses the idea of a unified experience of selfhood; this time, however, in relation to that experience in which one intuits one's full self in all its dimensions.[128] Elsewhere he says that the idea regarding the possibility of experiencing the full self in a single intuitive moment is also found in Hartshorne. Indeed in *Beyond Humanism*, the latter speaks of our dim consciousness of infinity, or the faint, slightly conscious background which embraces all past time, all the future, all space, and all possibility.[129] Of course, this needs to be understood in relation to the way Hartshorne conceives of the difference between human and divine consciousness. What to human experients is but a faint awareness, is for God distinct; that is, so long as we understand this to refer to finite values which happen to be anywhere *actualized*.[130] Still, the idea of being able to experience something like the full self, even intuitively and, as in the case of hypermnesia, in no more than a few seconds, seems to lend credence to the objection raised by personalists like Bertocci. He points out that the self is more readily—and according to common sense, it seems—experienced not only as a continuity, but also as a unity. The genuinely "person-al moment" is more readily experienced as "a person-al *now recognizing itself as it changes*, and anticipating what is not *now*."[131] At the same time, however, these critics, rather than completely rejecting the essence of the atomistic notion of the self, present us instead with several suggestions which they believe can provide a way of reconciling the epochal theory (which ensures that selfhood will no longer be equated with unchanging substance) and our lived reality of selfhood. These suggestions can be basically summed up in the notion that the human self, because it stands as a unique actual entity can, and must, be exempted from the epochal theory of becoming.[132]

The suggestion hinges on the argument that since God is exempt from the epochal theory of time, so may human entities be. In his article dealing with the question of whether or not the human self should be regarded as an actual occasion or a society, Rem Edwards argues that Whitehead did not extend the generalization of the discreteness of experience all the way to God.[133] Edwards then argues that Whitehead regarded this atomic theory of experience, not so much as a metaphysical theory, but as a cosmological one. The difference between these two is traced by Edwards to the distinction Whitehead makes between cosmological theories, which apply only to entities in our (or at least *some*) given cosmic epoch, and metaphysical theories, which apply to entities in all possible worlds. Whitehead's epochal theory of time, according to Edwards, is applied to all actual entities in our cosmic epoch, but not to all actual entities whatsoever. It is not, for instance, applied to God. The Whiteheadian God, according to Edwards, is not characterized in the same way:

> [I]n *Process and Reality* he [i.e., Whitehead] clearly exempts God from its application. There are no gaps in God's existence. He does not discontinuously flash in and out of existence, as do objects composed of societies of actual occasions. God is *always* there continuously assimilating data coming to him from the world and continuously acting upon the world. God does not exist in spurts, flashes, squirts, drops, or buds.[134]

The flow of Edwards' argument, however, is already problematic—from the very beginning. As Robert Fancher points out, contrary to Edwards' reading of Whitehead, "God is not exempt from the epochal theory of time, but it is precisely this theory of time which makes the actual entity Whitehead calls 'God' a nontemporal, continuous concrescence dependent upon the temporal world for his being."[135] There is a difference here of course between Whitehead for whom God is an actual entity, albeit "of a peculiar sort,"[136] and Hartshorne who approaches the notion of God as an actual entity, with much reservation. For instance, in his reply to his critics in *The Philosophy of Charles Hartshorne*, he states: "The main difference is that I find the idea of God as a single actual entity too close for comfort to classical theism and doubtfully consistent with the rest of the system."[137] This difference lies in the more radically temporalistic view of God as is found in Hartshorne.[138] This thoroughgoing temporalism leads him to seriously take into account Whitehead's idea that God's subjective aim, being infinite, is never satisfied, and as such he is never complete.[139] He also concludes that because of this, "a subject that never reaches completion but 'is always moving on' as it actualizes novel prehensions of novel states of the world is not a single subject or single actuality."[140] Nevertheless, both Hartshorne and Whitehead are in agreement that every actual entity is a single continuous concrescence until it is complete. This holds true, whether one regards God as an actual entity or not. Even God is God in the making.[141]

As such, the claim is made that there does not have to be a philosophical problem of exempting God from the principles of atomicity.[142] Edward's argument nonetheless is worth looking into, if only to drive home the point that the uniqueness of the self, in spite of the rejection of substantialism, is an issue that must be reckoned with by process thought. Even those sympathetic with the process perspective find the need to express caution that approaches to personal identity not be without the required nuance or qualification. Edwards argues that once it is realized that there is a possible exception to the epochal account, and that the theory itself is limited to entities belonging to our cosmic epoch (not to all actual entities whatsoever), one can then re-examine the question whether it applies to *all* entities within our own epoch or merely to *some* of them.[143] And he takes the argument even further by asking whether it is possible that the theory is not even applicable to all entities in our cosmic epoch. If it applies on the microscopic level of quantum physics, should we also take it to hold of entities on the macroscopic level? It is easy enough when we are dealing with electrons and other such subatomic particles. But is it just as easy when it is human beings that we are dealing with? Bertocci, for instance, has this to say:

> There is, methodologically, a radical personalistic experientialism in ... the insistence that every metaphysical theory is inadequate if it misconstrues or forces self-conscious experience into some mold that does not include personal self-consciousness—the one place where there is not only activity

but activity aware of itself as activity. The fact that we begin theorizing as self-conscious persons does not, to be sure, entail the conclusion that the person is the microcosmic model for the macrocosm.[144]

If it is methodologically questionable, as Bertocci suggests, to regard the person as the microcosmic model of the macrocosm, it appears likewise questionable to regard the character of the subatomic world of quantum physics as the microcosmic model of the macrocosmic reality which is personhood. There is something in this latter reality which seems to escape any attempt to explain, much less to reduce, it by means of the former.

Edwards therefore suggests that we loosen the analogy between the human person and the subatomic world of the electron, and focus instead on the analogy between the human person and God. Thus, he asks whether in regard to human beings the analogy with quantum phenomena could be justified, or whether it would be more appropriate to conceive of the human "soul" as a continuously concrescing actual entity, by analogy with God. And he adds that it appears much more reasonable to hold that human personality differs *from electrons*, but *not from God*, not in degree but in kind. He supports this claim by arguing from the same angle as the other critics, i.e., that it is more consonant with ordinary experience, to think of the stream of human experience and activity on the model of continuous concrescence rather than on the model of continuous pulsations.[145]

The question that arises, however, is how to characterize human selfhood as *similar to* yet *different from* God. Edwards' attempt to explain the similarity centers on the Whiteheadian notion—rejected by Hartshorne of course, for reasons already mentioned—that God is an actual entity. This means that there are basically two kinds of actual entities, God and actual occasions, both exemplifying (and not being exempt from) the *generic* characteristics of an actual entity, but with the latter existing discontinuously, but not the former. Edwards says that in the case of God at least, we have an instance of a continuously concrescing actual entity that *is* an actual entity, "to have continuous immediacy of self-enjoyment, to have continuous significance for itself ... to synthesize data continuously (concresce), to be continuously *causa sui* or self-creative (at least in part)."[146] The dipolar structure of deity is applied by Edwards to human beings in a much more radical way than do Hartshorne and Whitehead. The only difference between the unity of our experience of selfhood and God's is that unlike God, the human "*primordial self*, slumbers and sleeps and is not necessary, eternal, or nontemporal."[147] Nonetheless, there is in human selfhood, a creative agency which is characterized by a continuously enduring power to act and exercise such powers as thinking, feeling, choosing, synthesizing multifarious causal and sensory data into unified experience, during our wakeful moments. And is this not in fact how we ordinarily understand the self, namely, as having little to do with the epochal or atomistic notion espoused by both Whitehead and Hartshorne? Rather, as another critic expressed, we ordinarily experience the self as more of "a fluid unity in which the past so blends with the present in anticipation of the future that it is impossible, except artificially, to mark off its boundaries."[148]

The radicality of such a view, however—Edwards calls it "unorthodox Whiteheadianism"—lies in the fact that instead of being recreated every tenth of a second, the self has a continuous existence. The persistence of the creative agency secures such continuity while at the same time there is a sense in which the continuous self is likewise many and consequent. "The *consequent self* consists of the *specific* thoughts, emotions, feelings, choices, sensations, and experiences entertained by the enduring self from moment to moment. It is the concrete totality of the activities plus their objects at any given moment or during any period of time. Any given duration which is to count as such a moment is an abstraction from the continuing flow, however."[149] What this suggestion amounts to is a type of reinstitution of a new substance-type metaphysics, minus the idea of a *substratum* underlying the experience itself.[150] This manner of conceptualization would regard the self as "a unity within ongoing qualitative diversity."[151] Indeed, some critics point out that contrary to the Whiteheadian/Hartshornean way of looking at the matter, it is not merely the idea of an unchanging substrate that is an abstraction. Rather, it is the unqualified use of the concept that is. And in like manner, the unqualified use of the idea of discrete selves is also an abstraction for it is isolated from the ordinary commonsense experience of continuity.[152] Intelligence, it is argued, is what abstracts, leading us to reduce selfhood to either an unchanging substance on the one hand, or to an atomistic self on the other. On the contrary, it is intuition that tells us that the self is neither simply one nor the other but a unification of both.[153]

The problem of discreteness and continuity

Suggestions such as the ones just mentioned hinge on a thesis of reconciliation of continuity and discreteness. Some authors make a comparison here between the thesis of complementarity in physics in which the corpuscular theory of light, which had been held unchallenged for centuries, has been reconciled with the wave theory. It has led physicists to the realization of the inadequacy of the concepts of waves and particles, drawn as they are from the macroscopic world of ordinary human experience, as models of the microscopic world of light and the atom. That is to say, such models, however helpful for practical understanding and for prediction, must not be mistaken for exact images of reality.[154] However, there are two issues or considerations that must be noted with regard to this suggested need for complementarity.

First, notwithstanding the insistence on balance and complementarity on the part of these critics, their views are really for the continuity thesis rather than the notion of discreteness. The bottom line argument is that discreteness is simply not given in human experience—"no succession of experiences without experience of succession," as Bertocci puts it.[155]

Secondly, what is really being insinuated by their so-called suggestions is that what we are dealing with here is a dichotomy between atomicity and continuity.[156] Edwards, for instance, speaks of gaps between successive occasions during which nothing exists, since the occasions do not touch or overlap. He adds further that during these intervals the society of actual entities ceases to exist.[157] The fact of the matter, however, is that neither in Hartshorne nor in Whitehead does such a dichotomy exist.

Moreover, these two issues can be given an appropriate response, by going back to what for Hartshorne is the key to resolving apparent contradictories that underlie both issues and by noting that Hartshorne does not leave unreconciled any supposed dichotomy between discreteness and continuity. Hartshorne puts it in this way: "Perhaps some readers know or have guessed what my key to this problem is: the Aristotelian or ontological principle of Whitehead that the abstract is in the concrete, not vice versa. (Incidentally, I could have learned this *asymmetry* from C.I. Lewis rather than from Whitehead.)"[158] It is the asymmetrical relatedness between the two concepts of discreteness and continuity that provides an answer to those who suggest that balance and complementarity are the key. For Hartshorne, simple complementarity, i.e., balance understood to mean ordinary symmetry, fails to provide a resolution to such a problem. The situation can be compared to that relation which holds between the abstract and concrete poles of deity or even between ordinary concreteness and abstraction. The independent factor in deity is abstract, and *so is the consequent nature* as a mere nature. But concreteness is itself an abstraction. What is genuinely concrete are the instances of this particular abstraction. The abstract and the concrete *together* are instantiated in instances of the consequent (i.e., concrete) nature. In the same vein, neither continuity nor discreteness by themselves are the concrete reality. What is *really real* are the instances, "states"—as Hartshorne calls them, which embody both continuity and discreteness. These states are themselves atomic. Thus, Hartshorne states

> Continuity is an abstract mathematical concept, not a given actuality. Half a continuum is itself a smaller continuum, but half a man is not a smaller man, nor is half a molecule just a smaller molecule. If happenings are actualities, and even more concrete than individuals, they must be like molecules or men, not like mathematical schema. If experiencing were continuous, then half of a half of a half … of an experience would also be an experience. However, though in a tenth of a second we can have an experience, in half of a half of a tenth, it seems we cannot. Were experiencing a continuum, indeed, we should have an infinite number of experiences between waking and having breakfast.[159]

The relation between the concepts at issue is, as the critics say, one of complementarity. However, it is not such *simply*, for it is also, and more importantly, asymmetrical. Hence, there is no dichotomy between the concepts involved. And the suggestion that there are gaps in between the states that constitute a society, intervals in which no entity exists, is incorrect. As Fancher remarks, "there cannot be any *'gaps during which.'*"[160] Gaps only have duration if we suppose time to be an independent and fixed receptacle for actual entities. As Hartshorne notes, to involve such gaps in our consideration of time is to destroy the very unity itself of time. For time itself is the upsurge, the result of the communion of actual entities. It is the "sympathy (social continuity) of a creative present with a created or settled past and an uncreated, partially indeterminate future."[161] The communion of actual entities is fundamental to neoclassical philosophy. It is the very meaning of the doctrine of prehensions and of the denial of the Aristotelian doctrine that no substance is in another substance. The epochal theory of selfhood does not mean that there are gaps in which no self exists, for this would be tantamount to simple location in an independent continuum. And in no way does such notion represent the way by which Hartshorne distinguishes successive atomic events. These are distinct only in terms of the satisfactions in which they culminate. Each concrescence proceeds from the indeterminate many to the creatively synthesized determinateness of a unified subject. And the achievement of this determinateness is the achievement of a single, indivisible identity. Now due to the fact that any further change would destroy the atomic integrity of this novel event, the process of coming-to-be must come to an end. And the event becomes a datum amidst a plurality of other atomic events (data) out of which its successor event arises as the past event passes into (enters) the further concrescence of its descendant. Nevertheless, such passage does not nullify its atomic integrity. It remains a determinate datum for a concrescence which is yet-to-become fully atomic. It is the relations that hold between the completed and incipient events that constitutes the coming-to-be of the continuity of time.

It is such continuity that we ordinarily understand as given to us in experience. However, as Hartshorne points out, the case really is not so much that human experience is given to us as continuous, but rather that it is merely not given to us as discrete. The alleged continuity of the self—just like the so-called continuity of becoming criticized by Hartshorne—is already an interpretation. The only conclusion that one can reasonably make is that experience is merely vague as to any discreteness that there may be. It is this vagueness that is misread as a disclosure of actual continuity. "Experience," Hartshorne argues, "is at most quasi-continuous, or pseudo-continuous. To say more implies a fundamental error in theory of perception, of what it could possibly accomplish."[162] It is not accidental, for instance, that we do not distinctly or consciously perceive nature as composed of atomic and subatomic particles. Such distinct and conscious perception, says Hartshorne, is the prerogative of a radically superhuman intelligence. Anything other than such an intelligence merely glides over such facts as they are not significant for its everyday affairs. Thus, "individual atoms are not biologically significant, hence not perceived," Hartshorne explains. "But likewise individual events, even on the human level, are also insignificant for ordinary purposes, hence too they are not clearly perceived."[163] But just because these facts are not significant for our ordinary purposes does not mean that they are not the case nor that they are insignificant for philosophical query.

Indeed, the truth of the matter is that neither Hartshorne nor Whitehead denies this common sense experience of selfhood as a continuously existing reality. What is denied most emphatically is the notion that this continuity requires explanation by means of an appeal to an underlying substrate that remains basically unchanged throughout the career of a particular human individual. Just as Hartshorne admits that for normal, everyday purposes, the notion of substance is useful and hence, cannot be done away with, so too in the case of personal identity, the idea of something like personal identity that continues amidst the welter of transformations cannot simply be put aside. But this should not be interpreted as saying that it encompasses the whole reality of personhood.

There is no strict and unqualified denial of the self of ordinary experience in process philosophy. There is merely an attempt to free it from its bondage to substantialism and to reformulate the concept in terms of the category of becoming. There is hence no need to reintroduce the notion of the self as an integrating, unifying term to the atomic selves that make up the series of a person's life, for it was never denied. Neither Hartshorne nor Whitehead would agree that any such element of personhood analogous to the Platonic receptacle is simply an unchanging substantial entity like a selfsame ego. Whitehead is clear in his rejection of this concept as a foundation for what endures in a person. Even the receptacle, he says, which receives all occasions of the man's existence is changed and variously figured by the things that enter it so that it differs in its character at different times.[164]

Personal identity simply cannot be due to the possession of a particular unchanging content but, as Hartshorne says, to a principle of sequence of actualities. "The principle is the personality or character of the individual [the ordinary language equivalent of 'defining characteristic']; the actualities are states, experiences, or acts of expressing this character."[165] And just as causal connections are rigorous only retrospectively,[166] so in the case of persons, the "soul" of the individual is never fully determinate in content until the death of the individual.[167] One truly *is*, only when one is *no longer*; the Whiteheadian doctrines of the perishing of occasions and their objective immortality applies therefore to the case of personal societies as well. Hence, personal identity is regarded by Hartshorne as a special strand of the causal order of the world. It rests on the same principle of inheritance from the past as causality in general does.[168] Just as there is no such thing as a predetermined, already completed, and forever-unchanging reality, there is likewise no such thing as an identity already completed, substancelike and untouched by the innumerable changes that take place in the life of a person.

Personal identity thus does not depend upon the existence of some unchanging soul substance. Definiteness or concreteness belongs to occasions that make up a person, not to the concept of person simply. In the case of real causal connections, a certain neutrality holds with respect to the alternative future possibilities of becoming for a present event. This is also true with identity understood as the defining character of the sequence of events that constitute the life of an individual.[169] The consequence of this is that the individual person, like individual actual entities, possesses authentic freedom and creativity. There are of course, limiting factors to such freedom and creativity; they are not absolute. The genuineness of the past's immanence in the present—as this is disclosed by the structure of memory—ensures that the freedom and creativity that characterizes the coming-to-be of personal identity is confined within that area of experience. That area of experience can express or fulfill the particular purpose inherent in the entity's defining characteristic or, in the case of actual entities, the subjective form.

Furthermore, this doctrine of the past's immanence in the present also means that the present event, as Whitehead says, is "constituted by the *influx of the other* into that self-identity which is the continued life of the immediate past within the immediacy of the present."[170] This influx of the other which entails efficient causality or the literal transmission of energy from the past to the present likewise secures the nonabsoluteness of the freedom of a present subject. It does not emerge *ex nihilo*. Instead, the creativity which is internal to each event is both partially inherited from the antecedent others, antecedent determining conditions as well as partially spontaneous. Thus, personal identity, understood in terms of the defining characteristic of a society of occasions serially ordered and causally connected, is truly an affair of difference along a continuous historic route. The identity of a person is a chain of interconnected but genuinely other selves, each of which causally inherited from past selves what it is at the moment, and handing this inheritance *plus* the novelty it has contributed, to selves that shall come even later in the chain.[171]

The life of a person, therefore, is a series of experiences extending from birth to death. Each experience in this series is a subjective process of feeling innumerable past data and creatively synthesizing them into a complex experiential whole.[172] When the synthesis has come to fruition, the immediacy of the experience ceases, i.e., "perishes," in Whiteheadian terms, and the experience itself becomes an object to be remembered—consciously or subconsciously—by subsequent experiences. As an object remembered, an experience is a "superject"; as an immediate process of synthesizing, it is a "subject." Hence, to say that a human life is a series of experiences is to say that such a life is a series of "subjects" which become "superjects" for subsequent subjects. This theory of sequential societies of actualities, each of which is created and then persists thereafter as an objectified datum of prehension in later actualities, is better suited to explaining the complexities of personal identity.[173] The concrete subject cannot be things or persons as identical through change. Instead, they are the concrete momentary states, singular instances of becoming. When one remembers, it is not *A* simply remembering the identical *A*; rather, it is an experience remembering earlier, and definitely *not identical*, experiences.[174]

The relational self

The concrete subject is shot through and through with a dynamic relationality.[175] The self *here* and *now* is not simply a self existing in splendid isolation from the rest of the world. At every single moment, one is related in a most intimate way with other-selves which are coconstitutive of one's identity in space and in time.[176] Spatially, one is related first and foremost to the minute constituents of one's *internal* environment, i.e., the body as made up of genuine others whose experiences one immediately "feels." Secondly, one is related to the *external* environment to which one belongs, from the lowest to the highest level events that comprise one's world. There are genuine others as well, irreducible to an "I" which is both *different* from as well as *like* them. I do not constitute, but am actually *coconstituted by* them.[177]

In all these instances, the structure of pastness holds the real key to understanding the implicated relationality. For the relationality of the self is not only spatial, but temporal as well. As Hartshorne remarks: "The self ... is a temporal group mind as well as a spatial one. It focuses, in its present, what it knows of experiences belonging to other selves as well as experiences in its own past and future."[178] And it is in mnemonic awareness alone that this structure is given to us in ordinary experience. The mnemonic bridge between a present self and its past data is what finally enables us to make sense of the characteristically human experience of change and self-identity. We are what we remember, whether or not this remembering involves consciousness.[179] For the data which our present reality creatively synthesizes belongs genuinely to the past. That self which we shall eventually bequeath to our anticipated future, be this our own or any future whatsoever, is grounded and constrained by what the data of the past contributes to the creative coming-to-be of a novel event.[180] An event-in-process in Hartshorne's philosophy is derivative of the very otherness that lies at the heart of becoming as creative synthesis. It is the universal or generalized form of what we ordinarily experience as regard for self and regard for others.[181] And since pastness is itself the basis of interdependence, mnemonic identity is therefore inextricably bound with social identity.[182]

The most important consequence of the Hartshornean notion that personal identity is partial identity is that the nonidentity of one self with another self may also be partial. There is, to be sure, a difference between my relation to selves that belong to my own sequence, past and future, and my relation to other selves that do not belong to mine. But the difference is only relative, as Hartshorne states,

> Always ... in self relations and other relations, there are causal connections backwards and forward, these being prehensive relations, the prehending being always on the effect side and the prehended on the cause side. I expect to remember my present state in my future states and expect my friends, so far as they perceive my present, to remember it also. My awareness of my past tends to be more vivid and direct than of the past of others, but this is no absolute difference.[183]

A thoroughgoing sociality is foundational to a metaphysics of selves and persons in process philosophy. Here as well, the mnemonic structure of identity is the key, for in remembering, what one remembers is no less than the feelings or experiences of another.[184] Of course, it can be asked, if memory were constitutive of relationality, why then do we not know the memories of other persons? Experience tells us that what we remember is radically our "own." Hartshorne does not dispute this issue. But it hardly follows from the fact that we do not remember other's memories as vividly as our own that we can have no direct experience of concrete events other than our own past states.[185] Even our remembrance of our so-called own past states is never totally clear and distinct for we are not God. Moreover, as Hartshorne remarks, the maintenance of our personal integrity requires that we have a certain privacy or isolation of feeling from other human beings. Apart from any possible usefulness of telepathy, it is better for human beings that they are not in fact clearly and distinctly aware of the feelings and experiences of their fellows.[186] And yet, even if our awareness is not in fact as vivid as the divine, and even if we were not telepathic, the immediacy of our relation with our bodily components (cells especially) can be regarded as analogous to the relation that God has with the world body. For as Hartshorne observes we are in fact radically superior; consequently, we can synthesize their many trivial feelings into one feeling on our own higher level. This instance of relationality—since it spans the gap between metazoan and cellular individuality, together with the relationality involved in memory—shows that there can be an analogy between self-knowledge and a hypothetical direct intuition of "other" minds.[187]

This is what Hartshorne means by the broadening of memory. It must be shown to include not only nonhuman and even nonanimal forms but also to be conceivable for an individual to remember past experiences belonging to other individuals. Causality must connect enduring individuals with one another, not simply with their own pasts and futures. Whitehead has shown that there is no absurdity in this.[188] For Hartshorne, the otherness implicated in our experience of other persons, i.e., other-selves, is no more than the particular instance of the more general case which is disclosed by the relations we have, first to our bodily cells, and second, to our remembered past selves.[189] From the idea that personal identity involves partial identity and nonidentity—which therefore means that identity with one's past selves is relative rather than absolute—Hartshorne extrapolates to the notion that our difference from other human beings, other-selves of a much higher level on the scale of beings, is likewise relative than absolute. The same causal connections hold in self-relatedness and other-relatedness. One remembers one's past experiences in quite the same way that one would remember the past experiences of others with whom he is acquainted. The difference in vividness notwithstanding, no absolute difference exists between the two types of remembering. Neither self-identity nor nonidentity is absolute.[190]

This is the primacy of relatedness of which Hartshorne speaks.[191] It is the core of Hartshorne's account of personal identity and is also the most central concept of an ethical discourse in process philosophy. And foundational to this theory of relatedness is the mnemonic structure of personal identity, which enables us to regard ourselves as a society of innumerable individuals, each of which, could be regarded in its uniqueness, as another self.[192] A person, in his/her deepest and innermost being, is truly altruistic. And by this we do not mean that a person is always and immediately selfless or that because his/her nature is to be other-regarding, he/she will in fact act accordingly. Instead, what is meant by this altruism is that the nature of personhood is to be other-oriented, a person being a "society of past and future experiences bound together by a mode of sympathy which, in a specifically different but generically similar way, unites us also to the experiences belonging to the temporal societies constituting other personalities."[193] Hence, there can be no absolute independence of the self from other selves, both those belonging to its own sequence, as well as those not its own. And it can no longer be held, as did substantialistic theories of extreme individualism, that if all others were annihilated, the essential self would remain the same.[194] For the identity of a person, as against a substance, is—from the perspective of process philosophy—increased by its relations. As Whitehead says of an atom that it is a system of all things, we can say of self-identity, that it is a relational system of all selves. Personal identity is achieved by relationship. No entity is self-contained or absolutely unique in the sense of being unrelated to other entities and sharing nothing with them. This constitutes the most comprehensive and far-reaching statement that is an offshoot of the mode of philosophizing peculiar to process philosophy. Each person, like the world itself, is an indefinitely extended plenum of interrelated events, stretching all the way back to the events now shrouded in the mists of history, and all the way to the indefinite future which is the ever-growing consequent nature of God himself. It is the nature of the person to be relational, and the account of this nature as it is offered by process philosophy constitutes its most radical and comprehensive explanation.

Conclusion

The notion of identity in Hartshorne's philosophy is incurably abstract. This is why he regards the notion of a selfsame ego as a stumbling block to an account of personal identity. "Personhood," the concept that underlies theories of personal identity, simply resists accommodation within a framework of substance ontology. As we have tried to show in this work, there are difficulties with the notion that the self is a thinglike substance, and that whatever occurs in one's mind and one's thoughts is no more than the activity of a substantial entity of a certain kind, whether this is a physical brain or a substantial mind. Personal identity, for Hartshorne, encompasses a much wider domain than the simple question of the transtemporal sameness of a numerically identical self. It also involves delving into a far more complex conglomeration of ideas and concerns than theories dealing only with numerical identity.

This is not to say that the ideas and concerns that support Hartshorne's theory are totally different from those supporting accounts of personal identity as *sameness*. Concern for one's future and survival are very much part of the overall scheme by which Hartshorne discusses the problem of personal identity, as are questions that deal with an individual's relations with other persons. These concerns, however, serve both as a background for his reflections, as well as "existential" points of departure for his metaphysical generalizations.

Take the concern for one's future, for instance. That a difference exists between one's concern to survive and one's interest in another person's survival is beyond doubt. The question, however, is *how big a difference is it?* According to Hartshorne, while the difference is undeniable, its being absolute is not. The failure to realize that the difference is relative rather than absolute is due to our deeply entrenched notion of a self that remains untouched by change, a substancelike "I" standing over and against the fortunes and misfortunes of its "others." From this perspective, other-interest becomes no more than a function and offshoot of a more primordial interest and concern for one's "ownmost self." Hartshorne's rejection of this idea of the primacy of self-interest in our ethical and social relationships is what grounds his thesis of the nature of personal identity, as well as his analysis of the causal structure disclosed by the experience of memory. Like Locke, Parfit, and Ricoeur, this rejection serves as the foundation for his reflections on the identity of persons.

Still, a fundamental difference exists between Hartshorne and these philosophers. For while there is an almost unanimous rejection of a sub-stantial self in all of them, Hartshorne's theory—as we have tried to develop it in this work—unifies all the seemingly contradictory concepts involved. Locke's analysis paved the way for this by unfastening the bonds that tied the notion of personal identity onto the identity of "substance." In fact, Locke went farther. He created a somewhat artificial distinction between "men" and "persons." He wanted to emphasize the point that there is in the very idea of a 'person', and consequently in the concept of "personal iden-tity," an element irreducible to the identity of "substances," even if these be entities that belong properly to the domain of scientific discourse, viz., "men." Persons are entities that possess a *concern* unmatched by entities of the impersonal kind. "Concern" is an important term for Locke. It is how he ultimately understands the concept of memory as consciousness and utilizes this to expound his theory of person and his account of what constitutes a person's identity.

For Locke a person is a moral agent whose "concern" for and "appropri-ation" of his past thoughts, experiences, and deeds provide a key to under-standing what constitutes his identity. *Concern* and *appropriation* together constitute memory, which in turn constitutes personal identity. Without these two elements, there is hardly a way to make sense of the unity of the self without having to posit a substance onto which are attached the thoughts, experiences, and deeds that belong to one's past. But it also becomes difficult to explain the most important dimension of selfhood, namely, the fact that it involves the merging of two perspectives, the third person and the first. It is difficult enough to disentangle the self from sub-stance. And yet even if it were loosened from a too-easy connection with substance, the self still escapes any facile definition.

This is the main point of the criticism of Reid and Butler against the Lockean view. Against Locke, Reid and Butler held that the identity of selves is a strict-identity relation quite different from the identity of ordi-nary entities (nonselves) and ultimately irreducible to any description in the manner by which one would describe these objects. Hence, in regard to the criterion of memory as well, these critics hold that the identity of the self is already presupposed by memory, not the other way around. That one can remember—i.e., have "concern" for and "appropriate" one's past—only discloses the integrity and irreducibility of the self. Surreptitiously, how-ever, the notion of an underlying "thing" makes its return in the theories of these philosophers.

The concerns as well as a great deal of Locke's conclusions can be found in Derek Parfit's thesis, which also rejects the idea of a self untouched by change and existing in isolation from its others. Unlike Locke, however, Parfit goes much further, and actually dissolves the self, reducing it to its constituent states. He does not deny that for normal everyday purposes, there is a usefulness to the idea of a unified self akin to a substance enduring amidst the welter of change. However, the identity of such a self is not what ultimately matters, but rather, psychological continuity or connnectedness understood in the widest sense of the term. It does not matter that it is exactly I who will exist 10 or 15 years from now. The only thing that really matters is that there is someone *sufficiently continuous* with my present state of being.

Parfit calls it "Relation-R," and it is no more than a functional term. It does not say anything concerning the nature of personal identity as such. Instead it drives home Parfit's point concerning what he takes to be the unimportance of identity and the need to free our conceptions from the overwhelming hold of an unchanging self. Reducing the self to its states frees us to describe it in an impersonal way. But it also liberates us from too much concern for the fortunes, misfortunes, and interests of the self, thereby making us more available to consider the concerns and needs of others. As undue emphasis on the identity of the self is reduced, and we are set free from the concerns of strict selfhood, the "glass wall" that separates us from other persons is also removed. We come to realize that self-centeredness cannot be the rational basis of human action and that it cannot be more rationally compelling than any moral principle, as for instance, the principle of altruism.

It is in this regard that Parfit's thought is similar to Hartshorne's. However, as Paul Ricoeur's distinction between identity as *sameness* (*idem*-identity) and identity as *selfhood* (*ipse*-identity) makes clear, the simple reduction of the self to its states—even for the sake of escaping an ontology of substance— is not without its difficulties. Parfit's notion of identity freed from substantialism leads him to think that such a loosened connection frees us to be just as concerned, if not a little more concerned, with the interests of others. This shift appears a little too abrupt; and he has been criticized for this move. Ricoeur, for instance, says that the central phenomenon of personhood, upon which the entire problem hinges, and which Parfit reduces, is actually eluded. This, according to Ricoeur, is the "who," rather than the simple "what" of identity. And he insists that a considerable gap exists between a simple hermeneutics of selfhood and an actual philosophy of the "I," which is the innermost core of the self. These are two different things, as "to say *self* is not to say *I*."[1] In this regard, not only self-ascription, but other-ascription as well is untranslatable in terms of a mere impersonal description. Even my concern for the interests of others finds its ultimate foundation in the concern that an "I" has for the fortunes and misfortunes of its neighbors. The distinction that Ricoeur makes between identity-as-sameness and identity-as-selfhood drives home the point already found in Locke's philosophy and reemphasized by Butler and Reid; namely, the unique position occupied by the notion of selfhood in any theory of personal identity. It is an idea that Parfit, in his desire to break down the gulf between the self and its others, has seemingly passed by too quickly.

Hartshorne's own account of personal identity bears a close resemblance to these theories. However, the way by which he reaches his conclusions concerning selfhood and the need to transcend it involves a very different approach. Hartshorne agrees with these thinkers that the connection between the self and an ontology of substance must be rejected and that it can only be allowed insofar as there is a utility to the language of substance that serves us well in ordinary life. Parfit says as much. But unlike Parfit who reduces the question of selfhood to the question of the identity of its states, and unlike Ricoeur for whom the treatment of the question of *idem*-identity, important as this may be, is no more than a useful "detour" leading us all the way back to the even more important issue of *ipse*-identity, Hartshorne believes that the two perspectives of identity as *sameness* and identity as *selfhood* are related in a manner that merges one with the other.

In this work we showed how Hartshorne accomplishes this by grounding the notion of personal identity on a concept other than substance. In this way, both identity as sameness and identity as selfhood are based on a concept that integrates both perspectives and resolves the problems raised by Parfit and Ricouer. This is the notion of "event" as the basic *descriptum* of reality. Hartshorne's rejection of substance ontology as a foundation for a theory of personal identity is based on the thesis that "persons" and "selves" encompass a far greater and richer range of concepts than what belongs to an unchanging substrate localizable within a definite spatiotemporal locus. Of course, persons and selves are not unlike ordinary objects. They can be plotted onto a matrix with both spatial and temporal aspects. One can point to one's friend as "here" or "there" or "here yesterday" in much the same way as one can point to an important piece of paper as having been "there on the desk a week ago." Furthermore, one can point to the same friend and observe the difference that having his beard shaved has made to him in much the same way as one can spot the difference that having a room repainted has done to it. Accidental qualities may change, but we ordinarily believe that the entities remain the same; John is still John, and the room is very much the same room. Something remains the same. This is the traditional conceptualization of the identity of objects and persons. It is the notion that Hartshorne rejects. For taken simply, it fails to do justice to the fact that persons are not merely comparable to things. In spite of his rejection of any ultimate bifurcation in nature, and his refusal to believe that what is peculiarly human is an accident, completely detached from the nature out of which it arose, Hartshorne nevertheless rejects any suggestion that reduces what is human to what is not. For what is human is our "starting point," our way of approaching what is other to it by means of progressive generalization. This is the point of departure of metaphysical inquiry for Hartshorne, and he holds that there can be no other.

The classical conception of substance as located within a fixed spatiotemporal locus, existing in isolation from every other substance, and related to another only externally, far from being the reality itself, is already an interpretation of reality. That we encounter books, tables, chairs, trees, persons, far from being the primordial and original approach to the real, is already an interpretation on our part, conditioned to a very great extent, by the weakness of our senses and, to some degree, by the manner in which we have been accustomed to use them. According to Hartshorne, it is "events" (as process philosophy and much of contemporary physics tell us) that we actually encounter.

The mind abstracts from the overwhelming richness of reality, focusing on a specific locus in order to "get a handle" on things, in order to manage what would otherwise be an unmanageable complexity. It is this abstraction, harmless and useful as it may seem at first, that transformed into dogma becomes a hindrance to an adequate description of the richness and complexity of the real. Whitehead has termed it the "fallacy of simple location," and it has transformed what is merely a "way of approaching the real" into a complete and dogmatic description of reality itself, a map turned into the reality it attempts to describe: this is method transformed into metaphysics. It has likewise transformed what is no more than a useful way of starting an investigation into the nature of a "person" into a doctrine concerning this very nature. It is an *abstraction* that has come to define theories of personal identity.

The difficulties affecting this view of persons and of reality itself are not that obvious, says Hartshorne. This is what makes it more dangerous, but it is also why rejecting it is even more important. Like Parfit, Hartshorne regards the substantialistic notion of person as foundational to an ethics of self-interest and a morality that puts oneself and everything else that is closely or even remotely related to it over and above the interests, concerns, and needs of others. There is no question about the difference between one's concern for oneself and one's concern for another. Hartshorne does not deny the difference. But it is the absolutizing of this distinction which he most emphatically rejects. For it leads ultimately to the enshrining of an enduring self untouched by change, a selfsame *ego* in a metaphysics of the person, and consequently the raising to the level of dogma of an ethics that says (that in order to be able to love) one must love oneself *first* before others.

There is a difference between the self and its others. But it is relative, not absolute. Self-identity is always and inextricably bound up with other-identity. This represents the most comprehensive insight of process thought. The key to understanding this concept is Hartshorne's theory of personal identity based on a metaphysics of event, which reverses the very relation by which "stability" and "change" have been traditionally conceived. Although mutually dependent, one term expresses the complete reality of the entire relation. The other in fact acquires its content by being inserted into the descriptive domain of the more concrete concept. Change and stability are such kind of metaphysical pair. Traditionally, of course, the latter has been regarded as the more important and inclusive term. A substance remains unchanged, but not its accidents, just as a person remains identical throughout his/her lifetime, with only his/her accidental features changing. The self is untouched by these transformations, i.e., however close to the core of its being these changes may be, and even if the entire cosmos were to disappear, the person would still remain *himself/herself.*

Contrary to the traditional view, Hartshorne holds that change is the more original and concrete experience from which the derivative notion of stability is abstracted. The situation is analogous to the relation between being and becoming. For process thought, becoming is reality itself, and being is only an aspect of this reality. Becoming can be taken as inclusive, without suppressing the contrast between itself and being. The opposite case would destroy this contrast. As Hartshorne explains, "For no matter how much is uncreated, if the least thing is created, a totality results which embraces the uncreated and the created. *Creation is always the total reality*, never of a part merely."[2] That which remains the same in a person is no more than an abstraction derived from that which constantly changes. An unchanging identity is the abstract correlate of the concrete reality which is the self that is different at every moment. This does not amount to a denial of enduring individuality or of a specific subject having definite experiences. Instead, it is an assertion that each new experience that a subject undergoes represents a novel actuality for that subject.

It is the present subject of the experiences that is concrete; the "I *here* and *now*," not the subject *simply*. There is no denying a stable "I," therefore, but only an assertion that this stable "I" is no more than a limited portion of the entire sequence or series of "I"s. It is this series that Hartshorne calls a "personal society." It is constituted by innumerable other-selves, and is given integrity, not by some underlying substrate that remains unchanged throughout the vicissitudes of the personal society's career, but by a "defining characteristic" which is no more than a blueprint of possibilities for further becoming. It is held together as it realizes these possibilities by a "regnant member" of the society of events. Experience gives witness to the structure of such personal societies. Hartshorne's use of memory as an explanatory tool enables us to make sense of the causal structure involved in the coming-to-be of events on the one hand, and of persons on the other.

Hence, unlike other philosophers for whom memory is that which *actually* constitutes the identity of persons, Hartshorne understands memory as a conceptual apparatus which, by means of its asymmetrical causal structure, discloses the fact that causality, contrary to Hume, is actually *experientiable*. Consequently, this is true of the causal chain that unifies into a coherent life of a person what are actually innumerable "other-selves" which are both partially the same and partially different. Here too the situation is such that what is different encompasses a wider domain and actually includes within its compass what is selfsame. For what is likewise revealed by the experience of memory is that the self doing the remembering is not simply reducible to (or even deducible from) the thoughts, experiences, or deeds it is actually remembering. The present self doing the remembering is a new creation, fashioned out of the data of the past (which it remembers) but synthesized into a new reality by the present creative moment.

Mnemonic awareness represents a synthesis of past data which are "housed in," thereby "in-*forming*" the coming-to-be of a remembering event. But in the same manner that these past data are not merely constituted (created) by the present event, neither is the present event merely (or in its entirety) created by the data of the past, however many these might be. As Whitehead has said, and as Hartshorne has emphasized on numerous occasions, "The many become one and are increased by one." The reality that arises out of the creative synthesis of the present moment is a totally new event, a new "other" to the "others" belonging to its past which it had just integrated into itself. Finally, this novel event, this "new other" becomes a further ingredient in the coming-to-be of even newer "others" that will follow. Each event then inherits from others its past; it creatively synthesizes these in the present; it achieves satisfaction, i.e., becomes a fully actualized entity, then hurls itself into still a new other that will be yet another instance of creative synthesis in the future.

It is in this way that the coming-to-be of personal identity is explained. That there is simply no "I" that remains the same throughout the life of a particular person means first and foremost that there is only an *abstract* line, a "form" or "receptacle" of experiences that can be said to persist from a definite beginning to an anticipated future end. Even this form or receptacle is never completely fixed, at least not till the death of the individual. Second, that there is simply no "I" that remains unchanged also means that there is no absolute distinction between this "I" and its "others." In fact the "I" itself cannot be an "I" without its others, those that have come before it and have been "housed" in its present state and those that will come after it and will in turn "house" whatever its present state of creative synthesis makes of it. One is, in the most intimate sense, a *self* and an *other* to oneself. A person in Hartshorne's metaphysics is *both* processive and relational, in his very core.

Notes

Introduction

1. *The Economist*, December 23, 2006–January 5, 2007.
2. Charles Hartshorne's own brand of process thought is basically a theistic metaphysics. Indeed it is *natural theology*. In our investigation, therefore, we will keep in mind the close connection between Hartshorne's metaphysical concept of person and his idea of God. Hartshorne claims that wrong views about God lead to wrong views about human beings. This work therefore complements Santiago Sia's *God in Process Thought: A Study in Charles Hartshorne's Concept of God* (Dordrecht: Martinus Nijhoff, 1985).
3. Alfred North Whitehead, *Process and Reality: An Essay in Cosmology*, Corrected Edition, eds. David Ray Griffin and Donald W. Sherburne (New York: Free Press, 1979), 21n32. Henceforth cited as *PR*.

Chapter 1

1. The distinction between *strict* and *nonstrict* theories of personal identity has also been referred to in the literature as the "nonreductionist" and "reductionist," as well as the "simple" and "complex views." Cf. Harold Noonan, *Personal Identity* (London: Routledge, 1989). See also: Richard Swinburne, "Personal Identity," *Proceedings of the Aristotelian Society*, 74 (1973): 231–7; Derek Parfit, "The Unimportance of Identity," *Identity: Essays Based on Herbert Spencer Lectures Given in the University of Oxford*, ed. Henry Harris (Oxford: Clarendon Press, 1995), 16–20.
2. Paul Ricoeur, *Oneself as Another*, Trans. Kathleen Blamey (Chicago: University of Chicago Press, 1992), 116–17. English translation of *Soi-même comme un autre*, Editions de Seuil, March 1990.
3. Cf. J.L. Mackie, *Problems From Locke* (Oxford: Clarendon Press, 1976), 173.
4. Cf. Parfit, "The Unimportance of Identity," *Identity*, 14.
5. Jonathan Glover ed., *The Philosophy of Mind* (Cambridge: Cambridge University Press, 1967), 1.
6. See also: Gareth Evans, 'Can There Be Vague Objects?' *Identity*, ed. Harold Noonan (Aldershot: Grower House, 1993), 208; David Lewis, "Vague Identity: Evans Misunderstood," *Identity*, ed. Harold Noonan (Aldershot: Grower House, 1993), 359–61.
7. On a similar recognition but different interpretation of the ambiguity inherent in the notion of personal identity, see: Catherine McCall, *Concepts of Person: An Analysis of Concepts of Person, Self, and Human Being* (Aldershot, England: Averbury, 1990), 19–20.
8. Cf. David Lewis, "Counterparts of Persons and Their Bodies," *The Journal of Philosophy*, 68 (1971): 203–11.
9. Anthony Quinton, "The Soul," *Personal Identity*, ed. John Perry (Berkeley: University of California Press, 1975), 72.

10. Amélie Oksenberg Rorty alludes to this third group of theories and says that philosophers belonging to this group, who initially attempt to bridge the gap between defenders of a spatiotemporal criterion and defenders of a psychological criterion, eventually find themselves "forming third or fourth parties" to the debate. Cf. Amélie Oksenberg Rorty, "Introduction" to *The Identities of Persons*, ed. Amélie Oksenberg Rorty (Berkeley: University of California Press, 1969), 1.

11. David Lewis, *On the Plurality of Worlds* (Oxford: Blackwell, 1986), 192.

12. Noonan, *Personal Identity*, 19.

13. Lewis, *On the Plurality of Worlds*, 192–3. See also: Marc Slors, *Personal Identity and the Metaphysics of Mind*. "Questiones Infinitae," *Publications of the Department of Philosophy*, Vol. XVIII (Utrecht: Utrecht University, 1997), 3; Geoffrey Madell, *The Identity of the Self* (Edinburgh: Edinburgh University Press, 1981), esp. Chapter V, 3: "The Vindication of the Reid/Butler View of Personal Identity," 122–34.

14. Noonan, *Personal Identity*, 20.

15. James Baillie, *Problems in Personal Identity*, Paragon Issues in Philosophy (New York: Paragon, 1993), 8.

16. Cf. Sydney Shoemaker and Richard G. Swinburne, *Personal Identity* (Oxford: Basil Blackwell, 1984), 20: "The Simple View claims explicitly that personal identity is one thing, and the extent of similarity in matter and apparent memory another."

17. Madell, *The Identity of the Self*, 139.

18. Cf. Baillie, *Problems in Personal Identity*, 9–11. There are actually distinctions between the nonstrict and strict theories and the so-called reductionist and nonreductionist perspectives. These two sets, however, are often conflated with each other. Some authors, the most notable being Sydney Shoemaker, insist that the second distinction is not the same as the first. Cf. Sydney Shoemaker, "Critical Notice: Parfit's Reasons and Persons," *Mind*, 44 (1985): 443–53.

19. Cf. Evans, "Can There Be Vague Objects?" *Identity*, 208; Lewis, "Vague Identity: Evans Misunderstood," *Identity*, 359–61.

20. Lewis, "Vague Identity: Evans Misunderstood," *Identity*, 359–61. This position of course has been disputed. Instead of simply attributing the ambiguity to the *concept* of person, it is instead attributed to the *reality* of the person itself. As an objective entity, a person is itself an ambiguous object, and its vagueness is *in re* and not *in lingua tantum*. Cf. Peter van Inwangen, "How to Reason About Vague Objects," *Philosophical Topics*, 16/1 (Spring, 1988): 255.

21. Derek Parfit, "Personal Identity," *Philosophical Review*, 80/1 (January, 1971), 3–27. Reprinted in: John Perry ed., *Personal Identity* (Berkeley: University of California Press, 1975), 199–223. This 1975 reprint is the source we are using. Parfit specifies these beliefs as (i) the nature of personal identity and (ii) its importance (p. 223).

22. Derek Parfit, *Reasons and Persons* (Oxford: University Press, 1984), 201–2.

23. Parfit, "Personal Identity," *Personal Identity*, 219.

24. Parfit, "The Unimportance of Identity," *Identity*, 29.

25. Parfit, "The Unimportance of Identity," *Identity*, 44.

26. Henry E. Allison, "Locke's Theory of Personal Identity: A Re-examination," *Locke on Human Understanding: Selected Essays*, ed. I.C. Tipton (Oxford: Oxford University Press, 1977), 113.

27. Cf. Charles Hartshorne, "Causal Necessities: An Alternative to Hume," *Philosophical Review*, 43/4 (October, 1954): 479–99.

28. Paul Ricoeur, *Oneself as Another*, 130–9.

29. Joseph Butler, "Of Personal Identity," *Personal Identity*, ed. Joseph Perry (Berkeley: University of California Press, 1975), 100. Roderick Chisholm, another strict-identity theorist, makes use of Butler's terminology. Cf. Roderick

Chisholm, "Parts as Essential to Their Wholes," *Review of Metaphysics,* 26 (1973): 581–603.

30. Thomas Reid, "Of Identity," Chapter IV, Essay III: *Of Memory, Essays on the Intellectual Powers of Man* (1785); *Philosophical Works,* ed. William Hamilton (New York: Georg Olms Verlag, 1983), 346. Subsequent quotes from Reid will be taken from John Perry ed., *Personal Identity* (Berkeley: University of California Press, 1975), 112.

31. Reid, "Of Identity," *Essays,* 111–12.

32. Ibid., 111.

33. Reid, "Of Identity," *Essays,* 109.

34. Slors, *Personal Identity and the Metaphysics of Mind,* 3.

35. Reid, "Of Identity," 109.

36. Ibid.

37. Noonan, *Personal Identity,* 66.

38. Reid, "On Identity," *Essays,* 109.

39. Butler, "Of Personal Identity" [1735], in *Personal Identity,* 99–105.

40. E.J. Lowe, *Locke on Human Understanding* (London and New York: Routledge, 1995), 102.

41. Cf. Noonan, *Personal Identity,* 30: "It has been said that all subsequent philosophy consists merely of footnotes to Plato. On this topic, at least, it can be truly said that all subsequent writing has consisted merely of footnotes to Locke. Indeed many present-day philosophers writing on personal identity would still be happy to describe themselves as 'Lockean' or, at least, 'Neo-Lockean' in their approach to the topic, whilst many others would naturally define their positions by their opposition to Locke." The most significant difference, however, is the fact that while there was a tendency in Locke to conflate epistemic and ontological issues, the question as it is considered today is regarded as a purely metaphysical or ontological one. See also: Slors, *Personal Identity and the Metaphysics of Mind,* 25.

42. David Hume, *A Treatise of Human Nature* [1739], ed. L.A. Selby-Bigge, 2nd Edition, ed. P.H. Nidditch (New York: Oxford University Press, 1978), 259.

43. It was Locke's friend William Molyneux who provided the impetus to the Lockean account by suggesting that Locke would include a discussion of the *principium individuationis* in the new edition. See: William Molyneux, "Letter of Molyneux to Locke, 2 March 1693," *The Works of John Locke* (London, 1794), Vol. VIII, 310. Also: John Locke, "Letter to Molyneux, 23 August 1693," *The Works of John Locke,* 322–7.

44. Noonan, *Personal Identity,* 30.

45. Edwin McCann, "Locke's Philosophy of the Body," *The Cambridge Companion to Locke,* ed. Vere Chappell (New York: Cambridge University Press, 1994), 57–60.

46. Cf. Lowe, *Locke on Human Understanding,* 106. See also: Jonathan Bennett, "Locke's Philosophy of Mind," Part IV: Thinking Matter, *The Cambridge Companion to Locke,* ed. Vere Chappell (New York: Cambridge University Press, 1994), 98–100.

47. Cf. John Locke, *An Early Draft of Locke's Essay together with Excerpts from His Journal,* ed. R.I. Aaron and J. Gibb (Oxford: Clarendon Press, 1936), 121.

48. Cf. John Locke, *An Essay Concerning Human Understanding,* ed. Peter H. Nidditch (Oxford: Clarendon Press, 1975), IV, iii, 6, 542. Chapter 27 of this work is reproduced in Part II of *Personal Identity,* ed. John Perry (Berkeley: University of California Press, 1975), 33–52.

49. Ibid., II, xxvii, 21.

50. Ibid.

51. Charles Taylor holds that the Lockean enterprise is part of a larger movement characteristic of the time. He termed this a movement of "inwardness" which gave great emphasis to the first person point of view. Cf. Charles Taylor, *Sources of the Self: The Making of the Modern Identity* (Cambridge: Harvard University Press, 1989). See esp. Chapter 9: Locke's Punctual Self, 159–76.

52. Locke, *An Essay Concerning Human Understanding*, II, xxvii, 9.

53. Ibid., 17.

54. Such view has in fact been espoused by some authors. Although there are qualifications to their point, namely, that Locke was essentially an "empiricist" critic of Descartes, they nonetheless end up painting him a "Cartesian." Cf. Leon Roth, "Note on the Relationship between Locke and Descartes," *Mind*, 44 (1936): 414–16. See also: Richard Aaron and J. Gibb ed., *An Early Draft of Locke's Essay with Excerpts from His Journal* (Oxford, Clarendon Press, 1936). This identification has, as to be expected, been criticized by some authors. Thus, we read for instance: "Locke believed [...] that Descartes' foundational principles (e.g. that the true and immutable essence of body is extension) were purely fanciful, sheerly hypothetical, merely stipulative. He believed that in demonstrating the consequences of these principles [...] Descartes confused a verbal certainty with an extra-verbal uncertainty (in fact, in this case, an extra-verbal falsehood)." Cf. H.A.S. Schankula, "Locke, Descartes, and the Science of Nature," *Journal of the History of Ideas*, 41/3 (July–September 1980): 459, 475. This article contains a substantial refutation of theses which argue that Locke either "borrowed" from Descartes or was in fact influenced greatly by a reading of him, such that some authors have even argued that the empiricism and rationalism peculiar to the Lockean system developed through the impetus provided by Cartesian thought.

55. If there is a possibility of attributing truth to the Roth-Aaron thesis just spelled out, it might as well be this, but no more than this: it was with Descartes' insistence on clarity, that Locke found himself having a great sympathy for and not necessarily for the truth contained in his works. Cf. Shankula, "Locke, Descartes, and the Science of Nature," *Journal of the History of Ideas*, 463.

56. Thus, for instance, he states that it is possible that matter may think, and concerning the soul's immateriality, his comment is "Let men [...] resolve of that as they may please," and he insists that whatever resolution comes out, his theory of identity will remain. Finally, he also makes the telling assertion that there is the possibility of one person even where there are many spiritual substances. These alone, would be enough to make him a heretic in Platonic and Cartesian circles. Cf. M.W. Hughes, "Personal Identity: A Defence of Locke," *Philosophy*, 50/192 (April, 1975): 169.

57. For a discussion of this perspective see: Behan, "Locke on Persons and Personal Identity," *Canadian Journal of Philosophy*, 9/1 (March 1979), 53–75. Behan makes a clear distinction between Locke's understanding of person in terms of an individual understood in its particularity (we can say that this sense involves something one can point to, so to speak; "this specific person"; "this one and not that") and an individual understood in terms of its appropriating for himself a certain moral character for instance.

58. Locke, *An Essay Concerning Human Understanding*, IV, iii, 6.

59. John Locke, "Reply to the Bishop of Worcester's Answer to His Second Letter," *The Works of John Locke*, New Edition, Corrected, Vol. IV (London: Thomas Tegg, 1823. Reprint, Scientia Verlag Aalen, 1963), 460.

60. John Locke, "Reply to the Bishop of Worcester's Answer to His Second Letter," *The Works of John Locke*, 463.

61. Ibid.
62. Locke, *An Essay Concerning Human Understanding*, II, xxviii, 1.
63. D.J. O'Connor, *John Locke* (New York: Dover, 1967), 75.
64. Locke, *An Essay Concerning Human Understanding*, II, xxviii, 2.
65. Ibid.
66. Cf. Peter Alexander, "Locke on Substance-in-General," Part I, *John Locke: Critical Assessments*, Vol. IV, ed. Richard Ashcraft (London: Routledge, 1991), 185.
67. Aaron, *Locke*, 174.
68. We must point out here that Locke had made it his business to examine all the ideas in the mind, particularly those which initially appear to come from a source other than sensation or reflection. Substance appeared as such an idea. Substance is never directly experienced, either in sensation or reflection. Cf. John Locke, *An Essay Concerning Human Understanding*, I, iv, 18. Nor do we experience it through the enlargement or combination of the ideas. Thus the problem that Locke really deals with is *how* we come by the idea of substance; the question of *what* exactly a substance is, proceeds from this more primary purpose. See also: Alexander, "Locke on Substance-in-General," *John Locke*, 188–90.
69. Locke, *An Essay Concerning Human Understanding*, II, xxviii, 6.
70. Ibid., 37. The commonality between the two senses is of course that "substance"— particular or general—is that to which something incapable of independent existence inheres. Where the two diverge is with regard to how the details are spelled out concerning what inheres and what is inhered upon. The general idea of substance does not regard it as a synonym for "thing" simply. Rather, it is the idea of a *thinglike* item that is found at the basic level of one's ontology. Substances in this sense are simply the fundamental constituents of reality upon which all the rest depend for their existence and which themselves depend on nothing. For this interpretation, see: W.P. Alston and J. Bennett, "Locke on People and Substances," *Philosophical Review*, 97 (1988): 25–46. Thus, material substances are *thinglike* items at the most basic level of one's ontology of the material world, while thinking substances are *thinglike* items at the most basic level of one's ontology of the mental realm. On the other hand, particular substances are simply those things to which we ordinarily associate certain ideas. Also J.D. Mabbott, *John Locke* (London: Macmillan, 1973), 29.
71. Locke, *An Essay Concerning Human Understanding*, II, xxiii, 3.
72. Cf. Michael Ayers, *Locke*. Volume II: Ontology (London and New York: Routledge), 38. See also: Alexander, "Locke on Substance-in-General," Part I, *John Locke: Critical Assessments*, 185.
73. Locke, *An Essay Concerning Human Understanding*, II, xxvii, 2.
74. Ibid., 4.
75. Ibid., 2.
76. Locke, *An Essay Concerning Human Understanding*, II, xxvii, 4.
77. Ibid., 3.
78. Locke, *An Essay Concerning Human Understanding*, II, xxvii, 4. Locke differentiates the identity of a living organism from that of a mass of matter. Cf. also Noonan, *Personal Identity*, 39.
79. Locke, *An Essay Concerning Human Understanding*, II, xxvii, 8. Using this definition of the identity of man, Locke is able to refute notions of transmigration of an immaterial soul.
80. Ibid., 6. See also: Lowe, *Locke on Human Understanding*, 100; David A. Givner, "Scientific Preconceptions in Locke's Philosophy of Language," *Journal of the History of Ideas*, 23/3 (July–September 1962): 340. Concerning Locke's reaction

to the corpusuclar theory, see: Ayers, *Locke*, Vol. II: Ontology, Part III: Identity, no. 18: Locke on "Masses of Matter," 207–15.

81. John W. Yolton, *Locke: An Introduction* (Oxford: Basil Blackwell, 1985), 18.
82. Behan, "Locke on Persons and Personal Identity," *Canadian Journal of Philosophy*, 57.
83. M.W. Hughes observes that "though Locke does distinguish 'man' and 'person,' these terms do not correspond to the Cartesio-Platonic body and soul, and are more closely connected to each other [...] Locke may naturally be taken to have believed that bodily evidence is relevant to identity claims, since identity is a relationship by which bodily substances can be linked." Hughes, "Personal Identity: A Defense of Locke," *Philosophy*, 170–1.
84. P.T. Geach, *Reference and Generality*, 3rd Edition (New York: Cornell University Press, 1980), 63.
85. Cf. Baillie, *Problems in Personal Identity*, 58–9.
86. Concerning this distinction, see: Michael Dummett, *Frege: Philosophy of Language* (London: Duckworth, 1981), 73ff.
87. Lowe, *Locke on Human Understanding*, 95.
88. Locke, *An Essay Concerning Human Understanding*, II, xxvii, 7: "[...] for such as is the *Idea* belonging to that Name, such must be the *Identity*."
89. Cf. Noonan, *Personal Identity*, 2.
90. Behan, "Locke on Persons and Personal Identity," *Canadian Journal of Philosophy*, 566: "Identity was for Locke a sortal-relative concept."
91. Baillie, *Problems in Personal Identity*, 59.
92. See: Allison, "Locke's Theory of Personal Identity," *Locke on Human Understanding*, 106–7.
93. Locke, *An Essay Concerning Human Understanding*, IV, iii, 6.
94. W. Alston and J. Bennett, "Locke on People and Substances," *Philosophical Review*, 97 (1988): 43ff.
95. Locke, *An Essay Concerning Human Understanding*, II, xxvii, 18.
96. Cf. Givner, "Scientific Preconceptions in Locke's Philosophy of Language," *Journal of the History of Ideas*, 430–2.
97. Cf. Mabbott, *John Locke*, 61.
98. Cf. Ayers, *Locke*, 258–9. There was in Locke's mind, according to Ayers, a distinction between the idea of man simply as some sort of animal, and the formal idea of a *rational being*—the term which he regarded as appropriate to the ethical concerns of his theory.
99. Locke, *An Essay Concerning Human Understanding*, II, xxvii, 8.
100. John Locke, "Second Reply to the Bishop of Worcester," *The Works of John Locke* (London, 1824), Vol. III, 308.
101. Ibid., 15: "I do not take these two sounds, man and body, to stand for the same thing; nor the identity of man to be the same with the identity of the body."
102. Locke, *An Essay Concerning Human Understanding*, III, xi, 16.
103. Cf. Ayers, "Personal Identity Before the Essay," Chapter 22 of *Locke*, Vol. II: Ontology, 254–9.
104. Locke, *An Essay Concerning Human Understanding*, III, xi, 16.
105. That this difference cannot be stressed enough may be demonstrated by the fact that Locke is even willing to say that a brute, should it have the use of reason, has to be regarded as subject to law and in that sense, a man (Ibid.).
106. Cf. Ayers, "Personal Identity Before the Essay," Chapter 22 of *Locke*, Vol. II: Ontology, 258.
107. See: C.S. Lewis, *Studies in Words* (Cambridge: Cambridge University Press, 1967).

108. It is in this regard, synonymous with the word "conscience," which Locke himself also uses in a related context. Cf. Locke, *An Essay Concerning Human Understanding*, II, xxvii, 22.
109. Ayers, "Locke's Theory of Personal Identity," Chapter XXIII of *Locke*, Vol. II: Ontology, 260.
110. Locke, *An Essay Concerning Human Understanding*, II, xxvii, 9.
111. Noonan, *Personal Identity*, 53.
112. See Locke's lengthy discussion in: *An Essay Concerning Human Understanding*, II, i, 9–25.
113. Cf. Locke, *An Essay Concerning Human Understanding*, II, i, 11; 12.
114. Locke, *An Essay Concerning Human Understanding*, II, xxvii, 26.
115. Ibid., 11.
116. Behan, "Locke on Persons and Personal Identity," *Canadian Journal of Philosophy*, 59.
117. Paul Helm, "Locke's Theory of Personal Identity," *Philosophy*, 174.
118. Thomas Reid, "Mr. Locke's Account of Our Personal Identity," *Personal Identity*, ed. John Perry (Berkeley, California: University of California Press, 1975), 115. (From Chapter VI of "Of Memory," 3rd Essay of Reid's work *Essays on the Intellectual Powers of Man* [1785].)
119. Ibid.
120. Noonan, *Personal Identity*, 54.
121. Reid, "Mr. Locke's Account" *Personal Identity*, 115.
122. Butler, "Of Personal Identity," *Personal Identity*, 100.
123. Ibid. Usually, attributed to Butler, the objection in fact had already been made by John Sergeant that "one should really think it self-evident that consciousness of personal identity presupposes, and therefore cannot constitute, personal identity: any more than knowledge, in any other case, can constitute truth, which it presupposes." Cf. John Sergeant, *Solid Philosophy Asserted* (London, 1697), 14, sec. 12; cf. David P. Behan, "Locke on Persons and Personal Identity," *Canadian Journal of Philosophy*, 1.
124. Antony Flew, "Locke and the Problem of Personal Identity," *Philosophy*, 26/96 (January, 1951): 53–68.
125. Ibid., 57.
126. Cf. Sydney Shoemaker, *Self-Knowledge and Self-Identity* (New York: Ithaca, 1963), 199–200. See also: B.A.O. Williams, "Personal Identity and Individuation," *Proceedings of the Aristotelian Society*, 57 (1956–57): 229–52. (Reprinted in B.A.O. Williams, *Problems of the Self* [Cambridge: Cambridge University Press, 1973], 1–18.)
127. Locke, *An Essay Concerning Human Understanding*, II, x, 4.
128. Ibid., 4–5.
129. Helm, "Locke's Theory of Personal Identity," *Philosophy*, 177.
130. Helm, "Locke's Theory of Personal Identity," *Philosophy*, 177. (Italics added.)
131. Hughes, "Personal Identity: A Defense of Locke," *Philosophy*, 172.
132. Ibid. The difference between the two is shown by the fact that the connection that memory affords holds most of the time, but not always.
133. Helm, "Locke's Theory of Personal Identity," *Philosophy*, 179.
134. This notion must be tied in with the fact that we have explained "memory" in terms of Locke's idea of *concerned* consciousness as that which enables one to appropriate those thoughts, actions, and experiences as one's own—this act of appropriation being that which is constitutive of Locke's idea of "person."

135. Helm, "Locke's Theory of Personal Identity," *Philosophy*, 180.
136. Cf. M.W. Hughes, "Personal Identity: A Defense of Locke," *Philosophy* (1975); Behan, "Locke on Persons and Personal Identity," *Canadian Journal of Philosophy* (1979); Allison, "Locke's Theory of Personal Identity: A Re-examination," *Locke on Human Understanding* (1977); Helm, "Locke's Theory of Personal Identity," *Philosophy* (1979).
137. The logical property of transitivity holds that an identity relation *R* is transitive just in case, if *X* is *R*-related to *Y*, and, *Y* is *R*-related to *Z*, then *X* must be *R*-related to *Z*.
138. Noonan, *Personal Identity*, 12; see also, 67–8.
139. Behan, "Locke on Persons and Personal Identity," *Canadian Journal of Philosophy*, 69, 70. Behan remarks further that this is why the Lockean theory of person based on the requirement of accountability, contains a provision for moral change and growth.
140. Cf. Locke, *An Essay Concerning Human Understanding*, II, xxvii, 10.
141. Flew, "Locke and the Problem of Personal Identity," *Philosophy*, 56.
142. Ibid.
143. Behan, "Locke on Persons and Personal Identity," *Canadian Journal of Philosophy*, 70.
144. Flew, "Locke and the Problem of Personal Identity," *Philosophy*, 57.
145. Locke, *An Essay Concerning Human Understanding*, II, xxvii, 13.
146. Ibid. He says further that those plagued by this madness "put wrong ideas together, and so make wrong propositions, but argue and reason right from them."
147. Locke, *An Essay Concerning Human Understanding*, II, xi, 13.
148. Locke, *An Essay Concerning Human Understanding*, II, xxvii, 13. Mackie criticizes this view. See: Mackie, *Problems from Locke*, 184. Cf. also Helm, "Locke's Theory of Personal Identity," *Philosophy*, 176–7.
149. The notion of the "goodness of God" is a basic assumption in Locke. Cf. Locke, *An Essay in Human Understanding*, IV, iii, 18.
150. Locke, *An Essay Concerning Human Understanding*, II, xxvii, 22.
151. Ibid.
152. Helm, "Locke's Theory of Personal Identity," *Philosophy*, 178–9.
153. Galatians 2:20. *The Holy Bible. New Revised Standard Version* (Oxford: University Press, 1989). All subsequent biblical quotations are taken from this edition.
154. Taylor, *Sources of the Self*, 159.
155. Noonan, *Personal Identity*, 41.
156. As Locke insists, it is not important whether this underlying substance be "spiritual, or material, simple, or compound." Cf. Locke, *An Essay Concerning Human Understanding*, II, xxvii, 17. He makes a similar statement in, II, xxvii, 23: "For whatever substance there is, however framed, without consciousness, there is no Person."
157. Locke, *An Essay Concerning Human Understanding*, II, xxvii, 17.
158. Ibid., 26. Locke here was of course referring to "man" the "moral agent," and not the "physical" entity.
159. Ibid. "It is a Forensick Term appropriating Actions and their Merit; and so belong only to intelligent Agents capable of a Law, and Happiness, and Misery." A "forensic" term is basically one that is used in courts of judicature or in public discussion and debate.
160. Noonan, *Personal Identity*, 49. (Words in parenthesis added.)

161. C.C.J. Webb, *God and Personality*, The Gifford Lectures, 1919–1918, The Library of Philosophy (London: Allen and Unwin, 1919), 50.
162. Webb, *God and Personality*, 54.
163. Boethius, *The Theological Tractates*, trans. H.F. Stewart and E.K. Rand, The Loeb Classical Library (Cambridge, Massachusetts: Harvard University Press, 1973).
164. Cf. Ayers, *Locke*, Vol. II: Ontology, 268.
165. There is in fact a sense in which "person" is synonymous with "role" or "part" (cf. *dramatis personae*). The English word "person," in fact, is supposedly derived from the Latin *persona*, which is the name of the mask worn by actors in ancient dramatic performances. Now even with regard to this root, a distinction may be made—a "branching out," so to speak, such that in one direction, those words result which imply a substantive character—a "self," while in another, words which imply a performative character—a function or office. For a discussion of the historical evolution of the term "person," see: Adolf Trendelenberg, "A Contribution to the History of the Word Person," *Monist*, 20 (1910): 336–63. See also: Ayers, *Locke*, 268.
166. Cf. Roscoe Pound, *Jurisprudence*, Vol. IV: Application and Enforcement of Law (St. Paul, Minnesota: West Publishing Co., 1959), 191–2.
167. John William Salmond, *Jurisprudence or The Theory of Law*, 12th edition, P.J. Fitzgerald ed. (London: Stevens and Haynes, 1910; 12th edition, 1966): 299.
168. Taylor, *Sources of the Self*, 28–9.
169. Locke, *An Essay Concerning Human Understanding*, II, xxvii, 10.

Chapter 2

1. Hume, *A Treatise of Human Nature*, 252.
2. Glover, *The Philosophy and Psychology of Personal Identity*, 129.
3. William Barrett, *Death of the Soul: From Descartes to the Computer* (Oxford: Oxford University Press, 1986), 44.
4. Hume, *A Treatise of Human Nature*, 252.
5. Cf. T. Penelhum, *Hume*, (London and Basingstoke: Macmillan, 1975), 76.
6. But from where in fact do we get the idea of an unchanging self? Hume holds, in a vein not too different from Parfit, that our constitution is such that we find it natural to regard a succession of resembling perceptions as one continuously existing thing. Cf. Barry Stroud, *Hume,* The Arguments of the Philosophers, ed. Ted Honderich (London: Routledge and Kegan Paul, 1977, Reprint 1995), 119. Stroud continues his account of Hume's thesis in lines that mirror the Parfitian view of personal identity as a matter of convention.
7. W.L. LaCroix, *Four Questions on Persons: A Philosophical Dialectic* (Lanham: University Press of America, 1962), 24. Hume's method of considering the "theater" of his mind in probing the question of unified and abiding self is criticized by the author in terms that recalls the Kantian notion of the "transcendental unity of apperception" and in a way prefigures Ricoeur's distinction between *idem*-identity and *ipse*-identity, the former being the "what" of identity, and the latter, its "who."
8. Allison, "Locke's Theory of Personal Identity," *Locke on Human Understanding*, 113.
9. Cf. John Jenkins, *Understanding Hume*, eds. Peter Lewis and Geoffrey Madell (Edinburgh: Edinburgh University Press, 1992), 118. For a further exposition of this thesis see: E.B. Allaire, "The Attack on Substance: Descartes to Hume," *David*

Hume: Critical Assessments. Volume III, ed. Stanley Tweyman (London: Routledge, 1995), 73–6.

10. Cf. Roth, "Note on the Relationship between Locke and Descartes," *Mind*, 414–16.
11. Cf. Jenkins, *Understanding Hume*, 118.
12. Cf. Stroud, *Hume*, 123–4.
13. Hume, *A Treatise of Human Nature*, 219.
14. Ibid., 260.
15. Penelhum, *Hume*, 76.
16. Hume, *A Treatise of Human Nature*, 261. Penelhum explains it as a process of being "lulled by the similarity of the experience of the two types of objects into thinking of the related series as one identical object." Cf. Penelhum, *Hume*, 78.
17. Hume, *A Treatise of Human Nature*, 261.
18. Ibid., 262.
19. Allison, "Locke's Theory of Personal Identity," *Locke on Human Understanding*, 114.
20. Hume, *A Treatise of Human Nature*, 262.
21. Ibid., 261.
22. Jenkins, *Understanding Hume*, 115.
23. Jenkins, *Understanding Hume*, 115.
24. Cf. Penelhum, *Hume*, 80.
25. Hume, *A Treatise of Human Nature*, 635.
26. Ibid., 636.
27. Allison, "Locke's Theory of Personal Identity," *Locke on Human Understanding*, 115.
28. Here he subscribes to G.C. Lichtenberg's criticism that Descartes's certitude with regard to thought, although not mistaken, could have been expressed in a way that was not misleading. Hence Lichtenberg argues that it would have been equally sufficient to give an account of the Cartesian insight in an impersonal way, e.g.: "It is thought; thinking is going on." In this statement, or some similar one such as: "This is a thought, therefore at least one thought is being thought," our thoughts can be fully described without having to claim that they have thinkers. Cf. G.C. Lichtenberg, *Schriften und Briefe* (Sudelbucher II: Carl Hanser Verlag, 1971), 412. Quoted by Parfit, *Reasons and Persons*, 224–5.
29. Cf. James Duerlinger, "Reductionist and Nonreductionist Theories of Persons in Indian Buddhist Philosophy," *Journal of Indian Philosophy* 2/1 (March, 1993): 79–101. In this article, the author affirms the thesis that Parfit's belief concerning his peculiar kind of "no-self" theory is akin to that of certain Buddhist schools.
30. Derek Parfit, "An Interview with Derek Parfit," *Cogito*, 9 (1995): 123. (Italics added.)
31. Parfit, *Reasons and Persons*, 273. Cf. Appendix J: Buddha's View, 502–3, 532.
32. This thesis is not without its attendant problems. For while one can certainly appreciate attempts to render reality (including the reality of a person) more objectively verifiable, the more reasonable conclusion seems to be that the quandary of fluctuating delicately between a subjective and objective view of the world is a central and inescapable element of human nature itself. Cf. D.E. Harding, "On Having No Head" and "Reflections," *The Minds I: Fantasies and Reflections on Self and Soul*, eds. Douglas R. Hofstadter and Daniel C. Dennett (Brighton, Sussex: The Harvester Press, 1981), 23–33.
33. Parfit, *Reasons and Persons*, 275.
34. The perplexity evoked by the second half of this statement is captured by Thomas Nagel in his description of the problem of the relationship between

selfhood and objective reality, in the Introduction to his book *A View From Nowhere* (New York and Oxford: Oxford University Press, 1986), 3. Cf. also Thomas Nagel, "Physicalism," *The Mind/Brain Theory*, ed. C.V. Borst (London: Macmillan, 1970): 214–30.

35. Cf. Sydney Shoemaker, "Persons and their Pasts," *American Philosophical Quarterly*, 7 (1970): 269–85.

36. This notion is of course consistent with Parfit's rejection of a substantialistic self. With the rejection of the substantial "I" and its subsequent modification (or replacement) with "the temporal series of 'selves,'" it becomes possible to speak of an impersonal kind of memory, which is what quasi-memory is. It is important to note that Parfit is not eliminating personal identity, but merely suggesting a modification of it. With the concept of quasi-memory, one can attribute one's apparent memory to one or other of his previous "selves"—i.e., since there is no fixed "person," an "I" which must automatically assume ownership of whatever is being remembered. Albert Shalom criticizes this manner of arguing. Cf. Albert Shalom, *The Body/Mind Conceptual Framework and the Problem of Personal Identity: Some Theories in Philosophy, Psychoanalysis, and Neurology* (New Jersey: Humanities Press, 1985), 346–9.

37. Parfit, *Reasons and Persons*, 220.

38. Ibid., 222. (Italics added.)

39. Parfit's impersonal account of memory is but one dimension of the scheme that he develops. It is one that is characterized by a thoroughgoing impersonal character such that even indexical concepts, e.g. "here," "now," etc., are explained without the ordinary reference to an "I" which specifies them. In this he believes he is going against the Cartesian view according to which "a particular mental event occurs within a particular life solely in virtue of its ascription to a particular Ego." Cf. Parfit, *Reasons and Persons*, 252.

40. Cf. Ibid., 25.

41. Cf. Ibid., 275.

42. Cf. Ibid., 245.

43. He points to the results of R.W. Sperry's tests on split-brain patients displaying a duality of "spheres of consciousness" as a "striking evidence in favour of the Reductionist View." Cf. Footnote 33, Part III, section 12 of *Reasons and Persons* quotes from: R.W. Sperry, in J.C. Eccles ed., *Brain and Conscious Experience* (Berlin: Springer Verlag, 1966).

44. R.W. Sperry, "Hemisphere Deconnection and Unity in Conscious Awareness." Invited address presented to the American Psychological Association, Washington, DC, September 1967, and to the Pan American Congress of Neurology, San Juan, Puerto Rico, October 1967. (Reprinted in: Daniel Kolak and Raymond Martin eds., *Self and Identity: Contemporary Philosophical Issues* [New York and Toronto: Macmillan, 1991], 55–68.) Similar findings are set out in his other work: R.W. Sperry, "Mental Unity Following Surgical Disconnection of the Cerebral Hemisphere," *Harvey Lectures* (New York: Academic Press, 1968). Parfit mentions these cases and other related findings in: Parfit, *Reasons and Persons*, 247.

45. This, in fact, is not a far-fetched extrapolation as is further indicated by tests that were conducted by Sperry and his associates as well as the findings that have resulted from these. Cf. Sperry, "Hemisphere Deconnection and Unity in Conscious Awareness," *Self and Identity*, 58–60.

46. Parfit, *Reasons and Persons*, 247–8. Parfit's point of course is that our ordinary way of understanding "identity" requires that survival be nonbranching. He is

not saying that one who successfully undergoes the operation of "splitting" does not survive. Rather, he survives twice over. And it is precisely because the survival is doubly successful that we should not use the word "identity." Cf. Madell, *The Identity of the Self*, 11.

47. Cf. Sperry, "Hemisphere Deconnection and Unity in Conscious Awareness," *Self and Identity*, 60. See also the discussion by John Eccles on commissurotonomy in which he points out that after the said medical procedure, there results an unconsciousness of all the happenings in the minor, i.e., the right side of the brain, the unity of consciousness that the patient had experienced prior to the operation is in fact retained. What results is not a total disconnection of consciousness, which would allow us to posit the existence of two selves, but merely a "uniqueness and exclusiveness of the *dominant hemisphere* in respect of conscious experience." Cf. Karl R. Popper and John C. Eccles, *The Self and Its Brain: An Argument for Interactionism*, Part II, E5, p. 35: Investigations on the Human Brain After Commissural Section-Commissurotonomy (London and New York: Routlege, 1977, reprint 1993), 313–25.

48. Roland Puccetti, "Two Brains, Two Minds? Wigan's Theory of Mental Duality," *Self and Identity: Contemporary Philosophical Issues,* eds. Daniel Kolak and Raymond Martin (New York and Toronto: Macmillan, 1991), 69.

49. Ibid., 74.

50. See: Thomas Nagel, "Brain Bissection and the Unity of Consciousness," *Synthese*, 22 (1971): 396–413.

51. Parfit, *Reasons and Persons*, 206.

52. Ibid., 206, 222.

53. Ibid., 206.

54. Ibid., 204ff.

55. Ibid., 304–5.

56. Our ordinary way of regarding such instances would naturally try to dispel such perplexity and provide an antidote to our disorientation by pulling us back and reaffirming the way by which we have always understood such situations. George Orwell captured this ordinary way of seeing the issue when he said, "What can the England of 1940 have in common with the England of 1840? But then, what have you in common with the child of five whose photograph your mother keeps on the mantelpiece? Nothing, except that you happen to be the same person." George Orwell, *The Lion and the Unicorn* (London, Harmondsworth, 1982), 37. Alexander Solzhenitsyn, whom Parfit quotes, captures in a rather powerful way, the perplexing character of such experience in *The First Circle* (New York: Bantam Books, 1969), 232. Quoted by Parfit, *Reasons and Persons*, n64, Part III, 519n12.

57. Parfit, *Reasons and Persons*, 306.

58. Ibid., 215.

59. Ibid.

60. Ibid., 217.

61. Ibid., 262–3.

62. Noonan, *Personal Identity*, 203.

63. Parfit, "The Unimportance of Identity," *Identity*, 16–17.

64. Ibid., 16.

65. Parfit, "The Unimportance of Identity," *Identity*, 17.

66. Cf. Parfit, *Reasons and Persons*, 502–3. Quotes are taken from: The *Cila Mara*, quoted in Stcherbatsky, Th. "The Soul Theory of the Buddhists," *Bulletin de l'academie des sciences de Russie* (1919), 839. Also: The *Visuddhimagga*, quoted in Collins, *Selfless Persons*, 133.

67. Parfit, "The Unimportance of Identity," *Identity*, 17.
68. Parfit, "The Unimportance of Identity," *Identity*, 18.
69. Ibid., 16.
70. Ibid., 18.
71. Parfit, *Reasons and Persons*, 243.
72. Ibid., 199–201. Parfit buttresses this argument by means of thought experiments such as that involving Teletransportation.
73. Cf. Parfit, *Reasons and Persons*, 211–12. See also: Parfit, "The Unimportance of Identity," *Identity*, 18. This analogy of "person" with a nation is of course found in Hume's own account of identity. Cf. Hume, *A Treatise of Human Nature*, Book I, IV, Sec. VI, 261. Parfit quotes Hume in p. 211 of *Reasons and Persons*.
74. Parfit, *Reasons and Persons*, 214.
75. Ibid., 213.
76. He gives the example of the "callous neurosurgeon" who tampers with a person's brain and gives him the memories and character of Napoleon. Cf. Parfit, *Reasons and Persons*, 229–30.
77. In the teletransportation example, although there is no numerical identity, we can at least claim that the person on Mars is qualitatively identical with the one on Earth—in terms of psychological continuity at least. On the other hand, in the case of the mad neurosurgeon, although the person given Napoleon's memory and character is no longer psychologically continuous with the person whose memory was erased, there is no reason for the latter not to fear that the pain of the ordeal would continue, since he has no reason to expect that the pain will in fact stop at some point. And because of this it seems that physical continuity is sufficient to continue his existence throughout the ordeal. Cf. Parfit, *Reasons and Persons*, 230.
78. Parfit, "The Unimportance of Identity," *Identity*, 21.
79. Parfit, *Reasons and Persons*, 236–7.
80. Ibid., 237.
81. This view has of course been criticized as based on an ontology of object-phases, the possibility of which some have regarded as doubtful. Cf. Madell, *The Identity of the Self*, 14, 126. There are lines of similarity, if not convergence, between the way Process Thought views personal identity, and Parfit's own theory. And the object-phase ontology upon which Madell alleges Parfit to have based his account of personal identity bears an uncanny resemblance to the event ontology that Hartshorne espouses. Cf. John Cobb, "Man in Process," *Concilium*, ed. Franz Bockle (New York: Herder and Herder, 1972), 34.
82. Parfit, *Reasons and Persons*, 284.
83. Ibid., 215. Noonan calls this future entity which is psychologically connected with one's present self through Relation R, "Parfitian survivors." Cf. Noonan, *Personal Identity*, 24. In considering my future, it is not important that there be something alive who will be "exactly me." The only thing that matters is that there be at least one living person who is psychologically continuous with myself as I am at the present moment. Cf. Parfit, *The Unimportance of Identity*, 44.
84. Parfit, *Reasons and Persons*, 347.
85. Parfit does allow for the fact that bodily continuity is regarded by many as important. There is no irrationality in caring a little for one's physical continuity. But this should not be understood to mean anything more than a sentimental wish which he compares with the desire to keep something, e.g., a wedding ring, because it has a lot of sentimental value, rather than have it replaced with something similar. Cf. Ibid., 286.

86. Ibid., 3.
87. Parfit, Personal Identity, 200.
88. Parfit, *Reasons and Persons*, 341.
89. Ibid.
90. Parfit, *Reasons and Persons*, 282.
91. Shalom, The Body/Mind Conceptual Framework, 344.
92. Philippians 2:12. *NRSV*.
93. Shalom, The Body Mind Conceptual Framework, 344.
94. Parfit, "Personal Identity," 208.
95. Parfit, *Reasons and Persons*, 282.
96. Parfit, "The Unimportance of Identity," *Identity*, 29. This of course does not mean that ultimately, it is the "lowest-level" facts, e.g., subatomic particles, that matter. Parfit rejects this notion. What he is simply arguing for is that when a higher level fact such as personal identity is but a conceptual label for other lower level facts as physical and pychological continuity, the constituted fact cannot be *as important* as the constituting ones.
97. Parfit, *Reasons and Persons*, 446.
98. Hume, *A Treatise of Human Nature*, 262.
99. Parfit, *Reasons and Persons*, 282.
100. Ibid., 347.
101. Ibid., 446.
102. Ricoeur, *Oneself as Another*, 139.
103. This notion is summed up in the Hartshornean notion of "reciprocity" upon which his entire philosophy of societism is built. Cf. Charles Hartshorne, *Reality as Social Process: Studies in Metaphysics and Religion* (New York: Hafner Publishing, 1971). Hereafter cited as *RSP*.
104. This in fact is how Whitehead characterizes the paradigm that has given rise to the punctual or substantialistic view of self which, like the independent individualities of Newtonian physics, is conceived as fully describable apart from any reference to any other entity. Cf. Alfred North Whitehead, *Adventures of Ideas* (New York and London: The Free Press, Macmillan, 1933, Reprint 1967), 200–1. Whitehead's critique of the Newtonian atomistic worldview and the way such criticism gets played out in Hartshorne's objections to substantialist ontologies will be discussed in fuller detail in the succeeding chapters.
105. Charles Taylor criticizes this Lockean-Parfitian perspective on the self and argues that this perspective suffers from a fatal flaw as "the self is defined in abstraction from any constitutive concerns," its only constitutive property being self awareness. This, Taylor points out, is the "self that Hume set out to find and predictably, failed to find." Cf. Taylor, *Sources of the Self*, 49–50.
106. Cf. Madell, *The Identity of the Self*, 14. Madell argues that such a perspective based on an ontology of disconnected object-phases is simply not possible for persons. And he singles out Parfit in this particular critique, insisting that the unity of consciousness disclosed by thinking would not be possible if what were there was a mere succession of moments of consciousness.
107. Cf. Penelhum, *Hume*, 84–5.
108. See Derek Parfit's defense of G.C. Lichtenberg against Bernard Williams' objection to impersonal descriptions in which the latter attempts to modify Lichtenberg's thoroughly impersonal rendering of the Cartesian *Cogito*, by reasserting a subject of experience. Cf. Parfit, *Reasons and Persons*, 225–6.
109. Jenkins, *Understanding Hume*, 113.

110. Cf. Penelhum, *Hume*, 87–8.
111. Jenkins, *Understanding Hume*, 114.
112. Cf. Stroud, *Hume*, 132–3.
113. Here we agree with Capaldi's explanation of why Hume regarded his account as ultimately defective. Cf. N. Capaldi, "The Historical and Philosophical Significance of Hume's Theory of the Self," *David Hume Critical Assessments*, Volume III, ed. Stanley Tweyman (London and New York: Routledge, 1995), 632–3. Also, Jenkins, *Understanding Hume*, 114–15; Penelhum, *Hume*, 84–8. For an account of how the idea continued to reassert itself after the Appendix of the *Essay*, see: J. McIntyre, "Hume's Underground Self," *David Hume Critical Assessments*, Volume III, ed. Stanley Tweyman (London and New York: Routledge, 1995), 718–29.
114. Cf. David P. Behan, "Hume's Labyrinth," *David Hume: Critical Assessments*, Volume III, ed. Stanley Tweyman (London and New York: Routledge, 1995),730–4.
115. This is understandable given the more radical nature of the Humean thesis. Cf. Ibid., 730–4.
116. Stroud, *Hume*, 135.
117. "I had entertained some hopes, that however, deficient our theory of the intellectual world might be, that it would be free from those contradictions, and absurdities, which seem to attend every explication, that human reason can give of the material world. But upon a more strict review of the section concerning *personal identity*, I find myself involved in such a labyrinth, that, I must confess, I neither know how to correct my former opinions, nor how to render them consistent. If this be not a good *general* reason for skepticism, 'tis at least a sufficient one." Hume, *An Essay Concerning Human Understanding*, 636.
118. Ibid., 269.
119. Parfit, *Reasons and Persons*, 282.
120. This is something that Parfit himself recognized, pointing out that although Hume's view is largely inadequate, in all relevant respects, it is consistent with his own when it comes to challenging the Self-Interest theory in ethics. And he acknowledges that his views on selfhood and its relations to others "follows Hume." Cf. Parfit, *Reasons and Persons*, 139.
121. Shalom, The Body/Mind Conceptual Framework and the Problem of Personal Identity, 348.
122. Ricoeur, *Oneself as Another*, 27–39. These pages constitute the First Study of the *opus*, entitled "Person and Identifying Reference." In this section, Ricoeur endeavors to make a first stage analysis of what he believes we mean by the term "person." He does this by considering the ordinary notion of "identification." He says that it is along this path of identifying reference—which involves making "apparent to others, amid a range of things of the same type, that entity *of which* we intend to speak"—that we first encounter the idea of a "person." This first level idea is simply that of "something," just like anything else which we delineate from other "things." There is not yet any perspective of "identifying oneself." It is also in this section that Ricoeur discusses P.F. Strawson's notion of "persons" as basic particulars. Although he finds himself sympathetic with the Strawsonian viewpoint, Ricoeur says that the disadvantage of treating the idea of "person" in this way is that it leads to the obscuring of the self as "who," making room only for an understanding of the self as "what." Ricoeur thus concludes that Strawson's account, by and large, follows the route of *idem*-identity.

123. Ibid., 2.
124. Ibid., 118.
125. Ibid., 129–130.
126. Cf. Paul Ricoeur, "Intellectual Autobiography," trans. Kathleen Blamey, *The Philosophy of Paul Ricoeur*, The Library of Living Philosophers, Volume XXII, ed. Lewis Edwin Hahn (Chicago: Open Court, 1995), 49.
127. This explains why in spite of his agreement with P.F. Strawson who regarded "persons" as "primitive concepts" or "basic particulars," Ricoeur eventually finds Strawson's thesis inadequate. He agrees with Strawson's notion of "persons" as "basic particulars" in that he believes "there is no way of going beyond it, without presupposing it in the argument that would claim to derive it from something else." Nevertheless, the inadequacy of the Strawsonian account lies in the fact that the importance given by Strawson to the perspective of *ipse*-identity or selfhood is more apparent than real. First, explicit self-designation is weak in Strawson's account. His strictly referential problematic leaves no room for explicit self-designation. This, says Ricoeur precludes a real sense of *mineness* in which "the logical force of the self is acknowledged." Second, Strawson's overemphasis on "objective bodies" as basic particulars, and the neglect of "mental events and consciousness," leads only to "the increased concealment of the question of the self." As a commentator remarked: "To the extent that the body serves as a paradigm for the concept of a basic particular, the full reality of selfhood will be submerged in the physical" (Cf. Ronald G. Alexander, *The Self, Supervenience, and Personal Identity*, 108). Finally, Ricoeur argues that "one does not see how the property of selfhood could be placed in a list of predicates ascribed to an entity, even one as original as the person." The real problem, he insists, is "understanding how the self can be at one and the same time a person of whom we speak and a subject who designates herself in the first person, while addressing the second person." How do we in fact understand the manner by which the third person is designated in discourse as someone who designates himself as a first person." Cf. Ricoeur, *Oneself as Another*, 33–5.
128. Ricoeur, *Oneself as Another*, 123, n9. Quote taken from: Martin Heidegger, *Being and Time*, trans. John Macquarrie and Edward Robinson, English translation of *Sein und Zeit* (New York: Harper and Row, 1962), 351. In another work, Ricoeur compares the kind of identity encompassed by *idem* and the mode of being of ordinary things in the world as Heidegger characterized them in *Being and Time*, namely, as *present-at-hand* and *ready-to-hand*, *Vorhanden* and *Zuhanden*, respectively. These modes of being, he says, are not those that belong properly to personal identity understood from the perspective of *ipse*-identity. Cf. Paul Ricoeur, "L'identite narrative," *Esprit: Changer la culture et la politique*, 12/7–8 (July–August, 1988): 298.
129. Ricoeur, *Oneself as Another*, 130. In the reference (no. 21) to the quotation from Parfit, Ricoeur makes the observation that Parfit's expression, "Our identity is not what matters," cannot fail to introduce the question of ownership. Quote taken from: Parfit, *Reasons and Persons*, 245, 255.
130. Ricoeur, *Oneself as Another*, 133.
131. Ibid., 132.
132. Ibid., 17.
133. Ibid., 137–8.
134. Ibid., 18.
135. Ibid., 51.

136. "Limit" here refers to the fact that the privileged point of view on the world which the self possesses is a mark that sets it apart from any other standpoint in the universe.

137. Ricoeur, *Oneself as Another*, 53–4.

138. Ibid., 138.

Chapter 3

1. Charles Hartshorne, *Creative Synthesis and Philosophic Method* (London: SCM Press), xvi. Hereafter cited as *CSPM*.

2. Cf. Charles Hartshorne, "My Neoclassical Metaphysics," *Tijdschrift voor Filosofie* 42/1 (March, 1980): 3–10.

3. Commenting on the fact that the subtitle of Hartshorne's book *The Logic of Perfection* is "Essays in Neo-Classical Metaphysics," Huston Smith points out that "the author [Hartshorne] dissociates himself from the positivistic suspicion that such inquiries are misguided in principle and cognitively can come to nothing. The qualification 'classical,' in turn, distinguishes the inquiry from dominant continental quests—Heidegger's, Jaspers', Sartre's, Marcel's—which, though engrossed with the problem of being, doubt that traditional tools (objective reason directed toward system construction) can effectively come to grips with it. There remains the prefix 'neo,' which announces that we cannot perpetuate the past. In method as well as in content, twentieth century metaphysics must break new ground." Cf. Huston Smith, "The Death and Rebirth of Metaphysics," *Process and Divinity*. The Hartshorne Festschrift: Philosophical Essays Presented to Charles Hartshorne, eds. William Reese and Eugene Freeman (LaSalle, Illinois: Open Court, 1964), 37.

4. Cf. Santiago Sia, *God in Process Thought: A Study in Charles Hartshorne's Concept of God* (Dordrecht: Martinus Nijhoff, 1985), n32.

5. Cf. William Ernest Hocking, "Foreword," to Charles Hartshorne, *Reality as Social Process: Studies in Metaphysics and Religion* (New York: Hafner, 1971), 11–16.

6. Cf. J.C. Polkinghorne, "A Revived Natural Theology," *Science and Religion: One World Changing Perspectives*. Papers Presented at the Second European Conference on Science and Religion, eds. Jan Fennema and Iain Paul (Dordrecht: Kluwer Academic Publishers, 1990), 87–97. See also Arthur Peacocke, *Intimations of Reality: Critical Realism in Science and Religion* (Notre Dame: University of Notre Dame Press, 1984), 34.

7. Cf. Jan van der Veken, "God's World and Man Becoming: How can Science Possibly Help us to Transcend Dogmatism?" *Science and Religion: One World: Changing Perspectives*. Papers Presented at the Second European Conference on Science and Religion, eds. Jan Fennema and Iain Paul (Dordrecht: Kluwer Academic Publishers, 1990), 131–37. See also Arthur Peacocke, *Intimations of Reality*, 32; John Wild, "Devotion and Fanaticism," *Process and Divinity: The Hartshorne Festschrift*. Philosophical Essays Presented to Charles Hartshorne, eds. William Reese and Eugene Freeman (La Salle, Illinois: Open Court, 1964), 445–69.

8. *CSPM*, 175.

9. Cf. *CSPM*, xv. Hartshorne singles out Whitehead in the "Preface" to *Creative Synthesis*, as the philosopher whose thought is the closest parallel and probably the strongest influence upon his philosophy. There are not so insignificant differences between them of course, which Hartshorne also mentions, viz.,

(1) Whitehead's doctrine of "eternal objects," (2) the notion that God is a single "actual entity," and (3) the idea of "earlier" and "later" "phases" in the becoming of entities devoid of actual succession. These differences are spelled out and discussed in: David R. Griffin "Hartshorne's Differences from Whitehead," *Two Process Philosophers: Hartshorne's Encounter with Whitehead* (Tallahassee, Florida: American Academy of Religion, 1973), 35–57; Lewis S. Ford, "Whitehead's Differences from Hartshorne," *Two Process Philosophers: Hartshorne's Encounter with Whitehead* (Tallahassee, Florida: American Academy of Religion, 1973), 58–83.

10. Alfred North Whitehead, *Adventures of Ideas* (New York: Macmillan, 1967), 158. Hereafter cited as *AI*.

11. Ivor Leclerc, *Whitehead's Metaphysics: An Introductory Exposition* (London: Allen and Unwin, 1965), 18–19.

12. Aristotle, *Metaphysics* Z, I, 1028b, 2–8. Vol. VIII of *The Works of Aristotle*, Trans. W. D. Ross (Oxford: Clarendon Press, 1972).

13. This is how the medieval scholar Étienne Gilson describes the basic Aristotelian unit in *Being and Some Philosophers* (Toronto: Pontifical Institute of Medieval Studies, 1949), 42.

14. *CSPM*, 176.

15. Ibid., 173–4.

16. Cf. David Ross, *Aristotle* (New York: Barnes and Noble, 1964), 165–6. See also: A.H. Basson, *The Problem of Substance*, Proceedings of the Aristotelian Society, 17th Session, vol. XLIX (February 7, 1949): 65–72. The following treatment of the concept, including the major terminologies we are adopting follows in large part, a similar treatment to that of Ross.

17. Cf. Constantine Georgiadis, "Two Conceptions of Substance in Aristotle," *Substances and Things: Aristotle's Doctrine of Physical Substance in Recent Essays*, ed. M.L. O'Hara (Washington: University Press of America, 1982), 172–87. The author argues that it is possible to distinguish an earlier sense (found in the *Categories*), namely, substance as an individual thing (*res*), and a later sense (found in the *Metaphysics*), viz., substance as the constitutive nature (DPZ or 'principle') of the entity. The earlier sense he calls the "reistic" conception and the latter, the "archological" conception of substance.

18. *Metaphysics* , 8, 1017b, 13,14. For a treatment of the relation between these two passages and absence of any easy correlation between them, see: D.R. Cousin, "Aristotle's Doctrine of Substance," *Mind*, 42/167 (July, 1933): 320–1.

19. Aristotle, *Categories*, 2a, 11–18, *The Works of Aristotle*. Trans. W.D. Ross (Oxford: Clarendon, 1972).

20. Ibid., 21–2.

21. Ibid., 2b, 10–13.

22. This distinction is especially suggested by the phrase "present in a subject," the Greek work for "subject" here being *hupokeimenon* literally meaning "underlay." This does not mean of course that a substance can never be present in something else as part of a whole. Hands and heads, for instance, are themselves substances and yet are part of another substance, viz., the body (Cf. Ibid., 8b, 15).

23. The second Cartesian characterization of substance as it is found in the Principia Philosophiae reads: *Per substantiam nihil aliud intelligere possumus, quam rem quae ita existit, ut nulla alia re indigeat ad existendum.* ("By substance we can understand nothing other than a thing which exists in such a manner that it has need of no other thing for its existence.") Cf. René Descartes, Principia Philosophiae, Trans., John Veitch and A.D. Lindsay (London: Everyman's Library, 1969), I, 51.

24. Cf. Moltke S. Gram, "Substance," *Substances and Things*, ed. M.L. O'Hara (Washington: University Press of America, 1982), 125.
25. See: G.E.M. Anscombe and J. Körner, "Substance," *Proceedings of the Aristotelian Society*. Suppl., Vol. 38 (1964): 69–90, where the Cartesian definition of substance as that which exists without needing anything else apart from the divine operation, is traced to the Aristotelian notion, arguing, however, that what Descartes presumably meant was no more than that individual substances exist without either being predicated of or existing in anything else.
26. Gram, "Substance," *Substances and Things*, 125.
27. Thus, the second Cartesian sense of substance, when taken up and developed by Spinoza, for instance, resulted in consistent but rather startling conclusions. Spinoza demonstrated that if by substance is meant "that which is in itself and is conceived through itself," it becomes easy enough to show that there can only be one such being, namely, the whole universe, which he equated with God. Spinoza's theory or "hideous hypothesis"—in Hume's rather unfortunate phrase—demonstrates some of the most alarming consequences of the Cartesian inference, especially for religious orthodoxy. Cf. David Hume, *A Treatise of Human Nature*, 241. Rather ironically though, in a somewhat indirect way, Spinoza was able to show that nothing in the universe is totally independent of its environment, though some things possess more independence than others.
28. Cf. Alfred North Whitehead, *Process and Reality*, 50n79.
29. *Categories*, 4a, 10.
30. *Metaphysics*, Z, 1029a, 8.
31. Cf. Abraham Edel, *Aristotle and His Philosophy* (London: Croom Helm, 1982), 119.
32. Hartshorne himself does not treat this particular criticism in his works. However, it is a source of a significant amount of discussion in logic and the philosophy of language. For instance, in a rather original and penetrating critique of the notions of subject and predicate, Tsu-Lin Mei adopts the perspective of Carnap, expressed in *Philosophy and Logical Syntax* (London, 1935), and Quine, articulated in *From a Logical Point of View* (Cambridge, Mass., 1960) and argues that philosophical theses are language-relative. Cf. Tsu-Lin Mei, "Chinese Grammar and the Linguistic Movement in Philosophy," *The Review of Metaphysics*, 3/55 (March, 1961): 463–92. Using an analysis of the structural similarities and differences of English and Chinese, Tsu-Lin demonstrates that a strict subject-predicate distinction (valid in English and other Germanic languages) is invalidated by Chinese grammar. In a section of the work, the author criticizes P.F. Strawson's view that a predicate can never be part of a subject. (Cf. P.F. Strawson, "Proper Names," *Proceedings of the Aristotelian Society*. Suppl. Vol. 31 [1957]: 191–228, which asserts the classical notion that the subject-predicate distinction parallels the particular-universal distinction in logic. Tsu-Lin contests Strawson's grammatical criterion according to which a predicate expression demands a certain completion, namely, completion into a proposition or propositional clause. As far as English is concerned, such criterion is verified; its regional significance is assured. However, as the author shows, in Chinese, predicate expressions do not require, except for a few rare exceptions, completion into a proposition or propositional clause. This puts into question the global significance of the dependence of the notion of substance in terms of a subject-predicate structure.
33. *CSPM*, 174–5.
34. *PR*, 18n27.
35. *PR*, 79n122.
36. *CSPM*, 178.

37. Ibid., 179.
38. Charles Hartshorne, "Personal Identity from A to Z," *Process Studies*, 210.
39. It is what distinguishes time from space which in turn is "the symmetrical aspect of dynamic relatedness, the aspect of mutuality, whether mutuality of dependence or ... independence" (*CSPM*, 179). The asymmetry of temporal relatedness is best illustrated by the ancestor-descendant relationship. One is who he is because of the ancestors he has; these ancestors of his, however, were who and what they were, independent of the successors or descendants they might have had. This is the one-way relatedness of the ancestral relation.
40. Ibid., 180.
41. Ibid., xix.
42. Ibid., 180.
43. Ibid., 181.
44. Ibid., 184.
45. Ibid., 214.
46. The problematic relationship of Hartshorne's thought with relativity physics is nowhere more pronounced than here. This particular difficulty has to do with the fact that his system entails the existence of a definite cosmic "present" and its denial by relativity physics. Relativity holds that there may be a definite cosmic past and future, but no unambiguous "present." Hartshorne's system, however, entails a sharp demarcation between a determinate past and an indeterminate future, and this demarcation would require a definite "cosmic present" as the line separating past and future. Cf. John Wilcox, "A Question from Physics for Certain Theists," *Journal of Religion*, 40/4 (October, 1961): 293–300; Lewis S. Ford, "Is Process Theism Compatible with Relativity Theory," *Journal of Religion*, 47/2 (April, 1968): 124–35; Paul Fitzgerald, "Relativity Physics and the God of Process Philosophy," *Process Studies*, 2/4 (Winter, 1972): 251–73; Frederic F. Fost, "Relativity Theory and Hartshorne's Dipolar Theism," *Two Process Philosophers: Hartshorne's Encounter with Whitehead*, AAR Studies in Religion, No. 5, ed. Lewis S. Ford (Tallahassee: American Academy of Religion, 1973), 89–99; David Ray Griffin, "Hartshorne, God and Relativity Physics," *Process Studies*, 21/1 (Summer, 1992): 85–112. Hartshorne himself admits this to be a real problematic area of his system in terms of its dialogue with contemporary science. For instance, in a response to an article by William Reese, Hartshorne says that it is "a problem, even *the* problem, for me; how God as prehending, caring for, sensitive to, the creatures, is to be conceived, given the current non-Newtonian idea of physical relativity, according to which there is apparently no unique cosmic present or unambiguous simultaneity." Cf. Charles Hartshorne, "Bell's Theorem and Stapp's Revised View of Space-Time," *Process Studies*, 7/3 (Fall, 1977): 183–91. See also: Lewis Edwin Hahn ed., *The Philosophy of Charles Hartshorne*, Vol. XX of The Library of Living Philosophers (La Salle: Open Court, 1991), 616. While the discussion is of peripheral relevance to the issue with which we are concerned, we nevertheless cannot simply put it aside. And while it cannot be our intention to provide a reasonable solution to the problem, we intend to show that Hartshorne's way of viewing memory and perception—namely, that "both in memory and perception, the given entities are antecedent events"—and the notion of temporality entailed by such view, cannot but provide a way of clarifying certain difficulties involved in his thought's dialogue with science.
47. Cf. *Categories*, 41, 10.
48. *CSPM*, 181–2.
49. Ibid., 176.

50. Ibid., 176–7.
51. Charles Hartshorne, *Insights and Oversights of Great Thinkers* (New York: State University of New York Press, 1983), 55.
52. *CSPM*, 173.
53. *Metaphysics*, M, 1086b, 2–7.
54. Ibid., Z, 1036a, 28–9.
55. Ibid., K, 1059b, 25–6.
56. *CSPM*, 173.
57. Ibid., 173–4.
58. Ibid., 174.
59. Ibid., 174–5.
60. Ibid., 175.
61. P.F. Strawson, *Individuals: An Essay in Descriptive Metaphysics* (Garden City, New York: Doubleday, 1959, 1963).
62. Ibid., xiii.
63. Ibid., xiv.
64. Ibid., xv.
65. Ibid., xiv.
66. Hartshorne, *Insights and Oversights*, xv.
67. Strawson, *Individuals*, 27.
68. Ibid., 44–5.
69. Ibid., 30.
70. *CSPM*, 186.
71. Cf. Strawson, *Individuals*, xiv.
72. Ibid., 28–9.
73. Ibid., 35.
74. Ibid., 3.
75. Ibid., 35.

Chapter 4

1. Alfred North Whitehead, *Science and the Modern World*. The 1925 Lowell Lectures. (London: Free Association Books, 1985), 61–2 (First UK edition published in 1926, Cambridge University Press). Hereafter cited as *SMW*.
2. Ibid., 80.
3. Ibid., 62.
4. Ibid., 63.
5. Ibid., 49.
6. Cf. David C. Lindberg, *The Beginnings of Western Science: The European Scientific Tradition in Philosophical, Religious, and Institutional Context, 600 B.C. to A.D. 1450* (Chicago and London: The University of Chicago Press, 1992), 216. Lindberg discusses the steady growth of influence that a revived Aristotelianism enjoyed in universities of the West as well as the conflicts that ensued in terms of this philosophy's relationship with Christian faith. For a more detailed discussion of the works done by early medieval scholars see, Part VI (especially chapter I) of Etienne Gilson, *History of Christian Philosophy in the Middle Ages* (New York: Random House, 1955), 235–46. Van Steenberghen also discusses the reception of Aristotelianism in western universities as well as the difficulties attendant to this development. See: Fernand Van Steenberghen, *Aristotle in the West*. Translated by Leonard Johnston (Louvain: Nauwelaerts,1955). He has a similar discussion in

The Philosophical Movement in the Thirteenth Century (London: Nelson, 1955). See also David Knowles, *The Evolution of Medieval Thought* (New York: Vintage, 1964).

7. Cf. Philip Kitcher, "The Foundations of Mathematics," *Companion to the History of Modern Science*, eds. R.C. Olby, G.N. Cantor, J.R.R. Christie and M.J.S. Hodge (London and New York: Routledge, 1990), 679.

8. Cf. Lindberg, *The Beginnings of Western Science*, Chapter VIII: Science in Islam, Chapter IX: The Revival of Learning in the West, and Chapter X: The Recovery and Assimilation of Greek and Islamic Science,161–244.

9. Cf. Ian Barbour, *Issues in Science and Religion* (New York: Harper and Row, 1966), 23. Also: M. Kline, *Mathematical Thoughts from Ancient to Modern Times* (Oxford: Oxford University Press, 1972), 2.

10. *SMW*, 3.

11. Ibid., 28.

12. Ibid., 33.

13. Ibid., 27.

14. Ibid., 39.

15. Ibid., 41.

16. Ibid.

17. Ibid., 40.

18. Ibid., 40–1.

19. Ibid., 43.

20. *SMW*, 35.

21. Ibid., 37.

22. Ibid., 36.

23. *SMW*, 36.

24. Cf. Barbour, *Issues in Science and Religion*, 23.

25. Cf. Alexander Koyré, *Galileo Studies*, English trans. of *Etudes galiléennes* (Paris, 1939), European Philosophy and the Human Sciences, trans. J. Mepham (Hassocks: Harvester Press, 1978).

26. *SMW*, 37.

27. A. George Molland, "Aristotelian Science," *Companion to the History of Modern Science*.Eds. R.C. Olby, G.N. Cantor, J.R.R. Christie and M.J.S. Hodge (London: Routledge, 1990), 562–3.

28. Aristotle, *Posterior Analytics*, I.13, 78b35–79a6.

29. Aristotle, *Physics*, II.2, 194a7–8.

30. Aristotle, *Metaphysics*, XI.3.1061a30–5.

31. *SMW*, 37.

32. Ibid., 38.

33. Cf. Molland, "Aristotelian Science," *Companion to the History of Modern Science*, 561. Also: Hawking, *A Brief History of Time*, 15. Barbour, *Issues in Science and Religion*, 22–6.

34. *SMW*, 38.

35. *SMW*, 38.

36. N. Max Wildiers, for instance, discusses the decline of the medieval world picture in terms of a disintegration of the peculiar fusion of science and religion that had been accomplished by the medieval scholastics. "By the end of the seventeenth century," he points out, "the view of Galileo and Newton gained the day and the medieval picture of the universe was completely abolished. All certainties that were found on or supported by this medieval world picture lost all force of conviction." Cf. N. Max Wildiers, *The Theologian and His Universe:*

Theology and Cosmology from the Middle Ages to the Present, English translation of *Wereldbeeld en Teologie van de Middeleeuwen tot vandaag,* 1977. Trans. Paul Dunphy (New York: Seabury, 1982), 80–2. For a similar analysis see: Richard Tarnas, *The Passion of the Western Mind: Understanding the Ideas that have Shaped our World View* (New York: Ballantine Books, 1991), 224–71.

37. Paul Hazard has characterized this trend as a "crisis" of European consciousness, a "revolution," which reached its climax at the end of the 18th century. Notions held dear, almost sacred by the medievals became the very things that those who followed them "held in cordial detestation." Cf. his *The European Mind, 1680–1715* (Harmondsworth: Penguin, 1964), English translation of *La Crise de la conscience européene,* 1680–1715 (Paris,1935).

38. *SMW,* 43.

39. *PR,* 5n7.

40. Ibid., 5n7–8.

41. *SMW,* 25.

42. Ibid., 20.

43. Ibid., 49.

44. N. Max Wildiers points to these two as the "sources" of the world picture of the Middle Ages. Cf. Wildiers, *The Theologian and His Universe,* 19–35. See also the discussion in: Tarnas, *The Passion of the Western Mind,* esp. 73–105. There are, of course, criticisms of such views. In his book *Religion, Science and Naturalism,* for instance, Willem B. Drees, argues that by relying on such "global" pictures we promote the treatment of the alleged "sources" as if these were "monolithic entities" when there is in fact, a greater diversity that is involved in each of them. Cf. Willem B. Drees, *Religion, Science and Naturalism* (Cambridge: Cambridge University Press, 1996), 78–9.

45. *SMW,* 9–10.

46. Ibid., 13.

47. Ibid., 9–10.

48. *SMW,* 14.

49. Ibid., 14–15.

50. Cf. Schuster, "The Scientific Revolution," *Companion to the History of Modern Science,* 217.

51. Cf. Robert Fox, "Laplacian Physics," *Companion to the History of Modern Science,* eds., R.C. Olby, G.N. Cantor, J.R.R. Christie and M.J.S. Hodge (London: Routledge, 1990), 280–2.

52. David Bohm, "The Implicate Order: A New Approach to the Nature of Reality," *Beyond Mechanism: The Universe in Recent Physics and Catholic Thought,* ed. David L.Schindler (New York: University Press of America, 1986), 14.

53. Cf. Bohm, "The Implicate Order," *Beyond Mechanism,* 14–15. In Chapter 2 of his work *Insights and Oversights of Great Thinkers,* Hartshorne summarizes these characteristics into two: "Atomism meant: (i) the real, pervasive structure of the world, by which its changes are to be chiefly understood, is on too fine a scale to be directly apparent to sense perception and (ii) the imperceptibly small constituents of the world have permanent sizes and shapes and interact only by push-pulling one another." Hartshorne, *Insights and Oversights,* 17.

54. *SMW,* 72.

55. *PR,* 137n208.

56. Cf. Milič Čapek, *The Philosophical Impact of Contemporary Physics* (Princeton, New Jersey: Van Nostrand, 1961). This work is quoted by Hartshorne in *Creative Synthesis.* Cf. *CSPM,* 219.

57. Cf. A. d'Abro, *The Evolution of Scientific Though from Newton to Einstein* (New York: Dover, 1950), 343. Also, Erwin A. Esper, *A History of Psychology* (Philadelphia and London: W.B. Saunders, 1964), 9. The 18-page *Introduction* to this work is itself a reminder of the difficulties attendant to a less-than-critical exposition of possible "implications" of any developments in significant fields of study. He in fact singles out Gestalt psychology (in pp. 10–14) as a particular instance, the ideas of which must be approached and appropriated only with critical caution.

58. Cf. Joseph Needham, "A Biologist's View of Whitehead," *The Philosophy of Alfred North Whitehead*, The Library of Living Philosophers, ed. Paul Arthur Schilpp (New York: Tudor Publishing Company, 1951), 259–61, 271. In this article, Needham also briefly discusses the impact simple location has had on the development of biology and points to the fact that "in Whitehead's philosophy biologists find a view of the world which they are particularly well fitted to appreciate. [...] they see in him the greatest and subtlest exponent of organic mechanism."

59. Davies, *God and the New Physics*, vii: "The new physics soon revealed more than simply a better model of the physical world. Physicists began to realize that their discoveries demanded a radical reformulation of the most fundamental aspects of reality. They learned to approach their subject in totally unexpected and novel ways that seemed to turn common sense on its head and find closer accord with mysticism than with materialism." Also, Coveney and Highfield, *The Arrow of Time*, 68: "Quantum theory transformed our understanding of the 'fundamental' microscopic world beyond all recognition. And Einstein's theory of relativity swept away the notion of absolute time once and for all." Although still to wait for the dawning of the 20th century, Einstein's discovery was already being presaged by the thought and scientific advances of the 19th. Perhaps the impact of the change is captured in no more vivid terms than in John Squire's couplet that parodies the Alexander Pope's proposed epitaph to Newton: "Nature, and Nature's Laws lay hid in Night. God said, Let Newton be! and All was Light." D. Gjertsen, *The Newton Handbook* (London: Routledge and Kegan Paul, 1986), 439. Squire's couplet on Einstein reads: "It did not last; the devil howling Ho! Let Einstein be, restored the status quo." W. Gratzer ed., *The Longman Literary Companion to Science* (London: Harlow, Longman, 1989), 128.

60. Cf. J.C. Flugel and Donald J. West, *A Hundred Years of Psychology 1833–1933* (London: Gerald Duckworth, 1964), 205–206.

61. Čapek, The Philosophical Impact of Contemporary Physics, 79.

62. Milič Čapek, "Simple Location and Fragmentation of Reality," *Process and Divinity: The Hartshorne Festschrift*, Philosophical Essays Presented to Charles Hartshorne, eds., William Reese and Eugene Freeman (La Salle, Illinois: Open Court, 1964), 88–9. The summarization we are presenting here takes its cue from Čapek's article which deals specifically with the connections between the developments in physics and psychology which have influenced Whitehead's own critique of the notion of simple location.

63. Ibid.

64. Cf. Charles Hartshorne, "The Parallel Development of Method in Physics and Psychology," *Philosophy of Science* 1, 4 (October, 1934): 446–59.

65. Cf. Norton Wise, "Electromagnetic Theory in the Nineteenth Century," *Companion to the History of Modern Science*, eds. R.C. Olby, G.N. Cantor, J.R.R. Christie, and M.J.S. Hodge (London: Routledge, 1990), 647–8.

66. Wise, "Electromagnetic Theory in the Nineteenth Century," *Companion to the History of Modern Science*, 647–8.

67. Cf. Crosbie Smith, "Energy," *Companion to the History of Modern Science*, eds. R.C. Olby, G.N. Cantor, J.R.R. Christie, and M.J.S. Hodge (London: Routledge, 1990), 337.

68. Ibid.

69. Hartshorne, "The Parallel Development of Method in Physics and Psychology," *Philosophy of Science*, 450.

70. James Clerk Maxwell, *A Treatise on Electricity and Magnetism*, 3rd. edition, 2 (Oxford: Oxford University Press, 1891), 146.

71. See Maxwell's "Preface" to Treatise on Electricity and Magnetism.

72. Cf. Alfred North Whitehead, *The Concept of Nature* (Cambridge: Cambridge University Press, 1920), 146.

73. Čapek, "Simple Location and Fragmentation of Reality," *Process and Divinity*, 91–4.

74. Ibid., 91–2.

75. Ibid., 92–3.

76. Ibid., 93–4.

77. Hartshorne, "The Parallel Development of Method in Physics and Psychology," *Philosophy of Science*, 451.

78. Cf. Plato, *Phaedo*, Trans. Benjamin Jowett in *The Works of Plato*, The Modern Library, Ed. Irwin Edman (New York: Simon and Schuster), 131–32.

79. Cf. Hume, *Treatise on Human Nature*, Bk. I, Part IV, Sec. 5, 232–51.

80. Cf. E. A. Esper. *A History of Psychology* (Philadelphia and London, Saunders 1964).

81. Cf. Flugel and West, A Hundred Years of Psychology, 120.

82. Cf. Ibid., 121. The fifth chapter of Part III of this work (cf. 120–32) deals specifically with the development of psychological theories from the time of Franz Brentano's ground breaking work *Psychologie vom empirischen Standpuntke* to William James' *Principles of Psychology*.

83. Cf. Ibid., 124–5.

84. Cf. Ibid., 128–32.

85. Christian von Ehrenfels, "Über Gestaltqualitäten," *Vierteljahrschrift für Wissenschaftliche Philosophie* , 14 (1890): 249–92.

86. Cf. Richard Müller-Freienfels, *The Evolution of Modern Psychology*, Trans. W. Beran Wolfe (New Haven: Yale University Press, 1935), 98–101.

87. In 1912, Wertheimer wrote his *Experimentelle Studien über das Sehen von Bewegung*, which is commonly regarded as marking the beginning of the Gestalt movement in psychology. Cf. Max Wertheimer, "Experimentelle Studien über das Sehen von Bewegung," *Zeitschrift für Psychologie*, 1/71 (1912): 161–265. He also published a work in 1945 entitled "Productive Thinking" which deals with the intricacies involved in the study of problem solving. Cf. Max Wertheimer, *Productive Thinking*, eds., S.E. Asch and others (New York and London: Harper, 1945, reprint, 1961).

88. Köhler gave the William James lecture entitled, "The Place of Value in a World of Facts," which was published in 1938. Cf. Wolfgang Köhler, *The Place of Value in a World of Facts* (New York: Liveright, 1938). About ten years later, he published his work on the general principles involved in Gestalt theory. Cf. Wolfgang, Köhler, *Gestalt Psychology: An Introduction to New Concepts in Modern Psychology* (New York and Toronto: Liveright, 1947, reprint, New York: New American Library, 1966).

89. In 1924 Kofka wrote a book on child psychology from the point of view of Gestalt theory. Cf. Kurt Koffka, *The Growth of the Mind*, Trans. R.M. Ogden (London, 1924, reprint, New York: Transactio, 1980). In 1935, he also published a book that served as a comprehensive survey of all the hitherto relevant experimental work

that had been done in Gestalt theory. Cf. Kurt Koffka, *The Principles of Gestalt Psychology* (New York and London, 1935).
90. Cf. Čapek, "Simple Location and Fragmentation of Reality," *Process and Divinity*, 91–4.
91. Hartshorne, "The Parallel Development of Method in Physics and Psychology," *Philosophy of Science*, 451.
92. Alfred North Whitehead, *Modes of Thought* (Cambridge: Cambridge University Press, 1938), 199. Hereafter cited as *MT*.
93. Alfred North Whitehead, *An Enquiry Concerning the Principles of Natural Knowledge* (Cambridge: Cambridge University Press, 1925), 2. Hereafter cited as *PNK*.
94. Ibid., 2.
95. *AI*, 201–2.
96. *SMW*, 64.
97. Ibid., 72.
98. Ibid., 70.
99. *MT*, 12.
100. *CSPM*, 190.
101. Ibid., 184.

Chapter 5

1. *CSPM*, 90; 114.
2. Ibid., 90.
3. He cites the acts of intending or thinking as an example, saying that insofar as these occur, they are "realities." However, the other-orientedness of the act of thinking or intending may in fact not succeed; it may not be able to refer to its intended object. If it does refer to something other than itself, then both the act as well as its object are real. Otherwise, "reality" belongs only to the act; the object is unreal, there being nothing successfully designated. Cf. *CSPM*, 89. Or as he points out in another part of the book: "[...] acts of fancying or mistakenly believing are real occurrences, so that the unreal is also a form of reality." Ibid., 99.
4. Ibid., 167.
5. Ibid., 82–3.
6. Cf. Charles Hartshorne, *Man's Vision of God and the Logic of Theism* (Hamden, Connecticut: Archon, 1964), 235. Hereafter cited as *MVG*.
7. Cf. Charles Hartshorne, *The Divine Relativity: A Social Conception of God* (New Haven and London: Yale University Press, 1948), 64. Hereafter cited as *DR*.
8. *CSPM*, 168.
9. *DR*, 64.
10. Ibid.
11. *CSPM*, 89.
12. This, in essence, recalls the Whiteheadian "ontological principle" which, on the one hand, asserts the independent existence of "actual entities"—the Whiteheadian equivalent of Aristotle's *ousia*, by which is understood a "complete existent," while on the other, holds that whatever else exists, does so in a sense derivative from and dependent upon "actual entities." "Actual entities" and those that do not belong to this category form the contrasting pair; the total reality, however lies in the first term—this being the inclusive term; to the second belongs the dependent, included aspects of the first. Cf. Ibid., 90, 99.

13. Ibid., 99.
14. Morris R. Cohen, *Reason and Nature: An Essay on the Meaning of Scientific Method* (Glencoe, Illinois: Free Press, 1931), 165–168. See also: Morris R. Cohen, *Studies in Philosophy and Science* (New York: Henry Holt, 1949), 42–4.
15. Charles Hartshorne and William L. Reese, *Philosophers Speak of God* (Chicago: The University of Chicago Press, 1953), 2. Hereafter cited as *PSG*.
16. Cf. James P. Devlin, "Hartshorne's Metaphysical Asymmetry," *The Philosophy of Charles Hartshorne*, Vol. XX of The Library of Living Philosophers, ed. Lewis Edwin Hahn (LaSalle, Illinois: Open Court, 1991), 276. Hartshorne's own enumeration of the "five formally possible views" on the matter can be found in the chapter on methodology in *Creative Synthesis*: (i) Every (dyadic) relation is *internal* to *both* terms; (ii) Every relation is *external* to *both* terms; (iii) Some relations are *internal* to *both* terms; the rest *external* to *both*; (iv) Every relation is *internal* to *one* term, *external* to the *other*; (v) Some relations are internal to one term, external to the other; some internal to both terms; the rest external to both. The first three being purely symmetrical possibilities, are unacceptable, the fourth rules out symmetry altogether. The fifth is Hartshorne's notion.
17. Cf. Charles Hartshorne, "Absolute Objects and Relative Subjects: A Reply," *The Review of Metaphysics*, 15 1/57 (September, 1961): 175.
18. Cf. Ibid., 175–7.
19. *CSPM*, 206–7.
20. Ibid., 206.
21. Cf. *CSPM*, 211–12.
22. Hume, *A Treatise of Human Nature*, pt. 1.
23. Hartshorne, *Insights and Oversights*, 139.
24. At this point, we are still employing the word "event" in its usual sense, i.e., something that "takes place," and not yet in the sense peculiar to Hartshorne's philosophy, although this specific Hartshornean sense is already implied in our usage.
25. Hartshorne, *Insights and Overisights*, 139.
26. *CSPM*, 212.
27. Charles Hartshorne, *Beyond Humanism: Essays in the Philosophy of Nature* (Lincoln, Nebraska: University of Nebraska Press, 1969), 136. Hereafter cited as *BH*.
28. Hartshorne, *Insights and Oversights*, 165.
29. *CSPM*, 221.
30. Ibid., 219.
31. Ibid., 215.
32. Ibid., 205.
33. Ibid., 186.
34. Ibid., 187.
35. Ibid., 188.
36. Ibid., 188.
37. Ibid., 189.
38. *PR*, 23nn34–5.
39. *CSPM*, 190.
40. Ibid., 8.
41. Ibid., 3.
42. Cf. *PR*, 150n228.
43. *CSPM*, 14.
44. Ibid., 7–8.
45. Ibid., 10.

46. Cf. Charles Hartshorne, "Husserl and Whitehead on the Concrete," *Phenomenology: Continuation and Criticism: Essays in Memory of Dorion Cairns*, eds. F. Kersten and R. Zaner (The Hague: Martinus Nijhoff, 1973): 91.
47. *CSPM*, 188.
48. Cf. Nicholas Rescher, *Process Metaphysics: An Introduction to Process Philosophy* (New York: State University of New York Press, 1996).
49. *AI*, 202: "For physics, the thing itself is what it does, and what it does is this divergent stream of influence. Again, the focal region cannot be separated from the external stream. It obstinately refuses to be conceived as an instantaneous fact. It is a state of agitation, only differing from the so-called external stream by its superior dominance within the focal region."
50. Cf. Donald Davidson, *Essays on Actions and Events* (Oxford: Clarendon, 1980), see especially Chapter 8: The Individuation of Events, pp. 163–80, and Chapter 9: Events as Particulars, pp. 181–7.
51. Ibid., 175.
52. Strawson, *Individuals*, 53.
53. Davidson, Essays on Actions and Events, 173–4.
54. Ibid., 174.
55. Cf. Strawson, *Individuals*, 31, 34, 41.
56. P.F. Strawson, *Analysis and Metaphysics: An Introduction to Philosophy* (Oxford: Oxford University Press, 1992), 7.
57. Donald Davidson, "Reply to Quine on Events," *Actions and Events: Perspectives on the Philosophy of Donald Davidson*, eds., Ernest LePore and Brian McLaughlin, (Oxford: Basil Blackwell, 1985), 172.
58. Strawson, *Individuals*, xviii.
59. Whitehead calls attention to the "uncritical trust in the adequacy of language" as one of the errors to which philosophy is liable. (Cf. *AI*, 293) Elsewhere he declares with an uncharacteristic terseness: "Conventional English is the twin sister to barren thought." Cf. Alfred North Whitehead, "Remarks," *Philosophical Review*, 5/46 (March, 1937): 183. The problem of the adequacy of our ways of describing reality really hinges on two developments of contemporary philosophy. The first is a profound skepticism of language that has arisen from a purely Darwinian naturalistic view of its origin. The second is the growing depreciation of language in science and the progressive use of nonlinguistic symbols in the more exact sciences. Cf. Wilbur M. Urban, "Whitehead's Philosophy of Language," *The Philosophy of Alfred North Whitehead*. The Library of Living Philosophers, ed. Paul Arthur Schilpp (New York: Tudor, 1951), 303.
60. "Language," as Whitehead observes in *Modes of Thought*, "is the triumph of human ingenuity, surpassing even the intricacies of modern technology." Cf. Alfred North Whitehead, *Modes of Thought* (New York: Free Press, 1966), 44. (Hereafter cited as *MT*.) Elsewhere, he calls language an instrument devised by human beings to aid them in their adjustment to the environment in which they live. Cf. Alfred North Whitehead, *Symbolism: Its Meaning and Effect* (New York: Macmillan, 1927), 87.
61. Cf. A.H. Johnson, "Whitehead on the Uses of Language," *The Relevance of Whitehead*. Philosophical Essays in Commemoration of the Centenary of the Birth of Alfred North Whitehead, ed. Ivor Leclerc (Bristol: Thoemmes Press, 1993), 137.
62. Cf. *CSPM*, xix.
63. Cf. *PR*, n.78, 49.
64. A.H. Johnson, "Whitehead on the Uses of Language," *The Relevance of Whitehead*, 135. Johnson's quote from Whitehead is taken from *MT*, 55.

65. *CSPM*, xix.
66. Ibid., 175.
67. Cf. Davidson, *Essays on Actions and Events*, Chapter 8, "The Individuation of Events," pp. 163–80. Davidson admits events into his philosophy because he holds that there is a *need* to recognize the view of reality implicated by our language which, in its ordinary form, calls for a distinction between objects and events. An event for him is just as individual or particular as an object because it can be quantified over. Various grammatical structures and their logical forms designate event structures by individuating them. He gives several examples: "'Sebastian strolled': this may be construed along lines suggested by 'Sebastian took a stroll.' 'There is an *x* such that *x* is a stroll and Sebastian took *x*' is more ornate than necessary, since there is nothing an agent can do with a stroll except take it; thus we may capture all there is with 'There is an *x* such that Sebastian strolled *x*.' In this way we provide each verb of action or change with an event-place; we may say of such verbs that they take an *event-object*." (Cf. *Essays*, pp. 166–7) Davidson therefore urges that there is no reason to assign second-rank status to events. In fact, even with regard to what can be interpreted as a stringent requirement for individuation, namely, a particular susceptible to being "counted," Davidson holds that "events come out well enough." "Rings of the bell, major wars, eclipses of the moon, and performances of *Lulu* can be counted as easily as pencils, pots, and people." (*Essays*, p. 180) Yet again, such admission of events or any other particular for that matter, remains limited to the fact of their usefulness in epistemology. Davidson remains largely noncommittal, even skeptical when it comes to constructing conceptual frameworks (whether or not these center on events or substances). Cf. Donald Davidson, "On the Very Idea of a Conceptual Scheme," *Proceedings of the American Philosophical Association*, 47 (November 1974): 5–20.
68. Davidson, *Essays on Actions and Events*, 180.
69. *CSPM*, 187.
70. Ibid., 186.
71. *CSPM*, 187.
72. See: J.C. Polkinghorne, "A Revived Natural Theology," *Science and Religion: One World Changing Perspectives*. Papers presented at the Second European Conference on Science and Religion. eds. Jan Fennema and Iain Paul (Dordrecht: Kluwer Academic Publishers, 1990), Pp. 87–97; Ian G. Barbour, *Issues in Science and Religion*; "Attitudes toward Nature and Technology," *Earth Might Be Fair: Reflections on Ethics, Religion, and Ecology*, ed. Ian G. Barbour (Englewood Cliffs: Prentice-Hall, 1972), 146–68; Arthur Peacocke, *Intimations of Reality: Critical Realism in Science and Religion* (Notre Dame: University of Notre Dame Press, 1984; David Bohm, "The Implicate Order: A New Approach to the Nature of Reality," *Beyond Mechanism: The Universe in Recent Physics and Catholic Thought;* "The Implicate Order," A New Order for Physics," ed. Dean R. Fowler, *Process Studies* 8/2 (Summer 1978):73–102; *Wholeness: The Implicate Order* (London: Routledge and Kegan Paul, 1980).
73. Cf. Charles Hartshorne, "Some Not Ungrateful But Perhaps Inadequate Comments About Comments on My Writings and Ideas," *Process Studies*, 21/2 (Summer, 1992): 127.
74. Cf. Charles Hartshorne, "Beyond Enlightened Self-Interest," *Process Philosophy: Basic Writings*, eds., J.R. Sibley and P.A.Y. Gunter (New York: University Press of America, 1978), 397. Reprinted in: Mohammad Valady ed., *The Zero Fallacy and Other Essays in Neoclassical Philosophy*. (Chicago and LaSalle, Illinois, Open Court, 1997), 185–202. Hereafter cited as *BES*.

75. Hartshorne, "Some Not Ungrateful But Perhaps Inadequate Comments," 127.
76. *CSPM*, 191; also 198. The obstacle to obeying the Great Commandment, Hartshorne insists, is "not metaphysical or absolute, but psychological and relative."
77. Cf. *BH*, 121–2. The very possibility of understanding nonhuman nature by taking human reality as the point of departure is based on this notion.
78. *CSPM*, 49–50. The total absence of experience is an instance of what Hartshorne terms the "zero fallacy." "Zero," he says, "is an unthinkable extreme. (*RSP*, 32) It may indeed be a quantity, but with one exception, "an unobservable one." He insists further that "only where there is abrupt discontinuity can one observe a pure absence. Thus the zero of elephants in a room is observable because nothing else is much like an elephant, and the smallest elephant is still observably large. But natural laws of the kind required to predict what happens involve continuous variables, e.g., velocity, acceleration, angle of incidence. Observations of values under these variables are at best approximate." Charles Hartshorne, *Wisdom as Moderation: A Philosophy of the Middle Way* (Albany, New York: State University of New York Press, 1987), 98. Hereafter cited as *WM*.
79. *BH*, 169–70.
80. *PR*, 166n252. Cf. Charles Hartshorne, "Panpsychism: Mind as Sole Reality," *Ultimate Reality and Meaning*, 1/2 (1978): 242–55.
81. Ibid., 242.
82. *CSPM*, 129.
83. He defends what he calls the "principle of reasonable anthropomorphism." Cf. Charles Hartshorne, "Can We Understand God?" Inaugural Lecture at the Katholieke Universiteit Leuven, 4 October 1978. *Louvain Studies* 7 (Fall, 1978): 75–84. The same point is made by Louis Dupré, a philosopher of religion who defends a principle similar to Hartshorne's. Cf. Lous Dupré, "Evil—A Religious Mystery: A Plea for a More Inclusive Model of Theodicy," *Faith and Philosophy* 7/3 (July, 1990), 263.
84. *BH*, 121.
85. Charles Hartshorne, "The Development of Process Philosophy," Introduction to *Philosophers of Process*, ed. Douglas Browning (New York: Random House, 1965), xxi.
86. *AI*, 180.
87. Hartshorne, "Panpsychism: Mind as Sole Reality," 245.
88. W.E. Hocking, "Foreword," *RSP*, 15.
89. Hartshorne, "Panpsychism: Mind as Sole Reality," 245.
90. *RSP*, 29–43.
91. *BH*, 112.
92. *RSP*, 133.
93. *CSPM*, 49–50.
94. *RSP*, 59.
95. While the real differences among the various entities on the analogical scale is not dismissed, neither is the use of a cautiously employed "infinitely flexible analogy" based on the generalization of human experience eschewed. Cf. Charles Hartshorne, "Panpsychism," *A History of Philosophical Systems*, ed. Vergilius Ferm (New York: The Philosophical Library, 1950), 445.
96. Cf. *BH*, 112.
97. *PR*, n.37, 25.
98. *CSPM*, 141.
99. Cf. *CSPM*, 149–50.

100. *RSP*, 34.
101. Charles Hartshorne, "Whitehead and Contemporary Philosophy," *The Relevance of Whitehead: Philosophical Essays in Commemoration of the Centenary of the Birth of Alfred North Whitehead*, ed. Ivor Leclerc (Bristol, England: Thoemmes Press, 1993), 29.
102. *BH*, 117.
103. *RSP*, 35.
104. *BH*, 116.
105. Psalm 8:6. *NRSV.*
106. Hartshorne, "Whitehead and Contemporary Philosophy," 28–9.
107. *LP*, 123–4.
108. Ibid., 125.
109. Hartshorne, "Whitehead and Contemporary Philosophy," 29.
110. *LP*, 127.
111. Hartshorne gives a brief outline of the thinkers across varied disciplines who have espoused these or similar views: "This position ... was first clearly stated in one form by Leibniz, and has been repeatedly adopted in principle, but revised in various ways by philosophers (Peirce, 1935; Whitehead, 1929; Hartshorne, 1970), psychologists (Troland, 1922); biologists (Agar, 1951; Wright, 1953); Waddington, 1969; Rensch, 1970), physiologists, physicists (Burgers, 1965), and many other writers." Cf. Hartshorne, "Panpsychism: Mind as Sole Reality," 244.
112. Ibid., 242.
113. *CSPM*, xiii.
114. Cf. Hartshorne, "Response," *Charles Hartshorne and Henry Nelson Wieman*, ed. Wm. S. Minor (New York: University Press of America, 1969), 33.
115. *AI*, 176.
116. Ibid.
117. Ibid., 180.
118. *PR*, 52n81. "Prehension" is a technical Whiteheadian term which refers to the manner by which an actual entity can include, as part of its own essence, other entities without implying either consciousness or representative perception. Cf. *AI*, 300. An "actual entity" for Whitehead is basically a "concrescence of prehensions." Cf. *PR*, n.35, 23.
119. Hartshorne, "Whitehead's Revolutionary Concept of Prehension," *Philosophical Quarterly*, 19/3 (September, 1979): 256–7.
120. Cf. *AI*, 174–5.
121. Hartshorne, "In Defense of Wordsworth's View of Nature," *Philosophy and Literature* 4/1 (Spring, 1980): 82.
122. Hartshorne in fact considers it an error to suppose "that the preinterpretative datum must be consciously apprehended before being interpreted." Cf. Hartshorne, "Sensation in Psychology and Philosophy," *Southern Journal of Philosophy*, 1/2 (1963): 3.
123. *AI*, 175–6.
124. Cf. *The Works of William Wordsworth*, The Wordsworth Poetry Library (Hertfordshire: Cumberland House, 1994), 186.
125. Hartshorne, "In Defense of Wordsworth's View of Nature," 84.
126. They are not simply "things" or mere associated qualities. For as Hartshorne contends, "there are no merely neutral sense qualities," rather, "all so-called secondary qualities are intrinsically emotional." Cf. Ibid.
127. Hartshorne, "Sensation in Psychology and Philosophy," 4.

128. Hartshorne, "The Social Theory of Feelings," *Southern Journal of Philosophy*, 3/2 (Summer, 1965): 90.

129. Hartshorne, "Sensation in Psychology and Philosophy," 4–5.

130. Cf. *BH*, 195.

131. Hartshorne, "Sensation in Psychology and Philosophy," 5.

132. Cf. Nathaniel Lawrence, "Time, Value, and the Self," *The Relevance of Whitehead*, ed. Ivor Leclerc (New York, Macmillan, 1961), 147–50.

133. Hartshorne, "Sensation in Psychology and Philosophy," 10.

134. Wayne Viney, "Charles Hartshorne's Philosophy and Psychology of Sensation," *The Philosophy of Charles Hartshorne*, Vol. XX of The Library of Living Philosophers, ed. Lewis Edwin Hahn (LaSalle, Illinois: Open Court, 1991), 97.

135. Charles Hartshorne, "The Intelligibility of Sensations," *The Monist*, 44/2 (July, 1934): 175.

136. Hartshorne calls this theory suggesting the qualitative as well as structural similarity between feeling qualities and sensory qualities, "Affective Monism." Cf. Charles Hartshorne, "Monistic Theory of Expression," *The Journal of Philosophy*, 50/14 (July 2, 1953): 425–34.

137. Ibid., 434.

138. Charles Hartshorne, *The Philosophy and Psychology of Sensation* (New York: Kennikat Press, 1968), 128. Hereafter cited as *PPS*.

139. Cf. *PPS*, 54–5.

140. Ibid., 51–4. See also: Hartshorne, "Sensation in Psychology and Philosophy," 10.

141. Hartshorne, "Sensation in Psychology and Philosophy," 9.

142. Viney, "Charles Hartshorne's Philosophy and Psychology of Sensation," 98.

143. Cf. *RSP*, 38–40.

144. Hartshorne, "The Social Theory of Feelings," 89.

145. *BH*, 198.

146. Viney, "Charles Hartshorne's Philosophy and Psychology of Sensation," 104.

147. *BH*, 198. See also: Hartshorne, "Panpsychism: Mind as Sole Reality," 248.

148. Hartshorne, "In Defense of Wordsworth's View of Nature," 82.

149. What is directly given in experience, according to Hartshorne is cellular feeling as we ourselves feel it. Charles Hartshorne, "Sensation in Psychology and Philosophy," *Southern Journal of Philosophy*, 1/2 (Summer, 1963): 12. See also: Hartshorne, "In Defense of Wordsworth's View of Nature," 85.

150. Hartshorne, "The Intelligibility of Sensations," 171–2.

151. *CSPM*, 117.

152. Hartshorne, "Whitehead's Revolutionary Concept of Prehension," 256.

153. Hartshorne, "The Development of Process Philosophy," xix.

154. Hartshorne, "Whitehead's Revolutionary Concept of Prehension," 260.

155. As Whitehead says, it "expresses the *relation* of the entity, thus denoted, to one or more occasions of experiencing" (Cf. *AI*, 178. Italics added).

156. Cf. *CSPM*, 197–8.

157. Cf. Charles Hartshorne, "The Immortality of the Past: Critique of a Prevalent Misinterpretation," *Review of Metaphysics*, 7/1 (September, 1953): 98–112.

158. This conception is spelled out in chapters nine: "Science, Insecurity, and the Abiding Treasure," and chapter ten: "Time, Death, and Everlasting Life," of his book *The Logic of Perfection*. (Cf. *LP*, 234–62.) It also needs to be noted here that by "past" Hartshorne means both the objects of the vaguest possible recollections of detail as are found in human memory (which most often than not, exhibits a great deal of weakness), as well as the totality of actualities—human and otherwise—that belong to the domain of the "has been."

159. Thomas Aquinas, *Summa Theologica*, 1ª Q. 25, a. 4, r. 1. Vol. I, trans., Fathers of the English Dominican Province (Westminster, Maryland: Benziger, 1948), 139.

160. Ibid.

161. Hartshorne, "Absolute Objects and Relative Subjects," 181. Also: *LP*, 249.

162. Hartshorne, "The Immortality of the Past," 109.

163. *LP*, 245: "We are such stuff as dreams are made on, and our life is rounded with a sleep."

164. Ibid.

165. *BES*, 400.

166. *LP*, 254.

167. Cf. Charles Hartshorne, "Religion in Process Philosophy," *Religion in Philosophical and Cultural Perspective*, eds. J. Clayton Feaver and William Horosz (Princeton: Van Nostrand, 1967), 244–5, 264. The concept of an ultimately "deathless" personal existence in Hartshorne's view, together with the idea of heaven and hell, are the result of regarding the identity of individuals within an ontology of unchanging and eternally enduring substances. He categorically rejects the idea of a self-identical being existing after death and reaping its rewards or being given its due punishments.

168. Cf. Charles Hartshorne, "An Open Letter to Carl Sagan," *The Journal of Speculative Philosophy*, 5/4 (1991): 230.

169. Charles Hartshorne, "A Philosopher's Assessment of Christianity," *Religion and Culture: Essays in Honor of Paul Tillich*, ed. Walter Leibrecht (New York: Harper, 1959), 175. He even quotes Berdyaev who refers to the conjunction of the belief in personal immortality and the notion of reward and punishment after death as "the most disgusting morality ever conceived." Cf. Charles Hartshorne, "Religion and Creative Experience," *Darshana, An International Quarterly of Philosophy, Psychology, Psychical Research, Religion, Mysticism and Sociology*, 2/1 (January, 1962): 11.

170. Sia, *God in Process Thought*, 102: "Hartshorne looks on personal immortality as a rival to belief in God rather than a logical consequence of it since it seems to enshrine self-interest as ultimate."

171. Charles Hartshorne, "Some Causes of My Intellectual Growth," in *The Philosophy of Charles Hartshorne*, Vol. XX of The Library of Living Philosophers, ed. Lewis Edwin Hahn (La Salle, Illinois: Open Court, 1991), 43.

172. Cf. John B. Cobb, Jr., "Hartshorne's Importance for Theology," Ibid., 183.

173. *LP*, 254. Similar thoughts are expressed in: Charles Hartshorne, *A Natural Theology for Our Time* (La Salle, Illinois: Open Court, 1967), 107–111. Hereafter cited as *NT*.

174. *LP*, 253.

175. This particular distinction is consistent with Hartshorne's notion of the atomic or discrete nature of becoming as opposed to its continuous view as defended by thinkers such as Henri Bergson. He defends this idea in the chapter dealing with "events" in *Creative Synthesis*. (Cf. *CSPM*, 173–204, esp. 192–5.)

176. *LP*, 253. Similar sentiments are expressed in: Charles Hartshorne, "Philosophy After Fifty Years," *Mid-Twentieth Century American Philosophy: Personal Statements*, ed. Peter A. Bertocci (New York: Humanities Press, 1974), 148–9.

177. Marjorie Hewitt Suchocki, "Charles Hartshorne and Subjective Immortality", *Process Studies*, 21/2 (Summer, 1992): 121. See also, Santiago Sia, "Charles Hartshorne's Interpretation of Human Immortality," *Bijdragen, tijdschrift voor*

filosofie en theologie 54 (1993): 254–70 and Randall Auxier, "Why One Hundred Years is Forever: Hartshorne's Theory of Immortality," *The Personalist Forum* 14 (1998): 109–40.

178. Hewitt Suchocki, Ibid. By this is meant that even the minutest details of the complete reality of an actual entity—which, according to Suchocki cannot but include "consciousness in those cases where consciousness is the subjective form of immediacy"—are retained in God. This, she adds, for all intents and purposes, amounts to subjective and not merely objective immortality. In a response to this article, Hartshorne shows himself to be in essential agreement with Suchocki, with regard to the retention in the divine mind, of the totality of an entity's past experience, including consciousness. But he insists that it is God who is "conscious of our consciousness, or unit-instances of becoming." Entities that have died, according to him, "live everlastingly," and that such everlasting life includes the totality of their past, yet he says that he is not at all clear that this means "they can enjoy God's awareness of each of their experiences in those very experiences." Cf. Charles Hartshorne, "Inadequate Comments about Comments on My Writings and Ideas." *Process Studies* 21/2 (Summer, 1992): 127.

179. *LP*, 247.

180. Charles Hartshorne, *Omnipotence and Other Theological Mistakes* (Albany, New York: State University of New York Press, 1984), 35. Hereafter cited as *OO*.

181. Charles Hartshorne, *The Zero Fallacy and Other Essays in Neoclassical Philosophy*, ed. Mohammad Valady (Chicago and La Salle, Illinois: Open Court, 1997), 191. Hereafter cited as *ZF*.

182. Hartshorne, "Some Causes," *The Philosophy of Charles Hartshorne*, 44.

183. The five other "common mistakes about God," as he calls them, are: (i) the notion that God is absolutely perfect and unchangeable, (ii) the traditional notion of omnipotence which holds that God can do absolutely anything, (iii) the traditional notion of God's omniscience which holds that God knows past, present, and future as one single present actuality, (iv) the idea of an all-loving God who is nevertheless "unmoved" by the plight of the world, (v) the notion of the infallibility of revelation. Cf. *OO*, 2–5.

184. Cf. Charles Hartshorne, "The Divine Relativity and Absoluteness: A Reply to John Wild," *Review of Metaphysics*, 4/1 (September, 1950): 59.

185. Cf. *OO*, 110.

186. *BH*, 12; *RSP*, 49.

187. Sia, *God in Process Thought*, 103.

188. *RSP*, 42. In this he is in basic agreement with Whitehead for whom past actualities are also objectively immortal, and are primarily so on account of the everlasting value that they have in the divine mind. Cf. *PR*, n.527, 347.

189. *NT*, 57.

190. *MVG*, 298.

191. *LP*, 234.

192. *OO*, 124.

193. Cf. *LP*, 245, 249. The same ideas are expressed in several of his other writings: Charles Hartshorne, "Process Philosophy as a Resource for Christian Thought," *Philosophical Resources for Christian Thought*, ed. Perry LeFevre (Nashville: Abingdon Press, 1968), 145; also, "The Dipolar Conception of Deity," *Review of Metaphysics*, 21/2 (December, 1967), 288; and, "The Significance of Man in the Life of God," *Theology in Crisis: A Colloqium on 'The Credibility of God'* (New Concord, Ohio: Muskingham College, 1967), 40–3.

194. Charles Hartshorne, "The God of Religion and the God of Philosophy," *Talk of God: Royal Institute of Philosophy Lectures*, Vol II: 1967–1968 (London: Macmillan, 1969), 156.
195. Sia, *God in Process Thought*, 104.
196. André Cloots and Jan Van der Veken, "Can the God of Process Thought be Redeemed?" *Charles Hartshorne's Concept of God: Philosophical and Theological Responses* (Dordrecht: Kluwer Academic Publishers, 1990), 131.

Chapter 6

1. *CSPM*, 5; *BH*, 136.
2. *CSPM*, 5.
3. *BH*, 126–7.
4. *CSPM*, 11.
5. Ibid., 1.
6. Cf. Charles Birch, "Chance, Purpose, and Darwinism," *The Philosophy of Charles Hartshorne*, 54. Birch explains that the admittance of chance is a critically important feature of Hartshorne's philosophy of nature, as it allows for the genuineness of freedom, and therefore represents an important step in moving away from the concept of deterministic design. Both of these ultimately figure into Hartshorne's attempt to reconstruct a theistic metaphysics which eschews the idea of an omnipotent power—be this God or some inbuilt principle of nature—which has preordained the coming to be as well as the continuing and changing fortunes (and misfortunes) of all things down to their minutest details.
7. *BH*, 131.
8. Ibid., 134.
9. *NT*, 59.
10. *BH*, 133.
11. *NT*, 59.
12. *RSP*, 31–2.
13. *CSPM*, 7.
14. Ibid., 2–3.
15. Ibid.
16. *BH*, 133.
17. Charles Hartshorne, "A Metaphysics of Universal Freedom," *Faith and Creativity: Essays in Honor of Eugene H. Peters*, eds. George Nordgulen and George W. Shields (St. Louis, Missouri: CBP Press, 1987), 29.
18. Ibid. Antecedent data integrated by present experience are already devoid of process. Having already become, they are simply fodder for present actuality; there is no need for them to "become over again." Hartshorne, "The Immortality of the Past," 109.
19. Charles Hartshorne, "My Neoclassical Metaphysics," *Tijdschrift voor Philosophie*, 42/1 (March, 1980): 8.
20. Hartshorne, "A Metaphysics of Universal Freedom," *Faith and Creativity*, 32.
21. Ibid., 32.
22. *PR*, 75n116.
23. *MT*, 131.
24. This is consistent with the Aristotelian principle adopted by Whitehead and termed the "ontological principle," which states that "apart from things that are actual there is nothing—nothing either in fact or efficacy." Cf. *PR*, 40n64. A corollary to

this principle is that other entities exist in a manner dependent upon and derivative from the existence of such actual entities. Ibid., 73n113. As Whitehead remarks: "The ontological principle declares that every decision is referable to one or more actual entities, because in separation from actual entities there is nothing, merely nonentity—'The rest is silence'" Ibid., 43n68.

25. *PR*, 219n335.
26. *CSPM*, 181–2.
27. Ibid., 175.
28. *PR*, 41n65.
29. Thus concerning the last question for instance, Hartshorne writes: "This 'changing' subject is never complete or fully determinate until it ceases to endure through change—until it is dead in fact." Hartshorne, "Leibniz's Greatest Discovery," *Journal of the History of Ideas*, 7/14 (October, 1946): 420. See also: *PR*, 25n38, where Whitehead states: "… becoming is the transformation of incoherence into coherence, and in each particular instance *ceases with this attainment*" (Italics added). In words that parallel the quote from Hartshorne, Whitehead says in *Adventures of Ideas*: "The self identity of a society is founded upon the self identity of its defining characteristic and upon the mutual immanence of its occasions. But there is no definite nexus which is the nexus underlying that society, except when the society belongs wholly to the past. For the realized nexus which underlies the society is always adding to itself, with the creative advance into the future … until the death of the man and the destruction of the earth, there is no determinate nexus which in an unqualified sense is either the man or the earth" *AI*, 205–6.
30. *CPSM*, 192.
31. Ibid. See also: Hartshorne, *Insights and Oversights*, 163.
32. Hartshorne, *Insights and Oversights*, 164.
33. *CSPM*, 192.
34. Cf. James W. Felt, "Intuition, Event-Atomism, and the Self," *Process in Context: Essays in Post-Whiteheadian Perspectives*, ed. Ernest Wolf-Gazo (New York: Peter Lang Publishers, 1988), 137–52.
35. Ibid.,140–3. Felt quotes from Bergson's *The Creative Mind*, where the latter says: "The intuition we refer to [...] bears above all upon internal duration. It grasps a succession which is not juxtaposition, a growth from within, the uninterrupted prolongation of the past into the preset which is already blending into the future. It is the *direct vision of the mind by the mind* [...] Instead of states contiguous to states [...] we have here the indivisible and therefore substantial continuity of the flow of the inner life" (Quoted from: Henri Bergson, *The Creative Mind* [New Jersey: Totowa, 1963], 3). Felt draws from this quote, and from Bergson's distinction between the "object" of intelligence and that of intuition in *Matter and Memory*, the conclusion that intuition—which places us "in our attention *within* the immediate duration in which we act"—has to do with our experience of continuity, while intelligence—by which "the mind orders itself to practicality"—is concerned with the discreteness of process that Whitehead describes (cf. Henri Bergson, *Matter and Memory*, trans. Paul Palmer (London, 1970), 243f).
36. Felt, "Intuition, Event-Atomism, and the Self," *Process in Context*, 143–4, 146. This effectively reduces the notion of the discreteness of process as founded on an abstraction "derived artificially from the lived immediacy which is the experience of continuity."
37. Ibid., 149. The author readily admits this "reversion," but rather than further articulating how such appeal to a substance metaphysics need not be based on the idea of an unchanging substrate, what follows is a mere attack on "the

almost *a priori* assurance with which most process philosophers dismiss the notion of any substance-type philosophy as definitely discredited" and an insistence on the need "to reinstate something closer to a substance-type philosophy than the metaphysics of Whitehead allows."

38. Ibid., 145.
39. *CSPM*, 194.
40. Ibid.
41. Ibid., 194–5.
42. Charles Hartshorne, "Whitehead's Revolutionary Concept of Prehension," *International Philosophical Quarterly*, 19/3 (September, 1979): 253.
43. *PR*, 18n28.
44. *CSPM*, 192–6.
45. *PR*, 35n52. Concerning this relation, Whitehead notes that "there is a prevalent misconception that 'becoming' involves the notion of a unique seriality for its advance into novelty"—"an unfortunate generalization," he says, from the "experience of enduring objects."
46. Cf. *SMW*, 157–160.
47. *PR*, 35n53.
48. *CSPM*, 196.
49. It must be noted that in *Science and the Modern World*, we see that another strong reason for the adoption of the atomic view of process on Whitehead's part—aside from consideration of Zeno's paradox—was the increasing awareness among physicists of the importance of descriptions of nature in terms of quanta. Cf. *SMW*, 35. This "second reason" can also be traced in *PR*, 78n121 and 78n122.
50. *PR*, 35n53.
51. *PR*, 105–6, 68. Quote taken from: William James, *Some Problems of Philosophy*, chapter X (Italics added).
52. *PR*, 68n106.
53. Étienne Gilson, *Being and Some Philosophers* (Toronto: Pontifical Institute of Medieval Studies, 1949), 11.
54. Cf. *MT*, 97. This reconciliation of change and stability, shows that there is no inconsistency involved in the relation between an individual possessing a unified identity, and real change as also being constitutive of that individual's nature.
55. Cf. *PR*, 35n52.
56. *PR*, 35n52: "Actual Entities Perish, But Do Not Change; They are What They are."
57. *CSPM*, xv.
58. Ibid.
59. *CSPM*, 118. See also: Charles Hartshorne, "Whitehead's Novel Intuition," *Alfred North Whitehead: Essays on His Philosophy*, ed. George L. Kline (Englewood Cliffs: Prentice-Hall, 1963), 22.
60. *CSPM*, 118. Hartshorne is quoting from the last lines of the final paragraph of Whitehead's *Process and Reality*. Cf. *PR*, 351n533.
61. *AI*, 236.
62. *PR*, 219n335.
63. *AI*, 236.
64. Conceived as being in the process of activity, an actual entity can be nothing else save a unified and integrated whole. As Whitehead insists, "it can only be *understood* as well as *felt* as a process." Cf. *PR*, 227n347.
65. Cf. *PR*, 227n347.
66. Cf. Lewis S. Ford, "Inclusive Occasions," *Process in Context: Essays in Post-Whiteheadian Perspectives*, ed. Ernest Wolf-Gazo (New York: Peter Lang, 1988), 113.

Thus Lewis Ford explains that although becoming is not held to be extensive *simply*, this does not mean that it is not extensive in any sense, "for there can be genetic division." It is simply the case rather, that "if an occasion were divisible into many smaller acts of becoming, then it would attain determinate being along the way, before the final satisfaction, which is impossible."

67. Ford argues that the "genetic phases"—his term for the Whiteheadian "termini"— have no concrete determinateness. They are abstractions, means of analyzing or describing and "marking the successive degrees of determination."

68. Cf. *PR*, 222n339.

69. Ibid., 29n43.

70. Ibid.

71. Ibid., 60n94.

72. Ibid., 59n92.

73. That it does serve as data for future acts of becoming shows how mistaken are those interpretations that regard the "perished" entity as being no longer actual, and as such, no longer being an efficient cause. This would clearly be an extreme interpretation. Cf. John Blyth, "Whitehead's Theory of Knowledge," *Philosophy and Phenomenological Research*, 3/3 (March, 1948): 373.

74. *PR*, 60n94.

75. Ibid., 29n44.

76. Ibid., 45n71.

77. *AI*, 237.

78. *PR*, 45n71.

79. *AI*, 237.

80. Griffin, "Hartshorne's Differences From Whitehead," *Two Process Philosophers: Hartshorne's Encounter with Whitehead*, AAR Studies in Religion, No. 5, ed. Lewis S. Ford (Tallahassee: American Academy of Religion, 1973), 54. At the same time, Griffin notes that "although Hartshorne dislikes speaking of past occasions as 'dead,' he himself has done so: 'But only the dead or the abstract are mere objects.' The context makes clear he is speaking of past actual occasions, as he says 'only the dead can be (henceforth) absolute, immune to further influence'" (Griffin, 53; quote taken from *CSPM*, 120).

81. *PR*, 85n131. Quote taken from: Ezekiel 37: 10.

82. Ibid.

83. Cf. Charles Hartshorne, "Whitehead in French Perspective: A Review Article," *The Thomist*, 33/3 (July, 1969): 575.

84. Hewitt Suchocki, "Hartshorne and Subjective Immortality," *Process Studies*, 121. It is on account of this idea of the unsurpassability and supereminence of the divine prehension that Hewitt-Suchocki criticizes Hartshorne for not going beyond his idea of an actual entity's objective immortality in God. She notes that if the divine memory were indeed as supereminent as Hartshorne says it is, "objective immortality will also include consciousness in those cases where consciousness is the subjective form of immediacy. If the conscious immediacy of the subject is fully retained in God, this constitutes subjective, not objective, immortality."

85. Cf. Charles Hartshorne, "Review of Rasvihari Das on *The Philosophy of Whitehead*," *The Philosophical Review*, 48/2 (March, 1939): 231.

86. William Christian, *An Interpretation of Whitehead's Metaphysics* (New Haven, Connecticut: Yale University Press, 1959), 65.

87. John 12 : 24.

88. Christian, *An Interpretation of Whitehead's Metaphysics*, 65.
89. Cf. *PR*, 340n517.
90. *PSG*, 284.
91. In another place, Hartshorne shows how much importance he gives to this idea. Cf. Charles Hartshorne, "God and the Meaning of Life," *On Nature*, Boston University Studies in Philosophy and Religion, ed. Leroy Rouner (Notre Dame: University of Notre Dame Press, 1984), 162: "*All will be retained* as imperishable treasures 'where neither moth nor rust consumes and where thieves do not break in and steal.' (Italics added.)"
92. Griffin, "Hartshorne's Differences from Whitehead," *Two Process Philosophers*, 53–4.
93. Hewitt Suchocki, "Hartshorne and Subjective Immortality," *Process Studies*, 121.
94. Cf. Lewis S. Ford, "Whitehead's Differences From Hartshorne," *Two Process Philosophers: Hartshorne's Encounter with Whitehead*, AAR Studies in Religion, No. 5 (Tallahassee, Florida: American Academy of Religion, 1973), 73.
95. *PSG*, 284.
96. Griffin, "Hartshorne's Differences from Whitehead," *Two Process Philosophers*, 55.
97. *PSG*, 283.
98. Griffin, "Hartshorne's Differences From Whitehead," *Two Process Philosophers*, 54.
99. Hartshorne and Peden, *Whitehead's View of Reality*, 17. Whitehead likewise uses a similar expression in articulating the place of "God" among the metaphysical principles. God is, according to Whitehead, "their chief exemplification," and not an "exception invoked to save their collapse." Cf. *PR*, 343n521.
100. We use the word "limit" because even the divine characteristics, according to Hartshorne, are not *simply* absolute. For instance, God's power is not an absolute form of power that can do anything whatsoever. It is limited insofar as the past and the future are concerned. It cannot change the past, and it cannot know the future in full and perfect detail. It is also limited insofar as it cannot do what is contradictory. He cannot have me making decisions I might have made, but did not make. As Hartshorne notes, God cannot be the actualization of all possible perfections as 'it is logically impossible that there should be such an actualization, for possible values are in part mutually incompatible." Cf. Hartshorne and Peden, *Whitehead's View of Reality*, 17. For a more detailed analysis and exposition of the "limits" to which the divine reality is subject, see Hartshorne's short book, *Omnipotence and Other Theological Mistakes*. In *Creative Synthesis*, of course, he cautions against a wrong understanding of "limit," saying that we must be clear as to what we understand by the word. Thus, he says our using of the word is not meant "to make room for the freedom of the creatures (or to explain evil)" Cf. *CSPM*, 13.
101. Hartshorne, "A Metaphysics of Universal Freedom," *Faith and Creativity*, 33.
102. Charles Hartshorne, *Whitehead's View of Reality*, coauthored with Creighton Peden, Chapter I: The Basic Categories (New York: Pilgrim Press, 1981), 9.
103. *BH*, 30.
104. *CSPM*, 9. Here we must recall the notion that the causal antecedents of an entity are necessary to explain coming-to-be, but not sufficient to determine the result of its synthesis. This is on account of the fact that the causal antecedents always leave room for individual decision. An actual entity is ultimately responsible for what it becomes. This ability to create in accordance with an *ownmost* "ideal" is the essence of freedom. Thus in *Process and Reality*, Whitehead remarks that "the

freedom inherent in the universe is constituted by this element of self-causation." Cf. *PR*, 135n88. And it is by reason of this freedom that all actual entities share with the divine characteristic of transcendence; "every actual entity transcending all other actual entities, including God himself" Cf. Ibid., 339n222.

105. Cf. Charles Hartshorne, "Response to Paul Weiss," *Philosophical Interrogations: Interrogations of Martin Buber, John Wild, Jean Wahl, Brand Blanshard, Paul Weiss, Charles Hartshorne, and Paul Tillich*, eds. Beatrice and Sydney Rome (New York: Holt Rinehart and Winston, 1964), 346.

106. *CSPM*, 9.

107. *BH*, 215.

108. *CSPM*, 11.

109. Ibid.

110. The intertwinement of knowing and being influenced is most succinctly expressed by the statement: "To know is to receive influence. To be known is to exert influence." Cf. Charles Hartshorne, *Aquinas to Whitehead: Seven Centuries of Metaphysics of Religion*. The Aquinas Lecture, 1976 (Milwaukee: Marquette University Publications, 1976), 29.

111. Hartshorne and Peden, *Whitehead's View of Reality*, 16–17.

112. *CSPM*, 12.

113. Cobb, "Hartshorne's Importance for Theology," *The Philosophy of Charles Hartshorne*, 179.

114. This perspective represents a "cautious" way of articulating the relationship of the divine reality with ultimate creativity. Whitehead is careful not to identify these two too easily. In fact, some of those who have considered his view of the matter, have pointed out that there is a clear nonidentification of God and creativity in Whitehead. Cf. Van der Veken and Cloots, "Can the God of Process Thought be Redeemed?" *Charles Hartshorne's Concept of God*, 128, 131. There is a "clear and strong distinction" which Whitehead makes between the two. The reason that these commentators give for this move is not only the refusal on Whitehead's part, "to shower God with metaphysical compliments," but also to emphasize the fact that "creativity as such is neutral towards order, goodness, harmony, and intensity."

115. Cf. *CSPM*, 12.

116. Hartshorne, "A Metaphysics of Universal Freedom," *Faith and Creativity*, 33.

117. *PR*, 344n225.

118. Ibid., 372n244.

119. Ibid., 522n344.

120. Ibid., 373n244.

121. Hartshorne and Peden, *Whitehead's View of Reality*, 18.

122. Sia, *God in Process Thought*, 82.

123. *MVG*, 30.

124. God, says Hartshorne, "speaks to creatures so eloquently, beautifully, wisely, and hence relevantly to their natures that they cannot, except within narrow limits, even wish not to respond." Cf. Charles Hartshorne, "Religion in Process Philosophy," *Religion in Philosophical and Cultural Perspective*, 261. Divine power, as Whitehead describes it, "neither rules nor is unmoved." "It dwells upon the tender elements in the world which slowly and in quietness operate by love" (cf. *PR*, 343n520). As one commentator writes: "Although God cannot force human action, he can affect it by the lure of persuasion." See: James Luther Adams, "The Lure of Persuasion: Some Themes from Whitehead," *Process Philosophy and Social*

Thought, eds. John B. Cobb, Jr. and W. Widdick Schroeder (Chicago: Center for the Scientific Study of Religion, 1981), 116. See also: Jan van der Veken, "Love Neither Rules Nor Is It Unmoved," *Tripod,* 16 (1983): 45–59. This notion has its critics, for whom the primary difficulties range from the claim that God's power is reduced to that of a merely persuasive agent, an alluring ideal, to the claim that the Process God sees every occurrence of evil as completely contributory to an eventual harmonization of all experience. For a substantial treatment of the major criticisms of the Process view from the theological angle, see: Bernard Loomer, "Christian Faith and Process Philosophy," *Journal of Religion,* 29/3 (July, 1949).

125. According to Hartshorne, the definition of "optimal limits" is that "they are such that, were more freedom allowed, the risks would increase more than the opportunities, and were less freedom allowed, the opportunities would decrease more than the risks." The nonabsoluteness of divine power, in the sense of the classical notion of "omnipotence," is consistent with Hartshorne's insistence that a metaphysics must make room for the reality of "risk," if it likewise wishes to have room for real opportunity (cf. *RSP,* 41).

126. *PR,* 133n87.

127. Cf. Charles Hartshorne, "Religion and Creative Experience," *Darshana.* An International Quarterly of Philosophy, Psychology, Physical Research, Religion, Mysticism, and Sociology, 2/1 (1962): 10.

128. *PR,* 287n189.

129. Ibid., 374n245.

130. Cf. John B. Cobb, Jr. *A Christian Natural Theology Based on the Thought of Alfred North Whitehead* (London: Lutterworth, 1966), 154. Cobb explains this notion by saying that "while some particular possibility must be ideal, given the situation," closely related possibilities are available which are "appropriate to the situation, although deviating from the ideal."

131. This second suggestion creates difficulties with the Whiteheadian notion of "eternal objects." Hartshorne himself rejects the idea in some form (cf. *CSPM,* xv). We shall be looking into the differences between the two thinkers shortly hereafter.

132. Cf. Delwin Brown, *To Set at Liberty: Christian Faith and Human Freedom* (New York: Orbis, 1981), 32–3, 56.

133. Cf. *CSPM,* 240.

134. There is here a related difficulty which however marginal to the point of our discussion needs to be noted. This is the question raised by some critics as to whether God simply chooses not to coerce, but can in fact do so if he wanted to or if it simply does not belong to his nature to be able to do so. Cf. David Basinger, *Divine Power in Process Theism: A Philosophical Critique.* SUNY Series in Philosophy, ed. Robert C. Neville (Albany, New York: State University of New York Press, 1988). In the first chapter of the work entitled "Divine Persuasion: Could the God of Process Theism do more?," Basinger asks: "Is non-coercion a self-limitation? Or is it that God does not have the capacity to coerce other actual entities?" Given the structure of becoming in both Whitehead and Hartshorne, the notion of causality found in both, and finally, considering the full ramifications of Hartshorne's insistence on the benevolence of the "Eternally Secure" as well as the identification of the Whiteheadian God with the "tender elements of the world," it is no surprise that many process thinkers hold that divine non-coercion is not due to a decision on God's part which *could* be revoked from time to time. Cf. Hartshorne, "Religion in Process Philosophy," *Religion in Philosophical and Cultural Perspective,* 263.

135. Another interesting issue, albeit peripheral to our discussion, is the possibility that an entity will actually *reject* the divine lure towards goodness. It appears that there is no room in Hartshorne's philosophy for the possibility of an inherently evil entity. Even Kant in his work *Religion within the Limits of Reason Alone*, proposed, but immediately withdrew in horror at the possibility of a radical evil, an "insurmountable wickedness" inhabiting the heart of men, which they can "by no means wipe out." Cf. Immanuel Kant, *Religion within the Limits of Reason Alone*, trans. Theodore M. Greene and Hoyt H. Hudson (New York: Harper and Row, 1960), 66. For a relatively new collection of articles dealing with the problem of radical evil in relation to Kant's treatment of the reality of "wickedness, corruption, and perversity" vis-à-vis the Enlightenment's hopeful view of human progress, see: Joan Copjec ed., *Radical Evil* (London and New York: Verso, 1996). One possible way of reconciling the Hartshornean view is to say, with Maritain for instance, that "each time a free creature undoes for its part the work that God makes, God remakes to that extent—for the better—this work and leads it to higher ends. Because of the presence of evil on earth, everything on earth, from the beginning to the end of time, is in perpetual recasting." Cf. Jacques Maritain, *God and the Permission of Evil*, trans. Joseph Evans (Milwaukee: Bruce, 1960), 86. This notwithstanding, it has to be admitted that one encounters not a small degree of difficulty in making sense of the radical evil—the kind that liberation theology for instance seeks to define and combat—within Hartshorne's theodicy. See M. Sia and S. Sia, *From Suffering to God: Exploring our Images of God in the Light of Suffering* (Macmillan/St. Martin's Press, 1994).

136. The subsequent analysis takes its cue from David Griffin's work, "Hartshorne's Differences from Whitehead," *Two Process Philosophers*, 35–57. Griffin discusses the differences between the two thinkers relative to their particular conceptions of the nature of possibility in the first part of the article, especially pp. 37–40, which deal specifically with the "eternal possibilities."

137. Alfred North Whitehead, *The Function of Reason* (Boston: Beacon Press, 1958), 32. See also: *PR*, 44n70.

138. Cf. Ivor Leclerc, *Whitehead's Metaphysics* (London: Allen and Unwin, 1965), 92.

139. Ibid.

140. Griffin, "Hartshorne's Differences from Whitehead," *Two Process Philosophers*, 37.

141. Leclerc, *Whitehead's Metaphysics*, 92.

142. Ibid., 93. Leclerc quotes from Whitehead's work *Modes of Thought*, in order to bring home the point that the "forms" are entities that we in fact presuppose in our attempt to come to grips with experience: "We must admit that in some sense or other, we inevitably presuppose this realm of forms, in abstraction from passage, loss, and gain [...] It is always at hand, and there is no escape" (Quoted from *MT*, 68).

143. The "being" of actual entities as constituted by their process of becoming—both in terms of the "fact" of their existing as well as in terms of the "mode" in which they exist—lies in the fact that the very nature of their existence involves change. Actual entities *come into existence* in the sense of being *new creations*. Cf. Leclerc, *Whitehead's Metaphysics*, 93.

144. Ibid., 94.

145. In *Process and Reality*, Whitehead defines "ingression" as "the particular mode in which the potentiality of an eternal object is realized in a particular actual entity, contributing to the definiteness of that actual entity" (*PR*, 23n34).

146. Ibid., 40n63.

147. Ibid. Thus, as Leclerc points out, it must be from "past actualities" that eternal objects have ingression into present actualities, i.e., those entities in the process of becoming. As such they are "given" to the actualities as "objects." Cf. Leclerc, *Whitehead's Metaphysics*, 94–5.

148. Griffin, "Hartshorne's Differences from Whitehead," *Two Process Philosophers*, 37.

149. *CSPM*, xv.

150. Griffin, "Hartshorne's Differences from Whitehead," *Two Process Philosophers*, 37.

151. Cf. *CSPM*, 67f., 121f.

152. Ibid., 59.

153. *CSPM*, 59. In another place, Hartshorne emphatically states that only the absolutely general metaphysical categories should be regarded as eternal; the less general are contingent and therefore emergent. The latter moreover, "in their absolute definiteness are irreducibly relational and historical." Cf. Hartshorne, "Whitehead's Idea of God," 556–8. Also: *CSPM*, 64. However, Hartshorne does allow that mathematical ideas might also be eternal since they are extremely abstract and general (cf. *CSPM*, 65).

154. *CSPM*, 66.

155. Ibid.

156. *CSPM*, 65. (Italics added.)

157. See especially: Sia, *God in Process Thought*, 26–30.

158. Ibid., 36.

159. *DR*, 76.

160. Ibid., 20.

161. *PSG*, 509.

162. Cf. Charles Hartshorne, "Process and the Nature of God," *Traces of God in a Secular Culture*, ed. George F. McLean (New York: Alba House, 1973), 118.

163. *PSG*, 509; *RSP*, 119.

164. Hence, the absolute cannot be the all-inclusive, but it can be included in the concrete. The absoluteness and all-inclusiveness required by the philosophic and religious conceptions of God can both be retained only by restricting the former to an abstract dimension of God's being. Cf. *DR*, 87–8.

165. In this way, Hartshorne is in basic agreement with the idea of Thomism that in the knowing relation, the knower is the one who is internally related to the object he knows and is hence qualified by the object of his knowledge. But he objects to the reversal of this cognitive relation that Thomism does when it comes to God. According to the classical view, God knows the world without being related to or affected by the world. Hartshorne holds that on the contrary, "it is precisely the ideal case of knowledge—*God's in this case*—that must in some other aspect be literally and unrestrictedly relative" (*DR*, 9. Italics added). The error of classical theism is in its failure to distinguish between the two aspects of the divine reality.

166. *DR*, 134.

167. Cf. Charles Hartshorne, "Paul Tillich's Doctrine of God," *The Theology of Paul Tillich*, Vol. I of The Library of Living Theology, eds. Charles W. Kegley and Robert Bretall (New York: Macmillan, 1952), 183.

168. Cf. Charles Hartshorne, "A Philosopher's Assessment of Christianity," *Religion and Culture: Essays in Honor of Paul Tillich*, ed. Walter Leibrecht (New York: Harper 1959), 174: "The subordination of all to one power [...] means that all things are self-determining (and mutually determining) *within limits*, and it is the setting of these limits which constitutes the divine ordering of the world." In *The Logic of Perfection*, Hartshorne makes an analogy between the exercise of divine power

and the use of political power: "Statesmen know that beyond a certain point interference with the lives of citizens does more harm than good, and this is not solely because of the weakness or stupidity of statesmen but because of the meaning of good as self-activity. This is part of the reason for the ideal of democracy, that people need first of all to be themselves, and this selfhood no tyrant, human or superhuman, however benevolent, can impose upon them" (*LP*, 204).

169. *BES*, 408–9.
170. Charles Hartshorne, "Whitehead and Berdyaev: Is there tragedy in God?" *Journal of Religion*, 37 (April, 1957): 74.
171. *CSPM*, 240.
172. *NT*, 82.
173. *DR*, 50.
174. Restrictions to freedom which ensure that it is never absolute, are set by other acts, those of oneself or others, including the divine creativity. Cf. *CSPM*, 9.
175. Charles Hartshorne, "Review of Francis X. Meehan on Efficient Causality in Aristotle and St. Thomas," *Journal of Religion*, 25/1 (January, 1945): 30.
176. *CSPM*, 16.
177. *MVG*, 244.
178. Hartshorne, "Whitehead's Idea of God," 557.
179. *PSG*, 501.
180. Hartshorne, "Efficient Causality in Aristotle and St. Thomas," 30.
181. *PR*, 373n244.
182. *LP*, 273.
183. Cf. Belaief, *Towards a Whiteheadian Ethics*, 57; Cf. *AI*, 200.
184. In *Process and Reality*, Whitehead writes: "God's immanence in the world in respect to his primordial nature is an urge towards the future based on an appetite in the present. Appetition is at once the conceptual valuation of an immediate physical feeling combined with the urge towards realization of the datum conceptually prehended. Appetition is immediate matter of fact including in itself a *principle of unrest, involving realization of what is not and may be.*" *PR*, 32n47–8.
185. Cf. Charles Hartshorne, "Continuity: The Form of Forms in Charles Peirce," *Monist* 39/4 (October, 1929), 530. Also: *CSPM*, 67.
186. *AI*, 227.
187. *DR*, 81.
188. *PR*, 50, p. 34.
189. *DR*, 44–5.
190. Cf. Charles Hartshorne, *Whitehead and the Modern World: Science, Metaphysics, and Civilization*, Three Essays on the Thought of Alfred North Whitehead, Coauthored with Victor Lowe and A.H. Johnson (Boston: Beacon Press, 1950), 32–3.
191. *MVG*, 249. These two grades of identity of the divine reality parallel what Hartshorne calls the "two meanings of individual selfhood," namely: (i) "individual as what is concrete and determinate, rather than abstract, or admitting of further determination. The subject-complete-with-all-its-predicates is the individual in this sense. But (ii) the thing which continues to exist through change of states of itself is quite another matter." Cf. Hartshorne, "Leibniz's Greatest Discovery," 420.
192. *DR*, 143.
193. Peter Bertocci, *The Goodness of God* (Washington, DC: University Press of America, 1981), 267. There seems no reason to see a contradiction between Bertocci's notion of "creative insecurity" and Hartshorne's calling God the

"Eternally Secure." Bertocci's phrase refers primarily to the divine reality's taking on the supreme risk created by the reality of creaturely freedom. This type of risk, of which creatures are only able to take on in a much lesser degree, is possible only for an entity that possesses that unsurpassable security which Hartshorne ascribes to deity.

194. *NT*, 104. It is this multiplicity and authenticity of freedom, creativity, and power that characterize each and every entity, mingled with the genuineness of God's concern and interest in the world, which make for the reality of risk, suffering, and tragedy. Risk, for Hartshorne, is an element built into the very fabric of universal creativity and becoming. 'A world without risks, he says, is not conceivable" (*OO*, 12). These sentiments, as well as those expressed by Bertocci are echoed by Arthur Peacocke in his book *Intimations of Reality*, where he says: 'The law of "new life through death of the old" is inevitable in a world composed of common "building blocks" [...] death, pain and the risk of suffering are intimately connected with the possibilities of new life, in particular. Moreover, the very order and impersonality of the physical cosmos which makes pain and suffering inevitable for conscious and self-conscious creatures is, at the same time, also the prerequisite of their exercise of freedom as persons'. See: Arthur Peacocke, *Intimations of Reality: Critical Realism in Science and Religion* (Notre Dame: Notre Dame University Press, 1984), 69.

195. Cf. *CSPM*, 184–6; *BES*, 402.

Chapter 7

1. *LP*, 298. The final chapter of *The Logic of Perfection* is entitled, "The Unity of Man and the Unity of Nature." Quote taken from Albert Schweitzer, *Kultur und Ethik* (München: Beck, 1923), 241. (Italics added.)
2. In *Creative Synthesis*, for instance, Hartshorne's discussion of what constitutes the identity of persons, within the ontology of event includes a consideration of concerns dealing with responsibility for one's past acts, keeping a promise, feelings of remorse and making restitution for wrongful deeds, as well as the attribution of praise or blame to individuals. His responses to possible objections wrought by these and similar concerns are not too far removed from some of the responses that Parfit makes. Cf. *CSPM*, 198ff.
3. "Beyond Enlightened Self-interest," 398–406. That the ontology of event is made to bear upon this critique and its implications for his theory of personal identity is evidenced by the fact that embedded in the chapter dealing with event in *Creative Synthesis* is a similar critique as is found in "Beyond Enlightened Self-Interest." Cf. *CSPM*, 173–204. The seeming dispersion of his criticisms throughout this chapter, results from an obvious intent to draw from the event ontology, conclusions that could clarify his point vis-à-vis the theory being repudiated.
4. In their brief introduction to Hartshorne's article "Beyond Enlightened Self-Interest," the editors of the anthology *Process Philosophy: Basic Writings*, explain that the most central premise of Hartshorne's ethics is "the denial of psychological egoism; that is, the denial that human concerns are purely self-centered." Cf. J.R. Sibley and P.A.Y. Gunter, eds., *Process Philosophy: Basic Writings* (New York, University Press of American, 1978), 393–4.
5. Hartshorne, "Beyond Enlightened Self-interest," 398.
6. Ibid., 399. He does admit though that "there are times—as when one is close to death—that one may be able to do much more for another than for oneself."

7. Cf. Saul Newton and Jane Pearce, *The Conditions of Human Growth* (New York: Citadel, 1963), 223. See also: Paul Staes, *Positive Self-Regard and Authentic Morality*, Logos, No. 7 (Manila: Ateneo de Manila University, 1972). Staes discusses in this work the so-called "Third Force" school of psychology which attempted to reinstate what Carl Rogers calls an "unconditional positive self-regard" as an important driving force in the development of moral values among individuals.

8. Newton and Pearce, *The Conditions of Human Growth*, 108. We can here repeat Paul Ricoeur's criticism of Parfit's flight from the 'self': " If my identity were to lose all importance in every respect, would not the question of others also cease to matter?" Cf. Ricoeur, *Oneself as Another*, 139. Quoted in Chapter II, Cf. reference in footnote # 95, of the present work.

9. Hartshorne, "Beyond Enlightened Self-Interest," 399.

10. Thus Hartshorne expresses certain reservations when it comes to extreme conceptions of responsibility toward others. Asked whether the seemingly extreme notion that one is *"responsible for the Other without waiting for reciprocity,"* were congenial to his notion of responsibility, Hartshorne responded by saying that he agreed that our responsibility toward the other should not be limited to the possibility of his or her being able to reciprocate our act. "To exist," he says, "is to create value in oneself and in another." But he immediately adds that "there are many others and I do not see that any single other is more important than I am just because the other is other. And one does have a primary responsibility for oneself since no one else can as constantly and intimately know me as I can or influence me as I can." Cf. *ZF*, 23, see note 9. [The italicized quote is taken from: Emmanuel Levinas, *Ethics and Infinity: Conversations with Philippe Nemo*, trans., Richard A. Cohen (Pitsburgh: Duquesne University Press, 1985), 98.]

11. "Beyond Enlightened Self-Interest," 400.

12. Ibid., 401. In *Creative Synthesis*, he writes: "The Ultimate loyalty is not to any human person, including oneself. Perhaps it is not even to the totality of mankind, still less to a nation, class or party, but rather to that cosmic something or someone relation to which, or relation to whom, must ultimately embrace all our values, and which or who is above our narrow prejudices, and stands for the truly common or universal good of all creatures." *CSPM*, 316.

13. "Beyond Englightened Self-Interst," 402. For a discussion of death in relation to what Hartshorne calls its "aesthetic meaning," see: *WM*, 51–62.

14. "Beyond Enlightened Self-Interest," 402.

15. *ZF*, 11.

16. "Beyond Enlightened Self-Interest," 395.

17. Ibid., 396.

18. Cf. *SMW*, 72, 84; *AI*, 200. Such a notion of the self as fully independent of its environment is consistent with the major tenets of the seventeenth century atomistic metaphysics which Whitehead has criticized. It may be asked of course how different is such atomism from the one espoused by Process Philosophy. The difference lies in this, namely, that the atomism of Newton, Locke, Hobbes, and others, involved two distinct but related theses. (i) First, they held that all the changing material in the universe, even all apparent physical "substances," consist of certain indivisible and imperceptible elementary particles. However, in addition to this, they also held that (ii) the purely mechanical interactions between these atomic entities together with their own individual characteristics sufficiently explain all that happens and develops in nature. Cf. W. Von Leyden, *Seventeenth*

Century Metaphysics: An Examination of Some Main Concepts and Themes (London: Gerald Duckworth, 1968), 133. Although comparisons can be drawn between Process atomism and the atomism of 17ᵗʰ century metaphysics with regard to the first thesis, there is very little comparison between the 'scientific materialism' propounded by the second thesis of the older atomistic theory and the more organic theory of relations espoused by Whitehead and Hartshorne. The genuineness of relations that hold between actual entities—denied by the older atomistic theory—is a central doctrine of Process philosophy.

19. Cf. Alfred North Whitehead, *Religion in the Making* (New York: World Publishing, 1972), 95. Hereafter cited as *RM*.

20. Ibid.

21. See: Jan C. Smuts, "The Holistic Universe," *Process Philosophy: Basic Writings*, eds. J.R. Sibley and P.A.Y. Gunter (New York: University Press of America, 1978), 227–8. (Italics added.)

22. Cf. Alfred North Whitehead, "The Analysis of Experience," *Process Philosophy: Basic Writings*, eds., Jack R. Sibley and Pete A.Y. Gunter (New York: University Press of America, 1978), 256.

23. *AI*, 202.

24. "Beyond Enlightened Self-Interest," 12. See also: Charles Hartshorne, "Continuity: The Form of Forms in Charles Peirce," *Monist*, 39/4 (October, 1929): 531: "The essence of reason—generality—and the essence of emotional life—sympathy—are thus to coincide formally in the element of continuity." By "continuity" here Hartshorne is referring to the organic or dynamical relativity at work in the universe and experienced by us. See also: *CSPM*, xx; and *PR*, 15n23, where Whitehead states: "Morality of outlook is inseparably conjoined with generality of outlook." "Enlargement" is a term used by Henry Nelson Wieman to describe the outward directedness of concern that is a hallmark of Process philosophy. Cf. Henry Nelson Wieman, "Creative Good," *Process Philosophy: Basic Writings*. eds., Jack R. Sibley and Pete A.Y. Gunter. University Press of America, 1978.

25. Cf. Lynne Belaief, "A Whiteheadian Account of Value and Identity," *Process Studies*, 5/1 (Spring, 1975): 39. The author calls it a "creative ethics" or a theory of "creative evolution in the ethical life" which is founded on the idea that the essence of life itself is the gaining of intensity made possible by the genuineness of freedom.

26. Cf. Hartshorne, "Continuity: The Form of Forms in Charles Peirce," 531.

27. "Beyond Enlightened Self-Interest," 410. This is a view consistent with that perspective on reality that is peculiar to Process Philosophy, namely, the 'unbounded' nature of each entity. See for instance, *PR*, 67n104–5, where Whitehead states that the actual entities that constitute the extensive continuum "pervade the continuum," which in turn is "present in each actual entity." This view represents a repudiation of the 'punctual view' of entities such as is found in Newtonian physics and Cartesian philosophy, according to which there are atomic substances whose existence can be understood apart from the existence of any entity in its environment—the fallacy of "simple location" discussed in Chapter Two.

28. Ibid., 410.

29. See: Wieman, "Creative Good," 372.

30. "Beyond Enlightened Self-Interest," 409.

31. Ibid., 411. In words that parallel Hartshorne's ideas here expressed, Whitehead says that the "antithesis between the general good and the individual interest can be abolished only when the individual is such that its interest is the general

good, thus exemplifying the loss of the minor intensities in order to find them again with finer composition in a wider sweep of interest." Cf. *PR*, 15n23.

32. Ibid., 411.

33. *RSP*, 192. By this he means of course the adding of novel actualities to those that have already been realized.

34. John B. Cobb, "Two Types of Postmodernism: Deconstruction and Process," *Theology Today*, 47 (July, 1990): 153.

35. Cobb, "Two Types of Postmodernism," 152. With regard to the "points of contact" that Process Philosophy has managed to create between the philosophical, scientific, and theological disciplines, Leonard Sweet provides a kind of counterbalance to Cobb's more optimistic tone. Sweet recognizes the same advantage that Process Thought has with regard to bringing a more unified voice to human attempts at understanding the world, but sounds much more somber in tone than Cobb with regard to the actual contribution Process Philosophy has made, especially to the life of present-day religious communities. Sweet argues that not only deconstruction, but process thought as well, are "out of touch with the church." See: Leonard I. Sweet, "Straddling Modernism and Postmodernism," *Theology Today*, 47 (July, 1990): 159–64.

36. Cobb, "Two Types of Postmodernism," 153. A similar observation is noted by Gerald Heard who points out that "in the spiral of man's thought," the reappearance of creative speculation is a sign that "the phase of analysis, of breaking down as being the one way of finding out, is waning. Gestalt concepts are increasingly fruitful; the skeptical approach conversely barren." Cf. Gerald Heard, "Philosophy, Society and Civilization," *The Philosophy of C.I. Lewis*, The Library of Living Philosophers, ed. Paul Arthur Schilpp (La Salle, Illinois: Open Court, 1968), 308.

37. Cf. Charles Hartshorne, "Berdyaev as Philosopher," Preface to David Bonner Richardson, *Berdyaev's Philosophy of History: An Existentialist Theory of Social Creativity and Eschatology* (The Hague: Martinus Nijhoff, 1968), xi. See also: W. Widdick Schroeder, "Toward Belief: A Process Perspective on the Social Sciences and on Social Ethics," *Belief and Ethics: Essays in Ethics, the Human Sciences, and Ministry in Honor of W. Alvin Pitcher*. Studies in Religion and Society, ed. W. Widdick Schroeder (Chicago: Center for the Scientific Study of Religion, 1978), 425. The author explains that the ethical and the aesthetic are related in process thought in that it believes "the lure to accentuate harmony and intensity of feeling in the future is at the base of morality. Although one may be a bit oblivious to morals at certain times and in certain places, the lure for aesthetic satisfaction, truthful formulations, and good actions constitutes a basic trinity inherent in the nature of things."

38. Cobb, "Two Types of Postmodernism," *Theology Today*, 153–4.

39. Eva Schaper, "Aesthetic Perception." *The Relevance of Whitehead*, ed. Ivor Leclerc (New York: Macmillan, 1961), 264.

40. *CSPM*, 31 (Italics added). See also: Chapter XVII of *Adventures of Ideas*, for Whitehead's discussion of the relationship between the true and the beautiful. *AI*, 265–72.

41. Cf. Eugene Freeman, "The Interrelatedness of 'True,' 'Good,' and 'Beautiful,'" *Process and Divinity: The Hartshorne Festschrift. Philosophical Essays Presented to Charles Hartshorne*, eds., William Reese and Eugene Freeman (La Salle, Illinois: Open Court, 1964), 325, 334–5.

42. Cf. Ibid., 334. On the other hand, Freeman also recognizes that there is a real independence between aesthetic and moral values—at least in the sense in which he explains it. Thus, he says that "the aesthetic responses to what are

primarily aesthetic objects, such as, for example, works of art, are not only *not* linked to moral evaluations, but on the contrary, are so sharply demarcated from them that the very question of the moral worth of these aesthetic objects is irrelevant, and it is a category mistake even to ask the question." p. 335.

43. "Beyond Enlightened Self-Interst," 412. See also: *CSPM*, 308: "Since the intrinsic value of experience is by definition aesthetic value, and since goodness is the disinterested will to enhance the value of future experiences, ethics presupposes aesthetics."
44. *CSPM*, 76.
45. Cf. *PR*, 280n427: "… an actual fact is a fact of aesthetic experience. All aesthetic experience is feeling arising out of the realization of *contrast under identity*." (Italics added.)
46. See: John Hospers, "Hartshorne's Aesthetics," *The Philosophy of Charles Hartshorne*, Vol XX of The Library of Living Philosophers, ed. Lewis Edwin Hahn (La Salle: Open Court, 1991), 114.
47. *CSPM*, 76.
48. Ibid., 300.
49. "Beyond Enlightened Self-Interst,," 412.
50. *RSP*, 44.
51. Charles Hartshorne, "Idealism and Our Experience of Nature," *Philosophy, Religion, and the Coming World Civilization: Essays in Honor of William Ernest Hocking*, ed. Leroy Rouner (The Hague: Martinus Nijhoff, 1966), 70.
52. "Beyond Enlightened Self-Interest," 412. Hartshorne argues that there are two senses by which an act can be regarded as ethically good. First, it makes its contribution to the harmony and intensity of experience, both in itself and in others. "A good will enjoys a sense of harmony between self and others." And second, the repercussion of the act will be the enhancement of possibilities for intense and harmonious experiences among the other entities in the individual's environment.
53. *PR*, 346n525.
54. *AI*, 263.
55. Schroeder, "Toward Belief: A Process Perspective on the Social Sciences and on Social Ethics," *Belief and Ethics*, 247.
56. *SMW*, 251–2.
57. Whitehead, The Function of Reason, 14.
58. Ibid., 65.
59. *SMW*, 258.
60. "Beyond Enlightened Self-Intererst," 398; See also: *CSPM*, xx.
61. *RSP*, 204.
62. Ibid., 195.
63. *LP*, 310, 322.
64. *CSPM*, 316.
65. "Beyond Enlightened Self-Interest," 412: "Here ethics must lean upon aesthetics. For the only good that is intrinsically good, good in itself, is good experience, and the criteria for this are aesthetic. *Harmony* and *intensity* come close to summing it up." (Italics adde.) See also: *CSPM*, 303, where Hartshorne points out that harmony alone is not a sufficient condition of great value; intensity must likewise be present—hence the intertwinement of the two in his theory.
66. *CSPM*, 59.
67. Ibid., 303. The entire Second Chapter: "Harmony in Life and Nature," of Hartshorne's book *Reality as Social Process* is given to a discussion of the "essential" role "contrast" plays in the maintaining the harmony of life. Cf. *RSP*, 44–52.

68. *CSPM*, 304.
69. *RSP*, 45.
70. Ibid., 47.
71. Cf. Charles Hartshorne, "Contingency and the New Era in Metaphysics," *Journal of Philosophy*, 29 (1932): 466. Hartshorne remarks that the same holds true for painting, "which is not a wholly timeless art, since vision is perpetually shifting its attention from point to point." Also: *RSP*, 49, 51.
72. *CSPM*, 311.
73. Two possibilities can be brought against this claim. First, as Hartshorne points out, "communities that have no means of preserving the art experiences of the past in permanent records may not feel much monotony in repeating them" (*RSP*, 50–1). Thus an awareness of one's past is of utmost importance. The arising of novelty because the old has been exhausted presupposes an awareness of an "old" that can indeed be exhausted. Second, as Whitehead remarks in *Adventures of Ideas*, it is also possible for societies and civilizations to arrive at that point where novelty is downright rejected. Hartshorne calls this "conservatism in its unmitigated form." "In every civilization at its *culmination*," Whitehead says, "we should find a large measure of realization of a certain type of perfection. ... The *culmination* can maintain itself at its height *so long as fresh experimentation* within the type is possible. But when these minor variations are exhausted, one of two things must happen. Perhaps the society in question lacks imaginative force. Staleness then sets in. Repetition produces a gradual lowering of vivid appreciation. Convention dominates. A learned orthodoxy suppresses adventure" (*AI*, 277. Italics added).
74. Belaief, "A Whiteheadian Account of Value and Identity," *Process Studies*, 35. Belaief explains that in the same way that achievement of harmony and order provides endurance, nothing actual can retain a static identity. "Situations either advance into novelty or degenerate and decay, for there is no other alternative, metaphysically."
75. *MT*, 142. Even Whitehead would say that "the form of process is not wholly dependent upon derivation from the past. As epochs decay amid futility and frustration, the form of process derives other ideals involving novel forms of order."
76. *RSP*, 51. In a similar vein, but involving a civilization on a much larger scale, Whitehead makes the comment that "on the whole, the great ages have been unstable ages" (*SMW*, 208).
77. Hartshorne, "Contingency and the New Era in Metaphysics," 466.
78. *MT*, 19.
79. Thus both thinkers reject static and unchangeable moral codes as a dogmatic and dangerous error. Hartshorne thus says that "moral exhortations and disciplines which make life seem *ugly or boring* for self and for others are counterproductive" (*BES*, 413. Italics added). Instead, moral codes, according to Whitehead, must reflect "the behavior patterns which in the environment for which it is designed will promote the evolution of that environment toward its proper perfection" (*AI*, 291). And therefore, "the duty of tolerance is our finite homage to the abundance of inexhaustible novelty which is awaiting the future" (*AI*, 59).
80. *RSP*, 51.
81. Ibid., 46–8. These are the three areas which Hartshorne singles out as providing clear instantiations of harmony.
82. *BES*, 413.
83. *RSP*, 49.
84. *CSPM*, 92.

85. Ibid., 218.
86. Ibid, 75.
87. Cf. Charles Hartshorne, "Metaphysical Statements as Nonrestrictive and Existential," *Review of Metaphysics*, 12/1 (September, 1958): 35–47. In this article Hartshorne stresses that metaphysical statements are *existential*, i.e. they concern experience of what exists. They are "always embodied in experience." See also: Charles Hartshorne, "Metaphysics for Positivists," *Philosophy of Science*, 2/1 (January, 1935): 290.
88. *CSPM*, 90–1. See also: Hartshorne, "Metaphysics for Positivists," 289–94.
89. Cf. Hartshorne, "My Neoclassical Metaphysics," 3–10.
90. *BH*, 268.
91. *CSPM*, 75.
92. Cf. Hartshorne, "Metaphysics for Positivists," 292.
93. *CSPM*, xx.
94. *CSPM*, 77.
95. Hartshorne, "Sensation in Psychology and Philosophy," 6.
96. Hartshorne, "Idealism and Our Experience of Nature," 74, 75.
97. Hartshorne, "In Defense of Wordsworth's View of Nature," 85. This, of course is already a generalization beyond what is directly given, i.e. beyond feeling of the human form. At the same time, "it is important that this form is itself an indistinct participation in cellular feeling, which are more primitive than human ones."
98. Charles Hartshorne, "Husserl and the Social Structure of Immediacy," *Philosophical Essays in Memory of Edmund Husserl*, ed. Marvin Farber (New York: Greenwood Press, 1968), 227–8.
99. Hartshorne, "Sensation in Psychology and Philosophy," 6–7.
100. Cf. Hartshorne, "Metaphysics for Positivists," 295–6.
101. Cf. Hartshorne, "Husserl and the Social Structure of Immediacy," 220–1.
102. Cf. Hartshorne, "Sensation in Psychology and Philosophy," 7.
103. This is the essence of Hartshorne's notion of "Affective Monism" which he enunciates in: Charles Hartshorne, "Monistic Theory of Expression," *The Journal of Philosophy*, 50/14 (July 2, 1953): 426. See also: Hartshorne, "Idealism and Our Experience of Nature," *Philosophy, Religion and the Coming World Civilization*, 71: "... physical reality is not merely physical, neutral to psychical properties, but inextricably psychical as well." The objects of experience, are for Hartshorne, *experiences* themselves. See: *CSPM*, 7.
104. See: Hartshorne, "Absolute Objects and Relative Subjects: A Reply," 174–88.
105. Charles Hartshorne, "Husserl and Whitehead on the Concrete," *Phenomenology: Continuation and Criticism. Essays in Memory of Dorion Cairns*, eds. F. Kersten and R. Zaner (The Hague: Martinus Nijhoff, 1973), 97. See also: *LP*, 227, where Hartshorne rejects as absurd the idea "that any experience can thus furnish its own sole datum. A mere awareness of that same awareness is nonsense."
106. Hartshorne, "Husserl and Whitehead on the Concrete," 103.
107. Hartshorne, "Lewis' Treatment of Memory," *The Philosophy of C. I. Lewis*, ed. Paul Arthur Schilpp. The Library of Living Philosophers Vol. 13 (La Salle, Illinois: Open Court), 395–414.
108. Hartshorne, "Husserl and Whitehead on the Concrete," 103.
109. This, Hartshorne says, is a generalization of Bergson's notion that actual bodily states play the role of objects in dreams. He adds further that studying a universal in an imagined instance is not tantamount to studying it in a merely possible instance. Rather, it is to take an actual instance, e.g. a visual image—which is really a neurological process as it is intuited or felt—as standing for possible

instances which might exist in some form or other. Thus, the possible can only be studied in the actual, the universal only in the particular.

110. Cf. *LP*, 227. See also: Hartshorne, "Whitehead's Revolutionary Concept of Prehension," 257.

111. Hartshorne, "Husserl and Whitehead on the Concrete," 97. The basic point of this Hartshornean notion is that memory implicates a relation of a present event with past events that belong to a single sequence, namely, the personal event's own. Perception on the other hand implicates the relation of a present event with past events that do not belong to its own sequence. What both have in common is that there is no simultaneity between the event prehending and the event prehended. Instead, both belong to wholly the past. See also: Hartshorne, "Sensation in Psychology and Philosophy,", 7.

112. Charles Hartshorne, "Whitehead and Ordinary Language," *Southern Journal of Philosophy*, 7/4 (Winter, 1969–70): 437. Cf. *CSPM*, 75–7, 91–2: "Common to the two is what Whitehead calls 'prehension,' intuition of the antecedently real. This is a specimen of what I mean by metaphysical discovery. It is no mere matter of human psychology."

113. Hartshorne, "Whitehead's Revolutionary Concept of Prehension," *International Philosophical Quarterly*, 257.

114. Hartshorne, "Lewis' Treatment of Memory," 397. A similar exposition is found in: *CAP*, Chapter 13: "Lewis on Memory, Modality, and the Given," 159–81.

115. Hartshorne, "Husserl and Whitehead on the Concrete," 99.

116. Hartshorne, "Husserl and Whitehead on the Concrete," Ibid., 97. In *Creative Synthesis*, he cautions against an all-too-easy affirmation of "the view that perception gives us the absolutely simultaneous state of the environment, that there is no time lapse between perceiving and perceived." *CSPM*, 79, 80.

117. Cf. *CSPM*, 218. "An oddity" is how Hartshorne regards the notion of perception as being confined merely to the present moment.

118. Hartshorne, "Husserl and Whitehead on the Concrete," 97.

119. *CSPM*, 79, 109.

120. Hartshorne, *Insights and Oversights*, 258. See also: Hartshorne, "Lewis' Treatment of Memory," 396.

121. Hartshorne, "Whitehead's Revolutionary Concept of Prehension," 255.

122. Hartshorne, *Insights and Oversights*, 369. See also Hartshorne's discussion in: "The Logical Structure of Givenness," *The Philosophical Quarterly*, 312–16.

123. Popper and Eccles, The Self and Its Brain: An Argument for Interactionism, 91–3.

124. *CSPM*, 80.

125. *RSP*, 34.

126. Hartshorne, "The Social Theory of Feelings," 89. See also: Hartshorne, "Husserl and Whitehead on the Concrete," 94–5. Here Hartshorne states: "Bodily feelings are spatial, spatially separated in more or less definite degrees and directions ... And they are, in objective fact, spatially located, for so are the invisible bodily members, perhaps nerve cells, whose feelings they in the first instance are ... Precisely this is the mind-body relation. It is that of experience of one kind to experience of very different kinds, not of experience to mere physical things. It is a special form of the social relation, with the human experience being the "presiding spirit" in a society of extremely humble forms of experiencing." See also: *CSPM*, 80. Here Hartshorne states that it is actually "bodily experience, not vision of environmental objects" which should be the initial sample of perception.

127. Hartshorne, "The Social Theory of Feelings," 89.
128. Hartshorne, "Sensation in Psychology and Philosophy," 12.
129. Viney, "Charles Hartshorne's Philosophy and Psychology of Sensation," 104.
130. Cf. Hartshorne, "Husserl and Whitehead on the Concrete," 97.
131. Cf. *CSPM*, 79.
132. Cf. Ibid., 92. See also: Hartshorne, *Insights and Oversights of Great Thinkers*, 263, where he states that "only past actualities are prehended." This notion echoes Whitehead's own. See: Alfred North Whitehead, "The Analysis of Experience." *Process Philosophy: Basic Writings*, eds., J. R. Sibley and P.A.Y. Gunter. (University Press of America, 1978), 251: "The process of experiencing is constituted by the reception of entities, whose being is antecedent to that process ... These antecedent entities, thus received as factors into the process of experiencing, are termed 'objects' for that experiential occasion. Thus primarily the term 'object' expresses the relation of the entity, thus denoted, to one or more occasions of experiencing. Two conditions must be fulfilled in order that an entity may function as an object in a process of experiencing: (1) the entity must be *antecedent*, and (2) the entity must be experienced in virtue of its antecedence; it must be *given*."
133. *CSPM*, 75.
134. Ibid., 218. See also: Hartshorne, "Whitehead's Revolutionary Concept of Prehension," *International Philosophical Quarterly*, 255.
135. Ibid., 69–98: Chapter V: Some Principles of Method. The analysis of memory and perception (as well as imagination) is included in the discussion of the second principle enunciated by Hartshorne, namely, "experience." Cf. *Ibid* 75.
136. The very close relatedness of memory with perception in regard to the pastness of data has already been discussed, largely in terms of the objects of perception being events for which any further coming-to-be has already ceased and is now fodder for later acts of becoming. More will be said about the "pastness" even of the data of present acts of perceiving in the following section in which the notions of mediate and immediate memory are discussed.
137. Ibid 75. (Italics added.) For Hartshorne, the object of experience is *other*-experience. Hence, the italicized phrase should be read to refer to his conception of the "pervasiveness of mentality" as discussed earlier on in this work.
138. Ibid. See also: Hartshorne, "Lewis' Treatment of Memory," 403–5.
139. The "interconnection" of these ideas consists in the fact that each is built upon the foundations provided by the other. Thus, having already discussed the notion concerning the character of the data of awareness as belonging to the past—thesis (i)—Hartshorne is better able to discuss why he holds, against Hume, that we are capable of experiencing causal connectedness in nature—thesis (ii), and thus avoid the skeptical conclusion at which the latter arrived. Finally, since memory witnesses to the veracity of causal connections, it becomes possible to show there are genuine elements of unity and continuity as well as change and diversity in the notion of personal identity.
140. Hartshorne, "Husserl and Whitehead on the Concrete," 102.
141. This is the essence of "contrast" as the temporal aspect of harmony and intensity. Cf. *RSP*, 49.
142. Hartshorne, "Idealism and Our Experience of Nature," 76. Also: *CSPM*, 91–2.
143. Sia, *God in Process Thought*, 45. Concerning the reconciliation of constancy and change, the essence of personal identity will have to be sought within the bounds of Hartshorne's notion that the case is not of the "different" in the "identical," but of the "identical" being encompassed in the "different."

144. This criticism is found in an article analyzing C.I. Lewis' understanding of memory as enunciated in the latter's book, *An Analysis of Knowledge and Valuation*. Cf. Hartshorne, "Lewis' Treatment of Memory," 396. The work on which Hartshorne bases his article is Chapter 11: Probable Knowledge and the Validity of Memory in: C.I. Lewis, *An Analysis of Knowledge and Valuation* (La Salle, Illinois: Open Court, 1946).

145. Hartshorne, "Whitehead's Revolutionary Concept of Prehension," 256.

146. From which some conclude that what is involved in seeing is not the literal givenness of the object, but only of sense data. Cf. Hartshorne, "Lewis' Treatment of Memory," 396.

147. What constitutes the validity of memory, i.e. what enables us to have a degree of certainty that a correspondence exists between present "sign" and remembered reality, lies in memory's normal establishment of "the probability that *something like what is remembered* was really experienced." Hartshorne finds this notion questionable, saying that the "probability assurance" implicated in the relation of the present "sign" as an "interpretation" of a past reality is a little too "mysterious." Cf. Ibid.

148. Ibid., 398.

149. Cf. Hartshorne, "Whitehead's Revolutionary Concept of Prehension," 256–7.

150. Hartshorne, "The Social Structure of Experience," *Philosophy: Journal of the Royal Institute of Philosophy*, 35/137 (April and July 1961): 106.

151. Cf. Charles Hartshorne, "Synthesis as Polyadic Inclusion: A Reply to Sessions," *Southern Journal of Philosophy*, 14/2 (Summer, 1976): 250. See also: Hartshorne, "Whitehead's Revolutionary Concept of Prehension," 256.

152. Cf. Alfred North Whitehead, *Symbolism: Its Meaning and Effect* (Cambridge: Cambridge University Press, 1928). Parts of this work (together with selections from *Process and Realtiy* and *Adventures of Ideas*) are reproduced as: Alfred North Whitehead, "Symbolic Reference," *Process Studies: Basic Writings*, eds. Jack R. Sibley and Pete A.Y. Gunter. (New York: University Press of America, 1978), 51–78.

153. There are two modes of perception for Whitehead. "Presentational immediacy" which is one of them, refers to perception involving the clear, conscious, sensory discrimination that is characteristic of high grade experients. However, as Whitehead notes, "as we descend the scale, it seems that we find in the lower types [of creatures] a dim unconscious drowse, of undiscriminated feeling. For the lower types, experience loses its illustration of forms [sensa], and its illumination by consciousness, and its discrimination of purpose. It seems finally to end in a massive unconscious urge derived from undiscriminated feeling, this feeling being itself a derivation from the immediate past." Whitehead, *The Function of Reason*, 63–4. The initiation of this lower type of "reaction" does not depend on sense perception, as the "causal" reaction will still be there whether clear sense perception is present or not. This more primitive type of perception is what Whitehead terms "perception in the mode of causal efficacy" which is vague and essentially unconscious. Cf. *MT*, 154.

154. Whitehead, *Symbolist*, 19. Henry Nelson Wieman makes a similar distinction between a more primitive type of perception and a full-blown type found in higher forms of mentality, and whose object is the density and fullness of being, perceived when proper selection is made and the scope and complexity of awareness is involved. Cf. Henry Nelson Wieman, "Perception and Cognition," *Process Philosophy: Basic Writings*, eds., Jack R. Sibley and Pete A.Y. Gunter. (New York: University Press of America, 1978), 107–15.

155. Hartshorne, "Sensation in Psychology and Philosophy," 4.
156. Hartshorne, "The Social Structure of Experience," *Philosophy*, 106 (see esp. note 1). Hartshorne here refers to the work of H.H. Price, *Thinking and Experience* (Cambridge: Harvard University Press, 1953), 58–60, 79f.
157. Hartshorne, "Lewis' Treatment of Memory," 398.
158. Cf. Whitehead, Symbolism: Its Meaning and Effect, 18, 21.
159. *CSPM*, 79–80: "Mistakes of memory, about which we hear so much, are usually not carefully distinguished from mistakes of memory judgments." See also: Hartshorne, "Synthesis as Polyadic Inclusion: A Reply to Sessions," *Southern Journal of Philosophy*, 250: "... it is not our sensings which err, but the beliefs we form with regard to them."
160. Hartshorne, "Lewis' Treatment of Memory," 398. See also: *CSPM*, 79–80.
161. Ibid., 398–9. Hartshorne provides an illustration of his point: "Suppose I say that I remember a sentence uttered by Professor Lewis in 1919, and suppose it could be proved that what he actually said was somewhat different; would this mean that I am now merely imagining the incorrect words, and imputing them to the past? Not at all. If I have (inwardly or outwardly) repeated the sentence to myself at various times since hearing it, I may now be remembering, quite correctly, one of these earlier "repetitions." And when I thought up the false rendering, I may well have been trying, to guess, from fragments of memory, what some forgotten words would likely have been ... Sometimes I am quite aware of this element of guessing in my recollecting; perhaps never am I aware with absolute clarity and certainty, where the memory stops and the guessing begins."
162. Whitehead, "The Analysis of Experience," *Process Philosophy*, 253. See also: Charles Hartshorne, "A Reply to My Critics," *The Philosophy of Charles Hartshorne*, Vol. XX of The Library of Living Philosophers, ed. Lewis Edwin Hahn (La Salle, Illinois: Open Court, 1991), 573.
163. *CSPM*, 80.
164. Ibid., 89.
165. Hartshorne, "Lewis' Treatment of Memory," s, 398.
166. Hartshorne, "Husserl and Whitehead on the Concrete," 98.
167. Cf. Milič Čapek, "Immediate and Mediate Memory," 90–6.
168. Hartshorne, "Lewis' Treatment of Memory," 399. See also: Whitehead, "The Analysis of Experience," 253.
169. Hartshorne, "Reply to My Critics," 573.
170. Hartshorne, "Lewis' Treatment of Memory," 399.
171. Whitehead, "The Analysis of Experience," y, 253.
172. Čapek, "Immediate and Mediate Memory," 93.
173. Cf. Charles Michael Johnson, "On Prehending the Past," *Process Studies*, 6/4 (Winter, 1976): 265.
174. Cf. Charles Hartshorne, "The Development of Process Philosophy," Introduction to *Philosophers of Process*, ed. Douglas Browning (New York: Random House, 1965), xv.
175. Whitehead, "The Analysis of Experience," 253.
176. Hartshorne, "Lewis' Treatment of Memory," 399.
177. Charles Hartshorne, "Sprigge on Past, Future, and Eternity," *The Philosophy of Charles Hartshorne*, Vol. XX of The Library of Living Philosophers, ed. Lewis Edwin Hahn (La Salle, Illinois: Open Court, 1991), 674. This discussion is found in Hartshorne's reply to an article written by Timothy Sprigge in which the latter puts forward a more "eternalistic understanding" of time. The question

Sprigge raises in regard to his eternalistic viewpoint and its relation to Hartshorne's thesis is: *How do we know that the present is not already in the remote past?* Cf. T.L.S. Sprigge, "Hartshorne's Conception of the Past." *The Philosophy of Charles Hartshorne*, Vol. XX of The Library of Living Philosophers, ed. Lewis Edwin Hahn (La Salle, Illinois: Open Court, 1991), 397–414.

178. Hartshorne, "Lewis' Treatment of Memory," 397.
179. Hartshorne, "Reply to My Critics," 574.
180. Otherwise, as Hartshorne points out, we involve our theory in a vicious regress of "knowing, knowing its knowing, etc." Cf. Charles Hartshorne, "Sprigge on Past, Future, and Eternity," 674.
181. Hartshorne, "The Immortality of the Past: Critique of a Prevalent Misinterpretation," 109.
182. Cf. Hartshorne, "Lewis' Treatment of Memory," 400.
183. "Becoming is cumulative." Cf. *CSPM*, 273. See also: Charles Hartshorne, "Synthesis as Polyadic Inclusion: A Reply to Sessions," 245–55. It is certainly the case, as Hartshorne admits, that a present experience as well as its included memories is no more and no less than simply the experience itself. However, he quickly adds that "memory is at least intuition of a previous intuition of some data. Thus an experience includes an irreducible and considerable complexity."
184. Hartshorne, "Idealism and Our Experience of Nature," 78. See also: Hartshorne, "Synthesis as Polyadic Inclusion: A Reply to Sessions," 247–8.
185. Hartshorne, "Lewis' Treatment of Memory," 400. Also: "The Immortality of the Past: Critique of a Prevalent Misinterpretation," 99; "Personal Identity From A to Z," 211.
186. *DR*, 157. See also: Hartshorne, "The Immortality of the Past: Critique of a Prevalent Misinterpretation," 98. "The entire past," Hartshorne says, "not a mere portion of it," is what is preserved in the divine memory.
187. Frankenberry, "The Power of the Past," 133.
188. Ibid., 134. Quoted from *AI*, 230f.
189. Cf. *AI*, 227, 226, 241, 242.
190. Frankenberry, "The Power of the Past," 133.
191. Čapek, "Immediate and Mediate Memory," *Process Studies*, 94.
192. Čapek, "Immediate and Mediate Memory," 94.
193. It must be noted here that the "fading of the past" is an empirical, more than a logical observation. Hartshorne's explanations about the nature of human awareness are of the logical type. Empirically, i.e. from the standpoint of a biological theory of knowledge, what prevents human consciousness from possessing the past in its integral totality is explained by Čapek as such: "Just as our perception carves out of the whole physical realm only that zone which has practical importance for our organism, only those recollections which are relevant to our present situation are transmitted into our present moment." The limiting, selecting factor, he says is "our attention to life, embodied in our normally functioning nervous system." Adding further that since "the relevance of the remote past is practically negligible, it usually remains outside of our immediate memory, subsisting mainly in the form of imageless, virtual awareness."
194. *BH*, 122.
195. Milič Čapek, "Immediate and Mediate Memory," 94.
196. Hartshorne, "Lewis' Treatment of Memory," 402.
197. Cf. Charles Hartshorne, "The Logical Structure of Givenness," *International Philosophical Quarterly*, 8/33 (October, 1958): 308.

Chapter 8

1. Cf. *CSPM*, 7.
2. Hartshorne, "Lewis' Treatment of Memory," 401. Hartshorne has a substantial discussion of his assessment of Hume in several works. The ones most pertinent to our discussion are the following: Hartshorne, "Hume's Metaphysics and Its Influence," Chapter 13 of *Insights and Oversights of Great Thinkers*, 136–50; "The Structure of Givenness," *The Philosophical Quarterly*, 8/33 (1958): 307–16; "Freedom Requires Indeterminism and Universal Causality," *Journal of Philosophy*, 55 (1958): 793–812; and: "Causal Necessities: An Alternative to Hume," *Philosophical Review*, 479–99.
3. Hartshorne, "The Social Structure of Experience," 106.
4. Hartshorne, "Causal Necessities," 482.
5. Ibid., 480. These are likewise treated in Chapter 13 (on Hume's Metaphysics) in Hartshorne's book *Insights and Oversights of Great Thinkers*, 136–43.
6. Hartshorne, "Causal Necessities," *Philosophical Review*, 481.
7. See: Hartshorne, "Contingency and the New Era in Metaphysics," *Journal of Philosophy*, 465.
8. *AI*, 188.
9. Hartshorne, "Causal Necessities," 491.
10. Cf. Ibid., 480: (i) Causal relations, if necessities, must either be (a) logical necessities connecting events with subsequent events in their full particularity—or else (b) not logical necessities at all; (ii) Whether logical or not, the necessities must concern effected events in their full particularity; and (iii) They must, in some cases at least, connect states or bits of mere "matter" (rather than of experience of subjects). For purposes of facility, we shall combine the first and the second and thus end up with two assumptions rather than three.
11. Hartshorne, "Personal Identity From A to A," 210.
12. Hartshorne, "Causal Necessities," *Philosophical Review*, 480.
13. Hartshorne refers to an article by: H. Margenau, "Physical versus Historical Reality," *Philosophy of Science*, 19 (1952): 193–213, in order to call attention to the fact that the tendency to regard the world with deterministic lenses was much more pronounced with classical Newtonian physics than in contemporary physics, which regards the laws that govern the universe as for the most part approximate and statistical. Although Hartshorne also recognizes the fact that classical physics with its deterministic emphasis, "never pretended to deal with all aspects of events, for qualitative aspects were excluded (save as 'powers' to produce qualities in events of human experience)."
14. Hartshorne, "Causal Necessities," 480–1. (Italics added.)
15. Cf. *RSP*, 75. See also: Charles Hartshorne, "Whitehead's Differences from Buddhism," *Philosophy East and West*, 25/4 (October, 1975): 410.
16. Cf. Hartshorne, "Contingency and the New Era in Metaphysics," 466; also, Hartshorne, "Causal Necessities," 482.
17. The unit realites that are related to one another in a chain of successive events characterized by asymmetrical causality, are regarded by Hartshorne as "experient occasions." The analogy—admittedly remote—is to "momentary human experiences (occurring normally in the human case some 10–20 per second)." What Hartshorne is rejecting is the notion that causal relatedness involves only material entities. There are no such things as "merely material" entities in Hartshorne's philosophy. In this he admits partial agreement with the entire

"idealist" tradition which holds matter to be a "form of manifestation of 'mind'"—but "in the broad nonanthropomorphic sense." In this sense, Hartshorne's idealism is different from the Berkeleyan or Hegelian forms, as these are "essentially anthropomorphic." Cf. Hartshorne, "Personal Identity from A to Z," 210. The entities that are connected one to another in a causal series are themselves drops of experience, not "bits of mere matter."

18. Hartshorne, "Causal Necessities," 482.
19. Hartshorne, "Causal Necessities," *Philosophical Review*, 481. This in an important component of Hartshorne's understanding of the basic asymmetrical structure of time. Cf. *CSPM*, 218–19. The influence exerted by the present upon the future is, retrospectively regarded, the same as the influence of the past upon the present. An earlier temporal point exerts an influence on a later one only in the sense that the earlier creates an "outline," a range of possibilities for actualization. There is no determinate "fixing" of the result beforehand. See also: *RSP*, 73–5.
20. Cf. Hartshorne, *Insights and Oversights*, 286.
21. Cf. Hartshorne, "Lewis' Treatment of Memory," 402–9. Also: "Causal Necessities," 491.
22. This is the notion of a "generalized comparative psychology" enunciated in the chapter on "Cosmic Variables" in Hartshorne's book, *Beyond Humanism*. Cf. *BH*, 111–24. These "variables" refer to properties which entities on the "scale of being" possess in varying degrees. There are two kinds: "local variables," which are possessed by a limited portion of the entities on the scale. "Conscious mentality" is an instance of such variable. "Cosmic variables" on the other hand, are applicable to all entities on the scale. Thus mentality, for example, is possessed by higher level entities, such as human beings in a way far superior than the manner by which lower level animals, such as dogs or whales for example, possess it. Cosmic variables are possessed by all, but not in the same way. Thus although animals do not think the way humans do, they still cannot be regarded as not possessing what in humans is a very high degree of mind. Going down the scale of being, just as animals cannot be said to be without that which is found in a very high degree in humans, entities lower than animals on the scale cannot be said to be without that which is found in a higher degree in animals, and so forth as one goes even lower down the scale. The only inadmissible variable, if it can in fact be called such, is the "zero-instantiation" of mentality.
23. *CSPM*, 195; 221.
24. Hartshorne, "Causal Necessities,"493. See also: Hartshorne, "Sensation in Psychology and Philosophy," 6–9.
25. Hartshorne, "Lewis' Treatment of Memory," 403; "The Social Theory of Feelings," 90.
26. Hartshorne, "Lewis' Treatment of Memory," 404.
27. Hartshorne, "Sensation in Psychology and Philosophy," 6.
28. *RSP*, 80.
29. Ibid., 69–84.
30. Ibid., 81. (Italics added.)
31. For another example, this time involving the experience of pain, see: Hartshorne, "The Social Structure of Experience," 106–8. See also his explanation in: "In Defense of Wordsworth's View of Nature," 82–3.
32. *RSP*, 81. See also: Charles Hartshorne, "The Organism in Process Philosophy," *Process in Context: Essays in Post-Whiteheadian Perspectives*, ed. Ernest Wolf-Gazo (New York: State University of New York Press, 1987), 69–73.

33. Cf. Charles Hartshorne, "Leibniz's Greatest Discovery," *Journal of the History of Ideas*, 7/14 (October, 1946): 414–15.
34. For the argument concerning the limitations of nondivine intuition, see: Hartshorne, "The Social Theory of Feelings," 90, in which he states that "no subject other than God can adequately ... feel the feelings of another (thus we do not distinctly intuit the cellular or subcellular individuals in their unique individualities." For a similar explanation, see: "The Social Structure of Experience," 109.
35. Hartshorne, "Causal Necessities," 494.
36. *ZF*, 153.
37. Ibid., 157. See also: Hartshorne, "In Defense of Wordsworth's View of Nature," 82. "Our most direct contact with physical reality is with what happens inside our bodies. When we see or hear, first something physical happens inside ours skins, particularly in the nervous system, and only then do we perceive the extra-bodily happening." In *Creativity in American Philosophy*, Hartshorne quotes Montague who says that "the potentiality of external motion is the actuality of internal experience." Cf. *CAP*, 217. [Quote taken from: Montague, *The Way of Things*, 670.] Donald Sherburne also disccusses the relation of what transpires within the boundaries of the body (we could probably call it the "bodily map" as Hartshorne calls it in "The Logical Structure of Givenness," 314) in relation to the causal structure of experience involving data belonging to the past in: Donald W. Sherburne, "Whitehead's Psychological Physiology," *Southern Journal of Philosophy*, 7/4 (Winter, 1969): 401–7. Sherburne quotes from *Process and Reality* where Whitehead states: "It is by reason of the body, with its miracle of order, that the treasures of the past environment are poured into the living occasion. This final percipient route of occasions is perhaps some thread of happenings wandering in "empty" space amid the interstices of the brain. It toils not, neither does it spin. It receives from the past; it lives in the present. It is shaken by its intensities of private feeling, adversion or aversion. In its turn, this culmination of bodily life transmits itself as an element of novelty throughout the avenues of the body. Its sole use to the body is its vivid originality: it is the organ of novelty." See: *PR*, 339n516.
38. Charles Hartshorne, "The Organism in Process Philosophy," 72. Without such "independence," Hartshorne argues, "the escape from solipsism can only be a *tour de force*," as it is hardly a way to begin an epistemological inquiry by allowing even a logical possibility of an experience which is aware only of itself or its own creations .... An experience whose data are merely its own ideas or impressions is nonsensical."
39. *ZF*, 156.
40. Hartshorne, "The Organism in Process Philosophy," 69–71. Hartshorne explains that the neural correlates of our experience, even of "external realities" are "the absolute requirements for sensation, not the environmental conditions."
41. Ibid., 87.
42. Ibid., 73. In this Hartshorne breaks with traditional conceptualizations (and even the less fragmentary ones) of the relationship between mind and body. The so-called "two-aspect theories" hold that the two aspects occur simultaneously. Contrary to this, Hartshorne holds that the subject-object relation is one of "later-earlier." "What is sensed or felt is what has *just happened* in the body, not what is happening precisely now. Thus the bodily condition is cause in the normal temporal sense. And so we escape from the supposed need to assume an absolutely peculiar form of relatedness in the mind-body case."
43. *CSPM*, 221.

44. Ibid. This, Hartshorne states, is also the key to the resolution of the mind-body duality. "Since the idea of the psychical is that of experiencing or knowing, and since both soul and body must be known if there is a real problem, the key to the duality of mind and body is the relation of knowing or experiencing to the known or experienced. It is knowing which related itself to the known, not *vice versa* ... Thus the asymmetry of mind and matter can only be understood through some form of psychicalism" (p. 224).
45. Ibid., 220.
46. *CSPM*, 224.
47. *ZF*, 158.
48. Hartshorne, "Personal Identity From A to Z," 210.
49. Cf. Charles Hartshorne, "Whitehead's Differences From Buddhism," 407.
50. Hartshorne, "Causal Necessities," 494.
51. Ibid., 480–1.
52. *IO*, 141.
53. Hartshorne, "The Intelligibility of Sensations," 172.
54. Hartshorne, "Neville on Temporality and God," 672.
55. Hartshorne, "Idealism and Our Experience of Nature," 78.
56. Ibid., 78 (Italics added). See also: "Whitehead's Differences from Buddhism," 408.
57. *IO*, 141. An effect is internally related to its cause; hence, there are real necessary connections between events. Such relations, however, are not such as to make any particular event necessary, only that a certain *kind* of event—relatively, but not absolutely, particularized) shall not remain a null class. Every event has a cause, and this determines to some extent its effect. But when the question is asked with regard to the extent of this determination, Hartshorne virulently opposes the definition of a cause as a "condition or set of conditions, from which only one outcome is possible, or from which, in principle or ideally, the outcome is wholly possible." Cf. *LP*, 163. To say that something is possible—from an absolutely deterministic viewpoint—is to say that we are ignorant concerning some details of what is *already* actual. And that if we were not so deficient in our knowledge of actuality, we would not be ignorant at all about the future. Perfect prediction would be possible. Cf. Hartshorne, "Causal Necessities," 480.
58. Ibid., 483.
59. Hartshorne, "The Meaning of 'Is Going To Be'," 51.
60. Ibid., 46–7.
61. *CSPM*, 225. See also: Hartshorne, *IO*, 139–40.
62. Hartshorne, "Causal Necessities," 483–4.
63. *CAP*, 65.
64. Cf. *MVG*, 100–1. See also his analysis in: "Causal Necessities," 487.
65. Cf. *CSPM*, 100. He calls these triads: "all," "some," and "none," the "keys to all philosophical problems." Cf. *MVG*, 100.
66. Hartshorne, "The Meaning of 'Is Going To Be,'" 48. He also calls this "thinking in trichotomies instead of dichotomies." Cf. *CSPM*, 100.
67. Hartshorne, "The Meaning of 'Is Going To Be,'" 49.
68. *CSPM*, 204.
69. Cf. Hartshorne, "Metaphysical Statements as Nonrestrictive and Existential," 40.
70. *CSPM*, 71.
71. See: Hartshorne, "Metaphysical Statements as Nonrestrictive and Existential," *Review of Metaphysics*, 40. Here he points out that emergence itself or "the deviation from absolute order, admits of an infinity of degrees in particular cases," which is why relative indeterminism (or relative determinism) has the complete

flexibility characteristic of nonrestrictive or metaphysically valid ideas. Absolute determinism or "absolute order" on the other hand, is the special or limiting case (of zero freedom and creativity). It is, says Hartshorne, not only impossible, but coincides with "absolute nothing."

72. In *Beyond Humanism,* Hartshorne suggests that there are three ways of understanding the meaning of "possible." (i) The first is that it "is merely a name for our ignorance of what is actual." "Will it be sunny this coming weekend?" To respond "possibly" means that we do not know that it will be, but also that we do not know that it will not be sunny. If we had knowledge of what exactly the case would be, we would not be speaking of "possibility," but simply of "true" and "false." (ii) The second has to do with the distinction between possibilities within nature as it exists and possibilities involving other natures as conceivable. "On this view," he says, "the possible is that which is conceivably existent, but which nevertheless has never existed, at no time in the past could have existed, and never will exist." This is the supernatural view of possibility. (iii) The third view is the indeterministic one. Here the "possible" is the realm of "what might be," but also of "what might not be"—i.e., in the future. Such view regards possibility as "an element of indecision in reality with reference to the future of events. It could very well be settled today that it will be sunny this weekend, but just how much sun there will be, how much wind and clouds would affect the day, etc., these, Hartshorne insists, "may not be determined by the laws of nature." Within this range of indeterminism, various amounts of sunshine and cloudiness are possible. This possibility, Hartshorne holds, "is a real or natural fact." Cf. *BH,* 130.

73. Cf. *LP,* 163.

74. Hartshorne, "Causal Necessities," 485.

75. See also Hartshorne's explanation in: "The Meaning of 'Is Going To Be,'" 55. Hartshorne uses the example of "choice" in his explanation. What is "settled" beforehand, in making a choice is not the choice itself, but only the "*range* of possibilities," the "antecedent conditions," including "the chooser's 'previous character'." The "choice" that is actually made is settled, only when the individual himself, at that point when he makes the choice, "then and there, determines the precise action itself."

76. *CSPM,* 102. It is in this regard that Hartshorne cautions against the uncritical use of the phrase necessary and sufficient condition. ("Necessary" refers to that without which an event will not occur; "sufficient," to that with which it will certainly occur.) With regard to events, Hartshorne argues that the totality of the necessary conditions is always sufficient for real possibility. However, this is not always the case when what we are dealing with is the specific or certain actualization of this possibility. If it is fully concrete and definite events (or effects) that we are talking about, there are no such necessary and sufficient conditions, and the phrase is only a first approximation to an explication of the causal principle. See also: Hartshorne, "Causal Necessities," 487; Hartshorne, "A Reply to My Critics," 575. Hartshorne further explains this cautionary note in relation to the antecedence of physiological data to subjective experience. He says that if the given is to be the antecedent cause which at the same time is independent of its effect (human experience), the necessary condition must not be in the strict sense "sufficient." "For 'necessary and sufficient' is the same as sufficient and necessary, and implies complete symmetry of dependence between cause and effect." As such, he holds that the phrase "contradicts our natural intuition of one-way dependence of effects on causes, as well as our intuition that experiences

depend on things experienced, not conversely." Cf. Hartshorne, "The Organism in Process Philosophy," 73.

77. See: Charles Hartshorne, "Royce's Mistake—and Achievement," *Journal of Philosophy*, 53/3 (February 1956): 125. Hartshorne regards the notion of "time-less truth" as "the ghost of medieval theology." Cf. Hartshorne, "Whitehead's Revolutionary Concept of Prehension," 262. Hartshorne holds that truth must indeed have all the definiteness of reality. But if all events throughout time are already definite—as for instance in the case of deity—then there would be no gen-uine novelty and creativity at all. There would then be no "reality-in-the-making," but only "reality-already-made." To face, not such a kind of future where all things are already made but one with a degree of openness, is a more realistic view of the character of the given universe, i.e., as a potentiality for further determination. See also: *LP*, 165; *MVG*, 246.

78. Hartshorne, "Royce's Mistake—and Achievement," 125.

79. Hartshorne, "Causal Necessities," 488. As such, the future is the realm of the intertwinement of chance and necessity. The factor of necessity being that an experience must somehow become datum for *some* further experience, while the chance factor (or the lack of necessity), dwells in the freedom or indeterminacy with regard to just *how* or in just *what* further experiences this status as datum may be brought about. See: Hartshorne, "Whitehead's Revolutionary Concept of Prehension," 256.

80. See: Hartshorne, "The Logical Structure of Givenness," 316.

81. Hartshorne, "Causal Necessities," 491.

82. Cf. Hartshorne, "Personal Identity from A to Z," 213; Hartshorne, "Causal Necessities," 492.

83. *CSPM*, 106–7.

84. Cf. Hartshorne, "Personal Identity from A to Z," 210–11. See also: Sia, *God in Process Thought*, 44–5.

85. Hartshorne, "Metaphysical Statements as Nonrestrictive and Existential," 40.

86. Hartshorne, "Personal Identity from A to Z," 215.

87. Cf. Sia, *God in Process Thought*, 45.

88. Hartshorne, "Personal Identity from A to Z," 213. Although presenting a critical stance toward Hartshorne's account of personal identity, Albert Shalom and John Robertson capture the inadequacy of the simply symmetrical view when it is the identity of "persons" that is being dealt with. Attitudes, tendencies, dis-positions, inherited character traits, are among some of the concepts that can-not be adequately given meaning by the strict view. Now granted that these issues may not in fact readily fall within the orbit of this narrow perspective, it nonetheless remains the case that the concepts implicated in this limited field of inquiry originate in the much wider fact of human experience of which self-identity (in the narrow sense) is but a datum. It is because we experience change and identity that we seek to make sense of them. How can we do so if they are immediately detached from the source of our reflection and afterwards never reconnected with it? Cf. Albert Shalom and John C. Robertson, Jr. "Hartshorne and the Problem of Personal Identity," *Process Studies*, 8/3 (Fall, 1978): 177. A treat-ment not dissimilar to this is found in Peter Bertocci's article discussing Hartshorne's theory. Like the two earlier authors, Bertocci expresses reservations with the Hartshornean account, but acknowledges that there is much in it that is consistent with what he finds "in experience." See: Peter A. Bertocci, "Hartshorne on Personal Identity: A Personalist Critique," *Process Studies*, 2/3 (Fall, 1972): 216.

The reservations which these authors express can be summed up in terms of the implications of the theory of the atomicity of process as applied to personal identity. Against this view, these authors hold that our common experience of our identity is one of continuity rather than discreteness. As Hartshorne rejects the continuous theory of becoming, he likewise rejects the simple notion of the identity of persons as simply continuous. As we shall see, personal identity too is understood in the neoclassical metaphysics as quantized.

89. *CSPM*, 182–4.

90. Hartshorne, "Personal Identity from A to Z," 210.

91. The evidence for the constitution of an event is to be found in subjective experience. In fact, our occasions of experience are themselves instances of actual entities. The method employed is an analysis of these occasions of subjective experience so as to discover factors which are susceptible of generalization into principles applicable to all actual entities. Cf. *PR*, 112n172: "In describing the capacities, realized or unrealized, of an actual occasion, we have [...] tacitly, taken human experience as an example upon which to found the generalized description required for metaphysics." See also: Lewis S. Ford, "From Pre-Panpsychism to Pansubjectivity," *Faith and Creativity*, eds., George Nordgulen and George W. Shields (St. Louis, Missouri: CBP Press, 1987), 41–61, esp. 59–60. Ford explains how subjectivity even underlies efficient causation as the present appropriation of the past. Experience goes "all the way down," and hence there is no absolute gulf distinguishing the structure of human experience and experience in its lowest form, even though this latter is "canalized into slavish conformity."

92. Cf. *CSPM*, 184: "... the latest self as new is the total concrete reality containing the former." This represents a spelling out of the notion peculiar to Process Thought of the persistence of the past in the present, or the concept of an actual entity's immanence in another. See: Sheilah O'Flynn Brennan, "Substance Within Substance," *Process Studies*, 7/1 (Spring, 1977): 14–26. Brennan quotes Whitehead who says: "... an actual entity is *present in* other actual entities," and that Process Philosophy is mainly devoted to the task of clarifying this notion. Cf. *PR*, 50n79f. See also: Lewis S. Ford, "Inclusive Occasions," *Process in Context: Essays in Post Whiteheadian Perspectives*, ed. Ernest Wolf-Gazo (New York: Peter Lang Publishers, 1988), 107–36. Ford explains the inclusion of one occasion of another by means of the Whiteheadian doctrine that "prehension is inclusion." He also argues that this notion, if sufficiently adjusted to make room for "larger, more inclusive occasions," is well-equipped to express the persistence of being, not only on the submolecular and molecular levels, but to all natural events, including higher level entities.

93. *PR*, 161n244.

94. Hartshorne, "Personal Identity from A to Z," 219.

95. From a tape-recorded lecture on Self-Identity, given by Charles Hartshorne at the Salons of the Hoger Instituut voor Wijsbegeerte, Katholieke Universiteit Leuven, 1978.

96. Sia, *God in Process Thought*, 44.

97. Cf. Hartshorne, "The Development of Process Philosophy," xiii. An analogy can be made here in the manner by which Hartshorne conceives these two types of personal identity, the abstract and the concrete, and the two poles of the divine reality. God being dipolar, also has an identity that is abstract—the primordial nature, and one that is concrete—the consequent nature. Cf. Charles Hartshorne, "The Dipolar Conception of Deity," *Review of Metaphysics*, 21/2 (December,

1967): 274–89. Not only are these two poles unisolable when one wishes to speak in as adequate a way as possible about the nature of the divine reality, it is likewise the case that the concrete pole (God's relative aspect) encompasses the abstract pole (God's absolute aspect). The latter, separated from the former, is not only "not the Biblical God," it is also hardly a God that is worthy of worship. The "philosophical absolute" is not a God before whom "man can pray nor sacrifice"—to use Heidegger's phrase. Before it "man can neither fall to his knees in awe nor play music and dance." Martin Heidegger, *Identität und Differenz* (Pfullingen: Neske, 1957), 45. Quoted from: Van der Veken and Cloots, "Can the God of Process Thought be Redeemed?" 126.

98. See: Jay McDaniel, "Zen and the Self," *Process Studies*, 10/3–4 (Fall–Winter, 1980): 110.

99. *CSPM*, 184.

100. Hartshorne, "Husserl and Whitehead on the Concrete," 97.

101. Although it must be noted that this does not mean that the positing of a "third term" is wholly useless or even unnecessary. (This topic will be discussed shortly, in relation to the notion of personal identity as analogous to the Platonic idea of a "receptacle" found in both Whitehead and Hartshorne).

102. *CSPM*, 184.

103. *WMW*, 36. Here Hartshorne decries the neglect of this fact by a majority of philosophers. He says that "most philosophers seem to regard the discovery of cells in biology as merely a tale told to them when they were young. For they speak of the body as though it were essentially one entity, one mass of stuff, 'material' aspect of one human individual. In fact, the body is a vast 'society of cells,' none of which is a human being, and any of which could (with minor modifications) conceivably exist and live in a suitable medium outside of any human organism."

104. Cf. Charles Hartshorne, "The Compound Individual," *Philosophical Essays for Alfred North Whitehead* (New York: Russell and Russell, 1936), 212–15. Also: *BH*, 170–2.

105. Cf. *PR*, 34n51; *AI*, 206.

106. *PR*, 20n30.

107. Of course even Hartshorne admits that in normal everyday use, the idea of an enduring individual is not only perfectly acceptable, it is likewise scarcely dispensable as a way of putting what the event terminology analyzes into event sequences or "societies." *CSPM*, 204. Further, the use of the language of "societies" should not be regarded simply as an analogous manner to the way contemporary physics describes the old impenetrable atom as actually composed of more elementary particles. Rather, even the most fundamental unitary actual entity is itself a composite of other actual entities mnemonically related to one another. "No actual concrete entity includes but a single entity distinguishable from itself .... Every concrete entity is a case of awareness or experience and an experience includes an irreducible and considerable complexity." Cf. Hartshorne, "Synthesis as Polydadic Inclusion," 249; also: Brennan, "Substance Within Substance," 21; Robert C. Neville, "Whitehead on the One and the Many," *Southern Journal of Philosophy*, 7/4 (Winter, 1970), 389. Neville points out that from the viewpoint of Process, "it is inconceivable that there be a many or a one except that one is conceived as *a unification* of many and many is conceived as a disjunction of such unifications of manys. The process of unifying many into one is creativity." And he quotes from *Process and Reality*, where

Whitehead says: "The novel entity is at once the togetherness of the 'many' which it finds, and also it is one among the disjunctive 'many' which it leaves. ... In their natures, entities are disjunctively 'many' in process of passage into conjunctive unity." *PR*, 21n32.

108. *WMW*, 37. Here Hartshorne puts forward the notion of "the universality of societies in the cosmos, at all levels," and he argues that "what is called an individual in common life (and much philosophy) can only be understood as a *form of sequence* of particular actualities socially inheriting a common quality from antecedent members," and finally, that "personality itself is a special temporally linear case of such social—that is, sympathetic—inheritance."

109. Charles Hartshorne, *Whitehead's Philosophy*. Selected Essays, 1935–1970 (Lincoln, Nebraska: University of Nebraska Press, 1972), 181.

110. Cf. Ibid., 13.

111. The mnemonic structure of awareness, as it was discussed earlier, ensures that such inheritance is explainable.

112. *PR*, 34n50, 34n51.

113. Hartshorne, "Personal Identity from A to Z," 211.

114. Hartshorne, "The Compound Individual," 215.

115. The analogy between a person's relation to this bodily/spatial components (cells) and a person's relation to his temporal constituents (other-selves) is itself analogous to the transference of energy from particular occasion to particular occasion in physical nature and the transference of affective tone, with its emotional energy, from one occasion to another in a human person. As Whitehead points out: "the object-to-subject structure of human experience is reproduced in physical nature by this vector relation of particular to particular." *AI*, 242.

116. *WP*,13.

117. Hartshorne, "Leibniz's Greatest Discovery," 420.

118. Hartshorne, "Personal Identity from A to Z," 212.

119. *WP*, 13.

120. Cf. *PR*, 34n51, 35n52.

121. Cf. Ibid., 187.

122. Hartshorne, "Personal Identity from A to Z," 215.

123. *BES*, 403.

124. Cf. Bertocci, "Hartshorne on Personal Identity: A Personalist Critique," *Process Studies*, 216–21.

125. Albert Shalom and John C. Robertson, Jr., "Hartshorne and the Problem of Personal Identity,"170.

126. Felt, "Intuition, Event-Atomism, and the Self," 137–53. See also: Edwards, "The Human Self: An Actual Entity or a Society?," *Process Studies*, 5/3 (Fall, 1975): 199–200. Edwards also criticizes the epochal notion of personhood and says that contrary to it, our experience of the self is "the self-experience of a continuously existing entity with *continuous* immediacy of self-enjoyment, significance for itself, subjective aims, subjective forms, satisfactions, synthetic experiencing, and self-creativity."

127. Shalom and Robertson, "Hartshorne and Personal Identity," 171. See also: Edwards, "The Human Self: An Actual Entity or a Society?" 198. Edwards goes so far as to criticize Whitehead for over-hastily generalizing from the discontinuity of temporal change at the microscopic level of quantum phenomena to the discontinuity of all temporal change within the created world, including

changes within the stream of human experience and activity. Felt, says that "the atomic successiveness of personal identity ... belongs not to the immediacy of the experience of the subject or subjects, but rather to an abstraction derived artificially by the intelligence from this lived immediacy. The living reality of personal identity ... shows itself as an unbroken but growing and varied unity, a continuity of qualitative heterogeneity. The 'I' of personal identity is constituted by this very continuity" in "Intuition, Event-Atomism, and the Self,'" 152. Peter Bertocci expresses similar difficulties when he says that "at no point am I a succession of unit-events. I am an experient who is a self-identifying unity without which there would be no meaning for 'succession,'" and further that "there is nothing in my experience of myself that justifies my calling myself a synthesis of successive moments" in "Hartshorne on Personal Identity: A Personalist Critique," *Process Studies*, 217–18. See also Joseph A. Bracken, "Proposals for Overcoming the Atomism Within Process-Relational Metaphysis," *Process Studies*, 23/1 (Spring, 1994), 10. In this article Bracken acknowledges that Whitehead's notion that momentary subjects of experience are, like the physical reality of quantum physics, made up of discrete units, poses a certain difficulty in accounting for the experience of the human self as a continuously existing reality.

128. Cf. Milič Čapek, "The Reappearance of the Self in the Last Philosophy of William James," *The Philosophical Review*, 62/4 (October, 1953): 526–44.

129. *BH*, 122. Čapek quotes this line from Hartshorne in a footnote to the article on memory. Cf. Čapek, "Immediate and Mediate Memory," 95–6n4.

130. *BH*, 122. The "fullness" of God's awareness does not in any way change the basic doctrine espoused by Hartshorne that God, like us, knows the past as past, the present as present, the future as future. The difference is not absolute, but one of degree.

131. Bertocci, "Hartshorne on Personal Identity: A Personalist Critique," *Process Studies*, 219. The point being made here is not so much that the "unified" experience implied by hypermnesia is precisely what our normal experience of the self is. This obviously is not the case. Rather, the point is that what transpires in cases of hypermnesia seems much more congruent with our ordinary experience of selfhood, rather than the discontinuous account proposed by Hartshorne which, as other critics point out, "dissolves [the self] horizontally into a series of episodes." Cf. Shalom and Robertson, "Hartshorne and the Problem of Personal Identity," 176.

132. Cf. Edwards, "The Human Self: An Actual Entity or a Society?," 195–203.

133. He quotes from *Science and the Modern World*, where Whitehead calls attention to gaps between microscopic quantum events: "(i) An electron does not continuously traverse its path in space ... it appears at a series of discrete positions in space which it occupies for successive durations of time. It is as though an automobile, moving at the average rate of thirty miles an hour along a road, did not traverse the road continuously; but appeared successively at the successive milestones, remaining for two minutes at each milestone. (ii) The path in space of such a vibratory entity—where the entity is *constituted* by the vibrations—must be represented by a series of detached positions in space, analogously to the automobile which is found at successive milestones and at nowhere between.(iii) The discontinuities introduced by the quantum theory require revision of physical concepts in order to meet them. In particular, it has been pointed out that some theory of discontinuous existence is required. What is asked from such theory, is that an orbit of an electron can be regarded as a series

of detached positions, and not as a continuous line." Ibid. Quotes taken from *SMW*, 52, 54, and 196 respectively.

134. Ibid., 198.

135. Robert Fancher, "Of Time, the Self, and Rem Edwards," *Process Studies*, 7/1 (Spring, 1977): 14–26. The nontemporal dimension of God is of course reconciled with his dependence on the temporal world *via* the doctrine of divine dipolarity.

136. This is how Randall Morris describes the difference-within-similarity between God as actual entity, and other nondivine actual entities. Cf. Morris, *Process Philosophy and Political Ideology*, 35. Here as well lies the subtle distinction between the Hartshornean and Whiteheadian views. First, as Morris states, the deity for Whitehead is a nontemporal entity. Second, Morris argues that the Whiteheadian understanding of God as "an actual entity of a peculiar sort"—which Edwards has interpreted to mean that God is an exception—merely implies that "at this stage of his thought God is not yet a dipolar actuality." For the notion of God's consequent nature is in fact a "secondary development of Whitehead's metaphysical system." Originally Whitehead had conceived of God as a purely nontemporal actual entity. Lewis Ford corroborates this development in Whitehead's notion of God, pointing out that it was only during the fall and winter of 1927–8 that Whitehead "modified his view by attaching notes to what he had written and by composing the rest of part III (of *Process and Reality*), and it was only actually before the Gifford lectures were delivered that "he found that his researches into the nature of consciousness showed that if God were to be conscious, he would need a second, temporal, consequent nature." See: Lewis S. Ford, "A Guide to Whitehead," *Teaching Philosophy*, 7/2 (April, 1984): 145.

137. Hartshorne, "A Reply to My Critics," 642.

138. Cf. Cloots and Van der Veken, "Can the God of Process Thought be Redeemed?," 131.

139. Cf. *PR*, nos. 521–24, pp. 343–6. This, Hartshorne says, is also largely behind his refusal to use the Whiteheadian term "perishing." The essential structure of prehension, which for Hartshorne is "applicable even to God," requires that the creative synthesis must always have a structure of a one-way dependence of prehending upon prehended entities, and because of this, the creative synthesis itself is constituted by other-selves (past ones) that enter into the constitution of other-selves (presently concrescing ones), which then enter into still later ones, and so on until the subject is complete. God, of course, is never complete. Still, the foregoing notions, "requires us to define God as an enduring society of actualities, not a single actuality." Cf. Hartshorne, "The Dipolar Conception of Deity," 287.

140. Hartshorne, "A Reply to My Critics," 642.

141. Shalom and Robertson, "Hartshorne and the Problem of Personal Identity," 178. This incompleteness of deity is ultimately what is behind Hartshorne's rejection of the Whiteheadian notion of God as an actual entity. For as Hartshorne argues, it is "just what it cannot be, in the system in which every actuality is a unit-becoming in its concreteness." Cf. Charles Hartshorne, "Whitehead and Contemporary Philosophy," *The Relevance of Whitehead, Philosophical Essays in Commemoration of the Centenary of the Birth of Alfred North Whitehead*, ed. Ivor Leclerc (Bristol: Thoemmes Press, 1993), 26. The only point when something actually *is* is when it is no longer. For Hartshorne, there is no such thing as a "no longer" for God, no "perishing." "If God were a concrete singular, he would be

but an episode in cosmic becoming." See: Hartshorne, "Whitehead and Ordinary Language," 441.

142. Fancher, "Of Time, the Self, and Rem Edwards," 41.

143. Edwards, "The Human Self: An Actual Entity or a Society?," 198.

144. Bertocci, "Hartshorne on Personal Identity: A Personalist Critique," *Process Studies*, 217.

145. Edwards, "The Human Self: An Actual Entity or a Society?" 199. The reasons Edwards gives for his argument require some attention as he, like other critics of the epochal notion of selfhood, brings in a justified point of criticism, and a philosophically and experientially valid observation of the character of the self.

146. Ibid.

147. Ibid., 200.

148. Felt, "Intuition, Event-Atomism, and the Self," 141.

149. Edwards, "The Human Self: An Actual Entity or a Society?" 200.

150. Ibid. And this is in fact the case, notwithstanding Edwards' insistence that the "continuing self" is not the same as Descartes' thinking substance or Kant's noumenal ego which lies outside all space and time and which underlies the continuing creative agency.

151. Felt, "Intuition, Event-Atomism, and the Self," 149.

152. Edwards, "The Human Self: An Actual Entity or a Society?," 199; Shalom and Robertson, "Hartshorne and the Problem of Personal Identity,"172–3; Felt, "Intuition, Event-Atomism, and the Self," 143–4.

153. Felt, "Intuition, Event-Atomism, and the Self," 142–4.

154. Ibid., 150.

155. Bertocci, "Hartshorne on Personal Identity: A Personalist Critique," *Process Studies*, 217.

156. Robert Fancher points this out clearly in his rejoinder to the Edwards article. Cf. Fancher, "Of Time, the Self, and Rem Edwards," 42.

157. Edwards, "The Human Self: An Actual Entity or a Society?," *Process Studies*, 197.

158. Hartshorne, "A Reply to My Critics," 644.

159. Hartshorne, "The Development of Process Philosophy," xv.

160. Fancher, "Of Time, the Self, and Rem Edwards," 41. (Italics added.)

161. Hartshorne, "Continuity: The Form of Forms in Charles Peirce," 531.

162. *CSPM*, 194.

163. Ibid., 195.

164. *AI*, 187.

165. *WMW*, 31.

166. Hartshorne, "Metaphysical Statements as Nonrestrictive and Existential," 40.

167. Hartshorne, "Leibniz's Greatest Discovery," 420.

168. Cf. *CSPM*, 184–6.

169. *WMW*, 32: "*All* personal character, indeed, is abstract, neutral, free from wholly determinate limits, and is a principle or potency of actualization, rather than any actual entity."

170. *AI*, 233.

171. Charles Hartshorne, "The Ethics of Contributionism," 103. See also Hartshorne's related treatment of "contributionism" as the ultimate form of sociality, explained in terms of "the present, which enjoys contributions from past experience, regards itself as a contribution offered to the future as such." Cf. Hartshorne, "Idealism and Our Experience of Nature," 78.

172. Cf. Hartshorne, "The Development of Process Philosophy," xv.

173. Charles Hartshorne, "Response to Manley Thompson on Individuals and Continuity," *Existence and Actuality: Conversations with Charles Hartshorne*, eds., John B. Cobb, Jr. and Franklin I. Gamwell (Chicago and London: The University of Chicago Press, 1984), 147.
174. Hartshorne, "Whitehead's Revolutionary Concept of Prehension," 260. (Italics added.)
175. Cf. Hartshorne, "Lewis' Treatment of Memory," 407.
176. That which genuinely "individuates" us, namely, our relationality, is genuinely spatiotemporal. Cf. Hartshorne, "Personal Identity from A to Z," 214.
177. For the relation (continuity) between these two forms of relationality, see Part III: "From Physiological Data to Environmental Knowledge," Hartshorne, "The Organism According to Process Philosophy," 74–6.
178. *RSP*, 64.
179. Cf. Hartshorne, "The Development of Process Philosophy," xiii.
180. Shalom and Robertson, "Hartshorne and the Problem of Personal Identity," 177–8.
181. Hartshorne, "Whitehead's Differences From Buddhism," 407.
182. *CSPM*, 197.
183. Hartshorne, "Personal Identity from A to Z," 213.
184. Hartshorne, "The Social Structure of Experience," 106. Hartshorne states that the query "Can I know another's feelings as directly as I know my own?" is hardly distinguishable from the question, "Can I, as it were, 'remember' the feelings of another?"
185. Hartshorne, "Lewis' Treatment of Memory," 403.
186. Cf. Hartshorne, "The Social Structure of Experience," 108–9.
187. Hartshorne, "The Social Structure of Experience," 108. See also: Hartshorne, "Lewis' Treatment of Memory," 403.
188. Hartshorne, "Causal Necessities," *The Philosophical Review*, 493.
189. Hartshorne, "Whitehead's Differences From Buddhism," *Philosophy East & West*, 407.
190. Hartshorne, "Berdyaev as a Philosopher," xii. See also: Hartshorne, "Beyond Enlightened Self-Interest," 397.
191. See: Charles Hartshorne, "Martin Buber's Metaphysics," *The Philosophy of Martin Buber*, Vol. XII of The Library of Living Philosophers, ed. Paul Arthur Schilpp (La Salle, Illinois: Open Court, 1967), 50.
192. Ibid., 55.
193. *RSP*, 64.
194. Belaief, *Towards a Whiteheadian Ethics*, 56.

Conclusion

1. Ricoeur, *Oneself as Another*, 18.
2. *CSPM*, 13.

Bibliography

Works by Charles Hartshorne[1]

HARTSHORNE, Charles. "Continuity, the Form of Forms, in Charles Peirce." *Monist* 39/4 (October, 1929): 531–4.

"Contingency and the New Era in Metaphysics." *The Journal of Philosophy* 29 (1932): 457–69.

"The Intelligibility of Sensations." *The Monist* 44/2 (July, 1934): 161–85.

"The New Metaphysics and Current Problems." *New Frontiers* 1/1 (September, 1934): 90–101.

"The Parallel Development of Method in Physics and Psychology." *Philosophy of Science* 1/4 (October, 1934): 446–59.

"Metaphysics for Positivists." *Philosophy of Science* 2/1 (January, 1935): 287–303.

"The Compound Individual." *Philosophical Essays for Alfred North Whitehead.* New York: Russel and Russel, 1936, pp. 193–220.

"Review of Rasvihari Das." *The Philosophical Review* 48/2 (March, 1939): 230–1.

"Whitehead's Idea of God." *The Philosophy of Alfred North Whitehead.* The Library of Living Philosophers. Ed. Paul Arthur Schilpp. Evanston and Chicago: Northwestern University Press, 1941, pp. 515–59.

"Efficient Causality in Aristotle and St. Thomas." Review of Francis X. Meehan. Washington: Catholic University Press, 1940. *Journal of Religion* 25/1 (January, 1945): 25–32.

"Leibniz's Greatest Discovery." *Journal of the History of Ideas* 7/14 (October, 1946): 411–21.

The Divine Relativity: A Social Conception of God. New Haven and London: Yale University Press, 1948.

"Panpsychism." *A History of Philosophical Systems.* Ed. Vergilius Ferm. New York: Philosophical Library, 1950, pp. 442–53.

Whitehead and the Modern World: Science, Metaphysics, and Civilization; Three Essays on the thought of Alfred North Whitehead. Coauthored with Victor Lowe and A.H. Johnson. Boston: Beacon Press, 1950.

"Whitehead's Idea of God." *The Philosophy of Alfred North Whitehead.* The Library of Living Philosophers. Ed. Paul Arthur Schilpp. New York: Tudor Publishing, 1951, pp. 515–59.

"Paul Tillich's Doctrine of God." *The Theology of Paul Tillich.* The Library of Living Theology. Volume I. Eds. Charles W. Kegley and Robert Bretall. New York: Macmillan, 1952, pp. 164–95.

"The Immortality of the Past: A Critique of a Prevalent Misinterpretation." *Review of Metaphysics* 7/1 (September, 1953): 98–112.

"Monistic Theory of Expression." *Journal of Philosophy* 50/14 (July 2, 1953): 425–4.

---

[1]For a complete bibliography of Charles Hartshorne's works, see Santiago Sia, *Religion, Reason and God: Essays in the Philosophies of Charles Hartshorne and A.N. Whitehead* (Peter Lang Publishers, 2004): 195–223.

Philosophers Speak of God. Coauthored with William L. Reese. Chicago: University of Chicago Press, 1953.

"Causal Necessities: An Alternative to Hume." *Philosophical Review* 43/4 (October, 1954): 479–99.

"Royce's Mistake and Achievement." *Journal of Philosophy* 53/3 (February, 1956): 123–30.

"Whitehead and Berdyaev: Is There Tragedy in God?" *The Journal of Religion* 37/2 (April, 1957): 71–84.

"Metaphysical Statements as Nonrestrictive and Existential." *Review of Metaphysics* 12/1 (September, 1958): 35–47.

"The Logical Structure of Givenness." *The Philosophical Quarterly* 8/33 (October, 1958): 307–16.

"The Philosophy of Creative Synthesis." *The Journal of Philosophy* 55/22 (October 23, 1958): 944–53.

"A Philosophers Assessment of Christianity." *Religion and Culture: Essays in Honor of Paul Tillich.* Ed. Walter Leibrecht. New York: Harper, 1959.

"Hume's Metaphysics and Its Present-Day Influence." *The New Scholasticism* 35/2 (April, 1961): 152–71.

"The Social Structure of Experience." *Philosophy: The Journal of the Royal Institute of Philosophy* 37/137 (April and July, 1961): 97–111.

The Logic of Perfection. La Salle, Illinois: Open Court, 1962.

"Religion and Creative Experience." *Darshana: An International Quarterly of Philosophy, Psychology, Physical Research, Religion, Mysticism, and Sociology* (India) 2/1 (January, 1962): 47–52.

"Introduction to the Second Edition." *Anselm's Proslogium, Monologium, Cur Deus Homo, and Gaunilo's in Behalf of the Fool.* La Salle, Illinois: Open Court, 1962, pp. 3–21.

"Sensation in Psychology and Philosophy." *Southern Journal of Philosophy* 1/2 (1963): 3–14.

"The Social Theory of Feelings." *Southern Journal of Philosophy* 3/2 (Summer, 1963): 87–93.

Man's Vision of God and the Logic of Theism. Hamden, Connecticut: Archon Books, 1964.

"The Development of Process Philosophy." *Introduction to Philosophers of Process.* Ed. Douglas Browning. New York: Random House, 1965, pp. v–xii.

"The Meaning of 'Is Going to Be.'" *Mind* 74/293 (January, 1965): 46–58.

"Idealism and Our Experience of Nature." *Philosophy, Religion, and the Coming World Civilization: Essays in Honor of William Ernest Hocking.* Ed. Leroy S. Rouner. The Hague: Martinus Nijhoff, 1966, pp. 70–80.

A Natural Theology for Our Time. La Salle, Illinois: Open Court, 1967.

"Religion in Process Philosophy." *Religion in Philosophical and Cultural Perspective.* Eds. J. Clayton Feaver and William Horosz. Princeton: Van Nostrand, 1967, pp. 246–68.

"The Significance of Man in the Life of God." *Theology in Crisis: A Colloqium on 'The Credibility of God.'* New Concord, Ohio: Muskingham College, 1967, pp. 40–3.

"Martin Buber's Metaphysics." *The Philosophy of Martin Buber.* The Library of Living Philosophers. Vol. XII. Ed. Paul Arthur Schilpp. La Salle, Illinois: Open Court, 1967, pp. 49–68.

"The Dipolar Conception of Deity." *Review of Metaphysics* 21/2 (December, 1967): 273–85.

"Berdyaev as Philosopher." Preface to David Bonner Richardson, *Berdyaev's Philosophy of History: An Existentialist Theory of Social Creativity and Eschatology.* The Hague: Martinus Nijhoff, 1968, pp. ix–xiii.

"Husserl and the Social Structure of Immediacy." *Philosophical Essays in Memory of Edmund Husserl.* Ed. Marvin Farber. New York: Greenwood Press, 1968, pp. 219–30.

The Philosophy and Psychology of Sensation. Port Washington, New York: Kennikat Press, 1968.

"Process Philosophy as a Resource for Christian Thought." *Philosophical Resources for Christian Thought.* Ed. Perry LeFevre. Nashville: Abingdon Press, 1968, pp. 44–66.

Beyond Humanism: Essays in the Philosophy of Nature. Lincoln, Nebraska: University of Nebraska Press, 1969.

"Response." *Charles Hartshorne and Henry Nelson Wieman.* Ed. Wm. S. Minor. New York: University Press of America, 1969, pp. 33–42.

"The God of Religion and the God of Philosophy." *Talk of God: Royal Institute of Philosophy Lectures.* Volume II: 1967–1968. London: Macmillan, 1969, pp. 152–67.

"Whitehead in French Perspective: A Review Article." *The Thomist* 33/3 (July, 1969): 573–81.

Creative Synthesis and Philosophic Method. London: SCM Press, 1970.

"The Development of My Philosophy." *Contemporary American Philosophy.* Ed. John E. Smith. London: Allen and Unwin, 1970, pp. 211–28.

Reality as Social Process: Studies in Metaphysics and Religion. New York: Hafner, 1971.

"Whitehead's Metaphysics." *Whitehead and the Modern World: Science, Metaphysics, and Civilization.* Eds. Victor Lowe, Charles Hartshorne, and A.H. Johnson. New York: Beacon Press, 1972, pp. 25–41.

Whitehead's Philosophy. Selected Essays 1935–1970. Lincoln: University of Nebraska, 1972.

"Husserl and Whitehead on the Concrete." *Phenomenology: Continuation and Criticism: Essays in Memory of Dorion Cairns.* Eds. F. Kersten and R. Zaner. Den Haag: Martinus Nijhoff, 1973, pp. 90–104.

"Ideas and Theses of Process Philosophers." *Two Process Philosophers: Hartshorne's Encounter with Whitehead.* AAR Studies in Religion 5. Ed. Lewis S. Ford. Tallahassee: American Academy of Religion, 1973, pp. 100–3.

"Ideas and Theses of Process Philosophers." *Two Process Philosophers: Hartshorne's Encounter with Whitehead.* Ed. Lewis S. Ford. AAR Studies in Religion 5. Tallahassee: American Academy of Religion, 1973, pp. 100–3.

"Process and the Nature of God." *Traces of God in a Secular Culture.* Ed. George McLean. New York: Alba House, 1973, pp. 117–41.

"Philosophy after Fifty Years." *Mid-Twentieth Century American Philosophy: Personal Statements.* Ed. Peter A. Bertocci. New York: Humanities Press, 1974, pp. 140–54.

"Whitehead's Differences from Buddhism." *Philosophy East and West* 25/4 (October, 1975): 407–13.

Aquinas to Whitehead: Seven Centuries of Metaphysics of Religion. The Aquinas Lecture, 1976. Milwaukee: Marquette University Press, 1976.

"Synthesis as Polyadic Inclusion: A Reply to Sessions." *Southern Journal of Philosophy* 14/2 (Summer, 1976): 245–55.

"Bell's Theorem and Stapp's Revised View of Space-Time." *Process Studies* 7/3 (Fall, 1977): 183–91.

"Beyond Enlightened Self-Interest." *Process Philosophy: Basic Writings.* Eds. J.R. Sibley and P.A.Y. Gunter. New York: University Press of America, 1978, pp. 393–417. Reprinted from: *Ethics: An International Journal of Social, Political, and Legal Philosophy* 84/3 (April, 1974): 21–6. Reprinted as Chapter 12 of Mohammad

Valady ed., *The Zero Fallacy and Other Essays in Neoclassical Philosophy*. Chicago and La Salle, Illinois: Open Court, 1997, pp. 185–202.

"A World of Organisms." *Process Philosophy: Basic Writings*. Eds. Jack R. Sibley and Pete A.Y. Gunter. New York: University Press of America, 1978, pp. 275–96.

"Can We Understand God?" Inaugural Lecture at the Katholieke Universiteit Leuven, 4 October 1978. *Louvain Studies* 7 (1978): 75–84.

"Panpsychism: Mind as Sole Reality." *Ultimate Reality and Meaning* 1/2 (1978): 242–55.

"Whitehead's Revolutionary Concept of Prehension." *International Philosophical Quarterly* 19/3 (September, 1979): 253–63.

"In Defense of Wordsworth's View of Nature." *Philosophy and Literature* 4/1 (Spring, 1980): 80–91.

"My Neoclassical Metaphysics." *Tijdschrift voor Filosofie* 42/1 (March, 1980): 3–10.

"The Ethics of Contributionism." *Responsibilities to Future Generations: Environmental Ethics*. Ed. Ernest Partridge. New York: Prometheus, 1981, pp. 103–7.

Whitehead's View of Reality. Coauthored with Creighton Peden. New York: Pilgrim Press, 1981.

Insights and Oversights of Great Thinkers: An Evaluation of Western Philosophy. New York: State University of New York Press, 1983.

Creativity in American Philosophy. New York: State University of New York Press, 1984.

"God and the Meaning of Life." *On Nature*. Ed. Leroy Rouner. Boston University Studies in Philosophy and Religion. Notre Dame: University of Notre Dame Press, 1984, pp. 154–68.

Omnipotence and Other Theological Mistakes. Albany, New York: State University of New York Press, 1984.

"Response to Eugene Peters." *Existence and Actuality: Conversations with Charles Hartshorne*. Eds. John B. Cobb and Franklin I. Gamwell. Chicago: The University of Chicago Press, 1984, pp. 12–15.

"A Metaphysics of Universal Freedom." *Faith and Creativity: Essays in Honor of Eugene H. Peters*. Eds. George Nordgulen and George W. Shields. St. Louis, Missouri: CBP Press, 1987, pp. 27–40.

Wisdom as Moderation: A Philosophy of the Middle Way. New York: State University of New York Press, 1987.

"The Organism according to Process Philosophy." *Process in Context: Essays in Post-Whiteheadian Perspectives*. Ed. Ernest Wolf-Gazo. New York: Peter Lang Publishing, 1988, pp. 69–93.

"General Remarks." *Hartshorne: Process Philosophy and Theology*. Eds. Robert Kane and Stephen H. Phillips. New York: State University of New York Press, 1989.

"Devlin on Metaphysical Asymmetry." *The Philosophy of Charles Hartshorne*. Vol. XX of The Library of Living Philosophers. Ed. Lewis Edwin Hahn. La Salle, Illinois: Open Court, 1991, pp. 630–3.

"Hospers on the Aesthetics of Sensation." *The Philosophy of Charles Hartshorne*. Vol. XX of The Library of Living Philosophers. Ed. Lewis Edwin Hahn. La Salle, llinois: Open Court, 1991, pp. 600–5.

"Kane on Freedom and Sufficient Reason." *The Philosophy of Charles Hartshorne*. Vol. XX of The Library of Living Philosophers. Ed. Lewis Edwin Hahn. La Salle, Illinois: Open Court, 1991, pp. 606–13.

"Kegley on Royce and Community." *The Philosophy of Charles Hartshorne*. Vol. XX of The Library of Living Philosophers. Ed. Lewis Edwin Hahn. La Salle, Illinois: Open Court, 1991, pp. 620–3.

"King on Buddhism, Hierarchy, and Reason." *The Philosophy of Charles Hartshorne.* Vol. XX of The Library of Living Philosophers. Ed. Lewis Edwin Hahn. La Salle, Illinois: Open Court, 1991, pp. 624–7.

"An Open Letter to Carl Sagan." *The Journal of Speculative Philosophy* 5/4 (1991): 227–32.

"Reese on Panentheism and God's Goodness." *The Philosophy of Charles Hartshorne.* Vol. XX of The Library of Living Philosophers. Ed. Lewis Edwin Hahn. La Salle, Illinois: Open Court, 1991, pp. 616–17.

"A Reply to My Critics." *The Philosophy of Charles Hartshorne.* Vol. XX of The Library of Living Philosophers. Ed. Lewis Edwin Hahn. La Salle, Illinois: Open Court, 1991, pp. 567–84.

"Some Causes of My Intellectual Growth." *The Philosophy of Charles Hartshorne.* Vol. XX of The Library of Living Philosophers. Ed. Lewis Edwin Hahn. La Salle, Illinois: Open Court, 1991, pp. 3–45.

"Van der Veken on God and the Ultimate." *The Philosophy of Charles Hartshorne.* Vol. XX of The Library of Living Philosophers. Ed. Lewis Edwin Hahn. La Salle, Illinois: Open Court, 1991, pp. 617–19.

"Viney on My Psychology of Sensation." *The Philosophy of Charles Hartshorne.* Vol. XX of The Library of Living Philosophers. Ed. Lewis Edwin Hahn. La Salle, Illinois: Open Court, 1991, pp. 598–99.

"Inadequate Comments about Comments on My Writings and Ideas." *Process Studies* 21/2 (Summer, 1992): 123–9.

"Whitehead and Contemporary Philosophy." *The Relevance of Whitehead: Philosophical Essays in Commemoration of the Centenary of the Birth of Alfred North Whitehead.* Ed. Ivor Leclerc. Bristol: Thoemmes Press, 1993, pp. 21–43.

The Zero Fallacy and Other Essays in Neoclassical Philosophy. Ed. Mohammad Valady. Chicago and La Salle, Illinois: Open Court, 1997.

Secondary references

AARON, Richard I. and Joeelyn GIBB. Ed. *An Early Draft of Locke's Essay together with Excerpts from His Journal.* Oxford: Clarendon Press, 1936.

ADAMS, James Luther. "The Lure of Persuasion: Some Themes From Whitehead." *Process Philosophy and Social Thought.* Eds. John B. Cobb, Jr. and W. Widdick Schroeder. Chicago: Center for the Scientific Study of Religion, 1981, pp. 115–31.

ALEXANDER, Peter. "Locke on Substance-in-General: Part I." *Ratio* 22/2 (December 1980): 91–105.

———. "Locke on Substance-in-General: Part II." *Ratio* 23/1 (June 1981): 1–19.

ALEXANDER, Ronald G. *The Self, Supervenience, and Personal Identity.* Avebury Series in Philosophy. Aldershot: Ashgate, 1997.

ALLAIRE, E.B. "The Attack on Substance: Descartes to Hume." *David Hume: Critical Assessments.* Volume III. Ed. Stanley Tweyman. London: Routledge, 1995, pp. 73–6.

ALLISON, Henry E. "Locke's Theory of Personal Identity: A Re-Examination." *Locke on Human Understanding: Selected Essays.* Ed. I.C. Tipton. Oxford: Oxford University Press, 1977, pp. 105–22.

ALSTON, W.P. "Locke on People and Substances." Coauthored with J. Bennett. *Philosophical Review* 97 (1988): 25–46.

ANSCOMBE, G.E.M. "The First Person." *Self-Knowledge.* Ed. Quassim Cassam. Oxford: Oxford University Press, pp. 140–59.

AQUINAS, Thomas. *Summa Theologica.* Trans. Fathers of the English Dominican province. 5 Vols. Westminster, Maryland: Benziger, 1948.

————. "Recent Empirical Disconfirmation of Whitehead's Relativity Theory." *Process Studies* 4/4 (Winter, 1974): 285–7.

ARISTOTLE. *The Categories*. Trans. Harold P. Cooke. The Loeb Classical Library. Cambridge, Massachusetts: Harvard University Press, and London: William Heinemann, 1938. Reprint 1967, pp. 2–109.

————. *Metaphysics*. Books I–IX. Trans. Hugh Tredenick. The Loeb Classical Library. Cambridge, Massachusetts, Harvard University Press, and London: William Heinemann, 1936. Reprint 1968. (Books X–XIV, 1935, reprint 1962, pp. 2–320.)

————. *Physics*. Book II. Trans. Philip H. Wicksteed and Francis M. Cornford. The Loeb Classical Library. Cambridge, Massachusetts: Harvard University Press, and London: William Heinemann, 1934. Reprint 1968.

————. *Posterior Analytics*. Trans. G.R.G. Mure. *The Works of Aristotle*. Vol. I. Ed. W.D. Ross. London: Oxford University Press, 1928. Reprint 1971.

ARMSTRONG, D.M. "Introspection: The First Person." *Self-Knowledge*. Ed. Quassim Cassam. Oxford: Oxford University Press, pp. 109–17.

ASHMORE, Jerome. "Diverse Currents in Whitehead's View of Time." *Process Studies* 2/3 (Fall, 1972): 193–200.

AUGUSTINE. *The City of God*. Trans. Marcus Dodds. New York: Random House, 1950.

————. *Confessions*. Trans. E.B. Pusey. London: J.M. Dent and Sons, 1949.

AYERS, Michael, R. "The Ideas of Power and Substance in Locke's Philosophy." *Philosophical Quarterly* 25/98 (January 1975): 1–27.

————. *Locke*. Volume II: Ontology. London and New York: Routledge, 1991. Part I: Substance and Mode, pp. 15–28. Part III: Identity, pp. 205–96.

BAARS, Conrad. *Healing the Unaffirmed: Recognizing Deprivation Neurosis*. Coauthored with Anna Terruwe. New York: Alba House, 1972.

BAILLIE, James. *Problems in Personal Identity*. Paragon Issues in Philosophy. New York: Paragon House, 1993.

BAKER, John Robert. "Omniscience and Divine Synchronization." *Process Studies* 2/3 (Fall, 1972): 201–9.

BARBOUR, Ian. Ed. "Attitudes toward Nature and Technology." *Earth Might Be Fair: Reflections on Ethics, Religion, and Ecology*. Englewood Cliffs: Prentice-Hall, 1972.

————. *Issues in Science and Religion*. New York: Harper and Row, 1966.

BARRETT, William. *Death of the Soul: From Descartes to the Computer*. New York: Oxford University Press, 1987.

BARROW, John D. and Frank J. TIPLER. *The Anthropic Cosmological Principle*. Oxford: Oxford University Press, 1986.

BASINGER, David. *Divine Power in Process Theism: A Philosophical Critique*. SUNY Series in Philosophy. Ed. Robert C. Neville. Albany, New York: State University of New York Press, 1988.

BEHAN, David P. "Hume's Labyrinth." *David Hume: Critical Assessments*. Volume III. Ed. Stanley Tweyman. London and New York: Routledge, 1995, pp. 718–29.

————. "Locke on Persons and Personal Identity." *Canadian Journal of Philosophy* 9/1 (March 1979): 53–75. (Reprinted in John *Locke: Critical Assessments*. Volume IV. Ed. Richard Ashcroft. London and New York: Routledge, 1991, 564–85.)

BELAIEF, Lynne. "A Whiteheadian Account of Value and Identity." *Process Studies* 5/1 (Spring, 1975): 31–46.

————. *Toward a Whiteheadian Ethics*. Lanham, MD: University of America Press, 1984.

BENNETT, Jonathan. "Locke's Philosophy of Mind." *The Cambridge Companion to Locke*. Ed. Vere Chappell. New York: Cambridge University Press, 1994.

BERGSON, Henri. *The Creative Mind*. New Jersey: Totowa, 1963.

————. *Matter and Memory*. Trans. N. M. Paul and W. S. Palmer. New York: Zone Books, 1994.

————. *Time and Freewill*. New York: Harper and Row, 1910.

BERKELEY, George. *A Treatise Concerning the Principles of Human Knowledge*. Indianapolis: Bobbs-Merill, 1957.

BERTOCCI, Peter A. "Hartshorne on Personal Identity: A Personalistic Critique." *Process Studies* 2/3 (Fall, 1972): 216–21.

————. *The Goodness of God*. Washington, DC: University Press of America, 1981.

BIRCH, Charles. "Chance, Purpose, and Darwinism." *The Philosophy of Charles Hartshorne*. Vol. XX of The Library of Living Philosophers. Ed. Lewis Edwin Hahn. La Salle, Illinois: Open Court, 1991, pp. 51–63.

BLYTH, John. *Whitehead's Theory of Knowledge*. Providence, RI: Brown University Press, 1941.

BOETHIUS. *The Theological Tractates*. Trans. H.F. Stewart and E.K. Rand. Cambridge: Massachusetts, 1968.

BOHM, David. "The Implicate Order: A New Approach to the Nature of Reality." *Beyond Mechanism: The Universe in Recent Physics and Catholic Thought*. Ed. David L. Schindler. New York: University Press of America, 1986. 13–37.

————. "The Implicate Order: A New Order for Physics." Ed. Dean R. Fowler. *Process Studies* 8/2 (Summer, 1978): 73–102.

————. *Wholeness: The Implicate Order*. London: Routledge and Kegan Paul, 1980.

BOLTON, Martha Brandt. "Substances, Substrata, and Names of Substances in Locke's Essay." *Philosophical Review* 85/4 (October 1976): 488–513.

BOYLE, Marjorie O'Rourke. "Interpoints: A Model for Divine Spacetime." *Process Studies* 5/3 (Fall, 1975): 191–4.

BRACKEN, Joseph A. "Proposals for Overcoming the Atomism within Process-Relational Metaphysics." *Process Studies* 23/1 (Spring, 1994): 10–22.

————. *The Triune Symbol: Persons, Process and Community*. College Theology Society Studies in Religion 1. Lanham, MD: University Press of America, 1985.

————. "The World: Body of God or Field of Cosmic Activity." *Charles Hartshorne's Concept of God: Philosophical and Theological Responses*. Ed. Santiago Sia. Dordrecht: Kluwer Academic Publishers, 1990, pp. 89–102.

BRENNAN, Sheilah O'Flynn. "Substance Within Substance." *Process Studies* 7/1 (Spring, 1977): 14–26.

BRINTON, Crane. "Reflections on the Literature of Whither Mankind." *Philosophy, Religion and the Coming World Civilization: Essays in Honor of William Ernest Hocking*. Ed. Leroy Rouner. The Hague, Martinus Nijhoff, 1966, pp. 310–19.

BROAD, C.D. *Scientific Thought*. Paterson: Littlefield, Adams and Co., 1959.

BROWN, Delwin. *To Set at Liberty: Christian Faith and Human Freedom*. New York: Orbis Books, 1981.

BUTLER, Joseph. "Of Personal Identity." *Personal Identity*. Ed. John Perry. Berkeley: University of California Press, 1975, pp. 99–105.

CAPALDI, N. "The Historical and Philosophical Significance of Hume's Theory of the Self." *David Hume: Critical Assessments*. Volume III. Ed. Stanley Tweyman. London and New York: Routledge, 1995, pp. 627–40.

ČAPEK, Milič. "Immediate and Mediate Memory." *Process Studies* 7/2 (Summer, 1977): 90–6.

————. "Simple Location and Fragmentation of Reality." *Process and Divinity: The Hartshorne Festschrift; Philosophical Essays Presented to Charles Hartshorne*. Eds. William Reese and Eugene Freeman. La Salle, Illinois: Open Court, 1964, pp. 79–100.

——. *The Philosophical Impact of Contemporary Physics*. New York: Van Nostrand 1969.

——. "The Reappearance of the Self in the Last Philosophy of William James." *The Philosophical Review* 62/4 (October, 1953): 526–44.

——. "Toward a Widening of the Notion of Causality." *Process Philosophy: Basic Writings*. Eds. Jack R. Sibley and Pete A.Y. Gunter. Lanham, MD: University of America Press, 1978, pp. 79–103.

CAUTHEN, Kenneth. *Process Ethics: A Constructive System*. New York: The Edwin Mellen Press, 1984.

CHADWICK, Owen. *The Secularization of the European Mind in the 19th Century*. Cambridge: Cambridge University Press, 1990.

CHISHOLM, Roderick. "Parts as Essential to Their Wholes." *Review of Metaphysics* 26 (1973): 581–603.

——. "On the Observability of the Self." "The First Person." *Self-Knowledge*. Ed. Quassim Cassam. Oxford: Oxford University Press, pp. 94–108.

——. *Person and Object*. Murhead Library of Philosophy. Ed. H.D. Lewis. London: George Allen and Unwin, 1976.

CHRISTIAN, William A. "Some Uses of Reason." *The Relevance of Whitehead*. Ed. Ivor Leclerc. New York: Macmillan, 1961, pp. 47–89.

CLARK, Bowman. "Process, Time and God." *Process Studies* 13/4 (Winter, 1983): 245–59.

CLOOTS, André. "Can the God of Process Thought be Redeemed?" Coauthored with Jan van der Veken. *Charles Hartshorne's Concept of God: Philosophical and Theological Responses*. Ed. S. Sia. Dordrecht: Martinus Nijhoff, 1985, pp. 125–36.

——. "Towards a Dynamic Conception of Man." *God, Man and the Universe: Intercultural Dialogue*. Eds. Peter Jonkers and Jan van der Veken. Leuven: Center for Metaphysics and Philosophy of God, Institute of Philosophy, 1981, pp. 47–64.

COBB, John B. Jr. *A Christian Natural Theology Based on the Thought of Alfred North Whitehead*. London: Lutterworth, 1966.

——. "Bohm's Contribution to Faith in Our Time." *Beyond Mechanism: The Universe in Recent Physics and Catholic Thought*. Ed. David L. Schindler. New York: University of America Press, 1986, pp. 38–50.

——. Ed. with Franklin I. Gamwell. *Existence and Actuality: Conversations with Charles Hartshorne*. Chicago: University of Chicago Press, 1984.

——. "Freedom in Whitehead's Philosophy: A Response to Edward Pols." *Southern Journal of Philosophy* 7/4 (Winter, 1969): 409–13.

——. "Hartshorne's Importance for Theology." *The Philosophy of Charles Hartshorne*. Vol. XX of The Library of Living Philosophers. Ed. Lewis Edwin Hahn. La Salle, Illinois: Open Court, 1967, pp. 169–85.

——. "Man in Process." *Man in a New Society*. Concilium. Ed. Franz Bockle. New York: Herder and Herder, 1971, pp. 31–47.

——. Ed. with David Ray Griffin. *Mind in Nature: Essays on the Interface of Science and Philosophy*. Washington, DC: University Press of America, 1977.

——. "The Philosophy of Charles Hartshorne." *Process Studies* 21/2 (Summer 1992): 75–8.

——. "Two Types of Postmodernism: Deconstruction and Process." *Theology Today* 47 (July, 1990): 149–58.

——. "The World and God." *Process Theology: Basic Writings by the Key Thinkers of a Major Modern Movement*. Ed. Ewert H. Cousins. New York: Newman Press, 1971, pp. 153–70.

COHEN, Morris R. *Reason and Nature: An Essay on the Meaning of Scientific Method*. Glencoe, Illinois: The Free Press, 1953.

——. *Studies in Philosophy and Science*. New York: Henry Holt, 1949.

COPJEC, Joan. Ed. *Radical Evil*. New York: Verso, 1996.

CORNFORD, Francis Macdonald. *Plato's Cosmology: The Timaeus of Plato Translated with a Running Commentary*. International Library of Psychology, Philosophy, and Scientific Method. London: Routledge and Kegan Paul, 1937.

COVENEY, Peter. *The Arrow of Time: The Quest to Solve Science's Greatest Mystery*. Coauthored with Roger Highfield. London: Harper Collins, 1991.

CROSSON, Frederick J. "Man and the Meaning of the Whole." *Beyond Mechanism: The Universe in Recent Physics and Catholic Thought*. Ed. David L. Schindler. New York: University Press of America, 1986, pp. 51–63.

———. "Whitehead's References to the Bible." *Process Studies* 6/4 (Winter, 1976): 270–8.

D'ABRO, A. *The Evolution of Scientific Thought from Newton to Einstein*. New York: Dover, 1950.

DAVIDSON, Donald. *Analysis and Metaphysics: An Introduction to Philosophy*. Oxford: Oxford University Press, 1992.

———. *Essays on Actions and Events*. Oxford: Clarendon Press, 1980.

———. "Reply to Quine on Events." *Actions and Events: Perspectives on the Philosophy of Donald Davidson*. Eds. Ernest LePore and Brian P. McLaughlin. Oxford: Basil Blackwell, 1985, pp. 172–6.

———. "On the Very Idea of a Conceptual Scheme." *Proceedings of the American Philosophical Association* 47 (1974): 5–20.

DAVIES, Bryan. *The Thought of Thomas Aquinas*. Oxford: Clarendon Press, 1992.

DAVIES, Paul. *The Mind of God: Science and the Search for Ultimate Meaning*. New York: Simon and Schuster, 1992.

DENNETT, Daniel. "Conditions of Personhood." *The Identities of Persons*. Ed. Amélie Oksenberg Rorty. Berkely, Los Angeles and London: University of California Press, 1969, pp. 175–96.

———. "Where am I?" *The Mind's I: Fantasies and Reflections on Self and Soul*. Eds. Douglas R. Hofstadter and Daniel C. Dennett. Brighton, Sussex: Harvester Press, 1981, pp. 217–31.

DESCARTES, Réne, *Meditations on First Philosophy*. English translation of *Meditations de prima philosophia*. Ed. and Trans. John Cottingham. Cambridge Texts in the History of Philosophy. New York: Cambridge University Press, 1996.

———. *Principles of* Philosophy. English translation of *Principia Philosophiae*. Trans. John Veitch and A.D. Lindsey. London: Everyman's Library, 1969.

DEVLIN, James P. "Hartshorne's Metaphysical Asymmetry." *The Philosophy of Charles Hartshorne*. Vol. XX of The Library of Living Philosophers. Ed. Lewis Edwin Hahn. La Salle, Illinois: Open Court, 1991, pp. 275–90.

DE WACHTER, Frans. "Post Modern Challenges to Ethics." *Ethical Perspectives* 1/2 (1994): 77–88.

DOMBROWSKI, Daniel. "Hartshorne, Metaphysics and the Law of Moderation." *Process Studies* 21/3 (Fall, 1992): 152–65.

———. "Hartshorne and Plato." *The Philosophy of Charles Hartshorne*. Vol. XX of The Library of Living Philosophers. Ed. Lewis Edwin Hahn. La Salle, Illinois: Open Court, 1991, pp. 465–87.

———. "Process Thought and the Liberalism-Communitarianism Debate: A Comparison with Rawls." *Process Studies* 26/1–2 (Spring–Summer, 1997): 15–31.

DONNELLEY, Strachan. "Whitehead and Nietzsche: Overcoming the Evil of Time." *Process Studies* 12/1 (Spring, 1982): 1–14.

DREES, Willem B. *Religion, Science and Naturalism*. Cambridge: Cambridge University Press, 1996.

DUERLINGER, James. "Reductionist and Nonreductionist Theories of Persons in Indian Buddhist Philosophy." *Journal of Indian Philosophy* 2/1 (March, 1993): 79–101.

DUMMETT, Michael. *Frege: Philosophy of Language*. London: Duckworth, 1981.

DUPRÉ, Louis. "Ascent and Decline of a Self-Centered Culture." *Individuality and Cooperative Action*. Ed. Joseph E. Early. Washington, DC, Georgetown University Press, 1991, pp. 137–47.

———. "Evil–A Religious Mystery: A Plea for a More Inclusive Model of Theodicy." *Faith and Philosophy* 7/3 (July, 1990): 261–280.

ECCLES, John. *The Self and its Brain: An Argument for Interactionism*. Coauthored with Karl R. Popper. London: Routledge, 1990.

ECO, Umberto. *The Name of the Rose*. London: Picador, 1984. English translation of *Il nomme della rosa*. Sonzogno, Gruppo Editoriale Fabbri-Bompiani, 1980.

EDWARDS, Rem B. "The Human Self: An Actual Entity or a Society?" *Process Studies* 5/3 (Fall, 1975): 195–203.

EINSTEIN, Albert. "The World as I See It." *A Modern Introduction to Ethics: Readings from Classical and Contemporary Sources*. Ed. Milton K. Munitz. New York: The Free Press, 1961, pp. 621–3.

ELSTER, John. Ed. *The Multiple Self*. Cambridge: Cambridge University Press, 1986.

ELVEE, Richard Q. Ed. *Mind in Nature*. Nobel Conference XVII. San Francisco: Harper and Row, 1981.

ENGLEBRETSEN, George. *Speaking of Persons*. Philosophy in Canada: A Monograph Series 2. Halifax: Dalhousie University Press, 1975.

ESLICK, Leonard J. "Divine Causality." *The Modern Schoolman* 62 (1984–5): 233–47.

ESPER, Erwin A. *A History of Psychology*. Philadelphia and London: Saunders, 1964.

EVANS, Gareth. "Can There be Vague Objects?" *Identity*. Ed. Harold Noonan. Aldershot: Grower House, 1993.

———. "Self-Identification." "The First Person." *Self-Knowledge*. Ed. Quassim Cassam. Oxford: Oxford University Press, pp. 184–209.

FANCHER, Robert. "Of Time, the Self, and Rem Edwards." *Process Studies* 7/1 (Spring, 1977): 14–26.

FARADAY, Michael. *Experimental Researches in Electricity*. New York: Dover Books, 1965.

FELT, James W. "Intuition, Event-Atomis, and the Self." *Process in Context: Essays in Post-Whiteheadian Perspectives*. Ed. Ernest Wolf-Gazo. New York: Peter Lang Publishers, 1988, pp. 137–52.

FERRÉ, Frederick. "The New Solidarity: How Wide Our World?" *Individuality and Cooperative Action*. Ed. Joseph E. Early. Washington, DC: Georgetown University Press, 1991, pp. 165–71.

FITZGERALD, Paul. "Relativity Physics and the God of Process Philosophy." *Process Studies* 2/4 (Winter, 1972): 251–73.

FLEW, Antony. *Body, Mind and Death*. New York: Macmillan, 1964.

———. "Locke and the Problem of Personal Identity." *Philosophy* 26/96 (January 1951): 53–68.

FLUGEL, J.C. *A Hundred Years of Psychology 1833–1933*. 3rd Edition. Coauthored with Donald J. West. London: Gerald Duckworth, 1964.

FORD, Lewis. "A Guide to Whitehcad." *Teaching Philosophy* 7/2 (April, 1984): 143–7.

———. "The Concept of 'Process': From 'Transition' to 'Concrescence.'" *Whitehead and the Idea of Process*. Proceedings of the First International Whitehead Symposium. (*Whitehead und der Prozessbegriff*. Beitraege zur Philosophie Alfred North Whiteheads auf dem Ersten Internationalen Whitehead-Symposion, 1981.) Freiburg and Muenchen: Verlag Karl Alber, 1984, pp. 73–101.

———. "From Pre-Panpsychism to Pansubjectivity." *Faith and Creativity*. Eds. George Nordgulen and George W. Shields. St. Louis, Missouri: CBP Press, 1987, pp. 41–61.

———. Ed. with George L. Kline. *Explorations in Whitehead's Philosophy*. New York: Fordham University Press, 1983.

———. "God at Work: The Way God is Effective in a Process Perspective." *Encounter* 57/4 (Autumn, 1996): 327–40.

———. "Hartshorne's Interpretation of Whitehead." *The Philosophy of Charles Hartshorne*. Vol. XX of The Library of Living Philosophers. Ed. Lewis Edwin Hahn. La Salle, Illinois: Open Court, 1991, pp. 313–38.

———. "Inclusive Occasions." *Process in Context: Essays in Post-Whiteheadian Perspectives*. Ed. Ernest Wolf-Gazo. New York: Peter Lang Publishers, 1988, pp. 107–36.

———. "Is Process Theism Compatible with Relativity Theory?" *Journal of Religion* 47/2 (April, 1968): 251–73.

———. "The Origin of Subjectivity." *The Modern Schoolman* 62 (1984–5): 265–76.

———. "Whitehead's Differences from Hartshorne." *Two Process Philosophers: Hartshorne's Encounter with Whitehead*. AAR Studies in Religion 5. Ed. Lewis S. Ford. Tallahassee: American Academy of Religion, 1973, pp. 58–83.

Foss, Laurence. "Substance and Two Theories of Natural Language." *Substances and Things: Aristotle's Doctrine of Physical Substance in Recent Essays*. Ed. M.L. O'Hara. Washington, DC: University of America Press, 1982, pp. 213–23.

Fost, Frederick F. "Relativity Theory and Hartshorne's Dipolar Theism." *Two Process Philosophers: Hartshorne's Encounter with Whitehead*. AAR Studies in Religion 5. Ed. Lewis S. Ford. Tallahassee: American Academy of Religion, 1973, pp. 89–99.

Foster, John. *The Immaterial Self: A Defense of the Cartesian Dualist Conception of the Mind*. London and New York: Routledge, 1991. (Ch. 4: The Type-Identity Thesis; Ch. 5: Token-Identity and Metaphysical Reductionism; Ch. 6: Token-Identity and Psychophysical Causation; Ch. 7: The Mental Subject; and Ch. 8: Personal Identity, Embodiment, and Freedom.)

Fowler, Dean R. "Disconfirmation of Whitehead's Relativity Theory—A Critical Reply." *Process Studies* 4/4 (Winter, 1974): 288–90.

Fox, Robert. "Laplacian Physics." *Companion to the History of Modern Science*. Eds. R.C. Olby, G.N. Cantor, J.R.R. Christie and M.J.S. Hodge. London: Routledge, 1990, pp. 278–94.

Frankenberry, Nancy. "The Power of the Past." *Process Studies* 13 (1983): 132–42.

Freeman, Eugene, "The Interrelatedness of 'True,' 'Good,' and 'Beautiful.'" *Process and Divinity: The Hartshorne Festschrift*. Philosophical Essays Presented to Charles Hartshorne. Eds. William Reese and Eugene Freeman. La Salle, Illinois: Open Court, 1964, pp. 325–40.

Geach, P.T. "Identity." *Review of Metaphysics* 21/1 (September, 1967): 3–12.

———. *Reference and Generality*. 3rd Edition. New York: Cornell University Press, 1980.

Gerogiadis, Constantine. "Two Conceptions of Substance in Aristotle." *Substances and Things: Aristotle's Doctrine of Physical Substance in Recent Essays*. Ed. M.L. O'Hara. Washington, DC: University of America Press, 1982, pp. 172–87.

Geyer, Michael. "The Politics of Memory in Contemporary Germany." *Radical Evil*. Ed. Joan Copjec. New York: Verso, 1996, pp. 169–200.

Gier, Nicholas Fr. "Intentionality and Prehension." *Process Studies* 6/3 (Fall, 1976): 197–213.

Gill, Mary Louise. *Aristotle on Substance: The Paradox of Unity*. Princeton, New Jersey: Princeton University Press, 1989.

Gilson, Étienne. *The Elements of Christian Philosophy*. New York: The New American Library, 1960.

————. *History Of Christian Philosophy in the Middle Ages.* New York: Random House, 1955.

GIVNER, David A. "Scientific Preconceptions in Locke's Philosophy of Language." *Journal of the History of Ideas* 23/3 (July–September, 1962): 340–54.

GJERTSEN, D. *The Newton Handbook.* London: Routledge and Kegan Paul, 1986.

GLOVER, Jonathan. Ed. *The Philosophy of Mind.* Cambridge: Oxford University Press, 1967.

————. *The Philosophy and Psychology of Personal Identity.* London: Allen Lane, 1988.

GOSS, James. "Camus, God, and Process Thought." *Process Studies* 4/2 (Summer, 1974): 114–38.

GRAGG, Alan. *Charles Hartshorne.* Makers of the Modern Theological Mind. Ed. Bob E. Patterson. Waco: Word, 1973.

GRAM, Moltke S. "Substance." *Substances and Things: Aristotle's Doctrine of Physical Substance in Recent Essays.* Ed. M.L. O'Hara. Washington, DC: University of America Press, 1982, pp. 120–43.

GRATZER, W. Ed. *The Longman Literary Companion to Science.* Harlow: Longman, 1989.

GRIFFIN, David Ray. "Hartshorne's Differences from Whitehead." *Two Process Philosophers: Hartshorne's Encounter with Whitehead.* AAR Studies in Religion 5. Ed. Lewis S. Ford. Tallahassee: American Academy of Religion, 1973, pp. 35–57.

————. "Hartshorne's God and Relativity Physics." *Process Studies* 21/1 (Summer, 1992): 85–112.

HALLAMAA, Jaana. "The Concept of 'Person' and God as Trinity of Persons." *Paper presented at the 11th Conference of the European Society for the Philosophy of Religion.* University of Swansea, 1994.

HAMLYN, D.W. "Psychological Explanation and the Gestalt Hypothesis." *Mind,* 60/240 (October, 1951): 506–20.

HARDING, D.E. "On Having No Head." *The Mind's I: Fantasies and Reflections on Self and Soul.* Eds. Douglas R. Hofstadter and Daniel C. Dennett. Brighton, Sussex: Harvester Press, 1981, pp. 23–33.

HAWKING, Stephen. *A Brief History of Time: From the Big Bang to Black Holes.* New York: Bantam, 1988.

HAWLEY, Richard. "Mindless Lover to the Process Theologian." *Process Studies* 5/1 (Spring, 1975): 46.

HAZARD, Paul. *The European Mind, 1680–1715.* Harmondsworth, Penguin, 1964. English translation of *La Crise de la conscience européene, 1680–1715.* Paris: 1935.

HELM, Paul. "Locke's Theory of Personal Identity." *Philosophy* 54/208 (April 1979): 173–85.

HEWITT, Andrew. "The Bad Seed: 'Auschwitz' and the Physiology of Evil." *Radical Evil.* Ed. Joan Copjec. New York: Verso, 1996, pp. 74–104.

HOCKING, William Ernest. "History and the Absolute." *Philosophy, Religion and the Coming World Civilization: Essays in Honor of William Ernest Hocking.* Ed. Leroy Rouner. The Hague: Martinus Nijhoff, 1966, pp. 423–63.

————. *The Meaning of God in Human Experience: A Philosophic Study of Religion.* New Haven, Connecticut: Yale University Press, 1963.

HOFSTADTER, Douglas R. Ed., with Daniel C. Dennett. *The Mind's I: Fantasies and Reflections on Self and Soul.* Brighton, Sussex: Harvester Press, 1981.

HOSINSKI, Thomas. *Stubborn Fact and Creative Advance: An Introduction to the Metaphysics of Alfred North Whitehead.* Lanham, Maryland: Rowman and Littlefield, 1993.

HOSPERS, John. "Hartshorne's Aesthetics." *The Philosophy of Charles Hartshorne.* Vol. XX of The Library of Living Philosophers. Ed. Lewis Edwin Hahn. La Salle, Illinois: Open Court, 1991, pp. 113–34.

HUGHES, Christopher. "Is a Thing Just the Sum of its Parts?" *Proceedings of the Aristotelian Society* 86 (1986): 213–33.

HUGHES, M.W. "Personal Identity: A Defense of Locke." *Philosophy* 50/192 (April 1975): 169–87.

HUME, David. *A Treatise of Human Nature.* Ed. L.A. Selby-Bigg. 2nd Edition. Ed. P.H. Nidditch. New York: Oxford University Press, 1978.

JAMES, William. "On Some Omissions of Introspective Psychology." *Mind* 33 (January, 1884): 1–26.

JENKINS, John J. *Understanding Hume.* Eds. Peter Lewis and Geoffrey Madell. Edinburgh: Edinburgh University Press, 1992.

JOHNSON, A.H. *Whitehead's Philosophy of Civilization.* New York: Dover, 1962.

———. "Whitehead on the Uses of Language." *The Relevance of Whitehead: Philosophical Essays in Commemoration of the Centenary of the Birth of Alfred North Whitehead.* Ed. Ivor Leclerc. Bristol: Thoemmes Press, 1993.

———. *Whitehead's American Essays in Social Philosophy.* New York: Harper, 1959.

———. *Whitehead's Theory of Reality.* New York: Dover, 1962.

JOHNSON, Charles Michael. "On Prehending the Past." *Process Studies* 6/4 (Winter, 1976): 255–69.

JOHNSTON, Mark. "Is There a Problem About Persistence?" Coauthored with Graeme Forbes. *Proceedings of the Aristotelian Society* 61 (1987): 107–354; 137–55.

JONES, William B. "Bell's Theorem, H.P. Stapp, and Process Theism." *Process Studies* 7/4 (Winter, 1971): 250–61.

JUNG, Carl G. *Die Beziehungen der Psychotherapie zur Seelsorge.* Zurich: Rasher, 1932. (Quoted in Conrad Baars's *Healing the Unaffirmed: Recognizing Deprivation Neurosis.* Coauthored with Anna Terruwe. New York: Alba House, 1972.)

KANE, Robert H. "Free Will, Determinism, and Creativity in Hartshorne's Thought." *The Philosophy of Charles Hartshorne.* Vol. XX of The Library of Living Philosophers. Ed. Lewis Edwin Hahn. La Salle, Illinois: Open Court, 1991, pp. 135–55.

KANT, Immanuel. *Religion within the Limits of Reason Alone.* Trans. Theodore M. Greene and Hoyt H. Hudson. New York: Harper and Row, 1960.

KATZ, David. *Gestalt Psychology: Its Nature and Significance.* Trans. Robert Tyson. New York: Ronald, 1950.

KAZANTZAKIS, Nikos. *Report to Greco.* London: Faber and Faber, 1965.

KEGLEY, Jacquelyn Ann. "The Divine Relativity and the Beloved Community." *The Philosophy of Charles Hartshorne.* Vol. XX of The Library of Living Philosophers. Ed. Lewis Edwin Hahn. La Salle, Illinois: Open Court, 1991, pp. 215–34.

KERBY-MILLER, S. "Causality." *Philosophical Essays for Alfred North Whitehead.* New York: Russel and Russel, 1936, pp. 174–92.

KING, Sally B. "Buddhism and Hartshorne." *The Philosophy of Charles Hartshorne.* Vol. XX of The Library of Living Philosophers. Ed. Lewis Edwin Hahn. La Salle, Illinois: Open Court, 1991, pp. 235–52.

KITCHER, Philip. "The Foundations of Mathematics." Companion to the History of Modern Science. Eds. R.C. Olby, G.N. Cantor, J.R.R. Christie and M.J.S. Hodge. London and New York: Routledge, 1990, pp. 677–89.

KLINE, George L. Ed. *Alfred North Whitehead: Essays on His Philosophy.* Englewood Cliffs, New Jersey: Prentice-Hall, 1963.

KLINE, M. *Mathematical Thoughts from Ancient to Modern Times.* Oxford: Oxford University Press, 1972.

KNOWLES, David. *The Evolution of Medieval Thought.* New York: Vintage, 1964.

KOFFKA, Kurt. *Principles of Gestalt Psychology.* London: Routledge and Kegan Paul, 1962.

KOLAK, Daniel. Ed., With Raymond Martin. *Self and Identity: Contemporary Philosohical Issues*. New York: Macmillan, 1991.

KOLM, Serge-Christophe. "The Buddhist Theory of 'No-Self.'" *The Multiple Self*. Ed. John Elster. Cambridge: Cambridge University Press, 1986, pp. 233–65.

KOYRÉ, Alexander. *Galileo Studies*. Trans. J. Mepham. European Philosophy and the Human Sciences. Hassocks, Harvester Press, 1978. English translation of *Etudes galiléennes*. Paris: 1939.

KÖHLER, Wolfgang. *Gestalt Psychology: An Introduction to New Concepts in Modern Psychology*. New York and Toronto: Liveright, 1947. Reprint, New York: New American Library, 1966.

———. *The Place of Value in a World of Facts*. New York: Liveright, 1938. Reprint, New York: Harper, 1945.

KRIPKE, Saul. "Identity and Necessity." *Identity and Individuation*. Ed. M.K. Munitz. New York: New York University Press, 1971.

———. *Naming and Necessity*. Oxford: Blackwell, 1980.

KUNTZ, Paul G. "Charles Hartshorne's Theory of Order and Disorder." *The Philosophy of Charles Hartshorne*. Vol. XX of The Library of Living Philosophers. Ed. Lewis Edwin Hahn. La Salle, Illinois: Open Court, 1991, pp. 414–30.

LACROIX, W.L. *Four Questions on Persons: A Philosophical Dialectic*. New York and London: University Press of America, 1982.

LADRIÈRE, Jean. "Event." *Louvain Philosophical Studies* 7. Tradition and Renewal. Vol. III. Eds. David A. Boileau and John A. Dick. Leuven: Leuven University Press, 1993, pp. 147–164.

LAMBRECHT, Jan. *The Wretched 'I' and its Liberation: Paul in Romans 7 and 8*. English translation of *Het verscheurde 'ik' en zijn bevrijding. Paulus in Romeinen 7 en 8*. Louvain Pastoral Monographs 14. Leuven: Peeters Press, 1992.

LAWRENCE, Nathaniel. Ed. With D. O'Connor. *Readings in Existential Phenomenology*. Englewood Cliffs, New Jersey: Prentice-Hall, 1967.

———. "Time, Value, and the Self." *The Relevance of Whitehead*. Ed. Ivor Leclerc. New York: Macmillan, 1961, pp. 145–66.

———. *Whitehead's Philosophical Development*. Berkeley: University of California Press, 1956.

LEARY, Timothy. *Design for Dying*. San Francisco: Harper Collins, 1997.

LECLERC, Ivor. "Alfred North Whitehead: His Philosophy." *Process in Context: Essays in Post-Whiteheadian Perspectives*. Ed., Ernest Wolf-Gazo. New York: Peter Lang Publishers, 1988, pp. 25–43.

———. "Form and Actuality." *The Relevance of Whitehead*. Ed. Ivor Leclerc. New York: Macmillan, 1961, pp. 169–89.

———. "The Philosophical Problem of Individuals in Physics." *Individuality and Cooperative Action*. Ed. Joseph E. Early. Washington, DC: Georgetown University Press, 1991, pp. 109–115.

———. Ed. *The Relevance of Whitehead*. New York: Macmillan, 1961.

———. *Whitehead's Metaphysics: An Introductory Exposition*. London: Allen and Unwin, 1965.

LEE, Donald S. "Hartshorne and Pragmatic Metaphysics." *The Philosophy of Charles Hartshorne*. Vol. XX of The Library of Living Philosophers. Ed. Lewis Edwin Hahn. La Salle, Illinois: Open Court, 1991, pp. 529–50.

LEVINAS, Emmanuel. *Ethics and Infinity: Conversations with Philippe Nemo*. Trans. Richard A. Cohen. Pittsburgh: Duquesne University Press, 1985.

LEWIS, C.I. *An Analysis of Knowledge and Valuation*. La Salle, Illinois: Open Court, 1946.

LEWIS, C.S. *Studies in Words*. Cambridge: Cambridge University Press, 1967.

LEWIS, David. "Counterparts of Persons and Their Bodies." *The Journal of Philosophy* 68 (1971): 203–11.

———. *On the Plurality of Worlds*. Oxford: Blackwell, 1986.

———. "Vague Identity: Evans Misunderstood." *Identity*. Ed. Harold Noonan Aldershot: Grower House, 1993, pp. 359–61.

LEWIS, Douglas. "The Existence of Substances and Locke's Way of Ideas." *Theoria* 35/2 (1969): 124–46.

LINDBERG, David C. *The Beginnings of Western Science: The European Scientific Tradition in Philosophical, Religious, and Institutional Context, 600 B.C. to A.D. 1450*. Chicago and London: University of Chicago Press, 1992.

LOCKE, John. *An Essay Concerning Human Understanding*. Ed. Peter H. Nidditch. Oxford: Clarendon Press, 1975.

———. "Letter to Molyneux, 23 August 1693." *The Works of John Locke*. New Edition, Corrected. Vol. VIII. London: Thomas Tegg, 1794. Reprint, Germany, Scientia Verlag Aalen, 1963.

———. "Reply to the Bishop of Worcester's Answer to His Second Letter." *The Works of John Locke*, New Edition, Corrected. Vol. IV. London: Thomas Tegg, 1823. Reprint, Germany, Scientia Verlag Aalen, 1963.

LONERGAN, Bernard J.F. *Insight: A Study of Human Understanding*. 2nd Edition. New York: Philosophical Library, 1958.

LOOMER, Bernard. "Christian Faith and Process Philosophy." *Journal of Religion* 29/3 (July, 1949): 181–203.

LOWE, E.J. *Locke on Human Understanding*. London and New York: Routledge, 1995.

LOWE, Victor. "The Approach to Metaphysics." *The Relevance of Whitehead*. Ed. Ivor Leclerc. New York: Macmillan, 1961, pp. 193–216.

LUCAS, George R. *The Genesis of Modern Process Thought: A Historical Outline with Bibliography*. Ed. Kenneth E. Rowe. Metuchen: American Theological Library Association, 1983.

———. "Hartshorne and the Development of Process Philosophies." *The Philosophy of Charles Hartshorne*. Vol. XX of The Library of Living Philosophers. Ed. Lewis Edwin Hahn. La Salle, Illinois: Open Court, 1991, pp. 509–28.

———. *The Rehabilitation of Whitehead: An Analytic and Historical Assessment of Process Philosophy*. New York: State University of New York Press, 1989.

MABBOTT, J.D. *John Locke*. London and Basingstoke: Macmillan, 1975, pp. 15–69.

MACKIE, J.L. *Problems From Locke*. Oxford: Clarendon Press, 1976.

MADELL, Geoffrey. *The Identity of the Self*. Edinburgh: Edinburgh University Press, 1981.

MARCEL, Gabriel. "Solipsism Surmounted." *Philosophy, Religion and the Coming World Civilization: Essays in Honor of William Ernest Hocking*. Ed. Leroy Rouner. The Hague: Martinus Nijhoff, 1966, pp. 23–31.

MARGENAU, H. "Physics versus Historical Reality." *Philosophy of Science* 19 (1952): 193–213.

MARGOLIS, Howard. "Self-Interest and Social Motivation." *Individuality and Cooperative Action*. Ed. Joseph E. Early. Washington, DC: Georgetown University Press, 1991, pp. 129–35.

MARITAIN, Jacques. "Confession of Faith." *A Modern Introduction to Ethics: Readings from Classical and Contemporary Sources*. English trans. of *Confession de foi*. Ed. Milton K. Munitz. New York: The Free Press, 1961, pp. 604–12.

———. *God and the Permission of Evil*. Trans. Joseph Evans. Milwaukee: Bruce, 1960.

MARTIN, Norman M. "Taking Creativity Seriously: Some Observations on the Logical Structure of Hartshorne's Philosophy." *The Philosophy of Charles Hartshorne*.

Vol. XX of The Library of Living Philosophers. Ed. Lewis Edwin Hahn. La Salle, Illinois: Open Court, 1991, pp. 339–54.

MAXWELL, James Clerk. *Matter and Motion.* New York: Macmillan, 1920.

———. *A Treatise on Electricity and Magnetism.* 3rd Edition. Oxford: Oxford University Press, 1891.

McCALL, Catherine. *Concepts of Person: An Analysis of the Concepts of Person, Self, and Human Being.* Aldershot, Enland: Averbury, 1990.

McCANN, Edwin. "Locke's Philosophy of the Body." *The Cambridge Companion to Locke.* Ed. Vere Chappell. New York: Cambridge University Press, 1994.

McDANIEL, Jay. "Zen and the Self." *Process Studies,* 10/3–4 (Fall–Winter, 1980): 110–19.

McHENRY, Leemon. "Descriptive and Revisionary Theories of Events." *Process Studies* 5/25 (1996): 90–103.

McINTYRE, J. "Hume's Underground Self." *David Hume: Critical Assessments.* Volume III. Ed. Stanley Tweyman. London and New York: Routledge, 1995, pp. 718–29.

McMURRIN, Sterling M. "Hartshorne's Critique of Classical Metaphysics and Theology." *The Philosophy of Charles Hartshorne.* Vol. XX of The Library of Living Philosophers. Ed. Lewis Edwin Hahn. La Salle, Illinois: Open Court, 1991, pp. 431–44.

MELAND, Bernard Eugene. "Two Paths to the Good Life." *Process Philosophy: Basic Writings.* Eds. Jack R. Sibley and Pete A.Y. Gunter. Lanham, MD: University Press of America, 1978, pp. 423–34.

MERLEAU-PONTY, M. *Phenomenology of Perception.*Trans. Colin Smith. English translation of *Phénoménologie de la Perception.* London: Routledge, 1962.

MESLE, C. Robert. "Aesthetic Value and Relational Power: An Essay on Personhood." *Process Studies* 13/1 (Spring, 1983): 59–70.

MILLER, Peter. "Temporal Concepts: A Schematic Analysis." *Process Studies* 9/1–2 (Spring-Summer, 1979): 22–29.

MOLLAND, A. George. "Aristotelian Science." *Companion to the History of Modern Science.* Eds. R.C. Olby, G.N. Cantor, J.R.R. Christie and M.J.S. Hodge. London: Routledge, 1990.

MOLYNEUX, William. "Letter of Molyneux to Locke, 2 March 1693." *The Works of John Locke.* New Edition, Corrected. Vol. VIII. London: Thomas Tegg, 1794. Reprint, Germany, Scientia Verlag Aalen, 1963.

MONTAGUE, William P. *The Way of Things.* New York: Prentice-Hall, 1940.

MOROWITZ, Harold J. "Rediscovering the Mind." *The Mind's I: Fantasies and Reflections on Self and Soul.* Eds. Douglas R. Hofstadter and Daniel C. Dennett. Brighton, Sussex: Harvester Press, 1981, pp. 34–42.

MORRIS, Randall C. *Process Philosophy and Political Ideology: The Social and Political Thought of Alfred North Whitehead and Charles Hartshorne.* Albany, New York: State University of New York Press, 1991.

MORRIS, Thomas. Ed. *God and the Philosophers: The Reconciliation of Faith and Reason.* New York and Oxford: Oxford University Press, 1994.

MOXTER, Michael. "Human Subjectivity and Metaphysics." *Paper presented at the 11th Conference of the European Society for the Philosophy of Religion.* University of Swansea, 1994.

MÜLLER-FREIENFELS, Richard. *The Evolution of Modern Psychology.* Trans. W. Beran Wolf. New Haven, Connecticut: Yale University Press, 1935.

NAGEL, Thomas. "Brain Bissection and the Unity of Consciousness." *Synthese,* 22 (1971): 396–413.

———. *Mortal Questions.* Cambridge: Cambridge University Press, 1979.

———. "Physicalism." *The Mind/Brain Theory.* Ed. C.V. Borst. London: Macmillan, 1970, pp. 214–30.

————. *The View from Nowhere.* Oxford: Oxford University Press, 1986.

NEEDHAM, Joseph. "A Biologist's View of Whitehead." *The Philosophy of Alfred North Whitehead.* The Library of Living Philosophers. Ed. Paul Arthur Schilpp. New York: Tudor, 1951, pp. 241–71.

NEVILLE, Robert. *Creativity and God: A Challenge to Process Theology.* New York: Seabury, 1980.

————. "Genetic Succession, Time, and Becoming." *Process Studies* 1/3 (Fall, 1971): 104–8.

————. *God the Creator: On the Transcendence and Presence of God.* Chicago: University of Chicago Press, 1968.

————. "Time, Temporality, and Ontology." *The Philosophy of Charles Hartshorne.* Vol. XX of The Library of Living Philosophers. Ed. Lewis Edwin Hahn. La Salle, Illinois: Open Court, 1991, pp. 377–96.

————. "Whitehead on the One and the Many." *Explorations in Whitehead's Philosophy.* Eds. Lewis S. Ford and George L. Kline. New York: Fordham University Press, 1983, pp. 257–71.

New Revised Standard Version of the Holy Bible. Old and New Testaments. New York and Oxford: Oxford University Press, 1989.

NEWTON, Saul. *The Conditions of Human Growth.* Coauthored with Jane Pearce. New York, Citadel, 1963.

NOBO, Jorge Luis. *Whitehead's Metaphysics of Extension and Solidarity.* New York: State University of New York Press, 1986.

NOONAN, Harold. Ed. *Identity.* The International Research Library of Philosophy. No. 2. Aldershot: Dartmouth, 1993.

————. *Objects and Identity.* Den Haag: Martinus Nijhoff, 1982.

————. *Personal Identity.* London: Routledge, 1989.

————. "Personal Identity and Bodily Continuity." *Analysis* 43 (1983): 98–104.

ODEGARD, Douglas. "Locke as an Empiricist." *Philosophy* 40/153 (July 1965): 185–96.

O'HARA, M.L. Ed. *Substances and Things: Aristotle's Doctrine of Physical Substance in Recent Essays.* Washington, DC: Univeristy Press of America, 1982.

ORWELL, George. *The Lion and the Unicorn.* London: Harmondsworth, 1982.

PAILIN, David A. "God as Creator in a Whiteheadian Understanding." *Whitehead and the Idea of Process.* Proceedings of the First International Whitehead Symposium. Freiburg and Munich: Verlag Karl Alber, 1984, pp. 273–99.

————. "Narrative, Story, and the Interpretation of Metaphysics." *Hegel and Whitehead.* Ed. George R. Lucas. New York: Suny Press, 1986, pp. 268–81.

PANNENBERG, Wolfhart. "Atom, Duration, Form: Difficulties with Process Philosophy." Trans. John C. Robertson, Jr. and Gérard Vallée. *Process Studies* 14/1 (Spring 1984): 21–30.

PARFIT, Derek. "An Interview with Derek Parfit." *Cogito* 9 (1995): 115–25.

————. "The Indeterminacy of Identity: A Reply to Brueckner." *Philosophical Studies* 70 (1993): 23–33.

————. "Later Selves and Moral Principles." *Philosophy and Personal Relations: An Anglo-French Study.* Ed. Alan Montefiore. London: Routledge and Kegan Paul, 1973, pp. 137–69.

————. "Lewis, Perry, and What Matters." *The Identities of Persons.* Ed. Amélie Oksenberg Rorty. Berkely, Los Angeles and London: University of California Press, 1969, pp. 91–107.

————. "Personal Identity." *Philosophical Review* 80/1 (January, 1971): 3–27.

————. "Personal Identity, Rationality, and Morality." *Self and Identity: Contemporary Philosophical Issues.* Eds. Daniel Kolak and Raymond Martin. New York and Toronto: Macmillan, 1991, pp. 301–22.

———. *Reasons and Persons*. Oxford: Oxford University Press, 1984.

———. "The Unimportance of Identity." *Identity: Essays Based on the Herbert Spencer Lectures Given in the University of Oxford*. Ed. Henry Harris. Oxford: Clarendon Press, 1995, pp. 13–45.

PEACOCKE, Arthur R. "Natural Being and Becoming—The Chyrsalis of the Human." *Individuality and Cooperative Action*. Ed. Joseph E. Early. Washington, DC: Georgetown University Press, 1991, pp. 91–108.

PENELHUM, Terence. *Hume*. London and Basingstoke: Macmillan, 1975.

———. "Self-Identity and Self-Regard." *The Identities of Persons*. Ed. Amélie Oksenberg Rorty. Berkely, Los Angeles and London: University of California Press, 1969, pp. 253–80.

PERRY, John. Ed. "The Importance of Being Identical." *The Identities of Persons*. Ed. Amélie Oksenberg Rorty. Berkely, Los Angeles and London, University of California Press, 1969, pp. 67–90.

———. *Personal Identity*. Berkeley: University of California Press, 1975.

PETERS, Eugene H. "Methodology in the Metaphysics of Charles Hartshorne." *Existence and Actuality: Conversations with Charles Hartshorne*. Eds. John B. Cobb, Jr. and Franklin I. Gamwell. Chicago: University of Chicago Press, 1984.

PLANTINGA, Alvin. "Things and Persons." *The Review of Metaphysics* XIV 3/55 (March, 1961): 493–519.

POLKINGHORNE, J.C. "A Revived Natural Theology." *Science and Religion: One World Changing Perspectives*. Papers presented at the Second European Conference on Science and Religion. Eds. Jan Fennema and Iain Paul. Dordrecht: Kluwer Academic Publishers, 1990, pp. 87–97.

POUND, Roscoe. *Jurisprudence*. Volume IV: Application and Enforcement of Law. Saint Paul, Minnesota: West Publishing Co., 1959.

PRICE, H.H. *Thinking and Experience*. Cambridge, Massachusetts: Harvard University Press, 1953.

PTOLEMY. *Almagest*. Trans. G.J. Toomer. London: Duckworth, 1984.

PUCCETTI, Roland. "Two Brains, Two Minds? Wigans Theory of Mental Duality." *Self and Identity: Contemporary Philosophical Issues*. Eds. Daniel Kolak and Raymond Martin. New York and Toronto: Macmillan, 1991.

QUINNEY, Richard. *Social Existence: Metaphysics, Marxism and the Social Sciences*. London: Macmillan, 1982.

QUINTON, Anthony. "The Soul." *Personal Identity*. Ed. John Perry. Berkeley: University of California Press, 1975, pp. 53–72.

RAVETZ, J.R. "The Copernican Revolution." *Companion to the History of Modern Science*. Eds. R.C. Olby et al. London: Routledge, 1990, pp. 201–16.

REESE, William L. "The 'Trouble' with Panentheism and the Divine Event." *The Philosophy of Charles Hartshorne*. Vol. XX of The Library of Living Philosophers. Ed. Lewis Edwin Hahn. La Salle, Illinois: Open Court, 1991, pp. 187–202.

REEVES, Gene. "God and Creativity." *Southern Journal of Philosophy* 7/4 (Winter, 1969): 377–85.

REID, Thomas. *Essays on the Intellectual Powers of Man* [1875]. Ed. A.D. Woozley. London: Macmillan, 1941.

RESCHER, Nicholas. *Process Metaphysics: An Introductory Exposition*. New York: State University of New York Press, 1996.

RICOEUR, Paul. *Fallible Man*. Trans. Walter J. Lowe. English translation of *L'Homme faillible*. New York: Fordham University Press, 1986.

———. "L'identite narrative." *Esprit: Changer la culture et politique* 12/7–8 (July–August, 1988): 295–304.

———. *Oneself as Another*. English translation of *Soi-méme comme un autre*. Trans. Kathleen Blamey. Chicago: University of Chicago Press, 1992.

ROBINSON, John A.T. *Exploration into God*. Stanford: Stanford University Press, 1967.

ROGOZINSKI, Jacob. "It Makes Us Wrong: Kant and Radical Evil." *Radical Evil*. Ed. Joan Copjec. New York: Verso, 1996, pp. 30–45.

RORTY, Amélie Oksenberg. "A Literary Postscript: Characters, Persons, Selves, Individuals." *The Identities of Persons*. Ed. Amélie Oksenberg Rorty. Berkely, Los Angeles and London: University of California Press, 1969, pp. 301–23.

ROTH, Leon. "Note on the Relationship between Locke and Descartes." *Mind* 44 (1936): 414–16.

ROYCE, Josiah. *The World and the Individual*. New York: Dover Publications, 1959.

SALMOND, John William. *Jurisprudence or The Theory of Law*. London: Stevens and Haynes, 1910. 12th Edition, Ed. P.J. Fitzgerald. London: Sweet and Maxwell, 1966.

SANDERS, Andy F. "The Deconstruction of the Subject: Critiques of Subjectivity Based on Approaches to God." *Paper presented at the 11th Conference of the European Society for the Philosophy of Religion*. University of Swansea, 1994.

SANFORD, David Hawley. "Where Was I?" *The Mind's I: Fantasies and Reflections on Self and Soul*. Eds. Douglas R. Hofstadter and Daniel C. Dennett. Brighton, Sussex: Harvester Press, 1981, pp. 232–40.

SCHAFFER, Simon. "Newtonianism." *Companion to the History of Modern Science*. Eds. R.C. Olby, and others. London: Routledge, 1990, pp. 610–26.

SCHANKULA, H.A.S. "Locke, Descartes, and the Science of Nature." *Journal of the History of Ideas* 41/3 (July–September, 1980): 459–77.

SCHAPER, Eva. "Aesthetic Perception." *The Relevance of Whitehead*. Ed. Ivor Lecler. New York: Macmillan, 1961, pp. 263–85.

SCHINDLER, David L. "The Problem of Mechanism." *Beyond Mechanism: The Universe in Recent Physics and Catholic Thought*. Ed. David L. Schindler. New York: University Press of America, 1986, pp. 1–11.

SCHROEDINGER, Ernest. *Science and Humanism*. Cambridge: Cambridge University Press, 1951.

SCHROEDER, W. Widdick. "Toward Belief: A Process Perspective on the Social Sciences and on Social Ethics." *Belief and Ethics: Essays in Ethics, the Human Sciences, and Ministry in Honor of W. Alvin Pitcher*. Studies in Religion and Society. Ed. W. Widdick Schroeder. Chicago: Center for the Scientific Study of Religion, 1978, pp. 237–54.

SCHUSTER, John A. "The Scientific Revolution." *Companion to the History of Modern Science*. Eds. R.C. Olby and others. London: Routledge, 1990, pp. 217–42.

SCHWEITZER, Albert. *Kultur und Ethik*. Munich: Beck, 1923.

SENECA. *Moral Essays*. Trans. John W. Basore. Cambridge, Massachusetts, Harvard University Press, 1970.

SFEZ, Gérald. "Deciding on Evil." *Radical Evil*. Ed. Joan Copjec. New York: Verso, 1996, pp. 126–49.

SHALOM, Albert. *The Body/Mind Conceptual Framework and the Problem of Personal Identity: Some Theories in Philosophy, Psychoanalysis, and Neurology*. New Jersey: Humanities Press, 1985.

———. "Hartshorne and the Problem of Personal Identity." Coauthored with John C. Robertson, Jr. *Process Studies* 8/3 (Fall, 1978): 169–79.

SHELDON, Wilmon Henry. *God and Polarity: A Synthesis of Philosophies*. Westport, Connecticut: Greenwood Press, 1970.

SHERBURNE, Donald W., Ed. *A Key to Whitehead's Process and Reality*. Chicago: University of Chicago Press, 1966.

———. "Whitehead's Psychological Physiology." *Southern Journal of Philosophy* 7/4 (Winter, 1969): 401–7.

SHIELDS George W. "Hartshorne and the Analytic Philosophical Tradition." *Faith and Creativity: Essays in Honor of Eugene H. Peters*. Eds. George Nordgulen and George Shields. St. Louis, Missouri: CBP Press, 1987, pp. 196–225.

SHOEMAKER, Sydney. "Identity, Properties and Causality." *Midwest Studies in Philosophy* 4 (1979): 321–42.

———. "Introspection and the Self." *Self-Knowledge*. Ed. Quassim Cassam. Oxford: Oxford University Press, pp. 118–39.

———. *Personal Identity*. Coauthored with Richard Swinburne. Oxford: Basil Blackwell, 1984.

———. "Persons and their Pasts." *American Philosophical Quarterly* 7 (1970): 269–85.

———. *Self-Knowledge and Self-Identity*. Ithaca, New York: Cornell University Press, 1963.

SIA, Santiago. Ed. *Charles Hartshorne's Concept of God: Philosophical and Theological Responses*. Dordrecht: Kluwer Academic Publishers, 1990.

———. *God In Process Thought: A Study in Charles Hartshorne's Concept of God*. Dordrecht: Martinus Nijhoff Publishers, 1985.

———. "Process Thought as Conceptual Framework." *Process Studies* 19/4 (Winter, 1990): 248–55.

SLORS, Marc. *Personal Identity and the Metaphysics of Mind*. Vol. XVIII. Publications of the Department of Philosophy, Utrecht: Utrecht University, 1997.

SMITH, Huston. "The Death and Rebirth of Metaphysics." *Process and Divinity: The Hartshorne Festschrift. Philosophical Essays Presented to Charles Hartshorne*. Eds. William Reese and Eugene Freeman. La Salle, Illinois: Open Court, 1964, pp. 38–47.

SMITH, John E. "Neoclassical Metaphysics and the History of Philosophy." *The Philosophy of Charles Hartshorne*. Vol. XX of The Library of Living Philosophers. Ed. Lewis Edwin Hahn. La Salle, Illinois: Open Court, 1991, pp. 489–508.

———. "Is the Self an Ultimate Category?" *Philosophy, Religion and the Coming World Civilization: Essays in Honor of William Ernest Hocking*. Ed. Leroy Rouner. The Hague: Martinus Nijhoff, 1966, pp. 135–50.

SMUTS, Jan. "The Holistic Universe." *Process Philosophy: Basic Writings*. Eds. Jack R. Sibley and Pete A.Y. Gunter. New York: University Press of America, 1978, pp. 221–43.

SOLMSEN, Friedrich. *Aristotle's System of the Physical World: A Comparison with his Predecessors*. Ithaca: Cornell University Press, 1990.

SOLZHENITSYN, Alexander. *The First Circle*. New York: Bantam Books, 1969.

SPENCER, John B. "Meland's Alternative in Ethics." *Process Philosophy: Basic Writings*. Eds. Jack R. Sibley and Pete A.Y. Gunter. Lanham, MD: University of America Press, 1978, pp. 325–66.

SPRIGGE, T.L. "Hartshorne's Conception of the Past." *The Philosophy of Charles Hartshorne*. Vol. XX of The Library of Living Philosophers. Ed. Lewis Edwin Hahn. La Salle, Illinois: Open Court, 1991, pp. 397–414.

STALLO, J.B. *The Concepts and Theories of Modern Physics*. Cambridge: Harvard University Press, 1960.

STALNAKER, Robert. "Counterparts and Identity." *Midwest Studies in Philosophy* 11 (1986): 213–33.

STAPP, Henry Pierce. "Quantum Mechanics, Local Causality and Process Philosophy." Ed. William B. Jones. *Process Studies* 7/3 (Fall, 1977): 173–91.

STCHERBATSKY, Th. "The Soul Theory of the Buddhists." *Bulletin de l'academie des sciences de Russie* (1919): 937–58.

STRAWSON, P.F. *Entity and Identity*. Oxford: Clarendon Press, 1997.

———. *Individuals: An Essay in Descriptive Metaphysics*. Garden City, New York: Doubleday and Co., 1963.

———. "The First Person – and Others." "The First Person." *Self-Knowledge*. Ed. Quassim Cassam. Oxford: Oxford University Press, pp. 210–15.

———. "Proper Names." *Proceedings of the Aristotelian Society*. Supplementary Volume 31 (1957): 191–228.

STROUD, Barry. *Hume*. The Arguments of the Philosophers. Ed. Ted Honderich. London: Henley and Boston, Routledge and Kegan Paul, 1977. Reprint 1995.

SUCHOKI, Marjorie Hewitt. "Charles Hartshorne and Subjective Immortality." *Process Studies* 21/2 (Summer, 1992): 118–29.

SULLIVAN, William M. "Inwardness and Interdependence." *Individuality and Cooperative Action*. Ed. Joseph E. Early. Washington, DC: Georgetown University Press, 1991, pp. 149–55.

SWEET, Leonard I. "Straddling Modernism and Postmodernism." *Theology Today* 47 (July, 1990): 159–64.

SWINBURNE, Richard. "Personal Identity." *Proceedings of the Aristotelian Society* 74 (1973): 231–7.

TAYLOR, Charles. "Responsibility for Self." *The Identities of Persons*. Ed. Amélie Oksenberg Rorty. Berkely, Los Angeles and London: University of California Press, 1969, pp. 281–99.

———. *Sources of the Self: The Making of the Modern Identity*. Cambridge, Massachusetts: Harvard University Press, 1989.

TAYLOR, Mark C. *Erring: A Postmodern A/theology*. Chicago and London: University of Chicago Press, 1984.

THOMSON, Manley. "Hartshorne and Peirce: Individuals and Continuity." *Existence and Actuality: Conversations with Charles Hartshorne*. Eds. John B. Cobb Jr. and Franklin I. Gamwell. Chicago: University of Chicago Press, 1984, pp. 130–48.

TREDELENBERG, Adolf. "A Contribution to the History of the Word *Person*." *Monist* 20 (1910): 336–63.

UNGER, Peter. "The Physical View." *Self and Identity: Contemporary Philosophical Issues*. Eds. Daniel Kolak and Raymond Martin. New York and Toronto: Macmillan, 1991, pp. 192–212.

URBAN, Wilbur Marshall. "Whitehead's Philosophy of Language." *The Philosophy of Alfred North Whitehead*. The Library of Living Philosophers. Ed. Paul Arthur Schilpp. New York: Tudor, 1951, pp. 301–27.

VAN DE VATE, Dwight, Jr. "Strawson's Concept of a Person." *Southern Journal of Philosophy* 7/1 (Spring, 1969): 9–24.

VAN DER VEKEN, Jan. "From Modal Language to Model Language: Charles Hartshorne and Linguistic Analysis." *Hartshorne: Process Philosophy and Theology*. Eds. Robert Kane and Stephen H. Philipps. New York: State University of New York Press, 1989, pp. 33–51.

———. "God's World and Man Becoming: How can Science Possibly Help us to Transcend Dogmatism?" *Science and Religion: One World Changing Perspectives*. Eds. Jan Fennema and Iain Paul. Dordrecht: Kluwer Academic Publishers, 1990, pp. 131–7.

———. "Is Man the 'Result' of Evolution?" *God, Man, and the Universe*. Eds. Peter Jonkers and Jan van der Veken. Leuven: Center for Metaphysics and Philosophy of God, Institute of Philosophy, 1981.

———. "Love Neither Rules Nor Is It Unmoved." *Tripod* 16 (1983): 45–59.

———. "The Referent of the Word 'God.'" *Tradition and Renewal: Philosophical Essays Commemorating the Centennial of Louvain's Institute of Philosophy.* Eds. David A. Boileau and John A. Dick. Leuven: Leuven University Press, 1992, pp. 153–65.

———. "Process Thought from a European Perspective." *Process Studies* 19/4 (Winter, 1990): 240–7.

———. "Toward a Dipolar View on the Whole of Reality." *Louvain Studies* 7 (Fall, 1978): 102–13.

———. "Tracks to God." *God, Man, and the Universe: Intercultural Dialogue.* Eds. Peter Jonkers and Jan van der Veken. Leuven: Center for Metaphysics and Philosophy of God, Institute of Philosophy, 1981, pp. 5–18.

———. "Ultimate Reality and God: The Same?" *The Philosophy of Charles Hartshorne.* Vol. XX of The Library of Living Philosophers. Ed. Lewis Edwin Hahn. La Salle, Illinois: Open Court, 1991, pp. 203–14.

———. "Whitehead's God is not Whiteheadian Enough." *Whitehead and the Idea of Process.* Proceedings of the First International Whitehead Symposium. (*Whitehead und der Prozessbegriff.* Beitraege zur Philosophie Alfred North Whiteheads auf dem Ersten Internationalen Whitehead-Symposion, 1981.) Freiburg and Muenchen: Verlag Karl Alber, 1984, pp. 300–11.

VAN INWANGEN, Peter. "How to Reason About Vague Objects." *Philosophical Topics* 16 (1988): 255–84.

VESEY, Godfrey. *Personal Identity: A Philosophical Analysis.* Ithaca, New York: Cornell University Press, 1974.

VINEY, Wayne. "Charles Hartshorne's Philosophy and Psychology of Sensation." *The Philosophy of Charles Hartshorne.* Vol. XX of The Library of Living Philosophers. Ed. Lewis Edwin Hahn. La Salle, Illinois: Open Court, 1991, pp. 91–112.

VON EHRENFELS, Christian. "Über Gestaltqualitäten." *Vierteljahrschrift für wissenschaftliche philosophie* 14 (1890): 249–92.

VON LEYDEN, W. *Seventeenth Century Metaphysics: An Examination of Some Main Concepts and Themes.* London: Gerald Duckworth, 1968.

WEISHEPL, James A. *The Development of Physical Theory in the Middle Ages.* New York: Sheed and Ward, 1959.

Weiss, Paul. "History and Objective Immortality." *The Relevance of Whitehead.* Ed. Ivor Leclerc. New York: Macmillan, 1961, pp. 319–32.

———. "The Nature and Status of Time and Passage." *Philosophical Essays for Alfred North Whitehead.* New York: Russel and Russel, 1936, pp. 153–73.

WERTHEIMER, Max. "Experimentelle Studien Über das Sehen von Bewegung." *Zeitschrift ür Psychologie* 1/7 (1912): 161–5.

WHITE, Villard Alan. "Whitehead, Special Relativity, and Simultaneity." *Process Studies* 13/4 (Winter, 1983): 275–85.

WHITEHEAD, Alfred North. *Adventures of Ideas.* New York: Macmillan, 1961.

———. "The Analysis of Experience." *Process Philosophy: Basic Writings.* Eds. Jack R. Sibley and Pete A.Y. Gunter. Lanham, MD: University Press of America, 1978, pp. 247–71.

———. *The Concept of Nature.* Cambridge: Cambridge University Press, 1920.

———. *An Enquiry Concerning the Principles of Natural Knowledge.* Cambridge: Cambridge University Press, 1952.

———. *Essays in Science and Philosophy.* New York: Philosophical Library, 1948.

———. *The Function of Reason.* Boston: Beacon Press, 1929.

———. "Immortality." *The Philosophy of Alfred North Whitehead.* The Library of Living Philosophers. Ed. Paul Arthur Schilpp. New York: Tudor, 1951.

———. *Modes of Thought.* New York: The Free Press, 1966.

———. *Process and Reality: An Essay in Cosmology*. Corrected Edition. Eds. Donald Ray Griffin and Donald W. Sherburne. New York: Macmillan, 1979.

———. *Religion in the Making*. New York: Macmillan, 1926.

———. *Science and the Modern World*. Cambridge: Cambridge University Press, 1929.

———. "Symbolic Reference." *Process Philosophy: Basic Writings*. Eds. Jack R. Sibley and Pete A.Y. Gunter. New York: University Press of America, 1978, pp. 51–78.

———. *Symbolism: Its Meaning and Effect*. Cambridge: Cambridge University Press, 1928.

WHITMAN, William P.D. "Whitehead's Empiricism." *The Relevance of Whitehead*. Ed. Ivor Leclerc. New York: Macmillan, 1961, pp. 335–50.

WHITNEY, Barry L. *Evil and the Process God*. Toronto Studies in Theology. Vol. XIX. New York: The Edwin Mellen Press, 1985.

WIEMAN, Henry Nelson. "Creative Good." *Process Philosophy: Basic Writings*. Eds. Jack R. Sibley and Pete A.Y. Gunter. Lanham, MD: University Press of America, 1978.

———. "Perception and Cognition." *Process Philosophy: Basic Writings*. Eds. Jack R. Sibley and Pete A.Y. Gunter. Lanham, MD: University Press of America, 1978, pp. 105–15.

———. "The Revelation of God in Christ." *Process Studies* 10/1–2 (Spring–Summer, 1980): 2–17.

WIEHL, Reiner. "Hartshorne's Panpsychism." *The Philosophy of Charles Hartshorne*. Vol. XX of The Library of Living Philosophers. Ed. Lewis Edwin Hahn. La Salle, Illinois: Open Court, 1991, pp. 445–62.

WIGGINS, David. "The Concern to Survive." Chapter IX of *Needs, Values, Truth: Essays in the Philosophy of Value*. Oxford: Basil Blackwell, 1987.

WILBER, Ken. Ed. *The Holographic Paradigm and Other Paradoxes: Exploring the Leading Edge of Science*. Boston: New Science Library, 1982.

WILCOX, John. "A Question from Physics for Certain Theists." *Journal of Religion* 40/4 (October, 1961): 293–300.

WILD, John. "Devotion and Fanaticism." *Process and Divinity: The Hartshorne Festschrift; Philosophical Essays Presented to Charles Hartshorne*. Eds. William Reese and Eugene Freeman. La Salle, Illinois: Open Court, 1964, pp. 445–69.

WILDIERS, N. Max. *The Theologian and His Universe: Theology and Cosmology from the Middle Ages to the Present*. English translation of *Wereldbeeld en Teologie van de Middeleeuwen tot vandaag*, 1977. Trans. Paul Dunphy. New York: Seabury, 1982.

WILLIAMS, Bernard O. "Persons, Character and Morality." *The Identities of Persons*. Ed. Amélie Oksenberg Rorty. Berkely, Los Angeles and London: University of California Press, 1969, pp. 197–216.

———. "Personal Identity and Individuation." *Proceedings of the Aristotelian Society* 57 (1956–7): 229–52. (Reprinted in B.A.O. Williams, *Problems of the Self*. Cambridge: Cambridge University Press, 1973, pp. 1–18.)

———. "The Self and the Future." *Self and Identity: Contemporary Philosophical Issues*. Eds. Daniel Kolak and Raymond Martin. New York and Toronto: Macmillan, 1991, pp. 181–92.

WILLIAMS, Daniel Day. "Moral Obligation in Process Philosophy." *Process Philosophy: Basic Writings*. Eds. Jack R. Sibley and Pete A.Y. Gunter. Lanham, MD: University of America Press, 1978, pp. 393–418.

WILLIAMS, Donald. "Preface to Privacy." *Philosophy, Religion and the Coming World Civilization: Essays in Honor of William Ernest Hocking*. Ed. Leroy Rouner. The Hague: Martinus Nijhoff, 1966, pp. 81–93.

WILSON, Edward O. "Biological and Human Determinants of the Survival of Species." *Individuality and Cooperative Action*. Ed. Joseph E. Early. Washington, DC: Georgetown University Press, 1991, pp. 47–57.

WOLF, George. "The Place of Brain in an Ocean of Feelings." *Existence and Actuality: Conversations with Charles Hartshorne*. Eds. John B. Cobb, Jr. and Franklin I. Gamwell. Chicago and London: The University of Chicago Press, 1984, pp. 167–84.

WORDSWORTH, William. *The Works of William Wordsworth*. The Wordsworth Poetry Library. Hertfordshire: Cumberland House, 1994.

YOLTON, John W. *Locke: An Introduction*. Oxford: Basil Blackwell, 1985.

YORKE, "Chaos and Scientific Knowledge." *Individuality and Cooperative Action*. Ed. Joseph E. Early. Washington, DC: Georgetown University Press, 1991, pp. 37–45.

YOUNG, Louise B. "Cooperation and Individuality: Implications for the Future of Humanity." *Individuality and Cooperative Action*. Ed. Joseph E. Early. Washington, DC: Georgetown University Press, 1991, pp. 59–62.

Index